Cinematic Emotion in Horror Films and Thrillers

Routledge Advances in Film Studies

1. Nation and Identity in the New German Cinema
Homeless at Home
Inga Scharf

2. Lesbianism, Cinema, Space
The Sexual Life of Apartments
Lee Wallace

3. Post-War Italian Cinema
Daniela Treveri Gennari

4. Latsploitation, Exploitation Cinema, and Latin America
Edited by Victoria Ruétalo
and Dolores Tierney

5. Cinematic Emotion in Horror Films and Thrillers
The Aesthetic Paradox
of Pleasurable Fear
Julian Hanich

Cinematic Emotion in Horror Films and Thrillers
The Aesthetic Paradox of Pleasurable Fear

Julian Hanich

First published 2010
by Routledge
711 Third Avenue, New York, NY 10017

Simultaneously published in the UK
by Routledge
2 Park Square, Milton Park, Abingdon, Oxon OX14 4RN

Routledge is an imprint of the Taylor & Francis Group, an informa business

First issued in paperback 2011

© 2010 Taylor & Francis

Typeset in Sabon by IBT Global.

All rights reserved. No part of this book may be reprinted or reproduced or utilised in any form or by any electronic, mechanical, or other means, now known or hereafter invented, including photocopying and recording, or in any information storage or retrieval system, without permission in writing from the publishers.

Trademark Notice: Product or corporate names may be trademarks or registered trademarks, and are used only for identification and explanation without intent to infringe.

Library of Congress Cataloging in Publication Data
Hanich, Julian, 1975–
 Cinematic emotion in horror films and thrillers : the aesthetic paradox of pleasurable fear / by Julian Hanich.
  p. cm. — (Routledge advances in film studies)
 Includes bibliographical references and index.
 1. Horror films—History and criticism. 2. Thrillers (Motion pictures)—History and criticism. 3. Motion picture audiences. I. Title.
 PN1995.9.H6H355 2010
 791.43'6164—dc22
                       2009040612

ISBN13: 978-0-415-87139-6 (hbk)
ISBN13: 978-0-203-85458-7 (ebk)
ISBN13: 978-0-415-51657-0 (pbk)

For Henriette and Hans-Peter

Contents

List of Figures ix
Acknowledgments xi

PART I

Introduction 3

1 How to Describe Cinematic Fear, or Why Phenomenology? 38

2 Multiplexperiences: Individualized Immersion and Collective Feelings 52

PART II

3 Frightening Fascination: A Phenomenology of Direct Horror 81

4 Intimidating Imaginations: A Phenomenology of Suggested Horror 108

5 Startling Scares: A Phenomenology of Cinematic Shock 127

6 Anxious Anticipations: A Phenomenology of Cinematic Dread 155

7 Apprehensive Agitation: A Phenomenology of Cinematic Terror 202

PART III

8 Moments of Intensity: Lived-Body Metamorphoses and Experienced Time 221

9	Moments of Collectivity: The Cinema of Fear and Feelings of Belongingness	241
10	The End	252

Notes 257
Bibliography 281
Index 293

Figures

I.1	Pinhead (Doug Bradley), the fascinating monster in *Hellraiser*.	7
2.1	The shower murder in *Psycho*.	71
3.1	Direct horror: *House of 1000 Corpses*.	82
3.2	Daring a fearful look: Danny Torrance (Danny Lloyd) in *The Shining*.	96
3.3	Painful somatic empathy: Szell (Laurence Olivier) tortures Babe Levy (Dustin Hoffman) in *Marathon Man*.	105
4.1	Suggested horror: *Alien 3*.	109
4.2	Imagining Satan's son: Rosemary (Mia Farrow) in *Rosemary's Baby*.	124
5.1	Cinematic shock: *Alien*.	128
5.2	Unexpected Identity: Max Cady (Robert De Niro) dressed as a woman in *Cape Fear*.	132
5.3	Disrupted relief: Jason (Ari Lehman) attacks Alice (Adrienne King) in *Friday the 13th*.	139
6.1	Cinematic dread: *The Silence of the Lambs*.	156
6.2	A constricting experience: Frame-within-the-frame shot from *Dark Water*.	174
6.3	Motor mimicry: Bruno Anthony (Robert Walker) tries to recover his lighter in *Strangers on a Train*.	182
7.1	Cinematic terror: *Alien: Resurrection*.	203

7.2	Chase-and-escape terror: Leatherface (Gunnar Hansen) and Sally (Marilyn Burns) in *The Texas Chainsaw Massacre*.	208
7.3	Extreme camera angle: The death of Tatum Riley (Rose McGowan) in *Scream*.	209
10.1	Arthouse horror: Henry (Michael Rooker) in *Henry—Portrait of a Serial Killer*.	253

Acknowledgments

The way from the valley of darkness to the summit of light is not a straight ropeway drive up to the mountaintop. Writing an academic study does not imply that you enter the gondola at a station called "Ignorance" with your intellectual rucksack in your hands, store everything safely under your seat and leave the gondola after three or four years of idle reflection and some minor reshufflings and reorderings of your baggage at a station called "Understanding." Doing research means embarking on an extensive march on long and winding roads, hidden serpentines and rocky paths. Initially, you start out with little baggage, but gradually you add material on material, which makes your journey even more complicated and exhausting. Fortunately, on your way up you meet other hikers who sometimes lead you astray into dangerous fields, but more often recommend shortcuts, tell you where to find panoramic views and clear paths through the undergrowth when you are lost in dense woods. Sometimes they carry parts of your luggage or tell you what you can leave behind. The best and brightest are even strong enough to lift you up. Standing on the shoulders of giants has been a special privilege on my way. Without those other hikers, ramblers and giants I would have been lost, had given up or returned bewildered, confused, and defeated. Consequently, these intellectual companions deserve thanks—and more. Winfried Fluck, Vivian Sobchack, Gertrud Koch and Thomas Elsaesser were of particular importance. Jesco Delorme, Johannes Völz, Mario Grizelj, Robin Curtis, Philipp Hübl, Tarja Laine, Oliver Jahraus, Walter Metz, Stefan Brandt and Simon Remberger supported me in various other, important ways. Furthermore, I would like to send out a very special thanks to the Cusanuswerk, the foundation that more than generously supported my work for over three years. Thanks also goes to the University of California Los Angeles and the University of Amsterdam. Courtesy of those two places I was not only provided with a strong intellectual environment but also with a well-oiled infrastructure for a whole year. Last but not least I want to express my particular gratitude to the members of the Research Colloquiums of the Film Studies Department and the John F. Kennedy Institute of North American Studies at the Freie Universität Berlin.

Part I

Introduction

It is a common observation, that objects which in the reality would shock, are in tragical, and such like representations, the source of a very high species of pleasure. This taken as a fact, has been the cause of much reasoning.

(Edmund Burke)[1]

[T]he audience knows what they're coming to see, they've paid their six bucks. They're saying, 'Okay Mr. Barker . . . or okay, Mr. Cronenberg, okay, Mr. Lynch, or whoever the director is, horrify me.*

(Clive Barker)[2]

THE PARADOX OF FEAR: I'M AFRAID, THEREFORE I ENJOY

Can fear be pleasurable? In February 1949 the director Alfred Hitchcock publishes an article in which he raises this extraordinary question. Writing in the magazine *Good Housekeeping*, of all publications, Hitchcock tackles the matter in an amusing and anecdotal way: "I was discussing this point with an old friend not long ago. 'Fear,' he said, 'is the least pleasant of all emotions. I experienced it when I was a boy, and again during both wars. I never want my children to experience it. I think it entirely possible, if I have anything to say about it, that they'll live their entire lives and never know the meaning of the word.' 'Oh,' I said, 'what a dreadful prospect!' My friend looked at me quizzically. 'I mean it,' I went on. 'The boys will never be able to ride a roller coaster, or climb a mountain, or take a midnight stroll through a graveyard. And when they're older'—my friend is a champion motorboat racer—'there'll be no speedboating for them.' 'What do you mean?' he asked, obviously offended. 'Well, now, let's take the speedboat racing, for instance. Can you honestly tell me that the sensation you get when you cut close to a pylon, or rough water, with a boat riding close on one side and another skidding across in front of you, is anything but fear? Can you deny that a day on the water without fear, without that prickly sensation as the short hairs on your neck rise, would be an utter dead failure? It seems to me that you pay lots of money a year for fear. Why do you want to deny it to your sons?' 'I'd never thought of it quite that way,' he said. And he hadn't. Few people have. That's why my statement, made in all sincerity, that millions of people every day pay huge sums of money and go to great hardship merely to *enjoy* fear seems paradoxical."[3]

Can fear be pleasurable? Answering this unusual question will be the purpose of the approximately 300 pages that follow. Why do we, at times, deliberately and voluntarily expose ourselves to what seems to be a negative emotion—an emotion that we desperately wish to avoid in everyday life? How can we even think of spending our precious leisure time by driving to a movie theater and watch a film entitled, say, *The Texas Chainsaw Massacre* (1974)? Why pay at the multiplex box-office to be frightened and shocked by a movie that promises the *Dawn of the Dead* (2004), let alone *The Evil Dead* (1981)? Behind these questions lies the basic paradox that I will deal with in this study. I call it the *paradox of fear*.

Hitchcock was certainly not the first who pondered the question of pleasurable fear. The vexing character of the paradox can be gauged from its long tradition. Some 1,600 years ago, St. Augustine asked a very similar question in his *Confessions*.[4] Yet it was particularly during the 18th century that the problem created heated debates. Philosophers and aestheticians were interested in the question why *sublime nature*—enormous Alpine mountains, impenetrable forests, gaping gorges—could be an enjoyable spectacle. The most notable contributions were those of Edmund Burke in *A Philosophical Enquiry into the Origins of our Ideas of the Sublime and Beautiful* (1757) and Immanuel Kant in his *Critique of the Power of Judgment* (1790).[5] But the discussion also revolved around the pleasures of *tragic* and *sorrowful* stage plays, as can be judged from David Hume's "Of Tragedy" (1757) and Friedrich Schiller's "On the Reason Why We Take Pleasure in Tragic Subjects" (1792).[6] Last but not least, numerous authors like Joseph Addison ("Why Terrour and Grief are Pleasing to the Mind when Excited by Descriptions", 1712) or John and Anna Laetitia Aikin ("On the Pleasure Derived From Objects of Terror", 1773) were struck more specifically by *terror* and *horror* in works of art: in literature, on stage, in painting.[7] They put their astonishment in oxymoronic expressions like 'terrible joy,' 'pleasing horror,' 'terreur agréable,' 'schaudervolles Ergötzen' and 'angenehmes Grauen.' I will refrain from rephrasing their arguments in detail—not only because the interested reader might pick up Carsten Zelle's excellent studies, but also because these 18th-century analyses hail to us from pre-cinematic times and therefore do not take into account what is different in terms of the medium of film and its place of reception, the movie theater.[8] The pleasurable frightening situation *inside* the cinema, however, is precisely what interests me here.

Undeniably, in Hitchcock's wake a number of authors have—explicitly or implicitly—sought for the function of frightening movies and even set out to solve the present conundrum. Noël Carroll, for one, has devoted an important and highly controversial book to what he calls the "paradox of horror."[9] Yet Carroll's approach is only moderately convincing. First, by arguing that the viewer's main pleasure derives from the *satisfaction of cognitive interest* in the impossible being of the monster and the fascination for the narrative's gradual process of disclosing, discovering and proofing the monster's existence, Carroll overemphasizes the cognitive pleasure and thus overintellectualizes a rather somatic experience. Second, by maintaining that the emotion of art-horror—a commingling of fear and disgust—is unpleasant and merely *the price to be paid* for the pleasure of satisfied interest, Carroll both denigrates the viewer's emotional experience and situates pleasure outside of fear. Both arguments are counterintuitive. Hence there are good reasons for a new attempt in tackling the paradox of fear.

Because this study focuses on the U.S. and Hollywood movies, it does not help much to solve the paradox by taking into account the current cultural climate in the United States. Sociologists, political scientists, historians, media scholars and at least one filmmaker—Michael Moore in *Bowling for Columbine* (2002)—have concluded that Americans have for some time been living in a "culture of fear."[10] None of these scholars considers the situation healthy. None of them is particularly fond of fear. None of them believes that—against the backdrop of a society that is, across-the-board, safe and secure—the proportions of fear are adequate and rational. Peter N. Stearns, known as historian of emotions, locates this upsurge of fear within the time span of the last three decades. What are the reasons? On the one hand, "[t]oo many Americans have developed unrealistic hopes for a risk-free existence, and as such are open to excessive reactions when risk intrudes and to excessive worries about risks that may not eventuate," Stearns informs us.[11] As a result, there is a growing desire for safety and protection against risks. On the other hand, precisely this desire for safety and protection is capitalized on by various fearmongers who use fear as a means to unworthy ends. They manipulate and exploit their clienteles by evoking bleak scenarios and thus use fear as a political, economic or legal tool.[12] Hence the answer to why Americans harbor so many unnecessary fears is that power and money await those who tap into moral insecurities and provide symbolic substitutes.[13] As a consequence, many Americans were becoming easier to scare and ever more eager to escape their fears.[14]

And yet: the American cinema of fear thrives and thrives. But why do so many fearful Americans enjoy movies that scare them at the exact historical moment when they have more than enough of it in everyday life? On the face of it, America's culture of fear makes the puzzle even more striking.

MULTIPLE PLEASURES: NO PARADOX AFTER ALL?

Then again, some theorists have raised doubts if frightening movies involve a paradox at all. Matt Hills, for instance, rejects the idea that asking "Why horror?" could open up a conundrum since this would imply *essentializing* the genre by declaring scariness as *the* generic characteristic.[15] But why should we want to reduce horror movies to the experience of fear, if there are so many other pleasures to be gained? And if there are so many other pleasures, Hills suggests, why should watching horror movies be paradoxical? Indeed, distinguishing between a film's *function* (as the more general use-value) and the *pleasure* it generates (as one specific function), we have to admit that the horror film and its sister-genre the thriller not only fulfill various functions but also generate diverse pleasures. One reason is the filmmakers' active interest: in order to sell the same film to two or more audiences, a variety of pleasures and other functions are planted into the movie. As a consequence, there may be no ultimate essence to the pleasures of film viewing. Cinematic pleasures are dispersed and depend on film, genre, viewer, and cultural and historical context.[16] In this study I neither intend to present a grand theory about filmgoing in general nor do I want to fix the quintessential pleasures and functions of specific genres. A movie may be worthwhile for many reasons.

Think of information and knowledge: The fact that we can obtain information and learn from the movies not only goes for documentaries or sophisticated fiction films. Although frightening films often cannot be taken at face value, these films can nevertheless satisfy epistemophilia—our desire for knowledge—by creating vivid impressions of unknown places, times and works of art aesthetically. For instance, we can acquire sociological insights of how other classes or groups of society live. Examples comprise the Amish in Peter Weir's thriller *Witness* (1985), rural America (*Signs*, 2002), the lower class (*Henry—Portrait of a Serial Killer*, 1986), the young urban elite in a 'yuppie-horror movie' like *Basic Instinct* (1992), life in the projects (*Candyman*, 1992) or campus culture (*Scream 2*, 1997). And what about adaptations from other art forms, most notably literature? The film versions of *Bram Stoker's Dracula* (1992) by Francis Ford Coppola and *Mary Shelley's Frankenstein* (1994) by Kenneth Branagh tell us about and interpret classic novels.

But cinema can also function as a place for acquiring (sub-)cultural capital in Pierre Bourdieu's sense—that is, as a means of social distinction.[17] Discussing a David Fincher thriller around the water cooler helps those who have seen the movies to distinguish themselves from the rest. Another way of acquiring social recognition is the consumption of films which are taboo for a certain age group or might be considered as a test of courage (like R-rated horror movies). The one who has managed to see these films stands out from the group due to an act of social transgression that defies authority.[18] Moreover, the display of connoisseurship allows fans to demarcate the boundaries of the 'in-group', separating fans from non-fans, long-term aficionados from newcomers. Stressing media literacy, education and knowledge of the genre by pointing out intertextual allusions, previous work done by the *auteur*-director or recognizing the craftsmanship of special effects, sets those viewers apart.[19]

Watching frightening films certainly comprises the satisfaction of scopophilia. Think of 'gazing' at star performances such as Brad Pitt in *Seven* (1995) or watching good-looking, often highly eroticized people on the screen more generally; the stunning bodies in slasher films like *I Know What You Did Last Summer* (1997) come to mind. But pleasure of looking also involves the sight of well-crafted special effects: the convincing evocation of the monster via CGI (*The Lost World: Jurassic Park 2*, 1997) or hand-made (*Hellraiser*, 1987), the stunning depiction of violence (e.g., the famous decapitation scene in *The Omen*, 1976) or the creation of unknown worlds (*Alien 3*, 1992).

Moreover, pleasure might come from hermeneutic activity. Think of intertextual comparisons, ad-hoc interpretations and evaluations. An informed viewer will likely have fun following the allusions and drawing comparisons to other films while watching self-reflexive movies like *Wes Craven's New Nightmare* (1994) and *Scream* (1996). Or she may find it pleasurable to interpret Clarice Starling (Jodie Foster) in *The Silence of the Lambs* (1991) as a feminist heroine and evaluate the movie *Virus* (1999) as a trashy version of Goethe's poem "The Sorcerer's Apprentice."

There are more pleasures to be gained from frightening films if we think of aesthetic experience more narrowly defined—for instance the pleasure of cognitive and emotional self-expansion, imaginary role-play and self-fashioning.[20] Through an act of transfer of personal thoughts, emotions and body schemas the viewer concretizes and completes the characters and worlds offered by the film. The spectator transcends his or her own limited identity and can thus pleasurably stage himself or herself as someone else and somewhere else for a short period of time. In a terrifying movie like *The Silence of the Lambs* this not only comprises the heroine Clarice Starling, but also the fascinating and horrendous serial killer Hannibal Lecter (Anthony Hopkins). In fact, it necessarily comprises all the characters present in the film. Employing Nietzsche's concept of power-as-pleasure, Daniel

Figure I.1   Pinhead (Doug Bradley), the fascinating monster in *Hellraiser*.

Shaw claims that the horror spectator derives a feeling of self-empowerment by siding with the immensely powerful villain and the awesome havoc that he (or she) wreaks *as well as* the eventual triumph of the final girl (or boy) and the death and destruction of the villain.[21] Through imaginary role-play the viewer can have it both ways: empathy with the devil and satisfaction from the victim's victory.

Hence it would be blatantly reductive to restrict the aesthetic experience of frightening films to the aspect of emotion and the body. On the other hand, aesthetic experience certainly *does* involve sensory and sensual aspects. Particularly talking about the pleasure of *fear* without talking about the body and the way we experience it would certainly be an odd endeavor. Conceding that there are numerous pleasures to be gained *from* and functions fulfilled *by* frightening movies does not help to find an answer to the aesthetic paradox at the heart of my investigation. Let me underscore: unlike Hills and others who talk about the pleasures of *horror*, I do not ask for the function of one specific genre but for the pleasure of *fear* more generally. My guiding question is not: what functions do certain genres fulfill? But rather: what pleasures does the viewer gain from experiencing types of cinematic fear like horror, shock, dread or terror?

If we approach the problem from this angle, the essentializing tendency vanishes. We do not have to stipulate *one* single overarching function (like scaring the audience), but can concede a multiplicity of pleasures. What still remains unanswered, is the question how we derive pleasure from the *fearful* engagement with the movie. Studying the pleasure of cinematic fear implies, then, the deliberate disregard of other aspects of movie-going, since these aspects cannot answer the paradox. This also goes, incidentally, for such common affective responses as disgust and laughter, which are both largely ignored here even though being grossed-out is the central experience of splatter movies such as Sam Raimi's *The Evil Dead*. And laughing is a central response to a horror comedy like the same Raimi's *Army of Darkness* (1992).

WHY NOT CATHARSIS? THE INADEQUACIES OF A FUZZY CONCEPT

But why not simply refer to the concept of *catharsis* and leave it at that? When it comes to the viewer's body, the emotion of fear and a certain pleasure that goes along with it, the concept of catharsis could be an obvious choice. Most commentators agree that the body plays a crucial role in Aristotle's puzzling formulations from the *Poetics*. When he describes the function of tragedy as the stimulation of *eleos* and *phobos* and the subsequent purging or purification of these affects, he implies that a bodily transformation is brought about. The most widespread and popular interpretation therefore proposes a medical cure *from* (negative) emotions.[22] The emotions are intensified and then removed or discharged so that the viewer will experience, at the very least, a feeling of relief—which is pleasurable. Moreover, when Aristotle notes that tragedy is supposed to be "effecting through pity and *fear*" the riddance of these emotions, he explicitly talks about the very emotion in question here.[23]

However, even if the invocation of both the *body* and the emotion of *fear* could make catharsis an obvious candidate, the concept has a number of disadvantages. For one, catharsis remains not only one of the oldest but also one of the most frequently interpreted aesthetic concepts—in other words, a rather fuzzy concept. Moreover, while it is a staple rhetorical strategy to invoke catharsis in connection with the cinema of fear, the concept is often thrown into the debate like a bone the readers have to chew on, but the question *what* becomes purged *from* what and *how* is rarely answered.[24] While many commentators agree that Aristotle saw catharsis as the *main* purpose of tragedy, to my knowledge no one claims the same for frightening films; catharsis always remains an *ancillary* argument.[25]

But even if the concept was used in more than a supplementary fashion, it would still carry with it *three* major problems. First, there is the negative weight catharsis—at least in the sense of purgation—puts on emotions. The idea that we are in need of being purged or cleansed from specific emotions not only perpetuates the age-old prejudice against emotions, pervading our everyday language and dominating the philosophy of art from Plato through Augustine and Rousseau to Adorno. It also runs counter to my intuitive understanding of aesthetic pleasure. This is particularly true for the movie theater, a place that we visit primarily not in order to *get rid* of our emotions, but precisely to *experience* the lived-body transformations that are characteristic of being emotional. This study will show that this also goes for seemingly negative emotions like horror or shock.

The ambivalent view on emotions implicit in the concept of catharsis runs back to its origins in Aristotle's *Poetics*. Aristotle used the concept in order to defend tragedy against the political attacks from Plato (even if he never mentions him straightforwardly). Plato believed that tragedy numbs the wakefulness of reason by exciting irrational emotions—and therefore poses a threat to the community. In order to elevate tragedy and save it from Plato's reproaches, Aristotle cunningly argued that even though tragedy elicits pity and fear, it does so in order to eventually get rid of these harmful effects. In other words, with the concept of catharsis art becomes the sewer through which our emotional dirt can be dumped. This clever tactical maneuver might have defended tragedy as a whole, but it was a stab in the back of its main emotions.

A second aspect that strikes me as untenable vis-à-vis the cinema of fear—a point closely related to the first—is the fact that catharsis seems to be focused solely on the *end* of the experience: the feeling of *relief* after the negative pent-up emotions were discharged. Raising this issue begs the question of the temporal distribution of pleasure in frightening movies: does pleasure occur only *after* the emotion has vanished or already *during* the emotion? If catharsis were *the* pleasurable telos, we would have to endure an entire unpleasant film (or a series of literally horrible scenes) simply to feel the pleasure of relief at the end. Of course, one could argue that the film gives numerous small, episodic forms of catharsis at the end of *each* intense scene. Nevertheless, this would imply that we had to go through a negative experience every single time in order to arrive at a positive, pleasurable feeling of relief. Does this negative-positive arithmetic concur with the experience of frightening movies? I doubt it.

It is more likely that for many viewers there is a *double* pleasure in both bodily transformations: the transformation of the excitation *and* the subsequent change back to a less agitated experience. Our bodily experience is transformed to and fro, and most viewers enjoy *both* changes. In order to make this point more tangible, think about phenomena like bungee jumping or rollercoaster rides. Do we enjoy the free fall from the bridge and the speedy ride in the rollercoaster racing up and down the tracks? Or is it merely the joyful moment of relief after the frightening experience is over? I think *both* moments are pleasurable (albeit in different ways). These constant pleasurable ups and downs of emotions in a temporal form of art like film are precisely the reason why the rollercoaster is not only a convincing analogy but also recurs as a fitting metaphor in discourses about somatic types of movies (think of the discussion about action movies). But if the agitation of horror, shock, dread or terror is indeed pleasurable *itself*, there is no need to talk of catharsis with its anti-emotional connotations. We do not need to be purged or cleansed from something we enjoy.

This takes me to my third and final argument against catharsis. Norbert Elias has argued that in civilized societies emotions and affects have their place in culturally legitimized and clearly defined social spaces like sport arenas or movie theaters. In a modern twist on Aristotle, Elias asserts that within these clearly defined boundaries watching a soccer game, a movie or some other culturally acceptable social practice allows the discharge of otherwise controlled and repressed affects.[26] Some theorists took this model a step further and assumed that the spectator thus can get rid of a *surplus* of emotions. This idea of emotional surplus presupposes that our advanced modern world forces us to accumulate ever more emotions and tensions that for some reason cannot be discharged—until, just like a pumped-up tire, we are about to burst if the safety-valve is not opened. The emotion theory of Thomas Scheff is a case in point: "Because of the almost continuous interference with discharge, both by others and by one's own learned reflexes, most individuals accumulate massive amounts of repressed emotion, bodily tension which is always present but usually not recognized."[27] For our own health it is necessary to get rid of these bodily tensions and emotions. Otherwise the clarity of our thoughts and perceptions would be impaired. But is this really the case?

It is not difficult to see Freud's economic and mechanistic concept of drive reduction and tension discharge at work here. Freud's idea of the pleasure principle maintained that the basic movement of the living organism's psychic apparatus was toward an excitationless state of quiescence or at least toward a constant low level of excitation. This "principle of constancy" is achieved through tension reduction as well as avoidance *of* and defense *against* everything increasing the quantity of excitation.[28] Freud's ideal of a zero level of tension has been attacked from various sides. He was, for instance, criticized for not taking into account the individual's stimulation-seeking nature: from birth on humans show an eagerness to turn toward a variety of things in their environment; the sensory contact with them is enjoyed and not experienced as disturbing excitation.[29] Hence pleasure cannot be equated with a zero level of tension.

With this critique in mind, we may ask whether the cathartic principle of reducing tensions and emotions to a minimum can still be vindicated. The idea of tension reduction or emotional discharge stands in opposition to many of our most cherished experiences at the movies. Often watching a film does *not* reduce our tension or cleanse us from our passions. We often leave the cinema agitated, angry, aroused or afraid. Far from condemning these experiences as an unpleasant turmoil, we frequently consider those films the best. After a touching melodrama we experience an almost physical yearning for true love. After what one could call 'rage films'—films depicting blatant injustice or crass brutality against innocent people—we are often irritated far beyond the level of emotional equilibrium. Maybe the most effective prove that catharsis is not a valid concept for each and every film comes from a genre that is even more despised than horror. The concept of catharsis as a general constituent of aesthetic experience founders on the rock of pornography. The most important function of porn is to arouse. However, it is not the film itself that can cleanse us from our desire: it can only become a *means* to this end. Emotions, passions, affects are often not erased but enhanced. The same goes for frightening movies.

Sometimes the notion of catharsis merely implies a return to a less agitated state: a feeling of closure after an emotional turmoil. This is fair enough. But even this watered-down concept of catharsis is inconsistent with many film experiences. The most powerful movies manage to leave us afraid (or at least uneasy) after we have turned off the TV or entered our car to drive back from the theater. By denying full narrative closure and leaving the end open many contemporary filmmakers reveal that this is a goal they *deliberately* aim at.[30] Think of the surviving monster or psychopath in films like *Halloween* (1978), *The Texas Chainsaw Massacre*, *Henry—Portrait of a Serial Killer* or *The Silence of the Lambs*: Michael Myers, Leatherface, Henry and Hannibal Lecter are not dead or behind safe prison bars, but still haunt the imaginary streets—and possibly our imagination. Or consider the unsolved mysteries at the end of *Evil Dead*, *Lost Highway* (1997), *Rosemary's Baby* (1968) or *The Blair Witch Project* (1999). Is Rosemary's baby really the incarnation of the antichrist the Satanist conspirators longed for? And is there a rational explanation for the death of the three filmmakers, or were they killed by the ominous Blair witch? These questions remain open, as does the door through which these films may return and disturb us. Hence it is quite apposite that at the very end of *House of 1000 Corpses* (2003) we get to see the traditional insert "The End"—only to realize that after a short moment a question mark is added: "The End?"

When we go to the movie theater we do not get rid of a surplus of accumulated repressed emotions hoarded in our inner store room. This is the case simply because emotions cannot be stored in the first place—hence no need to discharge them. What we look for are the very emotions that the process of civilization through its leveling of emotions and affects *denied* us and what the process of modernization through its control of public crises and threat situations has *relieved* us of (see Chapter 8).[31] The cinema works as an efficient social institution that counterbalances the emotional and somatic *lack* (not surplus) within the disembodied culture of advanced modernity. Hence Norbert Elias writes: "what people seek in their mimetic leisure activities is not release from tension but, on the contrary, a specific type of tension, a form of excitement often connected [. . .] with fear, sadness and other emotions which we would try to avoid in ordinary life."[32] *With* Nietzsche, who famously exclaimed that art is "the great stimulant of life," and *against* most catharsis theorists I therefore want to stress a different function: I consider the cinema of fear not a purgative but a tonic.[33]

THE RETURN OF EMOTIONS: COGNITIVISM, DELEUZE AND PHENOMENOLOGY

Until recently, focusing on the pleasures of a cinematic emotion like fear would have been an eccentric undertaking. Emotions and affects—as well as bodily experiences more generally—were long neglected in film studies. In the 1990s this situation began to change: emotions and bodily experiences became a new field of research for a number of dissatisfied film scholars. The most interesting and prolific work on emotionality, sensuality and carnality comes from three directions: cognitivism, Deleuzian theory and phenomenology. In the following I will present a number of reasons why I do not subscribe to the cognitivist or the Deleuzian approaches. Stressing the differences also helps to put my own method, phenomenology, into sharper relief.

In the 1990s cognitivists like Noël Carroll, Torben Grodal, Carl Plantinga, Greg M. Smith, Murray Smith, and Ed Tan (to name but a few) were the first who meritoriously brought the nexus between film and emotion back on the agenda.[34] Their key assumption is: emotions involve cognitions. Apart from a bodily *feeling* (a) and an *object* to which the person is intentionally directed (b), there must be a thought, belief, evaluation, or judgment involved that connects a) and b). This cognition bridges, as it were, the gap between the object and the feeling. According to Carroll, the purpose of emotions for the overall effect of the film is twofold. First, emotions operate like "glue", "rivets" or "cement" which attach the viewers to the film and keep them engaged. The emotions are responsible for the *interest* the viewer takes in the characters and the narration. Second, emotions organize perception. They work as a spotlight guiding the viewer to important narrative aspects. It is the filmmaker who directs this activity: he or she *structures* or *pre-focuses* filmic emotions for the viewer—an aspect that distinguishes fictional works from real life.[35]

For this purpose the filmmaker uses stylistic and narrative devices. The cognitivist film scholar concentrates on these devices and asks: how are stimuli such as genre convention, mise-en-scène, sound, film music, editing pace, camera framing and movement, acting style and facial expression *causally* related to emotional reactions? The cognitivist typically takes a scene, a whole film or even a genre and looks at how emotional responses are generated—or as the cognitivists tend to say: 'elicited,' 'cued' or 'activated.'

When it comes to the *experience* of those reactions, however, the description remains one-dimensional (if it exists at all). It is here that I find the major shortcoming of the cognitivist camp. Carroll's analysis of the 'emotive address' of genres, for instance, states that melodramas generally elicit pity and admiration, and horror films evoke fear and disgust. But how these emotional experiences of pity or fear might *feel* like for the viewer and what pleasures they yield remains a secret. Although Carroll argues that cinematic emotions involve bodily states and phenomenological "qualia" he never describes them.[36] And even Carl Plantinga's recent book *Moving Viewers*—an impressive step away from orthodox cognitivism toward a more body-centered perspective—fails to live up to its subtitle's promise to tell us something about "the spectator's experience."

To be sure, refuting the cognitivist research agenda is not my point here. In fact, the cognitivists have generated the most comprehensive body of research in terms of cinematic emotions so far—insights that more than occasionally serve as a springboard for my own argument. In many ways the interests and goals of cognitivism and phenomenology are not oppositional but complementary: While the cognitivists try to explain *why* we feel certain emotions (and therefore focus on *explanation*), phenomenology is interested in *how* we feel them (and thus specializes on *description*). My point is simply that in order to arrive at a conclusion about the pleasures of fearful cinematic emotions, we have to take the viewer's emotional experience into account—an experience accessible only via first-person *descriptions*.

A more recent approach to cinematic "affects" and "sensations" is the one that follows in the wake of philosopher Gilles Deleuze. Attempts can be found, for instance, in studies by Steven Shaviro, Barbara M. Kennedy or Anna Powell.[37] Again, there is much to be lauded in their approach: the idea of film as an event that is a becoming-in-movement rather than a static being which represents; that confronts us with an enveloping reality at once actual and virtual rather than as an illusion; that has a sensory immediacy which enables somatic experiences like kinaesthesia or hapticity rather than remaining a disembodied mental phenomenon; that is always perceived synaesthetically rather than discretely by the disjointed senses of seeing and hearing; that necessitates a revalorization of aesthetics and thus sets it apart from anti-aesthetic psychoanalysis and psychosemiotics . . . In many respects the Deleuzian approach runs parallel to my project then. However, there are reasons why this is not a Deleuzian study.

While one might start by rebuking the opaque, almost hermetic language of the Deleuzians, the problem for my intent lies in the *origins* and the *use* of their highly metaphoric language. When Deleuze and his adherents import scientific concepts from biology, neurophysiology, physics and engineering—concepts like stimuli, excitation, vibration, pulsation, atoms, energy, resonance, organism, neuronal network, and molecularity—they sound much like empiricists.[38] This would suggest a scientific understanding of the physiological body that can be objectively analyzed and measured. The various hints at vibrating nerves, the structure of the cortex or the spinal cord imply as much. At the same time, Deleuzians claim that they have something to say about the somatic aspect of aesthetic experience. This, in turn, would imply a phenomenological body whose experiences can be described. But despite the continuous hints at the viewer's experience, it is never explored in more than an impressionistic manner.[39] This is, of course, part of the program. Barbara Kennedy, for one, negates what she calls "phenomenology's emphasis on subjectivity" and prefers "depersonalization" and a "subjectless subject" instead.[40] An extended description of the viewer's experience would undercut or even contradict this position. The Deleuzian account of affect as non-personal and desubjectified—as traversing the subject—is unfortunate because too much is lost: how would a Deleuzian account relate to a viewer who chooses or refrains from consuming horror films or thrillers?[41] Hence the talk of "depersonalization" and the "subjectless subject" is opposed to an investigation of the pleasures of fear, since pleasure is very much about the one who experiences it. In fact, Barbara Kennedy discards the question of pleasure altogether.

Positioned somewhere in-between, the Deleuzians are neither scientific nor phenomenological enough. Their studies are scattered with sentences like "The use of light and shade, and saturated color stock, initially affects the nerves of the eye, then spreads through the body's neuronal network via tonal vibrations."[42] Such sentences remain mere *assertions* not backed by either *causal explanations* based on scientific research (as done by empirical cognitivists) or *experiential descriptions* which can be intersubjectively verified or discarded (as done by phenomenologists). Often Deleuzians merely claim (*that*) what in fact needs rigorous explanation (*why*) or description (*how*). Not surprisingly, it has proven difficult for Deleuze's followers to apply his theory of affects and sensations to concrete cinematic experiences. Anna Powell's book on horror is a case in point. Despite claiming that "[h]orror's affective force is a potent experiential process" and promising "to explore the sensory affect of horror film *as* experience", her study remains almost purely interpretive.[43] Just like Kennedy's exuberant but sketchy ekphrastic evocations of filmic encounters, Powell's examinations contain occasional gestures to Deleuze that are supposed to prove the relevance—and truth—of Deleuze's concepts, but neither Kennedy nor Powell can put these concepts to concrete use for analysis. So far, the Deleuzian approach to affects and the body has sparked one brilliant polemical intervention that has helped to renew the interest in affects and body: Shaviro's *The Cinematic Body*. But to my knowledge an application that would tell us something profound about the spectator's somatic experience and its concomitant pleasures is still lacking.

Hence the *rue de Deleuze* is not the road taken here. Instead I prefer an option that has long proved its practicability: the phenomenological approach. In Chapter 1 I will give a detailed account of what this method implies. At this point I will restrict myself to some preliminary remarks. Phenomenology is defined by its focus on lived *experience.* It is a descriptive method that describes phenomena that are actually experienced—phenomena that we have at least a certain awareness of while living through them. However, in everyday life we often do not become aware of our own awareness. While sitting in the movie theater watching a frightening film I concentrate on what is happening in the filmic world. What I am not aware of is the *activity* of watching the movie itself, nor am I consciously attending to the *pleasures* this activity entails. If we want to find out about the pleasures of fear, however, we need a method that is able to re-capture these experiences. From its inception phenomenology aimed at broadening and deepening our understanding of experience: "the common concern is that of giving the phenomena a fuller and fairer hearing than traditional empiricism has accorded them," Herbert Spiegelberg notes.[44] Phenomenology tries to uncover what is buried in habituation and institutionalization, what is taken for granted and accepted as given, or what we have never been fully aware of in the first place. In its focusing on the subjectively experienced *phenomenal* or *lived-body* (the *Leib*)—as opposed to the objectively analyzable *physiological* body (the *Körper*)—and its thematizing of experiences of self and other, phenomenology will prove particularly suitable for my purposes. Applied to the study of film first and foremost by Vivian Sobchack, phenomenology can help us reflect on the plethora of aspects that define our fearful encounter with movies: the emotionalized body, the cinematic surroundings, the threatening film, the captivated co-viewers . . . [45] My project therefore takes a road barely traveled in film studies—a move towards a thick phenomenological description of the pleasurable experience of frightening films.

Unfortunately, we cannot expect much help from the literature on scary movies. Nor are there many studies on the emotional, sensual, carnal *experience* of the movies to be found elsewhere in film studies. Given that the body plays such an important role in any emotional cinematic experience, there is still a substantial deficit in academic discourse. Scholars like Sobchack or Shaviro have eloquently and forcefully lamented this absence.[46] This lack is particularly astonishing when it comes to the cinema of fear. Since film studies has counterintuitively preferred interpretive methods (and hence searched for meaning and investigated the politics of representation), the experiential level of frightening films has largely been ignored. To be sure, approaching the paradox of fear from an experiential standpoint does not deny this semantic dimension. This would be an absurd undertaking, at the very least because it would imply to discredit almost all the literature. As Hans Ulrich Gumbrecht has pointed out, aesthetic experiences oscillate between a *presence*-dimension and a *meaning*-dimension, between experiential and semantic levels. Depending on the aesthetic object one aspect is more prevalent than the other. Compare music and reading: while the former tends toward the presence-dimension, the latter is dominated by the meaning-dimension.[47] The same goes for the movies. A film by Jean-Luc Godard usually does not foreground bodily excitement, whereas pornography is seldom watched for meaning. This is not to say that porn movies cannot be interpreted; nor do I imply that Godard does not work on an experiential level. The same is true for the cinema of fear: While other genres or modes might call for meaning-locating, one must not overlook the experiential characteristics of frightening movies. On my way to answer the paradox of fear I intend to give the experiential aspect the detailed look which it was refused for the longest time.

Phenomenology can enlarge our capacities for conscious awareness, refine our cultural sensorium and change our perspective on the world. To say the very least, phenomenological descriptions enable an enrichment of our experience by pointing out aspects of everyday life that are almost too obvious to be noticed. It is an explicit aim of this study to create a novel awareness *of* and a more fine-grained sensibility *toward* some hitherto neglected aspects of movie-going. In the best of all cases, my phenomenological investigations would enable an expansion and enrichment of the cinematic experience by bringing into light what was previously left in the shade. This is not trivial. As Richard Shusterman claims in respect to the body, "If self-knowledge (rather than mere knowledge of worldly facts) is philosophy's prime cognitive aim, then knowledge of one's bodily dimension must not be ignored."[48]

THE MULTIPLEX EXPERIENCE: AN EMBODIED VIEWER INSIDE A THEATER

Focusing on experience implies that we stop treating films like de-contextualized 'texts,' but take them as events that take place in special environments.

We should refrain from looking at frightening films as autonomous aesthetic products, but situate the embodied viewer within the spatial and social surroundings of a specific site of exhibition. It obviously makes a difference if we watch a film like *The Strangers* (2008) on a big screen in a multiplex cinema—or on a tiny computer monitor, in the living room filled with afternoon light or under circumstances that allow for numerous interruptions, alone at home or with dozens of anonymous co-viewers. *How* we experience a film depends, of course, on *where* we experience it, with *whom* as co-viewer and presented by *what* technology. In this study I will concentrate on one specific viewing site as the place to experience scary movies: the contemporary American multiplex. This implies the exclusion of other types of cinema like the small art-house theater or the drive-in. Nor do I describe the experience of private DVD or VHS consumption on television screens and computer monitors. These various ways of looking, hearing, and feeling are sufficiently diverse and complex not to be lumped together. If we want to arrive at a clearer picture of the pleasures of fear, we have to take into account the specific characteristics of the media and reception surroundings. In Chapter 2 I will put this rallying call into practice by a phenomenological description of the multiplex theater.

The decision to limit myself to the medium of film consumed in the reception surroundings of the multiplex was made deliberately. I am aware that two counterarguments may be raised. First, there is the radical transformation of the cinematic public sphere with its viewing-habits shifting in the direction of the domestic space and its increased privatization of the modes and venues of consumption. In 2007 the average American spent 13 hours in the movie theater, whereas the home viewing of prerecorded VHS cassettes and DVDs took up 64 hours: private consumption surpassed public consumption by almost five times.[49] Second, critical voices might call attention to the fact that movies are heavily dependent on their revenues from sources *other* than the multiplex. On the U.S. market the distribution cycle generally moves from the movie theater to pay-per-view channels and video/DVD distribution to pay-TV and finally cable network TV screenings.

I have three arguments for choosing the multiplex. First, in order to be as precise *and* concise as possible I had to restrict my study to *one* viewing surrounding rather than a variety of places. Second, even if the box office revenues sometimes make up only a small percentage of the total turnover, the first-run multiplex is still the decisive place for the success of a movie. Generally, the more money a film makes at the box office, the more profit it promises from later distribution sources. At the very least, then, the multiplex theater acts as a means for testing and promoting a movie for the video and DVD release and setting its price for the sale to TV channels.

But this is certainly argued too defensively in light of the astonishing renaissance of the cinema sector. Between 1971 and 2002 the number of visitors per year rose from 820 million to 1639 million viewers.[50] This renaissance is strongly connected to my third argument: I am convinced that some types of film—frightening movies among them—reveal their full aesthetic potential only in the multiplex cinema as their implied viewing surrounding. I would take issues with critics who think that blockbuster aesthetics are partially geared to home viewing on small screens and that its dramaturgy is influenced by commercial breaks on TV. Instead, I argue that the two most important technological novelties of the last decades—digital sound and computer-generated images—lose most of their impact if not seen inside the multiplex. The digital sound plays out its full effect only in specially equipped movie theaters. And the success of digital special-effects relies heavily on the big silver screen. Paradoxically, then, the blockbuster does not make a movement *towards* the small screen (on which a large share of the revenues depends), but looks as it does due to a reaction *away* from the television set or computer monitor. This is why Conrad Schoeffter argues: "Television made cinema what it is today. The ride, the immersive experience, the special effects and digital sound systems are there because television has *not* got them."[51] In a 2006 survey the Motion Picture Association asked American viewers "What is the ultimate movie-watching experience?" Sixty-three percent answered: "the theater."[52]

DEFINING CINEMATIC FEAR: HORROR, SHOCK, DREAD AND TERROR

A consensus about what exactly constitutes an emotion has yet to be established among philosophers and psychologists. Are emotions a natural kind? Do 'basic emotions' like fear and disgust, 'higher emotions' like guilt and shame as well as 'emotion-like responses' such as frustration have enough family resemblance to belong to the same category? And what about love, boredom, sexual desire, regret, worry or vengeance? These longstanding questions are still up for debate, and it might well turn out that there is no structural essence found in all instances of what we ordinarily call an emotion.[53] Depending on our philosophical or psychological position, very different states acquire the name. If we are interested in facial expressions, *surprise* will be part of the emotion spectrum. If we consider physiological reactions and the autonomous nervous system the crucial elements of emotion, *startle* has to be included. And if we stress the role of cognitions, *interest* turns out to be an emotion. In short, emotions are very complex phenomena. In order to avoid oversimplifications of an intricate debate I will refrain from presenting a comprehensive grand theory of emotions.

What I will introduce, however, is an account of one single emotion, namely fear. This is a more modest intention, but a complicated endeavor nonetheless. For one, fear is a broader category than we usually think; it harbors a number of different if related phenomena. In everyday life there is fear of the dentist, fear of being mugged in an alley at night, fear of a future terrorist attack, fear of thunderstorms, fear of the final exam at the end of the semester, fear of dogs, fear of speaking in front of a large crowd etc. These phenomena are directed towards diverse intentional objects—objects that I am afraid *of*. But they also come with different experiences—they do *not* exactly feel identical. In contrast to many cognitivist emotion theorists I argue that we individuate types of fear not only according to their appraised intentional objects (we not only *think* emotions), but also according to their lived-body, temporal and intersubjective phenomenology (we also *experience* emotions).

This is, of course, also true for the various shades of *cinematic* fear, fear derived from an encounter with a film. In Chapters 3 to 7 I will show that in the movie theater fear exists—not exclusively, but predominantly—in five versions. Since canonical emotion terms may not do justice to the emotions evoked by many films, it is necessary to come up with new or rarely used ones to label those types of fear more accurately. I call them direct horror, suggested horror, cinematic shock, cinematic dread and cinematic terror (dread and terror are *frightening* versions of the larger category of suspense). Since these five types are identical neither in terms of intentionality nor in terms of experience, they veer into different directions and thus border on different emotions: shock is adjacent to surprise, horror to disgust etc.[54]

Hence the word *fear* functions as an umbrella term in my account. It encompasses a number of emotional states that are sufficiently close to *each other* as well as to *prototypical fear in everyday life* in order to deserve this single name. Yet how do I define the category of fear? I suggest an encompassing component theory: fear in the cinema (and elsewhere) consists of five components which can be separated analytically, but in fact form an integrated whole: intentionality, appraisal, action tendency, physiological change and phenomenological experience. The five components cannot be seen as separate parts that stand next to each other; they are aspects of the single state we call fear.

1) Intentionality: Fear is always about something in the world and hence related to an object or event. While anxiety is free-floating, in fear we are afraid *of* something, whether real or imagined. This intertwinement with an object or event—the "aboutness"—is called intentionality. As we shall see, in direct horror we are afraid of the vivid sound-supported *moving-images* of violence or a monster perceived on the screen, whereas in suggested horror we fear our own *mental visualizations* of violence or a monster instigated by the film. At a later point, I will complicate the notion of intentionality by drawing on an important distinction by phenomenologist Hermann Schmitz. Schmitz argues that in certain cases the *content*, to which the emotion is directed, and the actual *cause* of the emotion do not coincide but diverge.[55] In dread, for instance, I might be fearfully directed

to the plight of an endangered character alone in a dark house, but I am actually anticipatorily afraid of having to face a moment of cinematic horror or shock *myself*.

Note, furthermore, that my notion of intentionality does *not necessarily* entail the sentence-like form of thoughts, evaluations, judgments or beliefs: it *can* but *does not have to* involve propositional attitudes. Just think of animals and babies: It should hardly be contentious to claim that creatures who are either not capable of speech *at all* or *not yet* do experience fear *of* something. While intentionality often comes with propositional attitudes, this is not always the case. Some types of fear are intentional in a non-propositional way; others are certainly propositional and hence more cognitive. This lenient definition of intentionality has one advantage: it will allow me to include the cinematic shock (or startle) among the five types of fear.

2) Appraisal: In fear we narrow our attentional focus on an intentional object or event that we perceive, imagine or remember and register that this object or event is dangerous to our well-being. In other words, in fear we consider something we are confronted with as threatening. This appraisal, to use the most common psychological term, *can* but does not have to involve cognitions in any strong sense—a primitive visual or aural perception might be enough. Fear of loud noises or snakes might be hardwired and therefore unavoidable. But apart from innate emotional responses many of our associatively learned emotional reactions are mediated via perceptions as well. A visual or aural experience that frequently coincided with fear in the past can easily respark fear in the present simply through perceiving it.[56] Again, not considering cognitive judgments and evaluations an *essential* component of emotion leaves room for integrating shock in my list of fear at the movies. From a neuroscientific perspective we might say that *complex* cinematic emotions like dread or terror imply cognition (involving the sensory cortex), whereas a comparatively *primitive* type of fear like shock often relies on perception (heading straight for the amygdala) and therefore remains "quick and dirty," in Joseph LeDoux' words.[57] The danger posed by the film can be appraised both via simple percepts and complex judgments.

3) Action Tendency: Fear also comes with certain action tendencies that prepare and enable actions. The most noteworthy one is our inner preparation for flight. As we shall see, in the cinema this tendency to flee the threatening object might result in—may be followed by—proper actions like looking away or covering one's ears. However, these *actions* are not identical with the preparing and enabling *action tendencies* and are not a necessary part of fear.

4) Physiological Change: When we are afraid at the movie theater, we sometimes consciously realize physiological reactions like muscular contractions or sweaty palms. I stipulate that such physiological changes are an

essential part of fear, even if they often take place on a subconscious level. However, from arguing that our physiological body is somehow involved in fear we cannot conclude that types of fear can be individuated according to their physiology. For emotion researchers it is still an unanswered question whether emotions *in general* are physiologically distinct—and so is evidently the question whether we can separate the five types of cinematic fear according to their physiological changes. Future research might show whether heart rate, finger temperature or skin conductance response are correlated with certain types of fear or not. In this study I will not say anything profound about this topic. Yet the fact that the body clearly has an effect on our emotions seems more than evident. When I am tired after work, when I am exhausted after a session in the gym, when I am hungover from a cocktail party the night before, I have problems *feeling* the film. I might realize that the film is meant to be scary or I may remember that I found it frightening on another occasion, but under the current circumstances I cannot feel afraid. Hence physiology is crucial.

5) Phenomenological Experience: Cognitivist philosophers and film scholars emphasize the thinking part of an emotion—the evaluation or judgment about the object of the emotion—and often treat the emotional experience as epiphenomenal.[58] In contrast, phenomenologists consider *how it is like* to be in a certain emotional state essential. It is one of the main thrusts of this book to show that changes in phenomenological experience are more than a mere by-product. Even if the phenomenological experience is not measurable, it is inextricably and essentially bound up with the emotion of fear. In a thought experiment we might think of someone appraising a situation as a real threat for his or her well-being *without* experiencing what it is like to be in the state of fear. Would we refer to such a person as being afraid? Probably not. If you did away with the phenomenological experience, you would end up with a neutral state that has little to do with fear.

While the intentional intertwinement with an object or event that one appraises as threatening is a necessary condition for all five types of fear, intentionality and appraisal are often not sufficient to tell them apart. In order to overcome overly broad categorizations and arrive at fine-grained distinctions we should bring the phenomenological experience into play. This move could turn out to be particularly important when it comes to cinematic emotions (or more generally aesthetic emotions): Aesthetic emotions might be distinguished from utilitarian, pragmatic everyday emotions by an emphasis on their phenomenological quality. They are more felt than acted on. The phenomenological component will become most obvious in my distinction between dread and terror, two frightening versions of suspense. In both cases we are afraid of a potentially horrific outcome in the near future, but the phenomenological experience is quite different—not least because of the distinctive formal and stylistic elements that set these aesthetic strategies apart.

But what exactly do I mean by 'phenomenological experience'? It certainly comprises more than a mere change of the measurable, physiological body. What psychologists and philosophers call (bodily) *feeling*, often comes down to realizing one's sweaty palms or increased heart rate. But the emotion of fear also involves a remarkable change of the lived-body, spatial, temporal and intersubjective experience. In fact, fear generally brings about a gradual, sometimes sudden metamorphosis of ourselves and our taken-for-granted relation to the world. This transformation marks a breach—an inter-*ruption*—in the continuity of our experience, coloring the world differently and thus standing out from the more uneventful flow of life.[59] The narrowed attentional focus, for instance, comes with a phenomenological (not geographical!) closeness of the intentional object that seems to press in on us and that we wish to flee. At the same time, the lived-body is experienced differently; we literally feel it foregrounded in a specific way. For instance, a certain form of centripetal constriction—connected to the experiential closeness of the threatening object—seems to tighten and compress us (which, by the way, puts fear in opposition to the centrifugal expansion of joy or yearning). There is also a meaningful change in terms of our experience of time, which becomes very dense and intense. And we also pre-reflectively sense a different relation to our social environment: When we are afraid, we are no longer at one with the world, but thrown upon ourselves and somewhat distanced from the world around us. Hence there is an urge to leave this phenomenological aloneness, to be near to other people, to call someone on the phone or simply grab a hand (in later chapters we will see how the group experience of the movie theater and its collective fear sometimes alleviate this detachment).[60]

These metamorphoses—a phenomenological closeness of the threatening object, a constriction of the lived-body, a densification of time and a certain degree of social distance to the world—are constitutive parts of the magical transformation that comes with *all* types of cinematic fear. But we will see that horror, shock, dread and terror also vary sufficiently to tell them apart. Just to mention an example in terms of time. Horror and shock are thoroughly rooted in the present, whereas dread and terror are future-oriented. And while the cinematic shock bursts into the scene suddenly and lasts only briefly, a dread scene emerges gradually and can often go on for a considerable amount of time. To be sure, these transformative experiences are rarely reflected upon *during* our fearful encounter with the film. Prior to any explicit thematization of one's affective state, one is first and foremost experiencing the situation in an affective manner. It is only *after the fact* that phenomenological reflection can recover the experience. This is what Chapters 3 to 7 are about.

To summarize, in a fearful situation my attention is strongly intertwined with an object appraised as threatening. This dangerous object seems overly close to me, centripetally constricting my lived-body space, foregrounding and thickening time, detaching me from the world around me and implying an action tendency to flee the object. In order to avoid a simple stimulus-response model, let me stress the two-sidedness and reversibility of fear: even if we feel passively overpowered in fear, there is also an active dimension. Not only is it often *initiated* by our active decision to experience it as well as *followed* by specific actions like screaming or covering our ears. But the emotion itself has an active side both in our intentional relatedness to the threatening danger and our state of action readiness that prepares and enables actions like looking away. Hence being passively frightened or endangered by a threatening object or event means, simultaneously, actively fearing it—and vice versa.[61]

So far I have indiscriminately talked about shock or terror as both "aesthetic strategies" and "(cinematic) emotions." What is the difference? The aesthetic *strategy* is what aims at producing the emotion: it takes place on the filmic level and can therefore be *objectively described* and analyzed stylistically as part of the filmic object. Since these aesthetic strategies exist only in order to affect us, their implicit goal is to evoke *subjectively experienced* (cinematic) emotions of the exact same name. Hence the expressions horror, shock, dread and terror simultaneously refer to objective aesthetic *strategies* and subjective aesthetic *emotions*. The distinction is a heuristic one that analytically separates for descriptive reasons what in fact belongs together. When we experience horror or terror in the cinema, the film-as-aesthetic-object and the viewer-as-experiencing-subject are thoroughly intertwined. The affective dimension would not be there without the film's aesthetic strategy; but an aesthetic strategy that does not entail the proper phenomenological experience is not worthy of its name. We can certainly cognitively *judge* that a scene is supposed to be emotional but do not *feel* as such: I *know* that the scene wants to scare me because the filmic strategies employed normally evoke this reaction—nonetheless I am bored. My evaluative judgment does not coincide with my bodily response. Hence a unity must exist between the here and the there: an intertwining and reversibility of *emotional* dimension (the viewer's *fear*) and *evocative* dimension (the film's *danger*).[62]

Obviously, not every viewer experiences the examples used throughout this book identically. This is not necessary. What I strive for are not descriptions of *specific* experiences of single viewers but shared *types* of experience with a common structure—an endeavor that I will explain in more detail in Chapter 1. At this point I will only mention the fact that the shared dimensions of embodiment underlying all our experiences—for instance, temporality and spatiality—enable us to talk about a common structure (or core) of certain types of experience. If this common structure did not exist, we wouldn't be able to communicate about emotions in the first place.

What is more, it is easily conceivable that a single viewer experiences the exact same scene very differently, depending on the circumstances. There are the changing *spatial surroundings*, *media* and *co-viewers*: is the film shown in a cinema with numerous other viewers, or is it watched on a computer screen alone at home? There is the viewer's *bodily state*: is he or she ill, tired or even on alcohol or drugs? There is the viewer's *mood*: was he or she sad or angry beforehand? There is the question of how close or far the content is to *one's own concern* at a given moment: are the wants and interests at stake in this scene intensely important or not? For instance, watching *Don't Look Now* (1973) for the second time I might consider the scene of the drowning girl much more devastating, because a close relative had died since the first viewing. Last but not least, there is the problem of *repetition and habituation*: it makes a difference whether I watch *The Silence of the Lambs* for the first or the eighth time; and it matters whether I am confronted with the horror genre for the first time in my life or whether I am a regular horror buff.

PLEASURES AND COUNTERBALANCES: MOMENTS OF INTENSITY AND COLLECTIVITY

As the reader might have guessed, the rhetorical question posed at the very beginning will be answered affirmatively: cinematic fear *can be* pleasurable. It can be pleasurable because it consists of precious moments of subjective *intensity* including remarkable metamorphoses of the lived-body and the foregrounding of time as well as valuable instances of *collectivity*. Horror, shock, dread and terror foreground and transform us in stimulating ways just as they connect us in specific enjoyable manners to our co-viewers. The viewer undergoes a number of intensive metamorphoses that involve lived-body *constriction* and *expansion*, movements of immersion *into* and extrication *out of* the filmic world as well as pointed and extended experiences of *time*. These moments of intensity do not only take place on the individual level but also have a collective dimension. Sitting in the multiplex theater I am necessarily part of an anonymous group—and under specific circumstances I experience myself as part of this collectivity. For reasons to be explored in later chapters, I prefer the less emphatic notions of 'collectivity' and 'group' to the morally and politically charged expression 'community.' Community is often associated with collective values, mutual commitments, a common history and encompassing both private *and* public life.[63] I merely try to underscore the pleasure of *feeling together*. Consequently, I will talk of 'group feelings' and 'feelings of collectivity' (sometimes also of 'feelings of belongingness') rather than 'community feelings.' On the other hand, words like 'group' or 'collectivity' are obviously more positively connoted than mere 'accumulations' or 'gatherings' or even 'crowds' or 'masses.'

The phenomenological chapters will not only maintain that we *have* these pleasurable experiences but also *describe* them. But cinematic fear is pleasurable also because it helps to counterbalance some of the rapid transformations of our life-world. It is not implausible to argue that frightening films offer something life is not sufficiently able to provide us with, something the aesthetic experience of the movies possesses. The paradoxical question why we experience pleasure in the face of fear can be resolved more convincingly, I think, if we do not simply claim pleasures *per se* but regard them as intricately and inseparably interwoven with the larger sociocultural framework. At the end of this study, my pleasure arguments will therefore be discussed on the broader basis of advanced modernity and its discontents.[64] Frightening films help to reconcile two aspects that are fundamental characteristics of advanced modernity: a) a scarcity of deep and comprehensive experiences due to our *disembodied way of life* (calling for counterbalancing strategies of lived-body stimulation) as well as an *ever-accelerating lifeworld* (asking for ways of making time more palpable) and b) the *loosening of social bonds* as a result of individualization (requiring new forms of collectivity if a sense of isolation and loneliness is to be prevented). If people flee the real world in order to seek the pleasures of the cinematic world, we should look critically at the reasons that make this move so attractive. The last part of the book is therefore an attempt to raise awareness to the transformations of experience and collectivity in our advanced modern world, in short: to some current forms of what the philosopher Charles Taylor calls "malaises of modernity."[65] Since disembodiment, acceleration and the loosening of social bonds are not covered by one single, over-arching theory (even if both fields are highly significant aspects of modernization), I will bring together a number of European and North American sociologists and cultural theorists.

To be sure, this counterbalancing function is not identical with the pleasure of fear itself, even if I presuppose that both are strongly interwoven. It is important to differentiate properly here. In order to avoid mixing phenomenological description with cultural theorizing, it is methodologically necessary to distinguish the intersubjectively verifiable phenomenologies from the theoretical speculation about the counterbalancing function of frightening films. This is essential insofar as the later is not present to consciousness: while I watch a frightening movie I am not aware that I respond to my lifeworld—I can only become aware of the pleasure I experience. This line of argument entails both a different style and logic of argumentation as well as a change of perspective: from the *micro*-analytical poetics and phenomenology of fearful aesthetic devices and their concomitant lived-body, time and collective experiences to a *macro*-analysis of the cinema's place within advanced modernity and its counterbalancing function vis-à-vis the transformations brought about by the processes of civilization and modernization,

What I have sketched so far might sound like an apology. And indeed, by bringing into play the function of counterbalancing pleasure, my account legitimizes aesthetic experiences otherwise eagerly dismissed. Defending the pleasures of horror, shock, dread and terror is risky business for the advocate, since attacks await him from two camps equally loathing the kind of movies discussed here. On the one hand, there is the 'conservative right.' Since the inception of the medium, films that evoke strong emotions and bodily reactions were treated with suspicion and became the target of moral accusations. In particular the consumption of scary movies was—and is—seen as a dark road that leads to desensitization, moral corruption and dehumanization. In the worst case, the medium even effects an imitation of the heinous acts depicted. What is more, there is a constant fear among (neo-)conservatives that what was once considered unhealthy and abnormal, in the hands of overly liberal politicians will be turned into the norm by a shrewd act of "defining deviancy down" (Daniel Patrick Moynihan).[66] According to this view, American culture is trapped in a spiral of ever-more: ever more violence, ever more pornography, ever more decline of the civic order. Even if the high times of censorship movements have ended and the questionable privilege of being the scapegoat for teenage-misbehaviors has been handed over to computer games, watching frightening movies is still considered a dangerous pastime not to be defended. On the other hand, the 'progressive left' might claim that an apologetic defense of pleasures is reactionary and helps to stabilize the questionable politics of these films. From this camp demands might be raised to radically disclose the false ideologies at work and tear apart the veil thinly covering the misogynist, racist, xenophobic or homophobic forms of representation.

Both camps have a point. An exploration of the pleasures of frightening films cannot easily refute the potentially negative side-effects. My affirmative view is not meant as a blind and zealous apology. It is not supposed to rule out thinking about *what* forms of pleasure people prefer and hence does not mean an *excuse* for any and every form of pleasure. Just because emotions and the body were long ignored in films studies, we should not fall into the other extreme. Although I bracket the meaning-dimension *heuristically*, this does not imply that it is inexistent. At the same time, one cannot deny that these pessimist warnings contain a strong tendency to denigrate the audience as 'immature' (in contrast to the grown-up moralist), 'weird/strange/perverse' (as opposed to the decent, normal viewer) or 'duped/deluded/deceived' (unlike the critical, truth-seeing progressive).[67] The larger argument of this book might therefore also be considered an antidote to the pathologizing and belittling attitudes toward those who enjoy fear at the movies.

THE AESTHETICS OF FEAR AND THE PROBLEM OF CATEGORY FORMATION

But how can a film become dangerous to its viewers so that they are afraid of it? If we presuppose that film and affect are necessarily intertwined, we should not bracket the filmic level and simply talk about experience. Instead, we have to dare taking a long, hard look at the aesthetics of fear.

Hence this study aims to be more than a phenomenological description of our pleasurable fearful experience; it also sets out to understand where these emotions are rooted aesthetically. In other words, what scary aesthetic strategies are used to produce the concomitant frightened affects? This will become particularly evident in the chapters on suggested horror, shock and dread, which include detailed discussions of aesthetic strategies; but it is also part of the chapters on direct horror and terror. The *specific* examples I choose in these discussions are supposed to represent *general* types. However, the fact that *I* consider these scenes effective enough to present them as *typical* should not prevent the reader from adding his or her own convincing examples.

Just like descriptions of fearful cinematic *experiences*, however, studies on the *aesthetics* of fear are rare.[68] This bibliographical scarcity in terms of experience and aesthetics of fear allows and, in fact, necessitates the (re-) formation of categories. George Lakoff and Mark Johnson strongly suggest taking embodied experience into account: "the categories we form are *part of our experience*! They are the structures that differentiate aspects of our experience into discernible kinds. My categories are thus not a purely intellectual matter, occurring after the fact of experience. Rather, the formation and use of categories is the stuff of experience."[69] In other words, our lived bodily experience has a word to say when we form categories, and the closer we listen, the more convincing these categories will be. This is precisely where phenomenology comes in. Drawing on lived experience will ground my categorization of the five types of cinematic fear.

To a certain extent these categories are well established. However, some are defined too inconsistently or overly broad. In other cases taking into account the lived-body more closely suggests reshaping. In two cases— dread and terror—new categories have to be introduced. The definition of these frightening versions of suspense points to blatant cases of categorization-without-experience. Current definitions of suspense, under which dread and terror were hitherto namelessly subsumed, are almost exclusively based on narration and cognition, not listening to what the lived-body has to say.

To be sure, my analytic dissection separates aesthetic elements that during the act of viewing succeed or blend into each other and often occur simultaneously, with mutual influence and reinforcing consequences. The five aesthetic strategies that I will be looking at can be combined and permutated in almost all varieties. Studying them in idealized isolation as prototypes is problematic insofar as they always stand in a specific relation to each other and their environment—as specific figures on a ground. Watching a frightening movie does not mean that I perceive a succession of perfectly isolated aesthetic elements, but I always experience the movie as a whole. On the other hand, the kind of dissection I propose here also suggests itself to a certain degree because frightening movies *are* highly episodic. They often present a series of successive incidents, thus separating aesthetic strategies to a considerable higher degree than genres that stress continuity and development of plot. Moreover, conceding that cinematic experiences do not consist of absolute data independent of context does not mean that we should give up the kind of abstraction suggested here. In trying to establish generalities scientific category formation always comes at the price of de-contextualization.

Its benefits are considerable though. One major argument in favor of prototype categorization is that we do not have words for everything we experience aesthetically. We feel something but cannot point it out due to a lack of words, and yet we want and even need to communicate about it.[70] Language helps to grasp and make communicable what is, on the one hand, utterly fleeting and, on the other hand, very close to us in its affectivity. Only if we categorize can we hope to reflect on, compare, weigh and discuss experiences. The case of dread is a clear-cut example: every viewer certainly *feels* the difference to a terror scene but cannot name it since there is no word. If we want to investigate the experiential aspect, we need a more refined vocabulary.[71] But in the end, my definitions are not meant to erect barbed-wire fences. Their purpose is to enable a more nuanced vocabulary for describing what is, in fact, always a gradual and continuous process: aesthetic experience.

WHAT IS A SCARY MOVIE? THE SIGNIFICANCE OF GENRE

One significant question hasn't been answered so far: what exactly do I mean by *frightening* or *scary* movies? I take it that a frightening movie is able to color the viewer's experience in various hues of fear—most prominently terror, shock, dread and horror—and thus to bring about a considerable phenomenological metamorphosis of the spectator's everyday emotional tinge. Lay viewers and popular film critics describe frightening movies by a plethora of adjectives ranging from scary, gruesome, unnerving, chilling, terrifying, horrific, uncanny, eerie and creepy to intense, petrifying, nerve-racking, suspenseful, gripping, riveting, hair-raising and shocking.

We know that a film is scary because, as individual viewers belonging to a certain historical and cultural setting, we do not approach films as blank slates. We are always situated in a specific life-world that has influenced us before, shaping our horizon of expectations. First, there is the title that often informs us what the movie will be about: from *The Invasion of the Body Snatchers* (1978) to *Alien: Resurrection* (1997). Second, we usually do not go to the movies uninformed, but are predisposed by numerous forms of *discourse*: reviews and interviews; trailers, TV commercials and advertisements; word-of-mouth. Consider, for instance, the tag line from the *Scream* trailer: "From the first man in suspense—director Wes Craven—comes the last word in fear—*Scream*." Third, and most importantly, there is the communicative tool we call 'genre.' Genres make it easier for producers, distributors and spectators to have preconceived ideas about groups of movies. They are helpful instruments of orientation, expectation and convention that circulate between industry, film, and viewer. Due to their standardized, formulaic nature genres allow the spectator to judge in advance what he or she will encounter. The audience can choose what stories it wants to experience and, maybe even more important, what it tries to avoid.

Obviously this does not imply that every genre film is an utterly predictable reformulation of what the viewer already knows. In fact, variations are an essential part of audience expectations: viewers always also want to experience something new and different. Paradoxically it is something at the same time well-known: new variations of familiar pleasures.[72] These familiar pleasures vary: some genres put emphasis on cognitive pleasures (the whodunit mystery or many avant-garde films); others strive to enhance knowledge (the documentary). Still others have an affective focus.[73] Steve Neale argues that "particular genres can be characterized, not as the only genres in which given elements, devices and features occur, but as the ones in which they are dominant, in which they play an overall, organizing role."[74] Following Neale's approach, this study relies exclusively on genres in which *fearful* aesthetic devices and emotions are dominant.

The talk of genres implies, of course, one problem. Claiming that certain genres are dominated by fearful aesthetic strategies presupposes that I must have an idea how these genres are defined. Yet genre definition is not an uncontested field. Two roads can be taken. First, the *theoretical* genre: an authoritative proposal of a logically impeccable classification of films.[75] Such *ex cathedra* definitions have caused considerable problems in film studies because once the elaborate models were tested empirically they turned out to be too rigid for borderline cases or historical variations.[76] Overly fixed definitions cause associations and expectations that specific films might not fulfill. Or, to put it differently, every new film can potentially blur the boundaries because it may not be identical to the definition. Hence Jörg Schweinitz argues: "Genres are just as heterogeneous and constantly changing at their center as they are fuzzy at their edges, i.e. in differentiation to each other. Genres do not exist as scrupulously differentiated film-cultural fields that fit into a larger 'system of genres,' which is arranged according to homogenous aspects."[77] As a consequence, neither a coherent map of the genre *system* has been established successfully; nor has any strict definition of a *single* genre won widespread acceptance.[78] These recurrent empirical problems of the theoretical genre were one incentive to move away from rigid taxonomical genre theory towards more reception-oriented approaches.[79]

This is where the second option comes into play: the *historical* genre. In contrast to earlier attempts from structuralism or analytic aesthetics, the concept of the historical genre does not imply a stable, a-historical, essentialist category. Nor does it presuppose an inherent evolutionary development with a linear trajectory. Instead it accepts as true a constant dynamics of change. Any number of historical-contextual influences can be important. The influence might be cultural (moral restrictions) and political (state censorship), or be initiated from within the film industry itself (as a reaction to changing audiences). Below we will see how an increased tendency to create hybrid genres has influenced the cinema of fear. What we take to be a given genre is a historically variable, cultural construction whose meaning can change considerably.[80] It varies according to category shifts among producers and consumers who 'negotiate' or 'struggle over' genre definitions. Their broad cultural 'consensus' becomes evident in contemporary industrial publicity, the trade press, film criticism and popular forums such as internet sites like www.imdb.com. It is this second road that I will take when I discuss frightening movies.

Consider the changing content of the category of 'horror' in the last decades. In the 1970s and '80s the horror genre was dominated by the ferocious display of dismembered and disfigured bodies, aptly called 'body horror.' The original *Dawn of the Dead* (1978) or *The Evil Dead* come to mind. In the 1990s body horror all but disappeared. Instead, three strands dominated the decade. The first one was the comparatively tame, self-referential teenage slasher: *Wes Craven's New Nightmare*, the *Scream* series (1996–2000) or *Urban Legend* (1998). The second dominating trend marked the return of psychological horror in which the viewer does not know—or knows only very late into the movie—whether the seemingly supernatural events are 'real' or imagined by the protagonist. Ghost stories like *The Sixth Sense* (1999), *The Blair Witch Project* and *Stir of Echoes* (1999), haunted-house films like *The Haunting* (1999) and *What Lies Beneath* (2000) relied much more on psychological threats and suggestion of violence than on explicit gore. The third trend was the action-laden creature-feature containing plenty of comic relief: *Anaconda* (1997), *The Lost World: Jurassic Park II*, *Deep Rising* (1998) or *Deep Blue Sea* (1999). In this present decade, again, three cycles can be identified. There are remakes of Japanese horror movies, largely dealing with demons, possessions and haunted houses: *The Ring 1* and *2* (2002 and 2005), *The Grudge 1* and *2* (2004 and 2006), *Dark Water* (2005). There are numerous remakes of American horror classics like *The Texas Chainsaw Massacre* (2003), *The Amityville Horror* (2005) or *The Hills Have Eyes* (2006). Finally, there are gruesome torture films like *Hostel* (2005) or *Saw* (2004) and their various sequels (2005–2008). The last two cycles show a clear predilection for violence akin to the 1970s and 1980s. These considerable shifts in the meaning of the term 'horror' indicate that in order to function as a communicative tool, the definition of the historical genre needs to be comparatively basic and broad, displaying a generous leeway in terms of genre boundaries.

But even if we presuppose a broad cultural consensus we still need to know what we can minimally expect from a given historical genre. Since the *a priori* normativism of a clear-cut definition that harshly dictates what a genre should and should not do is impractical, a more open and pragmatic form of category formation is needed. In reality, historical genres are categorized by way of prototypes.[81] The viewer's expectations are organized according to a core-periphery schema. A paradigmatic, often cited or discussed 'core' film inherits the status of a prototype. These prototypes are automatically recognized as best averages, because they share attributes with most members of the category. The genre prototype is responsible for evoking the viewer's expectations of iconographic motives, character types, subject matters—or emotions. The 'peripheral' films, on the other hand, are grouped around the prototype because they contain less conventional characteristics and are therefore less prototypical. Peripheral films are close or distant relatives of—and therefore less 'generic' than—the prototype. Which films can claim the status of a prototype, depends precisely on the cultural consensus of the given period.

Now, if we presume a viewer broadly informed about today's historical genres—which one would he or she pick in order to experience the pleasures of fear? There are two genres whose name straightaway announces an intense corporeal experience that, at the very least, points in the direction of fear: the horror film and the thriller. To be sure, dominant genre elements—such as fear—are not necessarily exclusive elements; they not only occur in the genre concerned.[82] As a consequence, one can expect scary and hair-raising moments in a number of genres. *Unforgiven* (1992) might be judged by some as a nerve-racking western. For many viewers *The Fugitive* (1993) comes across as an intensely riveting action film. Or think of Jan Svankmajer's *Alice in Wonderland*-adaptation *Neco z Alenky* (1988)—certainly an unnerving animation film. There is shock in the disaster movie (*The Day After Tomorrow*, 2004). There is suspense in science-fiction films (*Terminator 2: Judgment Day*, 1991), caper movies (*Ronin*, 1998) and westerns (*High Noon*, 1952). And there is violence in war films (*Platoon*, 1986), gangster movies (*Casino*, 1995), comic-book adaptations (*Sin City*, 2005) as well as independent fare (*Totally Fucked Up*, 1993). However, when a viewer skims through newspaper ads for a frightening Saturday evening entertainment, he will most likely look for a horror film or a thriller. These genres quantitatively *condense* and qualitatively *intensify* the various forms of fear and therefore put them at the center of their generic promise.

This can be read directly from the etymological roots. The word 'horror' derives from the Latin 'horrere' meaning 'to stand on end, bristle, shake, shudder, shiver, tremble.' And the adjective 'horrific' comes from the Latin 'horrificus,' literally meaning 'making the hair to stand on end.'[83] It thus describes an intense fearful reaction of the body. 'Thriller,' on the other hand, comes from the Middle English word 'thrillen' meaning 'to pierce.'[84] Again, the etymological origin refers to a sharp somatic response: the thriller pierces, as it were, the viewer's body and ensures a visceral experience. Not to forget, there is the similarity between the words *thrill* and *thrall*: both words come together in the term *enthrall* which carries connotations of being enslaved, captured, spellbound. In a thriller we give ourselves up to be captured and carried away in order to be thrilled—to receive a series of sharp sensations.[85]

Yet etymology can only serve as a preliminary argument precisely because *historical* genres are so malleable. What else merits my confidence in these genres? The horror movie will most likely not pose much of a problem. Few would doubt that it counts as a clear-cut case in terms of fear. To repeat, I do not want to essentialize the horror film by imposing that a frightening experience is the *only* pleasure one could get out of it. I simply take it for granted that if someone prefers to be scared, the horror film would be the principal choice. Within this genre the fearful aesthetic devices analyzed in this study were employed with considerable persistence over the last decades—even if the preferences and the emphases changed. In this regard the thriller might seem a more questionable candidate. Why, then, is it integrated in this study? I have three arguments.

First, viewers have very different thresholds in terms of what they consider scary; what people experience as horrifying or terrifying varies a great deal. While some people remain unimpressed by the most shocking horror movie, others are deeply frightened by a tame (sometimes even lame) thriller. Many spectators even refrain from watching thrillers at all because they get scared too easily. Hence it is next to impossible to generalize about the effects horror films and thrillers have on viewers. This is exactly the advantage of the genre system and the reason why it is differentiated so meticulously. Just as the field of erotic excitement distinguishes between softcore and hardcore pornography, the field of frightening intensity knows horror movies *and* thrillers. Apart from other potential differences that need not concern us here, the thriller—by and large—implies a milder form of emotional involvement than the horror film. In fact, after a considerable blurring of the generic boundaries in the 1990s (to be described below), the disparity in intensity is often the most reliable difference today. On average, thrillers offer a lighter version of horror: less violence, fewer shocks and more moments of relief.

Second, the inclusion of the thriller suggests itself when we look at encyclopedias and academic research. Leafing through a random academic study—say Martin Rubin's *Thrillers*—we read the following definition: "In thrillers the mandate is 'Make me squirm.' Or, to put it another way: Pierce me with intense, even agonizing sensations that will transform my ordinary world and charge it with the spirit of adventure. This generic property raises the possibility of the thriller that is not thrilling akin to the comedy that is not funny or the erotic film that is not a turn-on."[86] What this quote implies is that even though the thriller might not have a clearly recognizable iconography (like the prairie and the cowboys in the western) or standard structural ingredients (like the songs in the musical), the genre gains its

Introduction 33

communicative value from the emotional experience it promises. It should be undisputed—and the only criterion important here—that thrillers thrill. Just like the horror film, the thriller is named after an intense emotional experience. What 'thrilling' means exactly, however, varies historically.

It will be my third argument that the word 'thrilling' became more and more associated with various forms of fear: in the late 1980s and 1990s developments took place that changed the historical genre of the thriller and further justifies calling it 'frightening' today. In those years what professional critics, average viewers and the studios described as *thrillers* came to include aesthetic elements formerly associated foremost with the *horror* movie. While terror and dread had been part of thrillers before, the aesthetic elements of *horror, cinematic shock* and even *disgust* became acceptable to a hitherto unknown degree. Even the most cursory look at films then categorized as thrillers will underscore this point. *Jacob's Ladder* (1990) uses monstrous and gory imagery such as demons, aliens and bloody, dismembered body parts. *Basic Instinct* contains nasty stabbing scenes in which an unholy amount of blood is spilled. In *Cape Fear* (1991) we are confronted with a horrifying rape scene in which the protagonist chews away parts of a woman's cheek. And *Seven* presents a foul-smelling, skeletal victim of torture, more dead than alive. Even the startle effect—cinematic shock in my terminology—is often part of mainstream thrillers: from *Fatal Attraction* (1987) to *The Bone Collector* (1999).

If we consider genres as a communicative tool relying on a cultural understanding about what a genre promises at a given time, public discourse must have captured this generic change. And, indeed, the blending of horror films and thrillers did not go unnoticed in journalistic and academic criticism. An extended debate centered on a distinct cycle of films that soon came to be known as 'yuppie horror movies'—frightening films in which bad things happen to good yuppies. The precursor of these films was soon identified as Adrian Lyne's *Fatal Attraction*. In its wake a whole series of movies entered the scene: *Pacific Heights* (1990), *Bad Influence* (1991), *The Hand That Rocks the Cradle* (1992), *Unlawful Entry* (1992), *Single White Female* (1992), *Final Analysis* (1992), *Whispers in the Dark* (1992), *Sliver* (1993), *The Vanishing* (1993) or *Malice* (1993).[87] Two important characteristics defined the cycle. First, the use of settings, protagonists and effects previously associated with the horror film: dark, terrible places and 'evil' houses; scenes in the constricted and disorienting space of basements and other labyrinth-like places; psychopathic stalkers or killers almost unstoppable in their rage; shock scenes that made the audience jump; and graphic violence. Second, these films were attractive for people that would usually not go to see horror movies: the very yuppies the name of the cycle refers to. (The audience extension is a point I will return to.)

Comprising most of the 1990s, a second, even more widely debated movie cycle equally destabilized the boundary between horror and thriller (also because it partly overlapped with the first one): the serial killer movie. From

Jennifer Eight (1992), *Copycat* (1995) and *Seven* to *Nightwatch* (1997), *Kiss the Girls* (1997) and *The Cell* (2000). Here the movie that most probably sparked the cycle was *The Silence of the Lambs*. Since serial killers often do not have a *motive*, the *depictions* and the *results* of the violent acts become pivotal: psychological or actual violence moves into the focus of attention. Why does Hannibal Lecter (Anthony Hopkins) crave human flesh for dinner? What is the motivation for Kathrine Tramell's (Sharon Stone) ice pick murders in *Basic Instinct*? The films often show crime for crime's sake. The lack of psychological and social motivation turned serial killers into close relatives of the slasher movie psychopaths. The slasher as a horror subgenre is clearly defined by a lack of sociological and psychological explanations in favor of a quick recurrence of visceral acts. Since the obsessive murderer will keep on killing till he is caught or killed, the seriality of his killings allows, by definition, for a whole series of terror, dread, shock or horror scenes. It plays, in Richard Dyer's words, on "the mix of repetition and anticipation, and indeed of the anticipation of repetition, that underpins serial pleasure."[88]

Due to these developments of the 1980s and particularly the 1990s the door is now open for thrillers to present more dread, more violence, and more shock effects than before. It is not surprising that they became more emotionally intense and frightening on average. Of course, it would be a blatant exaggeration to say that every thriller actually uses these devices. Nor would it be true to argue that thrillers are truly *scary* in every case— this is necessarily so because the genre closely borders on and overlaps with the action blockbuster (*The Bourne Identity*, 2002), the caper movie (*Inside Man*, 2006) and the whodunit mystery (*The Usual Suspects*, 1995). I simply argue that the stakes were raised: what is commonly understood as a thriller today can be much like horror in the past because both genres *can*—but not necessarily *do*—employ the same emotional aesthetic strategies. As a consequence, it became more difficult than ever to neatly tell them apart.

Yet the distinction between horror films and thrillers became fuzzy also because the industry deliberately influenced the labeling. Realizing that mainstream audiences could be lured into scary movies, the studios' advertising and marketing departments followed their own categorizing agenda: often they preferred the 'thriller' to the 'horror' badge.

Steve Neale argues that each era in the history of American cinema has its own transient generic system.[89] While some genres—like the travelogue or the phantom ride—were popular during the early cinema period, these genres vanished or changed considerably in subsequent decades. Quintessential American genres like the western and the musical—highly established in the 1930s and 1940s—largely disappeared during the last decades. In contrast, horror films and—to a lesser degree the more reputable and already established—thrillers came to move to the center very gradually.[90] Today's generic system would be unthinkable without them. Always a reliable indicator for mainstream acceptance is the box-office performance. Horror films like *Scream*, *The Blair Witch Project*, *The Sixth Sense*, *Signs*, *What Lies Beneath* or *The Ring*, hybrids such as *The Silence of the Lambs* and *Seven* as well as thrillers like *Sleeping With the Enemy* (1991), *Basic Instinct*, *The Da Vinci Code* (2006) and *Hannibal* (2001) were enormous successes. But acceptance might also be judged from the quality and reputation of the directors the two genres attracted. Since the 1990s a number of major directors have worked in the thriller field: Martin Scorsese (*Cape Fear*), Brian de Palma (*Raising Cain*, 1992), David Fincher (*Seven*), Sidney Pollack (*The Interpreter*, 2005), Gus van Sant (*Psycho*, 1998), Alan J. Pakula (*The Pelican Brief*, 1993) or Ridley Scott (*Hannibal*). Likewise, many arthouse directors, independent auteurs and reputable mainstream filmmakers in the U.S. and abroad (re-)turned to the horror genre or worked at its margins: from Neil Jordan (*Interview with the Vampire*, 1994), Lars von Trier (*Riget/The Kingdom*, 1994), David Lynch (*Lost Highway*), Roman Polanski (*The Ninth Gate*, 1999) and Danny Boyle (*28 Days Later*, 2002) to Alejandro Amenábar (*The Others*, 2001), Claire Denis (*Trouble Every Day*, 2001), Abel Ferrara (*The Addiction*, 1995), Jean-Pierre Jeunet (*Alien: Resurrection*) and Steven Spielberg (*Lost World: Jurassic Park 2*). Today the horror film is so firmly established at the heart of Hollywood cinema that even ultraviolent torture movies like *Hostel* and *Saw* are regular fare at the multiplex.

The development of the late 1980s and 1990s had important ramifications for the composition of the audience. It helped to open the field of frightening movies for other than the traditional patrons, male teenagers and horror buffs. Even if shockers occasionally had drawn mass audiences before (e.g., *Psycho* [1960], *The Exorcist* [1973] or *Jaws* [1975]), today consuming scary movies is more accepted than ever before. And women certainly belong to the regular patrons as well. Hence what Carol Clover had noted in her seminal study on the slasher film back in 1992—the fact that women compose a large part of the horror audience—has intensified in the meantime.[91] There is another upshot to this development: because the barriers to the cinema of fear have been reduced, the reception of movies in general has become more *direct* and *somatic*. It is, of course, one major goal of this study to demonstrate that there is a certain cultural logic behind this popularization and somatization—a development that points to the current state of advanced modern societies.

This study is not primarily intended as another entry in the long list of recent horror literature.[92] Nor does it specifically aim at extending the comparatively small inventory of studies on thrillers.[93] Yet it is an exploration of genres insofar as it aims to add to our understanding of the fearful aesthetic devices used in horror films and thrillers. And the concept of genre plays an important role also because it serves as a communicative tool that is essential for the decision-making process. The viewer's active decision to watch a frightening movie is based on what Gerhard Schulze calls "experience rationality" (*Erlebnisrationalität*), since more strongly than usual the viewer has to decide to watch the film *deliberately*.[94] No doubt, viewers are influenced by media hype, advertising and peer pressure, sometimes quite strongly. But these influences lose power once extreme experiences like horror, shock or dread are concerned. Experiences that might involve displeasure or even harm presuppose a much more active consent than tamer emotions and affects. Hence we are not passively pulled into but actively consent to go and watch a horror movie or thriller. Precisely for this reason we can also assume that the spectator expects the movie to yield some kind of reward.

This is not to say that every viewer can pinpoint precisely what he or she enjoys. After all, genres are means of communication that tell us what we can expect from a given movie *by and large*. It is certainly not necessary that we know *all* aspects of a genre's stylistics, subject matter, history etc. in order to come to a decision of what to look for and what to avoid. Instead this decision often functions *ex negativo*. Many avid fans of thrillers detest horror films. Even though they do not know a lot about the horror genre, it is pretty obvious to them that they know enough *not* to like it. I therefore agree with Ed Tan that most film viewers "have at the very least a strong intuitive feeling about what does *not* appeal to them, and it is not necessary to be a true film enthusiast to know approximately what type of film you are looking for."[95] Hence the decision to watch a scary film relies on two aspects. First, it depends on the experience the film—qua communicativeness of genre—promises. And second, it relies on what Ed Tan calls the "predisposition, sensitivity, preference, or motivation" of the viewer.[96] If both aspects match, the genre film and viewer will find together.

THE STRUCTURE OF THIS STUDY: AN OVERVIEW

Before we can start with the detailed discussion of the five types of fear, I have to set up the methodological fundament on which to build the larger argument. Since phenomenology is still relegated to the margins of film studies, I find it indispensable to introduce its major characteristics and ward off recurrent misunderstandings and unfounded criticisms. To avoid frustration among readers unfamiliar with phenomenology (but also to convince them of this fascinating approach), I will do my best to keep the discussion as accessible as possible. This is the goal of Chapter 1. In Chapter 2 I clarify how the multiplex cinema influences and skews our experience of the five types of fear under scrutiny here. This involves the enhanced attention of the cinematic experience in comparison to private home consumption. It includes the tendency to individualize and immerse the viewer as well as to increase his or her emotional experience. And it implies a look at the collective situation in the multiplex.

In Chapters 3 to 7 I eventually turn to cinematic fear itself. In order to grant the reader an easy entry into the discussion every chapter on cinematic fear starts with short summaries of three exemplary scenes as well as the definition of the respective type of fear. The first type of fear that I will look at is direct horror. This chapter is important also insofar as it explains the necessary preconditions for our pleasurable encounter with fear. In Chapter 4 I explore a second type of horror: not the drastically *direct* version, but the *suggested* one. In Chapter 5 I move on to cinematic shock. Just like the other chapters on fear, it contains an in-depth discussion of aesthetics and experience. Since the category of dread (as I define it) has not existed so far, Chapter 6 is longer than the others. Here I also take up issues like filmic atmospheres, empathy/sympathy and the phenomenology of time in fearful cinematic encounters. Chapter 7 introduces the category of terror, another frightening type of suspense. This chapter helps to set terror apart from other, more broadly conceived definitions of suspense *and* to distinguish terror from the notion of dread.

The last part of the book takes the phenomenological results and puts them against the backdrop of advanced modernity. In Chapters 8 and 9 I will discuss some of the malaises of advanced modernity that the cinema of fear helps to alleviate: disembodiment, acceleration and the loosening ties of communality. These chapters rely on the work of theorists of modernity like Norbert Elias, Karl-Heinrich Bette, Hartmut Rosa, Robert Bellah, Ulrich Beck and Zygmunt Bauman. Finally, in my conclusion I will present a list of aspects that did not make their way into this book, but are certainly valid to be explored. This last section is—*cum grano salis*—entitled "The End."

1 How to Describe Cinematic Fear, or Why Phenomenology?

> *[Phenomenology] is as painstaking as the works of Balzac, Proust, Valéry or Cézanne—by the reason of the same kind of attentiveness and wonder, the same demand for awareness, the same will to seize the meaning of the world.*
>
> (Maurice Merleau-Ponty)[1]

PHENOMENOLOGY—THE METHOD

Phenomenology is interested in subjectively experienced phenomena encountered in the world—whether these phenomena can be objectively accounted for scientifically or not. Genuine phenomenology therefore describes only what we have at least a certain awareness of; awareness-of-experience is a defining trait of conscious experience. What is not part of *conscious* experience does not fall in the domain of phenomenology since we do not have a chance to describe it.

However, we rarely become actively aware of our awareness. We are so involved in our activities that we do not notice or reflect upon the way in which we experience them. We therefore have to disentangle from the continuous flow of experience to reflect upon the structure of experience itself. In the words of Simon Glendinning, phenomenology is a work of "elucidation, explication or description of something we, in some way, already understand, or with which we are already, in some way, familiar, but which, for some reason, we cannot get into clear focus for ourselves without more ado."[2] Phenomenologists call this 'more ado' phenomenological reduction. It transforms the act I accomplish in a *natural* and *transparent* way into an *object for my attention*. Following Alfred Schütz, one could say we turn from a suspension of doubt to a suspension of belief.[3] Or, as Husserl, would call it: we move from the natural attitude to the phenomenological attitude.[4]

Phenomenology does not claim that all consciousness is simultaneously consciousness-of *and* self-conscious. It simply argues that all consciousness is consciousness-of and therefore *capable* of being reflected upon and brought under description. This occurs first and foremost after the fact: Afterwards I can reflect upon the experience and begin to thematize its structural features. During the *straightforward* activity of watching a film, for instance, the movie is the prime intentional object (with my lived body and the audience mostly at the periphery); during the *reflective* activity of phenomenological reporting, the past experience itself becomes the focus of attention. This reflection after the fact is possible only because I was *not* unaware or unconscious of these experiences. Don Ihde might be talking about intense cinematic involvements when he explains: "To say that self-consciousness is reduced to a minimum, that the 'I' of such experiences is not thematized or explicit, is not at all to say that such experiences are lacking in awareness or are opaque. Quite to the contrary, in ordinary or mundane life, such experiences can be a vivid example of the most valued type of experience. In reporting in the ordinary mode, I might well recall such occasions as those when 'I was most alive . . .'"[5]

In terms of cinematic fear there is a crucial difference between an adrenaline rush or high synaptic voltages and phenomena like a constricted lived-body experience and feelings of phenomenological isolation: The former cannot be reflected upon but only measured and observed from outside in a lab situation; the latter are supra-threshold in terms of consciousness and therefore open to phenomenological investigation. The former influence consciousness only indirectly; the latter have a direct manifestation in the experiential sphere. The former can be considered a form of *sub-personal* subjectivity, while the latter constitute *conscious* subjectivity (even though it is not necessarily a *self*-conscious one).[6]

Obviously, the contents of awareness vary in terms of how explicit, stable and easy to reflect upon they are. Experiences shade off into less overtly conscious phenomena: from *core* (or *focal*) experiences to marginal (or *peripheral*) experiences to experiences on the fringe (or *horizon*) of awareness. The cinematic experience is dominated by three foci: a) the film, b) the viewer's lived body, and c) the cinematic surroundings (with the rest of the audience in particular). The distribution of attention is not equal. In most cases the film will claim *focal* awareness, while we are only *marginally* conscious of the lived body and the cinema. Put differently, the film experience dominates consciousness, whereas body and cinema have receded—or, rather, were pushed—to the phenomenal background. However, and this will be a central argument, this distribution of attention is not static. At various points throughout the film the field of consciousness is reorganized. It comes into motion and flexibly shifts emphasis. The body as well as the cinema become foregrounded and claim attention, while the film as intentional object loses its center-stage position. This flexible shifting of emphasis is called the *conservation principle*: as something becomes clear, something else must become vague.[7] Or as something is excluded from the thematic *core* of awareness, something else moves in from the thematic *field*.[8] In cinematic shock, for instance, the lived body stands out and briefly relegates the film to the peripheral background: we gain self-awareness—a strong awareness-of-ourselves as embodied viewers—and consequently cannot fully devote attention to what happens on the screen. Or in moments of laughter—not uncommon in horror movies—the collectivity of the audience presses forward from its marginal status to a more focal position. While this is true for other genres as well, frightening movies are *dominated* by these fluid shifts in attention distribution between film, body and cinema. This is precisely the reason why I claim a transformative foregrounding of the body and feelings of collectivity as the prime pleasures of fear.

But what about all the idiosyncratic reactions to particular genres, movies and scenes? My mother keeps telling me that the most intense film she has ever seen was Hitchcock's *The Birds* (1963)—a comparatively unexciting film for someone who grew up with a shocker like *The Evil Dead*. On the other hand, I still consider *The Silence of the Lambs* the most frightening movie ever, whereas my students find it rather tame. What to do with the fact that some people have a hell of a boring time, while others are scared like hell? The answer is simple: uniformity in audience response to *specific* genres, films and scenes is not the point. Phenomenology does not want to explain how specific viewers respond to specific scenes. The question is rather: *if* a viewer is affected by a horror, shock, dread or terror scene, *how* does he or she experience it? It is therefore irrelevant if one specific viewer jumps out of his seat during a shock scene while another one remains untouched. What *does* have relevance, is the *common structure* that follows *when* these two viewers do experience a scene as shocking. But even if both are indeed shocked, I would not claim that they experience the scene identically in terms of intensity or length. I would simply argue that there is a common structure that unites their experiences. Hence I do not focus on *difference* but on *commonalities*; I do not want to particularize but look at what experiences have in common. In short, phenomenology is not interested in various and varying *specific* experiences but tries to capture *types* of experience.

If the phenomenologist was successful in suspending personal and institutional biases and has thoroughly reflected upon experience, he or she will approach the goal of bringing to light the core of a given subjective experience—its structural feature. Hence the description will be of what it is like—'invariantly' like—to undergo such an experience. To be sure, the 'invariant' core that phenomenology tries to uncover does not imply a universal or transcendental subject. This is the major move that led Merleau-Ponty and his *existential* phenomenology away from Husserl's *transcendental* phenomenology which sought to study 'pure' consciousness. Existential phenomenology claims that the subject of consciousness and experience is embodied and situated in the life-world. The lived body is always informed and qualified by the specific historical and cultural context lived in. Arguing otherwise would imply committing an essentialist fallacy.

Since there are no fixed essences, a fully exhaustive phenomenological reduction is impossible. This is why I put inverted commas around the word 'invariant.' Nevertheless, we can try to *approach* common structures, since we all share the ontological conditions of human embodiment. When we call 'emotions' subjective in everyday speech, we usually refer to empirical differences in terms of object, disposition and intensity. In other words, different people are afraid of different things, are scared easier than others and respond more intense to certain objects. But in what way does it make sense to say that we experience the structure of fear differently? To describe 'invariant' features is possible, as Vivian Sobchack notes, because experiences are lived both *generally* and *conventionally*: "in the first instance, according to general conditions of embodied existence such as temporality, spatiality, intentionality, reflection and reflexivity and, in the second instance, according to usually transparent and dominant cultural habits that are not so much determining as they are regulative."[9] It is not my point to ignore gender, race, class, sexuality, age etc. and quietly presume a male, white, heterosexual, middle-class spectator. However, before we can say in what way gender, race, class, sexuality and age qualify the common ontological conditions during a fearful cinematic experience, we need someone's account as a starting point. This starting point is, of course, marked by its own historicity: writing at this point in time reveals the author not as a transhistorical, a-cultural spectator but one rooted in a specific time and culture.

SUBJECTIVE OR SUBJECTIVISTIC? IN DEFENSE OF PHENOMENOLOGY

But isn't all this pure subjectivist blather? Both ignoramuses and people who should know better have repeatedly reproached phenomenology for registering mere private phenomena, for manifesting a relapse into introspectionism, for being an overly subjectivist approach that cannot provide scientific valid insights. Particularly its first-person accounts have provoked suspicion from the scientific community. Employing a method that draws on first-person descriptions at this historical point when some film scholars start to embrace the methods of the natural sciences might be considered a provocation, a methodical ignorance, or an outright stupidity.

This is clearly not the case. Phenomenology distinguishes sharply between simple introspection and higher-level reflection. While the former contains the straightforward accessible subjective data that are 'directly present to the mind,' the latter tries to reveal an experience's 'invariant' aspects that are genuinely discoverable but often not seen due to their habituated nature. Phenomenology is decidedly not interested in private opinions or spontaneous judgments. The merely personal idiosyncrasies that vary from person to person are precisely what phenomenology tries to avoid. Again, phenomenology is not interested in *particular* cases, but in *types* of experience. Closely related to the problem of introspection is the problem of self-observation: some scholars question it *per se* due to its call for a duplication of the subject. The observer cannot live through *and* monitor an experience. It is true that being in the grip of an emotion such as terror makes it difficult to observe it. An examining, observational position tends to neutralize the observer and detach him or her from the object of observation. A genuine emotion like fear, on the other hand, overwhelms the subject and involves him or her in a struggle with this emotion. This obviously stands in opposition to the neutral stance required by the observer. Yet from this we cannot jump to the conclusion that any self-investigation of emotional experiences automatically has to fail—otherwise there would be no account of them in the first place. If we did not relate to what others have to say about subjective experience, we would not be able to understand psychological novels or introspective poetry. Since it flies in the face of the evidence we have of convincing first-person descriptions, this accusation can be discarded. Hermann Schmitz gives another convincing reason. If emotions vanished once we tried to self-investigate them, we could easily get rid of negative emotions by switching into an observational mode.[10]

Another criticism put forward claims that first-person accounts are not viable because they modify the object of observation. This reproach is somewhat odd insofar as it uses the very method it tries to discard: in order to be informed about an eventual modification in viewpoint one would have to use a first-person account first. "For knowing about my internal state of mind, as also attesting to any transformation in it, presupposes in every instance the bringing into play of a first-person point of view!" Pierre Vermersch explains.[11] Obviously, this argument cannot wholly eliminate the problem. No methodological approach to experience is neutral. It inevitably introduces an interpretative framework into its gathering of data. Hence the hermeneutical dimension of the process is unavoidable: To a certain degree every examination is an interpretation—and all interpretation reveals and hides away at the same time. But from this we cannot conclude that a disciplined approach to experience creates nothing but artificial constructs or a 'deformed' version of the way experience 'really' is.[12] If phenomenology cannot deliver pure 'facts,' it nevertheless provides, at the very least, intersubjectively verifiable descriptions that we cannot do without if we want to talk about experience.

I need to issue a disclaimer, though. Phenomenology is not a magic potion, and first-person accounts are not suitable for every set of problems. If I want to find out about the amount of adrenaline male viewers discharge watching the famous chase scene in *Terminator 2: Judgment Day*, I would certainly not draw on first-person accounts. And if I am interested in the level of mirror neuron activity inside a viewer's brain while she listens to a frightened character in, say, *Candyman*, drawing on phenomenological description would be ridiculous. It all depends on the questions we ask. Just because some facts are inaccessible to consciousness and therefore unsuitable for first-person accounts does not necessitate that what we *are* aware of is *a priori* uninteresting or non-scientific.

LANGUAGE GAMES AND METAPHORS

As a descriptive method phenomenology yields predominantly descriptive knowledge and carefully avoids introducing aspects not consciously apprehended. One should therefore not expect explanations of unconscious or subconscious mechanisms. To illustrate: I will answer the question "how is it like to experience a cinematic shock?" not "what parts of my brain are stimulated when a monster suddenly attacks the protagonist?" Precisely because phenomenology is a descriptive method, however, so much depends on the script: the preciseness, density and accessibility of the language employed. This is far from being an easy task, since in describing a perceptual, imaginative or emotional experience one often reaches beyond where words can go. Our concepts seem too crude to express the infinite shades of experience. One way out of this tight spot is the use of metaphors. Employing figurative language is a characteristic that lies at the heart of many (maybe most) phenomenological investigations. Sobchack, for instance, argues that the vital but taken-for-granted figurative expressions of vernacular language—literally—speak of and tell us about our everyday experience. She quotes from Paul Ricoeur's work on metaphor: "Ordinary language . . . appears to me . . . to be a kind of conservatory for expressions which have preserved the highest descriptive power as regards human experience, particularly in the realms of action and feelings."[13]

Ricoeur's remark is easily underscored by a random look at journalistic criticism. Peter Travers, for instance, calls *Seven* a "skin crawler" with a "gut-wrenching climax".[14] Hal Hinson feels that in *Single White Female* "the psychological atmosphere that director Barbet Schroeder creates is so densely threatening that the air feels thick around you."[15] And in his review of *The Haunting* Roger Ebert portrays the old manor central to the film with the words: "We enter this space and feel enclosed by it . . ."[16] Is this mere language-playing? Certainly not. When we talk about films in metaphorical ways, we do so because metaphors help us to come closest to an adequate description of our lived-body experience for which we would otherwise have no words. Metaphorical language is thus irreplaceable.

The cognitivist linguist George Lakoff stresses the experiential roots of the figurative language we use in everyday life. Together with his co-author Mark Johnson he argues that metaphors cannot be comprehended independently of their *experiential* bases.[17] The concepts 'happy is up' and 'sad is down' might serve as simple but illuminating examples. On the one hand, we claim that we are feeling *up*, that we are *high* in spirits, that thinking about something positive gives us a *lift*. On the other hand, we feel *down*, our spirits *sink*, we *fall* into depression. Trying to explain the origin of these metaphors Lakoff and Johnson rightfully refer to the body as explanation: "Drooping posture typically goes along with sadness and depression, erect posture with a positive emotional state."[18]

We can easily confirm their third-person perspective by drawing on our own experiences in terms of the vertical impulses—the lifting and pressing down—of emotions like joy and happiness on the one hand and sadness and sorrow on the other. The most visible symptom of the former is the dido or caper: as if the earth had partly lost its gravitational force, the happy and joyful person experiences an upward urge not explicable in physical terms. For a limited period of time, these emotions bestow our existence with an incredible lightness of being. Sadness and sorrow, on the other hand, are characterized by experiential vectors pointing downwards: we feel as if carrying a weighty burden and possessing a heavy heart. Without difficulty, we can apply these examples to our cinematic experiences. After a 'high-spirited,' 'light' comedy we sometimes feel like dancing or flying out of the theater. A 'heavy,' 'depressing' tragedy, on the other hand, often causes the opposite experience: we trudge out into the night downhearted, unwilling to face the view of others.

Similarly, when we talk about a 'riveting' or 'gripping' film, as it is often the case with scary movies, we do not employ these metaphors as rhetorical embellishment. Instead, they function as indispensable bridges that cross language gaps. In fact, they describe quite literally the mode of our position in the seat: motionless and touched by the grip of the film. Ordinary expressions like 'riveting' and 'gripping' can therefore be considered as mini-phenomenologies. However, as *mini*-phenomenologies they are naturally not comprehensive enough. They can only serve as starting-points for more thorough-going descriptions. To be sure, the reliance on metaphor creates its own problems, since we still have to come up with the adequate expressions. As amateurs who clumsily imitate the work of professionals we face the danger of "being lousy poets," in Jack Katz's words.[19] The metaphors I employ throughout this study are therefore mere suggestions and might be replaced by the reader's own *mots justes*.

PHENOMENOLOGICAL DESCRIPTION AS SHARED KNOWLEDGE

All this is to say that doing phenomenology is not a readily-available practice. *Asking* empirical audiences is consequently no straightforward alternative: Many viewers cannot repress their prejudiced, habituated grasp of phenomena, which inevitably obstructs their viewpoint. Nor do they have words for their cinematic experience ready at hand. This is precisely the reason why we are doing phenomenology in the first place. If suspending the natural attitude, engaging in phenomenological reductions and providing rigorous descriptions were easily practicable activities, there would be no need for phenomenologists with special observational trainings, descriptive capabilities and temporal and institutional possibilities. As Simon Glendinning puts it, "the unreliability of the 'witness' in his own case is part of the motivation and difficulty of phenomenology."[20] Anticipating possible finger-pointing, let me say that this argument is meant no more elitist than an incontrovertible statement like 'not everyone is capable of repairing a car engine.' Just as looking at a car engine does not automatically turn me into a mechanic or a car engineer, to be in touch with one's own experience does not make me a good phenomenologist. Obviously not every phenomenological description is good phenomenology just as not every self-proclaimed phenomenologist is practicing phenomenology.

But how, then, can we judge whether a subjective description is more than mere subjectivistic blather? My constant high-sounding claims to work phenomenologically notwithstanding, there is obviously no guarantee of infallibility. Nevertheless there are certain criteria that distinguish good and bad phenomenology—and the prime authorities to judge over a successful phenomenological investigation are its readers.

First, the reader must consider the phenomenological description somewhat surprising. Phenomenology aims to uncover aspects of everyday experience that are buried beneath habituation and institutionalization and are thus known only implicitly. Through phenomenological description we get to 'see' something that was right 'in front of our eyes', but for which we were in some ways 'blind.' As a consequence, the results should have an air of novelty—otherwise they are not good phenomenology but remain descriptions of something familiar all along. This is all the more true in film studies where phenomenological descriptions of emotions and cinematic collectivity are few and far between. But novelty is not sufficient—eccentric and utterly false descriptions can be surprising as well.

The second and crucial criterion for a successful phenomenological description therefore demands that the established experiential 'invariants' should strike equal chords among others. Do the readers agree, because they can match the description with their own experience? Or do they get the impression that the analyst makes things up? Vivian Sobchack elaborates: "The proof of an adequate phenomenological description, then, is not whether or not the reader has actually had—or even is in sympathy with—the meaning and value of an experience as described—but whether or not the description is resonant and the experience's structure sufficiently comprehensible to a reader who might 'possibly' inhabit it (even if in a differently inflected or valued way)."[21] It is my hope that the subsequent descriptions are recognizable enough to evoke embodied understanding. There are no objective criteria of correctness in the sense of the natural sciences. Only an intersubjective validation can turn the subjective description into shared knowledge. But in order to be *inter*-subjectively verifiable, i.e. shared by others, it must have been noted by a *subjectively* experiencing individual first—otherwise we would have no idea of it at all.

Hence only making the descriptions public will help to find out whether they can be called objective (as opposed to merely private) in the first place. Herbert Spiegelberg notes: "What else can we do but first record our direct experiences as completely as possible and then see what others in the face of the same phenomena have to report? Only as the result of such comparing of notes (not an easy matter anyway) of these full experiences can we even think of selecting what is public. In fact, before this is done we cannot even say what is merely private."[22] Once written down, my phenomenological descriptions meet the criteria of scientific validation: they are publicly available, intersubjectively verifiable and can be repeated by anyone willing and able to describe phenomenologically. If inadequate, this will turn out in due time. Hence consider the phenomenological descriptions presented in the following chapters as a starting point: they offer grounded assumptions made available for the scrutiny of empirical research.

WHY NOT MEASURING? SOME NOTES ON SCIENTIFIC AUDIENCE RESEARCH

For a long time, most empirical research on audience responses was done outside of film studies, most notably in psychology and communication/media studies. Even though in the 1990s film studies began to focus more strongly on audiences (particularly in Janet Staiger's historical-materialist approach and the empirical research done in the wake of British Cultural Studies), the inadequacies are still prevalent.[23] Stephen Prince has therefore recommended the insights of psychophysiology or neuroscience.[24] This is precisely where one part of cognitive film theory, with its strong reliance on cognitive psychology and neuroscience, seems to be heading. The most empirically-inclined proponents have started to include technical devices that observe and record viewer responses: infrared cameras scanning facial expressions; electro- or magnetoencephalography (EEG/MEG), positron emission tomography (PET) and functional Magnetic Resonance Imaging (fMRI) mapping brain activity; biofeedback sensors with gloves sensitive to heart rate and skin temperature. Other physiological reactions measured are cardiac output, blood-sugar level, palmar conductance, saliva output, and endocrine activity.

Whatever the gains of these recordings (and there are certainly many), they cannot overcome a significant inadequacy: they are unable to provide a description of the viewer's experience. Experiments in cognitive psychology, psychophysiology and neuroscience deliver highly elaborate images, charts, diagrams and graphs. Yet these recordings document both too *much* and too *little* for the purposes of my study. On the one hand, a large amount of what is recorded does not make its way into awareness. The increase of blood-sugar level and the firing of mirror neurons certainly have a *causal impact* on my experience, but I am *not aware* of these unconscious physiological and neural transformations themselves. Hence, as useful as these scientific, third-person observations are in other respects, their problem in our context is: not everything recordable enters into a quantitative relationship with our experience. We need description rather than explanation and causality.

On the other hand, we cannot judge from these recordings *what* the viewer was experiencing, precisely because the recordings are unable to translate *every* aspect of conscious experience into a full-blown representation—the recording device simply documents too little. Of course, some neuroscientists might object that the search for *neural correlates* is all about finding a full-blown representation of, say, a headache and that one day we will be able to reduce mental states to its specific neural correlates. Until then, however, enormous technological shortcomings remain: fMRI devices, for instance, are not only expensive, slow and not fine-grained enough, but also very large. They can only be used under laboratory conditions, precluding recordings of ecologically valid film experiences (let alone theatrical experiences). But even if it was possible to overcome these technological problems at some point, the idea that consciousness could be reduced to biological processes might be far-fetched. Between the two there might always remain an "explanatory gap", as Joseph Levine has called it.[25]

The materialist accounts of the natural sciences—and those trends in film studies relying on them—focus exclusively on *physical* phenomena. They reject everything that is not recordable: what cannot be measured does not exist. Many rejections of phenomenological descriptions must therefore be ascribed to such limitations. This certainly goes for vital cinematic phenomena such as brooding atmospheres or the expansive lived-body experience vis-à-vis a vast, open landscape. The natural sciences cannot—and deliberately do not want to—account for these experiences because they are not measurable. As a consequence, they leave them untouched and thus ignore some of the most precious aspects of movie-going. This is where phenomenology must come into play. Fortunately, to a phenomenological approach the question whether or not the sciences can deal with these experiences is not decisive. The crucial question is whether they are phenomena entering awareness or not. In its characteristic openness phenomenology recognizes everything as real that becomes part of experience, including experiences that do *not* yield measurable data. If we remain methodologically open to what is experienced, the full cinematic reality is much more wide-ranging than what is accessible to scientific reconstruction.

One major move of my study will be to bracket the 'objective' anatomical body (*Körper*) of the natural sciences with its bones and brains, nerves and neurons and focus on the 'subjective' phenomenological concept of the lived body (*Leib*) as the site of experience. When I talk about *the viewer's embodiment* or *bodily stimulation* I predominantly refer to the latter. To be sure, the experienced lived body and the scientific physiological body overlap. Objectively measurable transformations of the physiological body— increased heart-rate or sweaty palms—can certainly become obvious in moments of cinematic fear. But the subjectively *lived* body is at the same much more than this. When we feel pulled down in sorrow, opened up to the world in joy, constricted in fear we cannot measure these phenomena.

But if we by-pass them as 'pseudo-problems' or 'metaphysical,' we brush aside a good deal of cinema's most intriguing aspects.

EXPANDING FILM PHENOMENOLOGY

To make one thing abundantly clear: I do *not* argue that phenomenology should replace other approaches. And I am far from rejecting the validity of cognitivist research. Phenomenology can happily co-exist with cognitivism simply because both present different questions and for that reason bring forth different answers. What I *do* claim is that the picture would be unfinished, unintelligible, left with white spots, if we solely rely on cognitivst strategies of explanation and causality and do not fill out the picture by phenomenology's detailed descriptions of experience. Not unsurprisingly considering its marginal status within film studies, phenomenology *itself* has left many parts of the painting untouched. This is why I consider it necessary to expand its current scope in three directions.

1) *Film Form and Style*: Phenomenological scrutiny is rarely directed towards film form and style, i.e. the way specific aesthetic strategies are related to specific viewing experiences. Clearly, our cinematic experience depends on the prime intentional object, the film. If this intentional object varies, so will our experience. The atmosphere of a movie changes when it takes place at night and not in plain daylight, in a constricted, labyrinth-like cellar and not in an open landscape. Disgust feels different when the slimy creature is shown in a close-up accompanied by repellent sound effects rather than in a silent panoramic shot. And the shock of an exploding time-bomb will be more effective if the bang disrupts a moment of silence rather than loud chaos. Experiences are deliberately produced, but filmmakers often rely on tacit practices rather than explicit understanding how to create these experiences. Phenomenology focuses on experiences and is therefore inclined towards the aesthetic recipient (*Rezeptionsästhetik*) rather than the aesthetic product (*Produktionsästhetik*). But the viewer's experience cannot be uncoupled from the intentional object. Hence it won't suffice to describe the viewer's experience; it will be necessary to take into account the ways horror movies and thrillers are intertwined with it. In other words, we need to describe phenomenologically the experience of various formal and stylistic strategies.

2) *Emotions*: Emotions have hardly played a role in film phenomenology so far. However, emotions merit a closer, non-cognitivist look. Fear in its different shades of horror, dread, terror and shock is such a dominant factor in contemporary cinema that phenomenological descriptions are overdue. Again, I will sharply differentiate between the *clinical, scientific account* of emotions with its emphasis on causality and the *phenomenological*

description of an emotional experience. In my account it won't be important which neurophysiological mechanisms are operative or what the biochemical substratum of emotions looks like. The focus will be on the *subjective lived-body and social experience*.

As defined in my introduction, the emotional experience can be described as a phenomenological metamorphosis—a transformation of our lived body and the world we relate to emotionally. The transformative process is manifest in the etymology of the word 'emotion' which derives from the Latin 'emovere' in which the notion of 'to move' and the prefix for 'out' are combined. The emotional experience is embedded in everyday life, but also stands out from it. When we are 'gripped,' 'moved,' 'carried away' by a film, we are *dis*-located from a non-emotional into an emotional experience.[26]

In the movie theater, the metamorphosis occurs when our routine, tacit intertwinement with the filmic world in a frightening moment of shock, horror or terror becomes problematic. Suddenly, both poles of the double structure of conscious experience are affected: the inner experiential dimension and the outer interactional dimension, the lived body and our relation to the filmic world (and the other viewers). In emotional experience, aspects of the body are foregrounded that usually remain outside of awareness: one turns, sensually rather than via thought, toward background corporeal foundations of the self. Moreover, our intertwinement with the film changes insofar as once a movie is experienced as frightening, the relation between viewer and film tends towards fascinated attachment (I will speak of *immersion*) or overwhelmed detachment (I will call it *extrication*). However, in most cases these bodily and interactional transformations do not enter *direct awareness*, even if we are peripherally *conscious* of the metamorphosis. To repeat, a non-reflective experience is not an unconscious one; being conscious does not necessitate *self*-consciousness. Through phenomenological reflection *after the fact* this state is nonetheless describable.

Clearly, frightening films belong to the movies with the strongest transformative potential. Chapters 3 to 7 will try to pave a way into the vast and mostly unexplored field of frightening and shocking emotional experiences in the movie theater. For this purpose I will frequently draw on the monumental work of German phenomenologist Hermann Schmitz, a scholar almost unknown in English-speaking countries and mostly neglected in his native country as well.[27] Schmitz' New Phenomenology (*Neue Phänomenologie*) is responsible for some of the most sensitive, detailed and illuminating descriptions of emotional experiences we have.[28] Chapters 3 to 7 contain close looks at the most significant fearful aesthetic strategies and affects: direct and suggested horror, shock, dread, and terror. Since I take into account both formal *and* experiential aspects, the current (rather rudimentary) taxonomy of these aesthetic strategies and their concomitant lived-body experiences will not be left untouched. Earlier text-based investigations characterized aesthetic strategies almost exclusively along narrative or formal lines, leaving the intended experiential differences aside.

The phenomenological section will be an exercise in concept formation and redefinition. Concepts are crucial for perceiving, remembering, talking and thinking about specific objects and events in the world. As such they are indispensable in academic debates as much as in everyday life. I prefer the *prototype* view of concepts: I assume that instances of a concept vary in the degree to which they share certain properties, and consequently vary in the degree to which they represent the concept.[29] There are prototypes that *epitomize* the concept, whereas other instances are *not as typical* and still others are *even less representative* etc.

This analytic dissection is not without pitfalls. It neatly separates what during the act of viewing succeeds or seamlessly blends into each other (e.g., dread and terror) and often occurs simultaneously (e.g., shock and horror), with mutual influence and reinforcing consequences. Studying them in idealized isolation as prototypes is problematic insofar as they always stand in a specific relation to each other and their environment. My remapping of frightening aesthetic strategies will therefore have to allow for blurs and overlaps if an overly sterile taxonomy is to be avoided. Plus, I see the definitions of my concepts as open-ended and corrigible rather than fixed and ex cathedra.

3) *Reception Surroundings*: My third and last point of critique refers to phenomenology's focus on the *film* experience and its simultaneous neglect of the *theatrical* experience. The interrelation of viewer and film is never a solitary engagement; nor does it take place in a spatial vacuum. Our experience always involves *other recipients* just as it implies *specific viewing surroundings*. As a consequence, the aesthetic object that we encounter in the movie theater with others is not identical with the one we watch alone at home—even if both rely on the same work of art.[30] When we sit in the movie theater what we could broadly call the 'social atmosphere' always co-determines our encounter with the film. In negative terms, co-viewers imply distractions caused by incessant talking, ill-timed laughing or inapt odors. In positive terms, the aesthetic object is perceived in common, creating a bond among the viewers. In the theater comprehending an aesthetic object means *grasping-together*. The cinematic experience can help to establish special kinds of collectivity. Describing these various feelings of belongingness will be a major goal of subsequent chapters.

Moreover, the cinemagoer is not a *dis*-embodied consciousness free-floating in a spatial vacuum. As an embodied being he or she is always part of the reception surroundings, influencing it as well as being influenced by it. Consequently, it is never the film alone that shapes our experience. The heat I feel on a warm summer day in a movie theater without air-conditioning has an effect on my cinematic experience just as the backache that troubles me when I have to endure an eight-hour Andy Warhol movie on a wooden seat. We cannot ignore these influences if we aim to give a complete account of the experience of frightening films.

As a pure concept the film experience is an ideal. It is nothing but a heuristically established subcategory of the *theatrical* experience which merges *film* experience, audience and viewing surroundings into a single whole. If we take this fact seriously, we have to abandon descriptions that rely predominantly on an artificially marked-off encounter between spectator and aesthetic object. Restricting the cinematic experience to a solitary encounter between viewer and film is ultimately incomplete and reductive. The phenomenological description of the film experience therefore needs to be rounded out by phenomenological descriptions of diverse theatrical experiences. This will be the focus of the next chapter in which I look at one specific site of reception: the multiplex cinema. Before I delve into the phenomenology of the five types of fear, it seems necessary to clarify in what way the cinema in general—and the multiplex in specific—influences and skews our experience *and* pleasure of these emotions. We will see that the multiplex favors a particularly strong immersive and individualizing experience that enhances the film's emotional impact, while at the same time allowing for specific kinds of collectivity. Among the prerequisites for these multiplex characteristics is the comparatively strong active and passive *attention* of the theatrical situation—the aspect that I will deal with at the beginning of the next chapter.

2 Multiplexperiences
Individualized Immersion and Collective Feelings

> *I insist that the film text be read in the architectural context of its reception rather than as an autonomous aesthetic product.*
>
> (Anne Friedberg)[1]

> *[T]here is no substitute for seeing a film in the theater. As scared as you might get sitting at home watching a flickering image, I think there's something more enveloping about the theater.*
>
> (Joe Dante)[2]

ENHANCED ATTENTION: AESTHETIC ATTITUDE AND ABSORPTION IN THE CINEMA

The heightened *attention* of aesthetic experience in general and the theatrical film experience in specific can be defined as a double movement—a reciprocity of subject and aesthetic object: I actively move towards the intentional object but I am also passively approached by it. On the one hand, I devote myself to the object in *active* attention: attention radiates from me. On the other hand, I experience the object pushing towards me and luring me into a state of *passive* attention: my attention is captivated. In the first case attention control is self-controlled; through my own effort I remain attentive. In the second case it is other-controlled; attention is achieved rather effortlessly. Aesthetic experience can never be exclusively one or the other but always consists of both sides—albeit to varying degrees. Henceforth I will use the traditional term *aesthetic attitude* for active attention. The notion *aesthetic absorption* will indicate passive attention. In the following paragraphs I show how I literally move towards the film and thus actively assume an aesthetic attitude and how the cinema—and the multiplex in particular—support the movie to captivate my passive attention.

Active Attention: Aesthetic Attitude

What distinguishes *aesthetic* experience from mundane, non-aesthetic experience and therefore makes it particularly effective in its affective dimension is the specific stance we adopt towards the world: an aesthetic attitude. What sets aesthetic attitude apart from other activities is our *disinterested perceptual attentiveness* to objects. Aesthetic experience is not a simple stimulus-response mechanism, but a voluntary encounter with an object that becomes an aesthetic object only through our active attention to it. If we focus on its perceptible properties and phenomenal characteristics and put its functional purpose out of gear, we can turn every object into an aesthetic one. Think of a chair. If we sit on it in order to study the latest book by, say, David Bordwell, we use the chair as a functional tool for other ends. If we forget Bordwell and lend our attention to the chair *as* a chair and remain *disinterested* in its function, it might enable an aesthetic experience. Mikel Dufrenne therefore argues in favor of an involvement for *its own sake*: "it is only when the spectator decides to exist wholly for the work, in accordance with a perception which is resolved to remain nothing but perception, that the object appears before him as an aesthetic object."[3]

Of course, this is also true for works of art. As a material thing the work of art can be used for all kinds of purposes: a Walker Evans photography might decorate a wall; a portrait by John Singer Sargent could be used to identify an historical individual; a Nirvana song might be employed to drown the neighbor's noise. Phenomenologists and phenomenology-inflected theorists like Dufrenne, Roman Ingarden and Wolfgang Iser have persistently underscored that the *work of art* needs a perceiver with an aesthetic attitude to become an *aesthetic object*.[4] The former is merely the structural foundation of the latter. If no one perceives the projection of *The Exorcist*, the film remains a material thing: its colors become light vibrations, its music and dialogues sound waves. A frightening movie as the intentional object of an aesthetic experience is completed, concretized, actualized only by the perceiving recipient who—through this constituting activity—turns the film into an aesthetic object.

However, in aesthetic attitude *we* also change. Constituting the aesthetic object implies a *self*-constitution: consciousness now tacitly understands itself as being properly attuned, as it were, for the possibility of further aesthetic experience. The more I lay myself open to the film, the more sensitive will I be to its effects. This implies more than merely being conscious of something—it means that we associate ourselves with it.[5] Adopting an aesthetic attitude implies that I attach myself to the aesthetic object and deliberately put myself in a position to be affected by it. I temporarily set aside the goal-oriented, instrumental attitude of everyday life and allow myself to be sensitive and vulnerable to what the aesthetic object might 'do' to me. Freed for roughly two hours from the pushes-and-pulls and pressures of non-aesthetic life, the cinematic viewer is open for other priorities. Only if I pay active attention and open myself to the object, I can be affected by it at all. Ordinary language has a rich vocabulary referring to this affective dimension: we say that a film 'touches,' 'moves,' 'overwhelms,' 'captivates' or 'spellbinds' us. In German one even talks about the film moving towards me: *Der Film geht mir nahe*. Deliberately directed at us, the film 'takes us seriously': it is *made* for us and hence literally *there* for us. Artistically pre-focused and selected, the film's approach is often made to affect us bodily: in the movie theater some genres are named precisely after their affective dimension—the horror film and the thriller are prime examples.[6]

Going to the movies implies a number of deliberate decisions that *prepare* an aesthetic attitude. In contrast to the 1940s, the heyday of movie-going in the U.S., watching television has long replaced the movies as the prime habit in terms of media consumption. Since the cinema is not engaged habitually anymore, moviegoers make much more *conscious* decisions when they leave their homes and drive to the theater. They choose a film they are convinced will affect them in a certain way. Surrendering to a specific timetable predetermined by the theater management, they give up the control they would have watching a DVD at home. They stand in line and pay several dollars. They enter the auditorium with dozens of other viewers. They tacitly agree to spend the next 90 or so minutes in a rigidly marked time slot that they know will bound them silently and motionless to their seats. Additionally, the fact that the viewer is willing to devote his or her active attention to the film can be judged from the changed atmosphere after the movie trailers and the advertisements. People start to sit quietly. Cell phones are turned off. Interaction between the spectators comes gradually to a halt.

The geographical distance, the choice of film, the financial investment, the implicit collectivity, the knowledge of considerable time spent in the theater with appropriate social behavior—all this suggests that the viewer *wants* to open up to the movie in aesthetic attitude. Active attention comes to light even more clearly when we compare it to the way we frequently choose a movie on TV. We often turn on the TV with no particular intention or goal. We channel-surf, follow the flow of television and eventually bump into a film by accident. While we actively go and leave for the movies, we passively sit in front of the television. These differences in aesthetic attitude influence the power of frightening movies.

Passive Attention: Aesthetic Absorption

Even if active attention never stops, once the movie starts *passive attention* largely takes over: we are *absorbed* by the film. Recalling the cinema's spatial structure, we find a number of factors supporting passive attention. We sit in a dark room. The only source of light is the illuminated screen. The main sources of sound are the speakers. The horizontally arranged seats face the dominating screen, thus restricting and minimizing perspective alternatives. Our eyes naturally turn to areas of light and are attracted by motion. The arrangement of rows and seats discourages bodily movement. Hence there is little with which we could actively distract ourselves. The attraction of seeing and hearing is indeed so strong that we have to become active in order to avoid it—a fact that has a considerable weight in terms of frightening movies. The enforced attraction of the screen is particularly apparent in fearful scenes of horror that we try to resist watching by looking away. As Linda Singer notes: "[I]t is hard to keep one's eyes diverted for long [and] resist the movement by which the eyes return to the screen and remain there horrified, but nonetheless fascinated. What explains this phenomenon, in part, is that in a situation where we are cut off from our habitual urgencies and commitments, we cannot help but look at the screen because there is very little else to do."[7]

Yet absorption is supported not only by the *spatial* situation; the *temporal* condition also has its share. In the movie theater we give ourselves over to an unstoppable and uncontrollable temporal sequence: "a segment, usually between 1½ and two hours, is marked off by a very strong caesura at either end (lights down—projection of film—lights up) giving the spectator a sense of closure and enclosure more radical than either watching television, a play or listening to a concert or the radio is able to produce," Thomas Elsaesser writes.[8] Neither can we stop the relentlessly forward-moving projection; nor can we change the predetermined narration. A film watched in a theater is set and unchangeable—it is an unwavering intention.[9] In contrast, the interactive spectatorship of watching a film on DVD allows for jumps to different chapters, fast forwards and backwards and what Laura Mulvey calls "delayed cinema": the slowing down of the film through interruptions, breaks, stills, repetitions and slow-motion. With the new technologies of home viewing the spectator gains considerable control—Mulvey even talks about the satisfaction of the "spectator's desire for mastery and will to power"—over the inexorable flow of the film at 24 frames per second.[10] What is more, halting the image and repeating sequences can result in a relieving shift of consciousness between temporalities, bringing to the fore a different relation to the image: the fiction might dissolve and the time of the registration can become foregrounded.[11] In other words, the indexical quality and the 'then-and-there-ness' of the filmic image dominate over the 'here-and-now-ness' of the narrative's own temporality. The remote-controlled mastery over the film's otherwise smooth linearity and narrative drive forward has a specifically relieving effect with regard to the cinema of fear. As we shall see, in the movie theater our inability to do anything against the film's narrative determinacy is one source of fear.

On the other hand, spectators enjoy the theatrical experience precisely because they can relegate the need for choice and decision to the film. This peculiar temporal character of watching a film in the movie theater becomes even more apparent when contrasted with the act of reading. In reading we have an even higher degree of control over time and pace than in watching a DVD. We can always stop or digress into daydreaming—there is nothing we would miss. Precisely because we can untangle ourselves more easily from the written world, reading is also more *active attention* in the sense that we must continuously decide anew whether we stay with the book. This is particularly obvious in overwhelming scenes of horror and disgust which sometimes make us force ourselves to keep on reading. Hence in the movie theater horror and disgust seem to *happen* to us *passively*, while reading a Peter Straub or Stephen King novel often creates the impression that we *actively inflict* horror and disgust on ourselves. The comparison to literature also points to another aspect of the movies: the reliance on direct perception rather than indirect language-inspired imagination. In the movie theater comparatively passive perception is primary and relatively active imagination comes in only second place. And even when strong imaginations are brought into play, they are often forced upon us rather than actively made up, as the section on suggested horror will show.

Moreover, the collective viewing situation also favors an atmosphere of passive attention. First of all, it suggests following the movie to its end. A film on TV is easily stopped if it is too boring or too frightening. Leaving the theater not only implies questioning the whole decision-making process described above, but also evokes a potentially shameful situation in front of other viewers. Second, cultural norms create an atmosphere that promotes being attentive insofar as the reactions of others rarely interfere. In the U.S. incessant talking or crying out loud is usually not-well received. When someone does not follow the rules of self-discipline, others discipline him or her. Third, passive attention is supported by the fact that the viewer does not have to control *responsive action* in the same way as in more socially interactive situations. The viewer can indulge in the film with little reflection on the image of self that he or she anticipates creating for the others. The participant of a more socially interactive situation, such as a private video or DVD party, where part of the appeal derives from the possibility to make comments and ask questions, cannot just passively *look*. He or she has to be on the *lookout* for emotional and bodily responses to a much greater degree than the viewer in the anonymous darkness of the cinema.[12] (Chapter 5 on cinematic shock will show, however, that we are not completely freed from the pressure to actively respond.)

Once we have made up our minds to buy a ticket, the structural features of the movie theater strips us of further burdens to choose. The focused active and passive attention eliminates what psychologists call 'the paradox of choice,' i.e., the fact that in advanced modern cultures the amount of choice—one of the hallmarks of individual freedom and self-determination—can become an overburdening problem.[13] We are not forced to think what else could I do and what else do I miss? The power of the movies takes over. We have put ourselves in a position of relative passivity which dramatically restricts our options: mostly sitting and watching.[14] While this is true for the cinema in general, the multiplex experience skews us even stronger towards attention.

MULTIPLEX EXPERIENCE: ENHANCED ABSORPTION, INDIVIDUALIZATION, EMOTION

In what follows I will look at the material object of the multiplex from a third-person perspective, as it were 'objectively from outside.' I shall describe what is specific in terms of construction and interior design, technology and theater policy (insofar as it concerns the viewing process). But this objectivist view can only be a preliminary step. Phenomenology rejects analyses of objects isolated from their relation to someone experiencing it. The *phenomena* of experience are always connected to and correlated with the *mode* of experience. We could enumerate all the multiplex characteristics in the world—this objectivist list would tell us nothing about the viewing experience. It is therefore necessary to look at the object also, so to speak, 'subjectively from inside.' We have to describe the way the viewer-as-subject perceptually and experientially engages the multiplex-as-object.[15]

This implies a special emphasis on the aspect of embodiment. The term *embodiment* describes the process of experiencing and making sense as a sensual human being in the world, as someone who lives inside and acts with a body. The viewer as embodied subject is never neutral to his or her surroundings. First, the viewer encounters the multiplex multi-dimensionally. We do not just look from a nowhere-position onto a two-dimensional screen, but take a seat inside a three-dimensional auditorium. Second, through the body the individual expresses him- or herself and thereby changes the surroundings. When we scream, others will hear us. When our neighbors talk, we might feel disturbed. And third, the viewer grasps the world in the cinema multi-sensually. Not just the eyes and the ears are engaged; the cinematic experience addresses the other senses as well. Think of the popcorn smell or an uncomfortable backrest.

As an overly familiar routine practice, awareness of the multiplex is clouded by habituation. Since familiarity tends to cover over what is most significant in our relations with the world, it will prove helpful to engage in occasional acts of *de-*familiarization. Confronting today's multiplex with the cinematic habits of the past, the multiplex will turn out to be one historical exhibition option among many—an option that differs considerably from the nickelodeon, the movie palace, or the drive-in. In order to extrapolate the specific viewing experience of the multiplex, we have to keep an eye on the *changes* that the boom of refurbishing old multiplexes and building new 'megaplexes' in the late 1980s and especially the mid-1990s brought to viewing habits. The introduction of these novelties stands as a key factor for the success of the new multiplex theaters—and thus for the renaissance of cinemagoing in general. A strong feeling existed that the 'old' was not adequate anymore and that something 'new' had to lure the audiences back.

Individualized Absorption

Two tendencies are intertwined in the multiplex. First, there is a movement towards *individualization*: the individual has increasing potential for private, idiosyncratic interaction with the film, while the presence of other viewers is reduced.[16] Second, there is a trend towards an even deeper *absorption* than known from other viewing venues. Both tendencies depend on each other. The audience's individualization allows the viewer to relate more strongly to the film—and the viewer's stronger relation to the film results in increased individualization during the act of viewing. The multiplex marks a tendency away from a more *socializing theatrical* experience to an increasingly *individualizing film* experience.[17]

a) **Seats and Seating:** One of the most palpable innovations of the multiplex concerns the seats and the seating. Seats are soft-cushioned and often bouncy, thus reducing distractions caused by more hard and immobile seats. The seat as a tool for film viewing becomes more easily 'incorporated.' The soft-cushioned seat is more easily absorbed as a symbiotic extension, which permits us to direct attention more fully towards the film. We experience the film *through* the seat; there is very little experience *of* the seat. Compare this to the American cinemas of the 1970s with their hard-backed, cushionless seats of plastic. Or compare it to India, where some seats are made of cement![18] In smaller theaters the almost seamless fusion between body and seat is frequently ruptured, thus turning the seat into an 'other.' This happens when someone sitting behind us, pushes or kicks against our seat. As a result the intruder almost literally becomes a 'pain in the neck.' Other instances include the 'struggle' for the armrest or the accidental foot contact with one's neighbor. These interruptions are often the cause for an upsurge of irritation, an emotion not derived from our filmic interaction. It disturbs our emotional involvement with the movie by drawing attention, at least partly, away from the screen. The film stops functioning as the sole source of our emotional experience.

In order to avoid bodily collisions the multiplex introduced increased arm- and legroom, thus blowing up, as it were, the imaginary 'space bubble' which surrounds every viewer. By increasing the space not to be trespassed by others, the multiplex at the same time prevents the viewer from entering the neighbor's territory. Bodily contacts with spectators to the right and left, back and front are reduced. Viewers are not as easily 'in touch' with each other. This tendency is further increased by the propensity to choose seats away from others. What some critics rather condescendingly lament as the multiplex' social coldness and anonymity, for many viewers might be one of its attractive aspects. These spectators cherish what V.F. Perkins calls the movie theater's "public privacy."[19]

But the intrusion of other viewers does not only occur via direct *physical* contact. Consider the sense of vision. One of the key innovations was the sloped stadium seating. As a consequence, practically all seats guarantee excellent sight towards the screen. There is no danger of tall neighbors in front blocking the *view* and intruding into one's field of vision; nor is there a danger of people blocking the *projection*. One is rarely forced to ask a tall person in front to "move down a bit," personal approaches to foreigners are unnecessary. Again, the *film* is supposed to be central to the experience—not our *social interactions*.

b) **Air-Conditioning**: Air-conditioning became part of many American theaters in the 1930s. And by 1950 almost three out of four theaters were air-conditioned.[20] But the fact that air-conditioning is not necessarily part of every viewing experience even today is easily shown. We only have to think of our private home-viewings. The main function of air-conditioning is to keep the room temperature at a pleasant level. Since the temperature does not change, the sense of warmth or coldness does not come to the fore and thus the room does not interfere with the viewer's feeling of being comfortably at home in the cinematic space. This is important: Since the viewer is not distracted by an unpleasant bodily feeling, he or she can stay captivated by the movie and thus be stimulated emotionally and corporeally first and foremost by the *film*. (This is not to say that overactive, ice-cold air-conditionings *never* disturb the viewer's attention!) Air-conditioning has a second effect: it keeps the audience from sweating and thus from penetrating other viewers' senses with unpleasant odors. This stands in stark contrast to beginning of the 20th century, when a substantial discourse was circulating about the odor of working-class patrons that violated the decorum of middle-class viewers.

c) **Tidiness**: The tendency to diminish smells and keep the room temperature steady is in line with another characteristic: tidiness as a response to surveys in which audiences listed dirty theaters as their biggest complaint.[21] Sticky floors were among the reasons why people over 35-years-old turned their backs on movie theaters by the late 1970s and early 1980s. Consequently, tidiness became part of the policy and the attraction of most multiplex cinemas. Preventing the spilling of sticky soft drinks, the cup holders on many multiplex seats can be seen as a *pars pro toto* tool of this policy. Drawing on Mary Douglas' concept of purity, Phil Hubbard argues that deep-seated anxieties about the despoilment of body and self through dirt draw the viewers to the clean space of the multiplex: "multiplexes are popular with specific audiences because they allow them to develop a clear sense of ontological security, knowing that they can enjoy an evening out without the boundaries of their body being brought into question by potential pollutants."[22]

d) **Interior Design**: Since its inception in the 1960s and its spreading in the following decade, the old generation of multiplex cinemas had been distinguished from earlier theaters partly by its reduced and minimalist interior design. The vocabulary used to describe their auditoria ranged from "unimaginative" to "dull." Especially in comparison to the lush, luxurious movie palaces of the 1920s the interior design of the earlier generation of multiplexes faded. Interestingly, this has not changed much with the new multiplexes of the late 1980s and 1990s. While the exterior architecture witnessed a change that, at least to a certain degree, tried to achieve some grandeur, the interior design of the new multiplex auditoria stayed functional at best. The auditoria of the movie palaces were often decorated with huge frescoes on the ceiling and contained highly ornamented walls with stucco, rococo-like pillars or pilasters in renaissance-style. The movie palace was a design feast for the eye. As Siegfried Kracauer underscored in 1926, the function of the lush inside was precisely to *distract* the viewer: "The interior design of the movie theaters serves one sole purpose: to rivet the audience's attention to the peripheral so that they will not sink into the abyss."[23]

Not so the multiplex. The function of its design is to direct the viewer to the screen and nowhere else. Its minimalist interior reduces visual distraction; it does not let the spectator's gaze wander and wonder in amazement. Since our vision is not identical with the film and we always see more than just the screen, it makes a difference whether the visual fringes of perception are kept neutral or not. On the one hand, there is the multiplex auditorium in which the walls are dark, monochrome, and flat. The reflected light from the screen is absorbed. Little visual tension exists at our visual fringes. On the other hand, the movie-palace had multi-colored walls. Often the auditorium was painted with white and gold—colors that reflected the light from the screen. Due to the decoration, the structure of the walls was uneven, creating visual tension and thus attracting attention of its own. Whereas the visual background stays unobtrusive in the multiplex, it pushed to the fore in the movie-palace.

The movie-palaces with their aura of fantasy and grandeur were designed and decorated to create a disarming atmosphere that would loosen the ties to the habitual world and offer entrance into another world.[24] In the multiplex this task is referred almost wholly to the film. In the multiplex we don't go to *the* movies—but to see *a* movie. We do not dwell in the building—but in the film.

e) **Noise:** By the 1980s talking and constant commotion had become the norm in the old shoebox multiplexes of the mall. Disagreeing with this tendency, theater owners began to react. At the end of the 1980s the Union Station multiplex in Washington, D.C., for instance, took the following measures: "Noisy patrons are issued one warning and then asked to leave without a refund. Ushers make the rounds of the nine auditoria every twenty minutes. One complaint and the usher remains through the rest of the program. Managers open half of the shows with a simple welcome and a reminder of the 'no talking' policy," Douglas Gomery recounts.[25] These measures and other analogous attempts to secure a quiet audience in the multiplex try to create an experience comparable to the movie palaces of the 1920s, which similarly worked to install 'tasteful' spectatorship. In the movie palaces it was so dark and ushers were so observant that silence became an obligatory part of the decorum. This tendency away from the unruly crowd of the old multiplex towards the quieter, disciplined audience of the new multiplex is an expression of a change in regard to what audiences (and theater owners) expect from the practice of movie-going. Of course, bourgeois discipline is not always the case. There are a number of cases where talking is quite common.[26] What is important for my argument is not so much whether there is *some* talking or *no* talking at all, but rather that there is a tendency to talk *less*.

f) **Screen and Screening**: During the 1990s a number of improvements in screening quality took place. First, the screens got bigger which reduces the sense that a machine mediates the film. A less alienated viewing experience was achieved, moreover, by eliminating a phenomenon called "keystoning." Douglas Gomery explains: "By shoehorning as many auditoria [. . .] as possible into a corner of a shopping center, projection booths rarely lined up with the screen. That is, one booth served two or more spaces, so the images invariably came out with one-half of the movie larger than the other."[27] Finally, improvement of the projection was also arrived at through curved screens. They do not only reflect the light and color directly back onto the audience, thus making the image brighter, but also enable a more precise focus of the image.

g) **Sound**: Arguably the most important feature of the multiplex theater is its advanced sound technology. Three aspects stand out: surround sound, the use of loudness, and the elimination of sound not originating from the film. These characteristics are so significant that some observers consider the once taken-for-granted dominance of the visible strongly challenged by the audible. One of the key technological innovations of the 1990s was the introduction of digital sound. Complex soundtracks can now be reproduced at almost zero distortion and noises are reduced even after various screenings. The introduction of digital sound also had a strong effect on the spreading of surround sound. Although surround sound has been around since the mid-1970s, the introduction of digital sound took the *analogue* Dolby sound systems one step further and turned high-class *digital* surround systems into an essential part of the multiplex brand.

The availability of multichannel technology enables filmmakers to explore off-screen sound both in the front and the rear of the auditorium, which implies a dramatic expansion of narrative space.[28] The one-directional, monophonic sound originating from the center of the screen made way for a multi-directional sound coming from different parts of the auditorium. This sound system emphasizes the three-dimensionality of the cinematic space. The resulting surround effect enables a bathing (if not drowning) of the viewer in an ocean of music, sound, and dialogue. While the viewer was originally placed *before* the filmic space, he or she was now placed *inside* of it.

Another essential characteristic is the use of loudness.[29] Again, this tendency was enabled by technological innovation. The new digital sound track permits acoustic pressure ten times as high (110–118 dB) as its analogue equivalent (90–95 dB). Acoustic pressure can now be boosted up to a level that is close to the human pain threshold (120–130 dB). An important result is the tendency to enhance passive attention and individualize the viewer. Two reasons interrelate. First, loudness draws the viewer's attention towards the film. Sound does not remain at a distance but forcefully penetrates. Plus, we cannot shut our ears the same way as we can shut our eyes. If loud enough, moreover, sound grabs the viewers' body even beyond the purely audible—thus underscoring the fact that we do not only hear with our ears (as the *focal organs* of our hearing) but with our whole body. Contemporary sound systems are powerful enough to move an amount of air that can 'hit' the spectator with sound, and thus make him or her experience the film with a far greater degree of physical involvement than ever before. But loudness also has a second effect: it guarantees that other sound sources are drowned. This, in turn, has ramifications for the social aspect of moviegoing: it becomes more complicated to talk as well as to listen to one's neighbor. Hence the individualizing effect. Whereas at the beginning of the century the nickelodeon served as a vehicle for informal socializing, this is not the purpose of the multiplex.

The third novelty regards distraction through unintentional noise. In the 1970s and early 1980s one of the major annoyances had been the spilling over of sound from other auditoria.[30] The viewer could be distracted from following an intimate dialogue passage from *Terms of Endearment* (1983) by gunshot noise from *Scarface* (1983). This problem was solved when the inadequately padded walls made way for soundproof walls. Sound-absorbent material was installed to minimize unwanted echo and reverberation. And the noise produced by air-conditioning equipment and projectors was quieted through improved sound insulation.[31] The result of the latter was the riddance of an oft-described aspect of older movie theaters, namely the rattling sound of the projector. In all cases, the idea was that distractions should be minimized. Sound was supposed to originate from the film and not from other sources.

In sum, there is a tendency to interfere as little as possible. Due to the construction of the auditorium, its interior design, the technology and theater policy used the viewer fuses easily with the surroundings and is quite effortlessly absorbed by the film.

An Enhanced Emotional Experience

The high degree of *passive attention* explains why frightening aesthetic elements are so powerful precisely at the multiplex. The less other aspects of the *theatrical* experience become focal objects, the more the *film* will turn into the primary object. At the multiplex it is first and foremost the film that sets into motion our emotions. To describe how frightening movies affect us powerfully will be the purpose of subsequent chapters. At this point I want to show how the cinematic situation makes possible—and the multiplex enhances—a pleasurable emotional experience in the first place. This requires a short detour into the field of emotions.

Researchers have long agreed that a major function of emotions is communication.[32] My lived body communicates through my emotions most conspicuously via three interrelated and often simultaneously occurring forms: facial expressions, vocal expressions, and bodily postures and movements. These emotional expressions cannot gallop away unbridled. They are subject to cultural norms and display rules. These norms and rules proscribe and prescribe specific emotional displays for certain situations and thus indicate the adequacy or impropriety of emotions.[33] In the movie theater this is just as true as elsewhere: the expression of emotions stops where other viewers feel bothered. To be sure, cinematic norms vary. While it was not uncommon to consume alcohol and exhibit drunken behavior in early nickelodeons, this would cause an outcry nowadays. Accounts that describe the movie theater as a place where one can give the emotions full and free expression are exaggerations.

Through socialization and habituation these cultural norms and display rules are firmly established. We do not need to actively remember them: the passive threat of the highly intersubjective emotion of shame keeps us from forgetting. The self is subconsciously looking at and listening to him- or herself, as it were, with the eyes and ears of the other. In negative instances this unreflective position becomes conscious: the individual realizes that he or she has failed to shape behavior according to the cultural norms and consequently feels exposed. This can happen easily in emotional situations whose foregrounding of the body implies a particularly strong form of social visibility. These instances of standing out negatively are experienced as shame. Gone is the taken-for-granted feeling of being folded into the cultural fabric of the group so as not to be subject to its devastating gaze.[34]

While this applies to all social circumstances, in the movie theater we confront a specific situation. The cinema owes its attractiveness, among other things, to its ability to partially relieve us from the burden of social interaction and the threat of shame. This is the case even though we sit there with dozens, sometimes even hundreds of other people. The reason? I call it the cinema's *hiding effect*. For one, there is the pervasive darkness that envelopes us. We instantaneously realize that the dark has a function beyond enabling the projection once the lights are *not* switched off. V.F. Perkins points out: "The deterioration of the image on the screen matters far less than the absence of the 'shield' which darkness customarily offers. The erection of the shield seems to be the precondition of involvement."[35] The few light sources not only enable us to direct attention to the screen while simultaneously concealing potentially distracting others from *our* view. They also cloak us in darkness and give *us* protection from *their* view. Due to the darkness the gaze of others—or, to be more precise, the viewer's *imagination* of this gaze—is less devastating.

While darkness—just as unidirectional seating—is an aspect that characterizes the cinematic situation in general, the multiplex amplifies the hiding effect. The sloped stadium seating supports invisibility because I can comfortably hide behind the backrest so that others have less viewing access. The generous arm- and legroom keeps the neighbors at bay. The loudness partially drowns my own noises. And the strong absorption makes it unlikely that the co-viewers will devote their attention to *me* of all people. Now, the protective shield of darkness, the bulwark of the backrest, the unidirectional seating position etc., have important ramifications for our emotional experience: emotions can be experienced with fewer repercussions. Precisely because we know that we are comfortably hidden, the threat of shame as a way of seeing-oneself-from-the-standpoint-of-another is reduced. We do not have to be afraid of 'losing our face' simply because our face is not as visible as in other circumstances.

The cinema's hiding effect has a double consequence. Since social interaction is limited and, in fact, often unwanted, we have to pay less attention to how we actively communicate our emotions. (Previously I have mentioned how this supports passive attention.) The fact that we are predominantly asked to passively bridle the *display*-part, in turn, allows us greater indulgence in the *feeling*-part of emotions otherwise spoiled by cultural constraints. A tough guy snivels surreptitiously as the star-crossed pair finally kisses each other? A sweet teenage girl feels her rage relieved when a killer takes bloody revenge? A father is more afraid of a monster than his son? While these constellations would cause moral inferiority and shame under regular circumstances, they are possible in the movie theater. The respective emotions are allowed to be *felt*. And, to a limited degree, they can also be *expressed*. The diminished force of the others' gaze grants us a certain leeway in terms of emotional display. Obviously this cannot mean loosening all restraints. An eye-catching emotionality would contradict the hiding effect and draw attention towards oneself. This is why we do not cry overtly but shed tears in silence. In sum, the emotional *display* remains controlled, even if the emotional *feeling* might be quite strong.

AN INTENSIFIED ABSORPTION: THE PRINCIPLE OF IMMERSION

Involvement vs. Appreciation, Immersion vs. Enthrallment

The passive attention of absorption with its enhanced emotional experience can veer in two directions. Hence we have to distinguish carefully. Following Ed Tan, I differentiate "experiencing the fiction"—I use his term *involvement*—and "experiencing the artefact"—like Tan, I talk about *appreciation*.[36] Fictional movies always present a filmic world, but they necessarily do it in a specific way. Hence we can distinguish between the

What and the *How* of the film's presentation. If we look at the *What* we are involved; if we follow the *How* we appreciate. To put it differently, *aesthetic involvement* describes our intertwinement with the filmic world, whereas *aesthetic appreciation* is the attention we pay to film form and style. The first case implies *looking-through* the film into its world; the second case means *looking-at* the film as a formal aesthetic object. (Sometimes the distinction between *depth* and *surface* perception is also used in this context.) We are able to fluently switch from one to the other—either actively and without much effort or more passively if the movie initiates the change by foregrounding form and thus temporarily relegates our involvement with the filmic world into the background. However, we cannot be fully involved and appreciate at the same time. If one aspect is foregrounded, the other must recede.

Both forms of absorption—involvement and appreciation—can be considerable. In order to specify *intensified* versions of passive attention I will use the terms *immersion* and *enthrallment*. In enthrallment as a heightened form of aesthetic appreciation we look *at* the movie spellbound. We are enthralled by the ingenuity of a plot twist, spectacular special effects, impressive acting, incredible cinematography or sound-design etc. The word immersion, on the other hand, describes a heightened form of aesthetic involvement during which we look so deeply *into* the filmic world that we almost seem to be lost in it: spatially, temporally and emotionally. A film that does not present a filmic world—whatever this world looks like—cannot be immersive. Immersion is a heightened form of attention—but this does not imply that every form of strong attention equals immersion. Watching a Stan Brakhage film, which unrolls painted or scratched celluloid, we can lose ourselves in enthralled appreciation (up to the point of near-hallucination), but we cannot be immersed. Moreover, the more immersed or enthralled we are, the more difficult it gets to move from one state to the other. Immersion and enthrallment are intensive states of passive attention that skew the viewer to remain immersed or enthralled and not switch into the opposite mode.

To be sure, emotions in the movie theater are not only derived from being involved *with*—or even immersed *in*—the filmic world (Ed Tan talks about "fictional emotions" or "F emotions"), but they also come from the aesthetic appreciation of the artefact's formal characteristics (Ed Tan calls them "artefact emotions" or "A emotions"). The latter include positive reactions such as enjoyment, admiration, astonishment, and a desire for the return of something enjoyable, but also negative responses like scorn, anger or embarrassment. Even though they hardly occur simultaneously, F emotions can spur subsequent A emotions.[37] Both A and F emotions can be pleasurable, albeit in different ways. My definitions are heuristic and do not imply value judgments. However, this study is interested first and foremost in the pleasure of emotions and affects that derive from an involvement with the frightening filmic world rather than the pleasures based on the film as artefact. I focus on emotions that derive *from* or in connection *to* immersion. Consequently, I sidestep further elaborations of enthrallment and concentrate fully on what I mean by immersion.

Not an Illusion: Immersion as Phenomenological Experience

I prefer the term *immersion* to the related concept of *illusion* for a number of reasons. First of all, as a comparatively new concept it carries less discursive burden and is less encrusted with evaluative prejudices. The term 'illusion' has often been discussed pejoratively. It could not have been engaged neutrally without prior defense against those critiques. Second, strictly speaking there is no such thing as an illusion from a phenomenological perspective. Phenomenology is interested in the experience of the things themselves. It does not distinguish between real being and false illusion: both are real phenomena that are experienced differently and must therefore be described in different ways.[38] This is not to say that the concept of illusion is invalid. From an objectivist third-person point-of-view the perception of movement, for instance, can clearly be described as an illusion. We know that the projector transports and projects 24 discontinuous still images per second interrupted by black spaces—and nevertheless we perceive continuous movement on the screen (the phi-effect). However, calling the perception of continuous movement an illusion presupposes a change of perspective. We need to look at the object from a second vantage point from which the seemingly real perception turns out to be false (for instance, by slowing down the projector). Changing the viewpoint, however, changes our phenomenological experience. Since the normal projection and the slow one are experienced differently, phenomenology treats them as different phenomena. Plus, who can tell that the second vantage point is the superior and thus the real one? Illusion is an epistemological concept, whereas the term immersion describes a phenomenological experience.

Third, and most importantly, the metaphor immersion is more apposite. The term *illusion* not only borders too strongly on *delusion*, but is simply a misleading exaggeration when it comes to our experience of the multiplex and fearful emotions.[39] As Menachem Brinker informs us, "the presence of an illusion can be indicated only by means of behavior toward the illusory object which resembles behavior toward a real object. Obviously only a few people will [. . .] flee from monsters depicted on the canvas."[40] Hence the term is a misnomer. We simply do not take the filmic world for real! Even from an objectivist perspective the cinema can be described merely as a perceptual-psychological illusion of the first-order (phi-effect), but not as a second-order "aesthetic illusion" that causes an impression of reality. Illusions by definition 'survive' all revelations of their false illusory character.[41] *Knowing* that we face a perceptual illusion does not change anything: we cannot *not* see continuous movement on the screen, whereas we can easily remind ourselves that it is only a movie—and thus withdraw from immersion.

Vivian Sobchack's phenomenology of the film experience clarifies why movies are not an aesthetic illusion: some proponents of filmic illusion erroneously presuppose a visual mind without a body—a subject-eye. Obviously the viewer is not a disembodied mind in a vat, but an embodied consciousness literally situated in the world. Because the viewer's embodiment comprises more than mere vision, the presence of the cinema as space and technological instrument will always be felt through our cooperative sensorium. Sobchack notes: "If my vision were merely a discrete sense, then perhaps Cinerama or some future holography might wear away the last of my abstract knowledge that my perception of the world was instrument-mediated. Indeed, my point of view and the film's would be the same, isomorphic, identical. However, I do not have a *point* of view. As a lived body engaged in intentional acts of perception in an intended world, I have a *place* of viewing, a *situation*. My vision is informed by and filled with my other modes of access to the world, including the tactile contact of my posterior with the theater seat."[42] To some degree, marginal consciousness always harbors elements that do not belong to the movie: the frame of the screen, the exit signs, the backrest of my seat, the auditory, olfactory, tactile and visible presence of my co-viewers, the proprioceptive discrepancies . . . Hence calling the movies an illusion flies in the face of our phenomenological experience.

Moreover, we shall see more clearly in the chapter on direct horror that films do not *re*-present *the* world but first of all *pre*-sent *a* world (if an irreal one).[43] I insist on the fact that we are not fooled to follow the illusion of the represented real world, but are invited to immerse ourselves in a presented irreal world. As the next chapter will show, this distinction puts us in a better position to account for the pleasure of frightening movies. And it averts all accusations that the viewer is duped into false believes. This is true despite the fact that I describe cinematic attention as largely passive.

Consequently, while certainly not entailing a full-fledged illusion, immersion enables a heightened form of involvement that is less inclined to the comparatively distanced experience of a theatrical performance than to the phenomenological proximity of computer games.[44] In fact, the term immersion originally emerged in discussions about virtual reality and computer games. Only more recently it traveled into the neighboring territories of other media and art forms.[45] Unfortunately, it lost part of the initial persuasiveness on its way because of vague and indistinct usage. Today people seem to use it in order to describe almost any kind of intensely pleasurable aesthetic experience or absorbing activity.[46] In the following section I will clarify the meaning of the term in my account.

Three Forms of Immersion: Spatial, Temporal, and Emotional

The quintessential precondition for cinematic immersion is the presentation of a filmic world. Marie-Laure Ryan claims: "For immersion to take place, the text must offer an expanse to be immersed within, and this expanse, in a blatantly mixed metaphor, is not an ocean but a textual world."[47] This textual or, more precisely, *filmic* world requires the presentation of a habitable environment in which objects and individuals exist and act. In other words, it must construct the setting for a potential narrative action to which the viewer can relate. Films that do not present at least some kind of world are few and far between (think of the Stan Brakhage example). However, the degree of immersion varies considerably from movie to movie, from genre to genre, from filmic mode to filmic mode. Obviously, the easily accessible stereotypical filmic worlds of popular culture favor immersion. In mainstream Hollywood films an easily accessible world is right there: spatial immersion takes place almost instantaneously.

The spatial aspect, indicated by the expression *filmic world*, is the foundation of immersion. Being spatially immersed can imply considerable pleasure without any specification of what the filmic world is about: the experience of being surrounded by another reality that takes over almost all of our attention.[48] This pleasure is the reason why being expulsed at the end can be such a harsh experience: the filmic ending does not only imply the problem of closure, but more generally the possibility to switch off, as it were, a whole world.[49] Recall the bad habit of turning on the lights abruptly after the last scene is over. With the eyes still used to the dark and consciousness still partly immersed in the filmic world, we feel the unexpected light almost like a physical intrusion. This is why it makes a difference whether a film ends with "The End," as in the classical Hollywood cinema, or not. Nowadays the credits often function as a kind of bumper, partially absorbing the impact of being thrown out of the filmic into the real world.

As the discussion about "The End" underscores, cinematic immersion also implies a *temporal* component. In comparison to non-temporal still photography or figurative painting, narrative film as an absorbing time-space art enhances immersion: the viewer is immersed both in the spatial world of the film *and* its temporal flow. Even if time plays a role in still photographic immersion as well (I am always immersed in the picture for *some* time), a different quality arises once a narration captures my interest. However, as the chapters on dread and terror will show, there are enormous immersive differences between scenes that play out rather uneventfully in blind progress and those that make me anxiously anticipate the outcome. Ryan therefore defines that temporal immersion is the viewer's desire for the knowledge that awaits him or her at the end of narrative time.[50] In some cases of temporal immersion experienced time stands out almost like a tangible gestalt.

Apart from spatial and temporal immersion Ryan also knows a third form: *emotional* immersion. In the chapters on suggested horror, dread and terror I will describe aesthetic strategies that strongly intend to immerse us emotionally. Their emotional immersion *depends* on spatial and temporal immersion: only because we are immersed in the filmic world and temporarily anticipate a negative outcome, we are opened up to react fully—and this implies fearfully—to the film. On the other hand, if we are immersed *emotionally* this reflects back on spatial and temporal immersion: we are all the more involved with the filmic world and its inhabitants. We feel 'glued' to what happens on the screen. Certain emotional experiences attach us much stronger to things, people and events than, say, mere perceptions.[51]

Presence and Absence in Immersion

This contrast between the strong tie of emotions and the more independent stance of perception implicitly refers to a key characteristic of immersion: the reduction of phenomenological distance to the fictional world in terms of space, time and emotions. When we are deeply immersed, we experience a close *proximity* to the filmic world and its characters. The types of fear that I will discuss offer two forms of phenomenological proximity. The first one, exemplified by dread, terror and pleasantly fascinating horror, is characterized by the *viewer* approaching the film. The second one, exemplified by shock and unpleasantly overwhelming horror, is defined by the *film* closing in on or even 'jumping' at the audience. While the first one pulls us in, the second one pushes us away—up to the point extrication. The film is obviously capable of pushing us away most effectively, when we are closest to it. Hence the spectacular effects of shock and overwhelming horror work best, when they are preceded by a strong immersive experience. This is also the reason why the surroundings of the multiplex support stronger effects of extrication: since its structural features encourage an immersive experience luring the viewer *into* the filmic world, he or she can be ejected more effectively *out of* it. But isn't this discussion of closeness and distance mere metaphorical talk? I don't think so. While cinematic forms of closeness and distance cannot be explained within the Cartesian paradigm and its model of space, phenomenology acknowledges them as actual experiences that can be described.

Since we are spatially, temporarily and emotionally close to the filmic world of the frightening movie, our immediate surroundings and everyday concerns are for the moment relegated to the margins. To repeat: being largely absent from the present world does not imply that we are tricked into an illusion. Being *close* to the presented world does not mean we are ontologically *in* the filmic world.

Obviously, I am talking about *tendencies* here. Arguing that frightening movies watched inside the multiplex cinema tend towards a strong immersive experience does not imply that every self-declared horror film and thriller guarantees immersion. If a bad film lacks the kind of immersion we rightfully expect, "the audience often produces 'fall-out' reactions, such as restlessness, aggressiveness (irritation, protective laughter, verbal comment) or a feeling of boredom, claustrophobia," Thomas Elsaesser argues.[52]

His expression *'fall-out' reaction* is particularly apposite here: a film that pretends to be scary but is merely boring causes the viewer to fall out of the immersive 'There' and arrive in the disenchanted, non-immersed 'Here'. If the film cannot open us a world, we have to face our own world. But what kind of world is this? With only slight exaggeration Elsaesser describes the cinematic situation vis-à-vis a bad movie as a "fixed term of imprisonment": the viewer is "pinned to his seat" and "enclosed in a darkened room, cut off visually from the surroundings and exposed to a state of isolation."[53] Small wonder that the viewer is not satisfied with these oppressive surroundings. I will not further deepen the discussion of boring movies since my goal is to answer the paradox of *pleasure* in fear. However, the reactions Elsaesser enumerates are important insofar as they remind us of other occasions when the tight connection between viewer and film is loosened or even severed. It is during these instances that the viewer becomes particularly active.

The Immersed Viewer: Passive but not Inactive

The film is actualized and completed only by the viewer. The spectator must perceive the film with the active attention of aesthetic attitude. Since he or she is actively devoted to the film experience, the viewer cannot be pictured as a passive receptacle bombarded by stimuli. The immersive experience of scary movies requires, for instance, the scanning of the temporal horizon in scenes of dread and the imaginative filling-in of incomplete perceptions in suggested horror. Even if I describe cinematic immersion as an intensified form of passive involvement, passive attention implies *attention* after all. However, immersion is an active act predominantly insofar as I decide to assume and keep an aesthetic attitude. To be sure, problem solving, hypothesis formation and inference-making certainly play a role while watching Hollywood movies. But we should not ascribe an overly strong agency to the spectator, particularly when it comes to the—by and large—effortless narrative comprehension of most horror films and thrillers.[54] This can help us to set the phenomenology of the film experience apart from more (inter-) active entertainment like playing a computer game. The effortlessness of watching films becomes even more striking when compared to reading literature. Using McLuhan's terminology, Marie-Laure Ryan argues: "A hot medium [like film] facilitates immersion through the richness of its sensory offerings, while a cold medium [like literature] opens its world only after the user has made a significant intellectual and imaginative investment. The media that offer data to the senses are naturally hotter than language-based media because in language all sensations must be actively simulated by the imagination."[55]

It is therefore appropriate to reserve the term *active*—apart from the active attention in aesthetic attitude—predominantly for a number of performative acts that will become crucial throughout the next chapters.

Horror, shock, dread and terror evoke "action tendencies", as philosophers and psychologists tend to say.[56] In particular cases action tendencies turn into action: When we close our eyes. When we put our hands in front of our ears. When we scream in shock. When we reach out for the hand of our partner. When we turn our head away from the screen and look for eye-contact with likeminded viewers. Consider the audience response to Hitchcock's *Psycho* in Linda Williams' description: "I vividly remember a Saturday matinee in 1960 when two girlfriends and I spent much of the screening with our eyes shut listening to the music and to the audience's screams as we tried to guess when we might venture to look again at a screen whose terrors were unaccountably thrilling. [. . .] From the very first screenings, audience reaction, in the form of gasps, screams, yells, even running up and down the aisles, was unprecedented."[57]

These deliberate bodily responses underscore that we are not hypnotized, dreaming or hallucinating, but actively answer the movie's emotional challenge. We actively undertake measures to stop (or lessen) an immersive experience that is threatening to become unpleasant. Since displeasure is not something we crave for, we take shelter from a negative emotional avalanche. Or, to put it in a more Sartreian vein: we play the sorcerer who magically re-transforms the emotional world. The discussions in the following chapters will present various degrees of immersion: from being deeply lost in the filmic world to a precarious balancing on the boundary between emotional fascination and abhorrence to a full-fledged rejection of the immersive experience—I call it extrication. Extrication either means that I simply withdraw from the film; or it implies, more productively and pleasurably, that I become aware of the *collectivity* inside the multiplex cinema—an aspect so far largely ignored in my account.

Figure 2.1 The shower murder in *Psycho*.

THE COLLECTIVE EXPERIENCE

In one sense it is fair to say that watching a film inside a multiplex is mainly an individual experience amongst other individuals: the *theatrical* experience is dominated by the *film* experience. But what about this other crucial aspect of the cinema: the group experience? In focusing on the act of viewing in the cinema my description excludes—by definition—any solitary viewing processes.[58] In contrast to reading or watching movies at home, viewing films in the theater is an inherently social activity. It is true that our *film* experience is an *individual* not a *social* one. My relation to the filmic world and its events is experienced as *my* relation—not as ours. But, once again, the film experience can never be uncoupled from the theatrical experience. Since the latter includes other viewers sitting next to me, the social is always part of the whole. In fact, I would go further: although we eagerly look for an individualized experience, there is a simultaneous tendency to watch films with others. We appreciate that the multiplex blocks interferences but still need others around: the cinema can become an eerie space if empty—a particularly true observation in case of frightening films. Even if there is little social *interaction* between those private individuals, the multiplex is nonetheless a place where the viewer can experience rewarding *feelings of collectivity*.

In fact, we can go so far as to credit the multiplex for a renaissance of the collective experience. The new generation of multiplex cinemas was—at least partly—responsible for the pull that drew the crowds back into the theaters. Go to a Saturday evening screening of the newest blockbuster and see. In the 1970s the number of average admissions per year was down to 985 million; in the 1980s it rose to 1,117 million; during the 1990s it climbed up to 1,297 million, with the highest numbers occurring at the end of the decade when the new generation of multiplexes was firmly established. The numbers peaked in 2002 with 1,639 million admissions, the highest number since 1957.[59] In comparison to the worst year ever—820 million spectators in 1971—this meant an increase of almost 100 percent. The renewed prevalence of collective viewing can also be judged from the increase in seats per screen. While in the 1970s and 80s the viewer would most generally share the auditorium with 50 to 100 other spectators (if sold-out), the current generation of multiplex cinemas hosts between 250 and 650 patrons. It certainly makes a difference if you watch a film with 50 people or with 650.

Now, what is true then? Is the multiplex experience an individualized or a collective experience? Curiously, it is both. Often it is precisely *because* the audience is so individualized and immersed that the single viewer becomes part of a larger whole. At other times we smoothly switch from an individualized to a collective state. Hence in the cinema we can enjoy the presence of others, even if we interact with them only minimally. Why?

In order to answer this question I have to come back to the enhanced *hiding effect*. The dark auditorium, the unidirectional viewing position, the backrest in combination with sloped stadium seating, the enhanced personal space, the loudness of the soundtrack, and the passive absorption not only hide *me* (as argued before)—but they also make it difficult for me to judge what *others* feel. The hiding effect works in both directions: in the literally face-less anonymity of the auditorium we do not only hide our faces—but also have a hard time reading the emotional expressions of our co-viewers. This has a peculiar effect: the viewers take for granted a state of *intersubjective objectivity* since they assume that they share the same intentional object with the rest of the audience. Since everybody is—or at least *seems* to be—in the grip of the movie, the individual viewers are never led to believe that anyone else would *see* or *hear* anything else. And why should they in light of the film's formidable capacity to demand passive attention? Consider the situation in the auditorium before the screen is turned from a grey rectangle into a colorful world. People eat their popcorn, talk on the cell phone, read a magazine. The viewers either sit alone, somehow occupied, often awkwardly killing time. Or they have come in groups and talk with each other quietly. Seen as a whole, the attentions of these people are scattered. A sense of collectivity hardly exists. Once the screen is illuminated, however, it becomes the prime center of attention.

But seeing and hearing the same object is only half of the story. Since the viewers direct their senses almost fully towards the film and are simultaneously kept at a distance from each other, they perceive the reactions of others primarily in exceptional cases like laughing, moaning and screaming. Now, precisely because reactions are not made explicit—or rather because they are cloaked in darkness, drowned in loudness, hidden behind the back of the seat etc.—one can only speculate about the film experience other audience members might have. Supported by the fact that in American theaters no social hierarchy exists and that everybody can feel like an equal individual among many, the viewers tacitly presuppose that the others have the *same* film experience—they also *think* and *feel* alike. When the movie starts it seems as if an invisible Toscanini or Karajan lifts his baton and orchestrates the experience of the audience. And while some of the instrumentalists might not be perfectly in tune with the rest of the orchestra, the film, by and large, leads the common reactions of the spectators. And even if this is—in fact—often not the case, it is what the viewers—tacitly and without reflection—*assume* under the special circumstances of the multiplex.

Hence, while before the film we have an accumulation of scattered foci, during the screening there is a strong (if obviously not a total) equality. When the viewers take their seats in the movie theater they are merely *attached* as a group of physically close viewers, but they do not yet share the *intersubjective intimacy* of phenomenologically close spectators.[60] This gradually changes once the film gets underway—and the chapter on dread will show that it can become particularly striking in moments of fearful emotional intensity. *Physical* closeness can turn into *phenomenological* closeness.

In this context, the fact that we watch *fictional* films becomes vital. As Sobchack argues, viewing a fiction film results in the strongest possible relatedness to the screen. Drawing on Jean-Pierre Meunier's phenomenology of cinematic identification, Sobchack asserts that in the fiction film we are highly dependent on the screen for specific knowledge.[61] Because the objects presented onscreen do not exist elsewhere but only in the filmic world, i.e. because the objects onscreen are differentiated from the reality of the spectator's life-world, the viewer has to rely on the screen as the only source of information. In contrast to home movies and documentaries the viewer can hardly see, as it were, beyond the screen's boundaries and back into his or her life-world. Hence the attention to the objects on the screen is more focused and intense than in home movies and documentaries. This, in turn, has an effect on the collective thoughts and feelings within the audience. If someone is familiar with the topic of a documentary he or she has a strong advantage in terms of *knowledge*. If someone knows the persons shown in a home movie his or her *feelings* will be different from those who don't. In the fiction film, however, the audience's common relatedness to unknown—because non-existent—objects facilitates the impression of a commonly *shared* intentional object.

To be sure, most of the time we do not actively think about the rest of the audience. Consciousness is directed toward the film. The other spectators stay in the *background* of awareness. The concept of background is employed by phenomenology and analytic philosophy in order to indicate that intentional states—states in which we are conscious *of* something—always rely on something that is unintentional: the background. An example from the phenomenological literature is Drew Leder's discussion of the *absent body*. Leder makes clear that whatever we do, there are always regions of body that we do not focus upon.[62] While we follow the onscreen action, we predominantly use our eyes and ears to relate to the filmic world as our intentional object. But this is only possible because the legs, buttocks and back support our position on the seat. Even though these bodily regions are necessary to follow the film, they are not thematized and therefore relegated to the phenomenological background—unless the back starts to hurt. Analytic philosopher John Searle employs the concept of background similarly. He argues that intentionality in such forms as understandings, interpretations, beliefs, desires, and, most important for our purposes, experiences only function with a set of background capacities that are themselves not intentional.[63] Think of the solidity of the floor we stand on. We generally take for granted that the earth under our feet does not move. Under normal conditions it is nothing that we would think of. When an earthquake occurs, however, this background presupposition suddenly becomes foregrounded.

In both cases—sore back and earthquake—we become aware of the background under extraordinary circumstances.[64] I think it is especially helpful to consider the collectivity inside the cinema as such a tacit background. And the extraordinary circumstances under which collectivity can play a crucial role are provided precisely by frightening movies.

Obviously, collectivity is not necessary for the *film* experience. At home, we often watch films alone and find nothing strange about it. When it comes to the cinema, however, the collectivity of the audience is taken for granted as an invariant component. Most of the time it is not part of our focal awareness. But just as we realize that we stand on solid ground only when the earth shakes, we are conscious of the movie audience when it is somehow—actively or passively—made explicit. This can happen, as it were, *ex negativo*. When we sit alone in the auditorium, the eeriness of the empty place reminds us of what we miss. The phenomenal background of the other viewers becomes foregrounded by its non-presence. The room not only *looks* empty, but also *feels* empty.

Furthermore, some of the most familiar moments of crisis in terms of the multiplex collectivity take place when other viewers make explicit their individuality by expressing their own thoughts and feelings. Consider the differences in *thoughts*. They often become noticeable when someone tries to signal that he or she has understood an allusion or a pun that others might have overlooked by breaking out into 'connoisseur laughter.' This connoisseur laughter does not communicate an emotion, but a thought or understanding. Often it is an understanding that indicates: I see, hear, or know more than you. As an act of social distinction it threatens the taken-for-granted collectivity. Regarding the differences of *emotions*, we all know the anger that fills us when we are deeply involved in a sad love scene and someone starts to laugh derisively. Or the irritation that arises when we follow a terrifying moment and another viewer yawns audibly. We get angry not only because we are dragged out of deep immersion against our will, but also because we are glaringly reminded that *not* everybody sees, hears, thinks and feels alike. The cloak that envelops us as a collectivity is forcefully torn apart. Precisely because we do not want the taken-for-granted collectivity to be destroyed by someone who positions him- or herself outside the group, we use our own instruments to discipline and punish. We feel an urgent drive to achieve a quick reintegration: we shush him or her or threaten to take other measures.

The cinematic collectivity works only if everybody plays by the (display) rules. Every viewer needs to sign a cinematic contract, as it were, in which he or she agrees to follow the implicit cultural norms. Whether the individual is willing to follow these social display rules depends on the *outcome* of his behavior in terms of rewards and costs. Paradoxically, while in India the overt expression of individual feelings has positive effects, it is different in a more individualized society like the U.S. Here the viewer must be aware that the consequences of *not* adhering to the rules—that is, of displaying emotions too overtly—are twofold. The viewer will give up the personal experience of collectivity, because he or she deliberately places him- or herself outside the group. And he or she might be disciplined and thus marked even further as an outsider. The bonds that unite the interrupter with the group are broken twice over. The fact that most viewers behave properly most of the time goes a long way to explain their willingness to become part of the special cinematic collectivity.

So far, I have described moments in which the taken-for-granted collectivity is made explicit *ex negativo*. However, the collective situation can also be thematized in a positive way: either when we actively focus on it or when the backgrounded collectivity itself comes to the fore. In these instances the viewer experiences what I will call 'feelings-in-common' or even a 'collective body.' While the collectivity of the audience constitutes an essential background most of the time, throughout the film moments occur in which we are consciously aware of this collectivity. Admittedly, the two categories of 'feelings-in-common' and 'the collective body' are somewhat broad, leveling the numerous degrees and shadings of collectivity in between. As broad categories, however, they help to highlight what might otherwise be overlooked. It will be part of this study to describe the back-and-forth movement between individualized immersion (being There in the filmic world *alone*) and collective presence (being Here in the cinematic space *together*). I argue that horror films and thrillers allow for a smoother and more fluid back-and-forth movement than most other genres. In more individualized and immersive genres like pornography or melodrama it is neither necessary nor desired to get an impression of the other viewers' reactions. In more collective genres like the comedy the reactions of others are much more strongly forced upon us; nor should we ignore the problem that our own shaking body in laughter poses to immersion.

How do moments of collectivity manifest themselves? When we are overwhelmed by fear and actively look for confirmation in the audience or grab the hand of our partner, this not only implies that we temporarily loosen (or even cut) our immersive ties to the filmic world—it also opens a door to others. We try to counter the isolating experience of fear by reverting to the collective viewing situation. Realizing that our co-viewers are also quietly and fearfully following the film, we become aware that we all sit in the same boat, so to speak. We are rewarded with the reassuring impression that we are similarly afraid. Even more obvious are instances of the 'collective body'. Its phenomenological experience might be described as an emotional fusion of oneself with otherwise heterogeneous others that results in a momentary feeling of a social whole. Let me give some quick examples. The first of these is laughter. In comedies the common outburst of laughter not only reinforces one's own feeling of hilarity; it also creates a bond within the audience. A similar thing can be said about moaning in disgust and screams of shock in thrillers and horror movies. To be sure, 'collective body' moments depend on a variety of empirical variables like the movie, the number of spectators or the density of seating. Nonetheless, common laughter, moaning and screaming exemplify moments in which the viewer can directly adhere to the *conscious* impression that others are not only *seeing* and *hearing* the same thing, but are also *thinking* and *feeling* alike.

As individual members of the audience we enjoy being part of this homogeneous collectivity. And even if in actuality we often do *not* think and feel the same—a point that recent reception studies have made quite clear—the viewer in the audience still *believes* so as long as not contradicted or proved otherwise because he or she *wants* to believe so. I take it as a human characteristic that we wish that others think and feel as we do in aesthetic experience.[65] As a result, our individual experience seemingly becomes the norm that we subconsciously project onto others. The cinematic collectivity—built from various similar but not identical individual experiences—appears as formed in the likeness of our own experience. The multiplex cinema becomes a place where common emotions create an impression of social belongingness.

For many viewers familiarity and similarity are key incentives to attend a screening in a multiplex. Regardless to which company the theater belongs (United Artists Theaters, Cineplex Odeon or any other U.S. competitor), the word 'multiplex' describes a kind of super-brand. This homogeneity stands in stark contrast to the individuality and uniqueness of 1920s and 1930s movie palaces.[66] Today no matter what theater the viewer-as-consumer picks, the multiplex-as-product guarantees specific features. Consequently, the viewer can decide *in advance* whether he or she chooses the multiplex product—or prefers another one. As was explained previously, similar things account for genres. The viewer is able to select from a variety of options: comedies, melodramas, tragedies . . . or frightening horror movies and thrillers. Each one promises a different (emotional) experience. Taken together, the decision to watch a scary movie in a multiplex theater suggests a very specific experience that is quite unlike other viewing experiences.

Having looked at how the multiplex skews our cinematic experience towards individualized immersion, heightened emotionality and specific forms of collectivity, I will now move on to explore the fearful effects of the films themselves. In order to avoid misunderstandings, I need to prime the reader that the following five chapters are more detailed than the phenomenological discussion of the pleasures of fear—and hence my answer to the paradox that provides the title to this study—would warrant. As pointed out at the beginning, this study also aims to contribute to the neglected field one could call 'aesthetics of fear.' Readers interested first and foremost in my phenomenological descriptions might skip the aesthetic parts and move directly to the phenomenological sections. The first of the five chapters contains an in-depth discussion of what I call *direct horror*. Horror stands at the beginning because in many ways it is the *conditio sine qua non* of other types of cinematic fear. Without the fear of a confrontation with violence or the monster, dread or terror would not be possible. This chapter helps to clarify the question how an experience of fear at the movies—and hence the pleasure derived from it—is possible in the first place. And it also touches upon aspects that will figure more prominently in later chapters, for instance the lived-body experience of fear.

Part II

3 Frightening Fascination
A Phenomenology of Direct Horror

Since time immemorial people have craved spectacles permitting vicariously to experience the fury of conflagrations, the excesses of cruelty and suffering, and unspeakable lusts—spectacles which shock the shuddering and delighted onlooker.

(Siegfried Kracauer)[1]

The strongest emotion is fear. The oldest emotion is fear. We all have it, and it is a very deep pool inside every human on the planet. So there are some of us who dive into that pool because we are both repelled and attracted by it.

(John Carpenter)[2]

DIRECT HORROR: THE DEFINITION

- After being raped and almost strangled by her brother, a young woman is rescued in the nick of time by a friend. The two men start a violent, fatal fight. When the brother smashes a bottle over his opponent's head and sets out to finish him off with the words "Adios, motherfucker!", the woman grabs a metallic comb and pierces it into her brother's eye. He recoils heavily, winces and screams in pain. The friend takes the comb and stabs it several times into the brother's stomach. Soon both men are soaked in blood.
- A man walks through a graveyard at night. Suddenly he is surrounded by two monsters. One of them keeps him in check with a knife. The other one threatens him by its sheer monstrosity: piercing, at times blinking eyes, metallic teeth, skin from which snake-like hair emanates, a deep, dark, distorted voice, and a self-assured, highly aggressive demeanor. The monster laughs at the man, threatens him "You came to die" and calls him an "asshole." At one point, it starts roaring like a deadly, werewolf-like beast, shakes the snake-hair and suddenly transforms, now flashing sharp, pointed teeth, a drooling mouth and rotten skin. It roars loudly and screams: "I want meat!" Eventually it attacks the man.
- It is night. A girl clad in a grotesque Halloween bunny costume flees from a murderous, knife-wielding, blond woman into a dark graveyard. Her escape is in vain. The woman overwhelms her and stabs the screaming girl several times aggressively and with hysterical laughter in the chest until both are splattered with blood. The woman licks her bloody lips and smiles.

Figure 3.1 Direct horror: *House of 1000 Corpses*.

The sample scenes are taken from *Henry—Portrait of a Serial Killer*, *Nightbreed* (1990) and *House of 1000 Corpses* respectively. They exemplify an aesthetic strategy I call 'direct horror.' The viewer experiences direct horror—the first type of cinematic fear—as a frightening, engrossing and potentially overwhelming confrontation with vivid *sound-supported moving-images* of threatening acts of *violence* or a dangerous *monster*. In the face of the perceptible violent event and/or monstrous object the viewer is both frightened and fascinated. In contrast to suggested horror (discussed in the next chapter), direct horror presents the threatening violent event or monstrous object in full vision and thus as directly as possible.

When he or she experiences direct horror, the viewer is involved in a balancing act between the luring pull *towards* the frightening object of fascination and the threatening push *away* from the fascinating object of fright. The experience vacillates between pleasurably frightening, fascinated *immersion* and displeasing overly frightened *extrication*. The former turns into the latter when the frightening aspect obliterates the fascinating side, when pleasurable fear turns into displeasing fear, and when all pleasure components are gone and fear is experienced pure and simple. Moreover, we are horrified by an *instantaneous* event or object: it is what we perceive right now that scares us, not what has happened in the story's past or what might occur in the immediate future. Although we often draw on preceding information or perceptions, the present threatening moving-images are the causes for our horror. Hence remembering and anticipating are subordinate to the concrete event. Since we *are in the face of* the horrific there is a high degree of intentionality and no uncertainty about its coming-into-being. These aspects distinguish horror from anticipatory types of suspenseful fear like dread and terror: the latter are rooted in the present *and* the future; both are dominated by uncertainty and a more complicated kind of intentionality (see Chapters 6 and 7).

But what is it that connects threatening *acts* of violence and the dangerous *object* of the monster? Why do I subsume both under the category of cinematic horror and why, for instance, do natural disasters not qualify? In contrast to the latter, violent events and monstrous entities indicate *intentional* and *disproportional immorality* in combination with *disturbing brutality*. It is precisely this combination of intentional immorality and brutality that we experience as horrifying and that we usually do not ascribe to natural disasters or other threatening events. (Note, that I include the adjectives 'disproportional' and 'disturbing,' because they allow for idiosyncratic differences among viewers: what some consider disproportionally immoral and disturbingly cruel, others might regard as tolerable and hence not horrifying.) While we might consider a greedy character delivering nuclear arms to a terrorist group in a political thriller disproportionally immoral, we do not experience this act as cinematic horror because of a lack of disturbing brutality. The disturbingly brutal depictions of a devastating hurricane killing dozens of people in a disaster movie cannot be considered horror either, since a natural disaster cannot be judged in moral terms (unless it is anthropomorphized). And when in a movie like *The Descent* (2005) a female character breaks her leg and we get to see the bloody bone sticking out, this might cause disgust or feelings of pain via somatic empathy. But we do not experience the type of fear I call cinematic horror since no one behaves immorally here. In order to qualify as cinematic horror it does not suffice that a lot of blood is spilled.

Surely, immoral and cruel *acts of violence* should not pose a problem for my definition. But what about moving-images of a monster, say, wandering through the streets of Houston? While such a scene need not *necessarily* evoke horror, the monster often hints at horror so strongly and lets it shine through so vividly that it starts to personify horror: We are frightened by the sheer presence of the monster either because it reminds us forcefully of an act of violence we have already witnessed or have inferred from the plot; or because it points toward an impending cruelty indicated by the monster's aggressive behavior and/or dangerous appearance. Think of the example from *Nightbreed*: although the monster in the graveyard has not attacked the man yet, its menacing looks, its aggressive demeanor and its hostile comments reveal so much immoral and cruel intention *already*, that many viewers might experience it as horrifying *before* the act of violence has begun. Yet if the definition of the monster hinges on a disproportional intentional immorality combined with disturbing cruelty, the monster does not need to be an ontologically impossible being. This is the reason why we do not call anomalous, supernaturally powerful but likeable characters like Yoda or Albus Dumbledore monsters, whereas vicious animals can become horrifying creatures—i.e. monsters. Consider

The Birds, *Anaconda* or the killer shark in *Jaws*. Most viewers probably find their intentional attacks on innocent human beings unjustified, overly brutal and hence horrifying. This definition also helps to explain why human characters can be regarded as (realist) monsters. Just think of Norman Bates, Henry or Hannibal Lecter. To be sure, they evoke cinematic horror only during threatening moments, i.e. in most cases when an act of violence takes place or is at least imminent.

Horror is easily intensified. Two strategies come to mind. First, the victim has to be a character for whom we have developed a strong allegiance and whom we like. This might happen because a star plays the victim, because the actor is attractive, because the character has features or preferences similar to ours, or because he shares an affiliation along race, class, ethnicity, gender, age or religion lines.[3] More importantly, an act of violence can horrify us because we strongly approve of the victim on moral grounds, particularly if he or she is sympathetic and innocent. Second, horror can be intensified through an increase in immorality and cruelty. When a bank robber takes great pleasure in cutting off a policeman's ear while dancing rhythmically to a pop song (as in *Reservoir Dogs*, 1992) or a serial killer deeply enjoys eating from a victim's open brain (as in *Hannibal*), these heinous acts of violence are particularly horrifying.

To be sure, the film cannot merely show an act of violence or a monster, but must present the filmic content in such a vivid and impressive way that the content comes across as *threatening*. That is, in order to be effective cinematic horror must seamlessly combine content and form, semantics and aesthetics. If one component lags behind, there will be no horror. Hence a vivid, impressive presentation of a ripe banana will create just as little horror as a barely audible monster crossing a cornfield in the far-away distance. Aesthetic choices like proximity through close-ups, precision and volume of the sound track, but also the inconspicuousness of the special effects that draw our attention toward the artefact and away from the scary object play a fundamental role when it comes to threatening the audience.

Threat is crucial for my definition of horror, insofar as there are funny presentations of violence and the monster as well. Let us look at *violence* first. Stephen Prince has suggested a broad distinction between dominant forms of what he calls "ultraviolence": a) the aestheticized, balletic violence of Arthur Penn, Sam Peckinpah, John Woo and the likes relying on slow motion, multi-camera filming and montage editing; and b) graphic imagery of bodily mutilation exemplified by horror movies of the 1970s and 1980s which employed new makeup special effects to convincingly portray the destruction and dismemberment of the body.[4] According to Prince, both forms of 'ultraviolence' are horrifying, if to varying degrees. However, Prince does not take into account that ultraviolence can be hilarious. Think of a funny, violent splatter movie like *Evil Dead II* (1987). The film would clearly fall into Prince's second category, even though it does not have the same horrifying effect as the first *Evil Dead* installment simply because, due to various aesthetic strategies, it does not want to and cannot be taken seriously. Similarly, for most people the violence in Quentin Tarantino's *Pulp Fiction* (1994) does not come across as horror, since it is clad in distancing humor and irony and therefore loses its threatening character. Hence one could argue that a "violent" movie is only experientially violent as long as it affects the viewer in a menacing way. It not only matters *what* is presented, but also *how* it is presented.

The same goes for the monster. Depending on the context, the same creature can be a horrifying monster or a funny creature. In *House of Frankenstein* (1944) and *Abbott & Costello Meet Frankenstein* (1948) the creature looks the same and is even played by the same actor (Glenn Strange), but evokes very different reactions.[5] Displaying the monster is not enough to convince us that it is dangerous. The monster must be characterized as a menace by presenting its capabilities and the consequences of its actions. If the monster is not frightening, it might cause all kinds of responses—ranging from laughter to disinterest and even boredom. What is at stake in horror is not violence or the monster *per se* but their threatening side.

Incidentally, these violent and monstrous moving-images need not be repulsive. My definition of horror rests on a separation between *horrifying* and *disgusting* moving-images and sounds. A frightening film like *Cape Fear* uses horrifying imagery but works almost completely without disgust, while a splatter parody like *Braindead* (1992) is predominantly revolting without being scary. Obviously, the line between horror and disgust can be quite thin. On the one hand, images of cruel acts of torturing mean pure *horror* and a rotting body full of pus evokes *disgust* and nothing else. On the other hand, a scene in which a character's stomach is sliced open and the intestines can subsequently be seen gushing forth seamlessly blends horror and disgust. Sometimes both emotions occur simultaneously: for instance, when a disgusting monster violently kills a character. Despite the frequent coexistence of these various responses, however, I see no need for a new emotional category. In Noël Carroll's account fear and disgust are welded together and constitute an emotion he terms "art-horror."[6] His prime instance of art-horror is the monster: it is both threatening and disgustingly impure. But why introduce a new emotion, when the viewer simply feels fear and disgust simultaneously?

THE FASCINATION FOR VIOLENCE AND MONSTERS

Cinematic horror clearly casts an attractive spell. It thrives on a similar kind of fascination that makes people flock around the site of a murder, causes traffic jams at scenes of accident due to slow-driving gapers and made people stare at the TV images of the collapsing World Trade Center on 9/11. The snake-headed Gorgo Medusa might be seen as a mythological precursor of today's monsters: a horrible entity highly tempting to look at.

The popularity of movies containing violence and monsters clearly points to a high acceptance among viewers. It is hard to deny that graphic violence has generally increased over the last decades. Since the late 1960s, when the Production Code was revised and the Code and Rating Administration introduced its new classification scheme, Hollywood has drastically changed its stance towards violence. At the same time the craft of special effects (makeup) enabling highly graphic depictions of monsters has made considerable progress. Stephen Prince even goes so far as to describe the history of American cinema as a history of ever-more explicit presentational techniques of violence and monstrosity.[7]

Horror movies and thrillers deliberately put the viewer into contact with moving-images that normal life—fortunately—withholds to a large degree, making them both alluring and threatening. This goes in terms of *violence*: the immoral shooting, burning, stabbing, raping, piercing, slicing, smashing, torturing, opening-up, tearing-apart, fragmenting, mutilating, exploding of the body; the cruel disclosure and exposure of the human insides; the death and destruction of the flesh. But it also true in terms of the *monster*. In most cases monsters are unseen and unheard of entities, often transcending the limits of the human: extremely cunning aliens; deadly living deads; lethal ghouls; mutated, slime-spitting bugs; abnormally intelligent serial killers; haunted, vengeful houses; indestructible slashers; beastly werewolves; outrageously aggressive snakes, dogs or sharks . . . Noël Carroll explains: "[Monsters] arouse interest and attention through being putatively inexplicable or highly unusual vis-à-vis our standing cultural categories, thereby instilling a desire to learn and to know more about them."[8]

Direct horror is, then, a particularly forceful example of what Mirjam Schaub dubs the cinema of visibility (*Kino der Sichtbarkeit*).[9] It is a type of cinema that focuses on everything potentially visible and audible. It wants to present what cannot be seen and heard: the more precise, more lasting, more explicit, the better. The depictions of monsters lay bare the cinematic wish—*and* capability—to make visible and audible even non-existent entities. Schaub calls this the 'logic of optical omnipresence.' Seen from a reception perspective, the *cinema of visibility* manifests the disposition of its viewers: an urge to see and hear as much as possible.

The extent of this urge can be gauged from our reactions to scenes that deliberately *withhold* the horrific—and thus lure and titillate us. In such scenes of blocked or deferred visual access, there is often a *longing* for a better view: we almost bend to look from a different angle—we are all eyes. David Fincher's *Seven* belongs to those movies that incessantly play with the viewer's wish to confront the horrific. It variously uses photographs that cannot be seen properly or are glimpsed only shortly. In a crucial scene a policeman urges Detectives Somerset (Morgan Freeman) and Mills (Brad Pitt): "You better see this!"—only to keep back what *they* get to see from our view. In this scene the two detectives enter the bedroom of the prostitute who has become the serial killer's fourth victim. The policeman withdraws a blanket from her corpse like a curtain, as if to say '*Voilà*, here you go!' When the victim is revealed, however, Detective Mills blocks our view. What we see are her legs, slightly covered with blood. However, the fatal wound is—frustratingly?—kept back. Another baiting strategy involves the reaction shot of a horrified character confronting a monster or watching an act of violence. In order to heighten our curiosity for the monster or the effects of violence (and thus to maximize the impact of their presentation), the horror movie often turns around the logical cause-and-effect sequence of storytelling, in which the *re*-action shot *follows* the action, by offering the reaction shot *first* and thus creating heightened curiosity.[10]

The terms curiosity, interest and fascination explain—at least in part— our strong attention: we are drawn to violence and the monster because we can see and hear things usually unseen and unheard.

MINDING THE ONTOLOGICAL DISTANCE, OR THE VIEWER'S RELATIVE SAFETY

This strong attention would not be possible, however, if a certain precondition was inexistent: the viewer's relative safety. In *Seven*, Detective Somerset tells an anecdote that can function as a parable about our fascination with violence and the monster: "First thing they teach women in rape prevention is: Never cry for help. Always yell: 'Fire.' Nobody answers to 'Help.' You holler 'Fire,' they come running." What Somerset bleakly points out is not only our *fascination* with death and destruction, but also the *safety* aspect. No one comes to rescue if there is a demand for active involvement, as implied in the imperative "Help!" If they can take a distanced position, people gather. As a particularly salient part of the cinematic experience, this crucial form of distance enables the vicarious experiences of horror films and thrillers in the first place. I call this detachment *ontological distance* since the movie theater's Here and the filmic world's There are of different existential orders: they are, literally, worlds apart.[11] In Stanley Cavell's reflections on the ontology of film as a *succession of automatic world projections* the fact that the world of the film is present to us, while we are absent from it, that we are save from it by way of the ontological boundary that is the screen, plays an essential role: "A screen is a barrier. What does the silver screen screen? It screens me from the world it holds— that is, makes me invisible. And it screens that world from me—that is, screens its existence from me," Cavell notes.[12] The ontological distance implies the viewer's physical absence from the scene of action, and thus provides us with a form of safety: we are not threatened by the serial killer Henry or the monster Freddy Krueger *in the same way* as their victims are. This physical absence has important ramifications.

First, we do not have to take action in terms of *geographical* flight from the diegetic threat. When the devil sets about his work of destruction in

The End of Days (1999), we do not run out of the theater; when all hell breaks loose during the dinosaur attacks in *The Lost World*, we do not call 911. Without this sense of safety the emotional experience of the movies would be unbearable. The idea of a crucial nexus between safety, fear and pleasure goes back, at least, to the discussions of the sublime in Burke, Kant and Rousseau.[13] Since then it has resurfaced, among various other places, in the classical film theories of Balázs and Kracauer.[14] A more recent theory that underscores the importance of the ontological (or, as he calls it, "safe") distance is Ed Tan's description of film as an "emotion machine." Tan notes: "A terrifying situation is entertaining precisely because you can do no more than watch; if you were in a position to intervene, in order to protect yourself and others, then you would feel responsible and would no longer be able to enjoy the fictional events on the screen."[15]

Tan points out the second important aspect implied by the notion of ontological distance: it excuses us from action also in the sense of practical *intervention*. In the movie theater we feel no ethical or legal obligation to step in. We cannot cross the film's ontological boundary to heroically throw ourselves in front of the woman and thus prevent her from being stabbed in the shower. And rushing to our cars and heading for Texas to stop the local chainsaw massacre would be utterly in vain. Being relieved from the burden of intervention is closely tied to narrative determinacy. Since in the movie theater the film unrolls without mercy and we cannot stop it, the relieving helplessness is mechanically assured. Hence we could replace Laura Mulvey's afore-mentioned argument for the viewer's "desire for mastery and will to power [over the movie]" with Stanley Cavell's argument for the viewer's "wish not to need power, not to have to bear its burdens."[16] In terms of frightening movies being exempted from practical intervention is a blessing—but, as we shall see, it is sometimes a blessing in disguise: precisely because we have no options to intervene we can only hope and fear. In other words, the viewer's passivity is also one of the reasons for the frightening power of moving images.

Third, when the ontological distance is coupled with the *fictional* distance, we are also granted a certain leeway in terms of *moral evaluation*. Since we know that the filmic events are neither live and real *right now* nor have they ever taken place *in the past*, we do not have to be morally outraged as much as in real-life when we watch the burying of two well and alive innocents (as in *House of 1000 Corpses*) or the hideous rape of a female protagonist (as in the 2007 *The Hills Have Eyes II*). Indeed, projecting ethical norms onto the fiction film might well reduce the intensity of aesthetic experience by drawing us away from the filmic world. This fact becomes quite obvious in cases when the real shines through the irreal and the fiction film unwittingly develops a documentary quality due to its indexical character. All of a sudden we are not interested in what *is taking* place in the fictional filmic world at this moment anymore, but what *has taken* place in front of the camera in the profilmic past of the real world.

When in Andrej Tarkovsky's *Andrej Rubljov* (1969) a *real* horse really falls from a staircase or in Jean Renoir's *La règle du jeu* (1939) as well as in Robert Bresson's *Mouchette* (1967) a *real* rabbit is really shot, chances are good that we are morally upset.[17]

The uncoupling of perceiving from active participation and moral outrage has an important consequence: since there is nothing we can do, we are free to watch and listen in order to satisfy our curiosity. Even more importantly, we can dwell more deeply in our immersive experience. If the disengagement of the practical did not exist and we were to witness a scene of violence in reality, we would act practically, evaluate morally and be captivated more *strongly* by our emotions—but we would be *less* aware of the whole experience. We would be absorbed completely, whereas in the movie theater the experience is always partial. It is partially there, but simultaneously here, in our body, as well. Hence we need the ontological distance as a prerequisite to devote our awareness more strongly to the fascinating-perceptual and the frightening-emotional experience of violence and monstrosity. Last but not least, add the fact that we know from the outset that this experience is not going to be an endless one: the cinematic experience is a pre-packaged, finite, bounded encounter with fear after which we can always return to our everyday life.

GLARING IMAGES, STRIKING SOUNDS: THE IMPRESSIVENESS OF THE MOVIES

But are we that safe after all? I think we have to answer this question with both 'Yes' and 'No.' *Yes*, we are safe insofar as we can always rely on the ontological distance between cinematic surroundings and filmic world. However, just because we are not subjected to the *same* danger as the characters does not imply we confront *no* danger at all. Readers might have noticed that I have talked about *relative* safety. In fact, some films can have such strong emotional and corporeal effects that we consider them a literal threat to our well-being. They make us feel psychologically mistreated and even physically harmed.[18] Consider the numerous viewers who couldn't cope with *Henry—Portrait of a Serial Killer* and had to leave the theater. Or take the spectators who got sick and even vomited because of *The Exorcist*. These examples do not represent run-of-the-mill horror or thriller experiences. Yet they accentuate quite spectacularly that fear and shock are *real*.

The fact that films *do* sometimes have these overwhelming effects is—implicitly or explicitly—conceded by the existence of four discourses or classificatory systems. First of all, *censorship*: in this case a powerful political or religious group decides to put a ban on a film (or parts of it), because it deems the respective film too harmful for society as a whole. The idea is that some films might harm the moral order of a society or trigger dangerous acts of imitation so that these films need to be concealed from view. Second, *the rating system*: the Motion Picture Association of America (MPAA) judges films according to the well-known rating system that classifies films from G to NC-17. The goal of the rating system is to protect a part of society, namely children and adolescents, from psychological disturbances or the danger of imitation. Obviously, people judge these media effects quite differently. Hence there are often fierce controversies about censorship and ratings. Third, *academic ideology critique and criticism of the politics of representation*: by exposing films and their representations of women, African Americans, homosexuals and other minority groups (but also the representations of animals and nature) as agents of ideological manipulation, this form of intellectual iconoclasm also ascribes a harmful effect to movies.[19] Fourth, there is the *genre* as the last, but certainly not the least important classificatory system. The genre as a communicative tool guarantees that the individual knows by and large what to expect from a movie. It thus functions as a means of self-protection. Many people frankly admit that they are not able to bear horror movies, because these films are too frightening—be it, because their personal constitution *in general* or their personal phobias vis-à-vis particular presentations *in specific* do not allow for such intense experiences.

But how can something as fleeting as the cinema have such strong effects? Phenomenologists of perception tell us that sight and sound *per se* have pathic affective quality. The pathic is always a necessary part of perception—we cannot disconnect perception (*Wahrnehmung*) from feeling and affect (*Empfindung*).[20] To be sure, there are differences between the 'higher' and the 'lower' senses in terms of what Erwin Straus calls *gnostic* and *pathic* moments of experience: the gnostic (recognition) dominates in a sense like sight; the pathic (feeling) prevails in a sense like touch. Hence the change from one prevailing sense modality to another implies a change in dominance of the gnostic to the pathic moment (or vice versa). However, it would be wrong to understand seeing merely as a *distance sense* that relates the perceiving subject to the perceived object via distance and thus keeps the object at bay. "In seeing, too, we not only experience the seen but also ourselves as someone who sees," Straus notes.[21] What I see is not excluded and distant from me—simply *out there*—but always stands in a pathic relation to me. While we might not be aware of this in everyday circumstances, it becomes all the more obvious in extraordinary cases in which the pathic is so strong that we experience it as affective.[22] Think of visual objects that glare or strike: the sun, the putrefying corpse of a dog at the roadside, the gaze of a beautiful passer-by. The third stanza of Baudelaire's famous poem "To a Woman Passing By" is apposite here. At the sight of a beautiful woman the thunderstruck poetic "I" exclaims: "A gleam. . . .then night! O fleeting beauty, /Your glance has given me sudden rebirth . . ."[23] While the glaring of the sun might be explained (away) physiologically, the strong effects of the disgusting dead animal and the female gaze (or male, for that matter) cannot. Seeing is a form of touching at a distance, as is exemplified in the notion *eye contact*.[24]

In what way does this relate to the violent and monstrous moving-images of the cinema? The answer is as simple as it is obvious: the pathic moment of seeing does not stop in front of moving-images in which the object is not *really* there but merely *artificially* present. We cannot deny that we are affected by reality *and* images (which does obviously not imply that both experiences are identical phenomenologically). In his book *The Power of Images*, David Freedberg marvels about the effectiveness, efficacy and vitality of images and the unrefined, basic, pre-intellectual, raw responses they entail: "People are sexually aroused by pictures and sculptures; they break pictures and sculptures; they mutilate them, kiss them, cry before them, and go on journeys to them; they are calmed by them, stirred by them, and incited to revolt."[25] And they are, of course, afraid of them. Where does this power of dead material come from, Freedberg wonders? His provocative answer veers in two directions. First, his elaborate cross-cultural research implies that approaching images from the perspective of response means giving up the belief that our response to pictures must be radically different from the way we respond to the world around us: "To respond to a picture or sculpture 'as if' it were real is little different from responding to reality as real," he writes.[26] It would certainly be wrong to deduce from Freedberg's empirical argument that we experience images and reality *identically*. He simply states that we respond *intensely* in both cases. Nor does he argue that images *represent* reality—the second direction he moves into. "I do not wish to suggest that response should be based on the perception of representation as the more or less successful imitation or illusion of nature," he writes.[27] Here lies the simple but important lesson to learn from Freedberg's empirical intervention: we are able to respond vividly to something that is not really there.

As a consequence, we should abandon the third-person standpoint of comparing images to reality. Otherwise we will always and necessarily notice an essential lack. If we expect images to imitate or represent reality, we cannot help but see them as deficient and hampered illusions.[28] Which would take us back to the point where we began: how do we explain the strong effects of a deficient illusion? The same is true for the cinema. One of the traditional ways to explain its strong effects was precisely to invoke the "reality effect" of illusion. As my discussion of the differences between immersion and illusion has shown, in the movie theater we do not respond to an illusion—we respond to a fictional filmic world evoked by sound-supported moving-images. Phenomenologically, this implies a crucial difference: we are not tricked into experiencing the onscreen action as real, but always experience it as a film. This has troubled illusion theorists a great deal. They couldn't cope with the problem how a deficient illusion might result in such intense responses. Since its inception phenomenological aesthetics has rejected the idea of illusion or *Schein*.[29] Hence it suggests itself to go back to the things themselves and describe the filmic image not as a (deficient) illusion but as a phenomenon in its own right.

We should think of images not as acts of *representation* but as acts of *presentation*.[30] To show something via image does not mean that the image has to *refer* to something, but that something is presented artificially.[31] What images present, are visible entities with specific ontological features: quasi-things present even if they are not real and cannot be seen outside the image. Lambert Wiesing calls them *phantoms* in order to indicate their ontological ambiguity and to distinguish them from real things and illusions. W.J.T. Mitchell treats images quite similarly when he talks about the "living image" or "the image-as-organism," when he calls images "ghostly semblances" or "pseudo-life-forms," when he speaks about our double consciousness toward images torn between "magical beliefs and sceptical doubts, naive animism and hardheaded materialism, mystical and critical attitudes".[32] This double consciousness is not something one could safely ascribe to primitives, children, the uneducated or illiterate masses, but it is a deep and abiding feature of human responses to images in general: "It is not something we 'get over' when we grow up, become modern, or acquire critical consciousness," Mitchell notes.[33] Hence what might sound mysterious from a naturalist-objectivist point of view is recognized as an actual phenomenon from a phenomenological standpoint: consciousness of something that has no real and material substance, that does not follow the laws of physics, that cannot be analyzed and measured scientifically—the phantoms of imagery.[34]

Since they are actual, perceptible phenomena, the phantoms of imagery are not exempt from the pathic quality of seeing. Their pathic element is even more striking when we confront *moving*-images supported by *sound*. Before this account becomes too iconocentric, let me hasten to add the pathic quality of sound. Sound is always present: once we hear it, it has already pressed in upon us, taken hold of us, captivated us.[35] We can only avert it *after* it has had an effect on us. The strong pathic aspect of sound, in fact, propels the pathic moment of the image, as can be seen when both are fused into the single gestalt of sound film.[36]

Searching for a solution to the intricate 'paradox of fiction,' a number of scholars from the field of philosophical aesthetics have recently argued that the quality, vividness and impressiveness of a filmic presentation are responsible for the viewer's feelings—not the *beliefs* in the reality of the filmic world and its fictional characters. The vivid appearance of a visually and aurally present cinematic object is sufficient for real feelings. It all depends on the concrete presentational qualities; it needs to be presented vividly enough.[37]

Hence we are neither tricked by a literal illusion nor do we foster the *belief* that what is presented *re*-presents something real in documentary fashion. While the question of *illusion* implies the problem that what we perceive *is* real right *now*, the question of *belief* implies the problem that what we perceive *was* real in the *past*. As to the latter, we rarely lose knowledge of the fact that what we see is fictional (who could forget that slime-spitting giant bugs or rampaging dinosaurs are not really out there?). However, there is a difference: in contrast to illusion *belief* can be added—and this clearly influences our response. Think of the shocked early audiences who thought that *The Blair Witch Project* was a documentary and not a fiction film. And remember the response to the harmed animals in the Tarkovsky, Renoir and Bresson movies mentioned previously. When we assume a documentary consciousness—i.e., when we belief that the film not only presents but also *re*-presents what *was* once real and thus lose the fictional distance—the quality of the ontological distance changes. We are, at the very least, more strongly challenged on moral grounds. But the cases under consideration in this study do not presuppose a belief in the reality status of the images and sounds in order to be affective. What the images and sounds *present,* artificially makes us respond vividly.

To repeat, the question of a literal illusion is not at stake when we watch a frightening film. Instead, how strongly we respond is a matter of the vividness and impressiveness of the filmic presentation—and the cinema of fear offers some prime examples of highly effective and affective presentations. We are not afraid of the monster or the violent act as if they were real, but of the vivid presentation of the monster and violent act via moving-image and sound. The easiest and most obvious proof is the fact that we do not jump up and run out of the theater in order to escape the *monster,* but simply avoid looking and listening to the images and sounds of the *film*. Thus fear in the face of a non-existent filmic object or event should be far from astonishing. A tacit assumption of the illusion thesis is that we can only fear the *real* things of *perception*. But this is clearly not the case. There are numerous modes of consciousness in which we are afraid but do not confront the real things of perception: dreams, hallucinations and memories come to mind. The same goes for images. David Freedberg's search for psychological invariants in response to images suggests that human beings throughout history and across cultures have reacted powerfully: the affective quality of images seems to be an anthropological constant.[38] Why, then, should we *not* be afraid of something that is felt as vividly and impressively as the presentation of the filmic world (even if it is simultaneously irreal)? Even though they are immaterial, cinematic images and sounds literally affect the viewer.

REDUCING THE PHENOMENOLOGICAL DISTANCE, OR A REAL THREAT TO THE VIEWER

When the images and sounds of a frightening movie become literally impressive, when they press in upon us and leave an affective trace, when we stop feeling safe from what we see and hear, we get the feeling that something has broken away or has been extremely diminished: we experience a dangerous *proximity* of the threatening movie. The ontological distance might be the movie's safety net. But a safety net presupposes some kind of risk. Even if we might cut the intertwinement with the horrifying film at any time, the fact that we *are* intertwined implicates a possible exposure to and contact with the unbearable. In fact, the moment we turn away often comes too late: we have already crossed the boundary between the fascinating still-watchable and the abhorrent un-watchable. While the *ontological* distance cannot be bridged, we often face the vanishing (or dwindling) of what I call the *phenomenological* distance. The viewer experiences the phenomenological distance to the film as *vacillating* on a continuum from *growing* to *decreasing*, depending on the relative position beforehand. When the film really closes in on us with all its frightening potential we can grasp what Carol Clover might have had in mind when she wrote that the "horror movie is somehow more than the sum of its monsters; it is itself monstrous."[39] Hence ascribing a genuine threat to the movies is no rhetorical exaggeration.

But what if the phenomenological distance shrinks radically? In her famous essay *On Photography* Susan Sontag underscores an important precondition for the frightening impact of (moving) images: "One is vulnerable to disturbing events in the form of photographic images in a way that one is not to the real thing. That vulnerability is part of the *distinctive passivity* of someone who is a spectator twice over, spectator of events already shaped, first by the participants and second by the image maker."[40] Sontag develops her argument with Michelangelo Antonioni's China documentary *Chung Kuo* (1972) in mind, but her remarks are valid for the experience of fiction films as well. When we watch a gruesome thriller in the multiplex we are also forced to follow events with a double passivity: the events onscreen are determined, first, by the fictional narrative (*what* is presented) and, second, by the aesthetic choices of the filmmaker (*how* it is presented). As real-life spectators of the gruesome events we would have modest possibilities for—potentially relieving—participation, whereas in the movie theater we are bound to our seats, motor activity largely inhibited, with little else to do but looking.

Moreover, while in reality we would be able to direct our attention according to our own will (hence choosing the details we consider appropriate), in the movie theater we are forced to confront what the filmmaker has pre-selected for us. Furthermore, the film also condenses the temporal extension of the event—the interesting parts presented in an interesting way—generally with regard to maximum effect. Hence what I have described as an essential blessing is simultaneously a curse: our passivity and ontological absence from the scene of action. However, only because the viewer is forced into this ambiguous passivity, he or she can enjoy fear in the first place. Without the restrained viewing position vis-à-vis the horrifying film the viewer would simply not be afraid (or, at least, be afraid in a very different way). This ambiguity is essential: we do *not have* to do anything against what happens inside the filmic world, but we also *cannot* do anything. As Sontag puts it: "the camera looks for me—and obliges me to look, leaving as my only option not to look." [41]

The last part of the sentence points to a potential way out the movie theater's distinctive passivity. When all classificatory measures of protection are ineffectual and we are faced with a film that threatens to approach, overwhelm and harm us despite the barriers of censorship, rating system and genre, we can still keep the cinematic experience an endurable one. Despite the passivity that the cinematic dispositive forces on us, we often *do* take very specific actions—even though we neither run away nor intervene in the filmic world. When we look away, close our eyes or cover our ears, we *literally* try to escape from the filmic threat. This is not meant in a metaphoric sense. Depending on what we consider more threatening—the visible or the audible—we might proceed by first looking at the exit sign and then covering our ears or vice versa, creating a sort of hierarchy of the horrific aspects and thus a hierarchy of different levels of flight. I have talked about *geographical* flight in the sense of running out of the theater. These geographical flight reactions would imply that we took the diegetic threat literally. Obviously, we are not that naïve. To be sure, there are viewers who *do* leave the theater. However, this is less a direct flight-reaction to a certain scene—viewers do not *run* out of the theater in panic—rather than the avoidance of an overall, accumulated unpleasant experience.[42]

This does not entail, however, that covering our eyes and ears is not an actual flight from a real threat. As phenomenologist Aurel Kolnai notes: "Flight need not literally mean running away, traveling to a distant place, or going into hiding. It is not the spatial proximity of the feared object but the agent's being actually or virtually exposed to its *impact* that matters."[43] You don't have to *duck* away from gruesome images, it is sufficient to *look* away. You don't have to *run* out of the theater, it's enough if you *cover* your ears. These are *active* decisions. We have to let loose and purposely untangle ourselves from the tight grip of the movie. But why try to escape if not for the sake of our endangered well-being? The film may be fictional; the threat to the well-being of our lived bodies and psyches is not. The danger to the characters might occur at a safe *ontological* distance; what we see, hear and feel can easily bridge the *phenomenological* distance. Stanley Kubrick has illustrated this difference quite appositely. In a highly self-reflexive sequence in his horror masterpiece *The Shining* (1980) the young boy Danny Torrance (Danny Lloyd) stands in a hallway of the huge Overlook Hotel in which he spends the winter with his family. Suddenly he sees bloody images of mutilated bodies flash up in front of him. Rather than trying to escape, the shocked boy raises his hands in front of his eyes. After a while he hesitantly dares to peek through his fingers. A voice soothes him: "It's just like pictures in a book, Danny. It isn't real." The wise boy does not trust the voice, however. He knows that even if the images are of a different order than reality, they nevertheless have a real effect on him. The boy acknowledges it by raising his hands protectively.

Figure 3.2 Daring a fearful look: Danny Torrance (Danny Lloyd) in *The Shining*.

Our various aversive reactions do not have to involve physical movement, though. There are other—albeit less secure—strategies of temporary avoidance (or flight, if you will). The first is looking *at* rather than *into* the movie: by withdrawing from immersion into appreciation—i.e. by stressing the film-as-artifice rather than the filmic world—the filmic phantoms might disappear and lose their power to haunt us. Second, one can also look *onto* the movie by either focusing on the material basis of the film through foregrounding an awareness of the screen and the flickering dance of lights and shadows (which is not the same as appreciating the style and technique of the movie); or by taking an elevated, distanced position by emphasizing the film's fictional status. Rather than looking *into* the movie, the viewer looks *away*, looks *at* it or looks *onto* it. Annette Hill usefully distinguishes between "*physical* barriers, where participants use their body to withdraw from viewing violence, and *mental* barriers, where participants choose on anything other than violent depictions on screen."[44]

What distinguishes looking-at and looking-onto from looking-away (or even covering one's eyes and ears) is the degree of conspicuousness and security. While the activity of the latter is characterized by treacherous movements, other avoidance strategies remain more inconspicuous. This is an advantage for those who are not supposed to reveal fearfulness. Not astonishingly, then, flight reactions seem to be separated roughly along gender lines. While men are supposed to display fearlessness, women are expected to cower and look away. Hence men might more often look for ruptures in realism or try to admire the quality of the special effects as counterparts to looking away. Yet there is a downside to it: looking-at and looking onto the movie is risky business, since the horrifying phantoms of imagery return easily; or we might not be able to get rid of them in the first place, because they sturdily occupy a central position in our field of consciousness and thus defy straightforward cognitive detachment. It takes an effort to resist the initial urge to look into rather than at or onto the film.[45] Once my *active* decision to admire, say, special-effects artist Tom Savini's ingenuous design of the monster is ruptured—either because the fictional content crosses the threshold of attention or because I am tempted by curiosity—I end up back in the filmic world after all.

Note that these various degrees of control are possible only because the *ontological* distance between reality and filmic world exists. The ontological distance relieves us from deeply involved action in terms of ethical or legal interventions even if the phenomenological distance breaks down momentarily. Once we have looked away, covered our ears or concentrated on the formal aspects, the phenomenological distance jumps back into place. Since the ontological distance is always present as background knowledge, what would in real life consume our whole attention, in the cinema becomes a cause of pleasure: the foregrounding of the body due to a diminished phenomenological distance. To be sure, even if the impressive and vivid presentation of violence and monstrosity poses a genuine threat, to perceive extreme violence and a powerful monster by way of a *film* does not endanger us identically as *real* violence and monstrosity would—precisely because it endangers us like a *film*. Comparing the resulting forms of fear would be a category mistake—as if I said "I am more afraid of bungee-jumping than losing my job." Being afraid of a film and being afraid of a murderer are two kinds of fear.

TRUE FRIGHT: AFRAID OF THE HORRIFIC

If a genuine threat exists, it is not astonishing that there is also some kind of fear. To put it differently, if we are frightened, we assume a real danger. People are generally frightened only, if they consider a situation dangerous. Think of the behavior in front of a cage containing a lethal animal: there is little trace of fear. Of course, there are situations that are—statistically speaking—not dangerous, and we are frightened anyway. These fears are often judged irrational. The fear of flying is a classic case in point. But calling this form of fear irrational implies a third-person perspective: someone waving a statistic and arguing for the safety of flying. For the person *experiencing* fear, however, the danger of flying is very *real*. Trying to convince the scared person with statistics—i.e. *rational* arguments—is often futile. This is, by the way, another argument against the central position of beliefs in emotions.

The same goes for the movies. If we find a film frightening, its threat is indisputable. Attempts to soothe us with the argument that this is only a movie might be convincing—often they do not succeed. This is the case precisely because I am afraid of the vivid and impressive presentation of the movie *itself* and not by its status as a failed illusion referring to the extra-filmic world. And even if these arguments *are* successful, it takes an active step to create a distance from the filmic world and look *at* or *onto* it. Being afraid of a movie therefore does not imply that we actively suspend *disbelief.* Far from it. Just as the person afraid of flying does not willingly suspend disbelief in something he or she is rationally aware of (namely the safety of flying), the viewer in the movie theater does not suspend disbelief in the movie's irreality. He or she is simply afraid, even though the awareness that the movie is irreal does not disappear. In fact, a conscious act of volition would be counterproductive for any emotion. Volition is involved only in our readiness to enter the reception process and our effort to concentrate.[46] Insofar, the talk of a "willing suspension of disbelief" does not make sense in terms of frightening movies. But Coleridge's famous phrase is doubtful also because we do not suspend our disbelief and then consider the fictional world as though it was real: this is precisely the reason why we do not *run* away from the *monster* but *look* away from the *images* of its evil conduct.

What are we afraid of then? The cause of fear is nothing more and nothing less than the onscreen appearance of the *disproportional immorality* and *disturbing brutality* of the violent act or monster, forced on us through the *vividness* and *impressiveness* of threateningly close cinematic images and sounds. Its emotional impact is clearly rooted in the *present*: in our momentary confrontation with dangerous moving-images and sounds. However, we must also take into account the possibility that we are instinctively and unconsciously afraid of a *future* effect. The *episodic* appraisal ("This is threatening to my well-being right now!") might be interlinked with a *long-standing* appraisal ("This can harm my psychical integrity for a long time!"). It is always possible that we fear that we will have to remember these perceptions. They might haunt us in our dreams and daydreams. They can turn into lasting threats. The film critic Pauline Kael once commented on the effects the famous shower scene in *Psycho* had on her: "The shock stayed with me to a degree that I remember it whenever I'm in a motel shower."[47] Or consider this quote from a participant in Annette Hill's empirical study: "I went to see *The Shining* when I was quite young and this film scared me so much I just decided never to go and see another horror movie. The thrill while you're in the cinema isn't worth the risk when you get home, when you can't sleep."[48] Hence in the face of cinematic horror we also look away, because it can pose a long-term threat to our psychical well-being. We intuitively know that once the frightening film haunts us, hardly any flight reaction will help: we cannot look, let alone run away from our fearful memories.

Cinematic horror does not need to take a detour via characters, then, but affects us *directly*. The directness of horror would help to explain why horror movies are so effective despite our notoriously low allegiance with their—often—unpleasant cardboard characters. It is me who is *directly* frightened by the violent onslaught onscreen, and it is me who is *directly* afraid of the threatening appearance of the monster. Neither a *personal* character involvement nor his or her *observational* facial and bodily responses are *necessary* for our reaction (even if they certainly help to increase it).

This becomes quite clear when we are confronted with the *result* of a violent act that has already occurred unseen earlier in the film. Take the scene in *The Silence of the Lambs* in which a dead lieutenant (Charles Napier) is revealed slit open and crucified against Hannibal Lecter's cage. The fact that this disclosure frightens (rather than disgusts) me cannot be explained by *empathy* since I do not feel fright together *with* (let alone identical to) the policeman—who is dead after all. Nor can *sympathy* account for my frightened reaction, because I am not afraid *for* the lifeless character.[49] I might feel pity or sorrow for him, but that wouldn't explain the frightening aspect. In terms of the monster let me note that in direct horror proper we are not afraid of what the monster might do to the characters in the *immediate* future—in this case we would experience the anticipatory fright that I call *terror*. It is the monster's immoral and brutal intention that appears threatening to us. This is not to deny that terror and horror often occur simultaneously, thus reinforcing each other. However, there are instances in which we are afraid of the monster's presence itself even when no character is around. Think, again, of *The Silence of the Lambs*, when the weirdly dressed, make-up- and wig-wearing serial killer Jame 'Buffalo Bill' Gumb (Ted Levine) tells himself "I'd fuck me. I'd fuck me so hard" and dances in front of a video camera, facing us directly. This scene still scares me after numerous viewings even though there no character is threatened by the strange demeanor.

THE PLEASURE OF DIRECT HORROR

If the threat wasn't real and the potentiality of being overwhelmed was nonexistent, we would follow the film emotionless. Only because a genuine danger lurks are we frightened at all. The emotional captivation, on the other hand, has ramifications for our intertwinement with the horrific: it is fright that immerses us and thus creates an *emotional* fascination beyond the simple curious *cognitive* fascination that I have talked about at the beginning. The *interest* in violence and the monster itself couldn't explain this immersive effect. If curiosity was the whole story, we would merely pay remote attention to the horrific as something unusual, comparable to a visit to a botanical garden or a zoo. But we do not only confront these sound-supported moving-images in order to satisfy a quasi-scientific curiosity. We are fascinated and drawn to the filmic world because of the very emotional, corporeal effect these exposures entail—namely fear.

Even if correct in one sense, Carroll's overly rational terms 'interest' or 'curiosity' are therefore too limited.

Instead, what we enjoy in horror is precisely the emotional immersion of *Angst-Lust*, i.e. pleasurable fear.[50] Co-existentialist versions of pleasure in horror such as Carroll's—in which the cognitive pleasure of interest and the emotional displeasure of fear exist *next to each other*—have to be replaced by an integrationist one. Moritz Geiger is right when he argues: "When aesthetic pleasure is mixed with moments of displeasure, pleasure acquires a different character. It might become bitterer, more ambivalent, less uniform, but displeasure does not exist next to pleasure. In pleasurable pain, in enjoyable anguish these feelings merge with pleasure. And pleasurable horror is [. . .] not simply pleasure plus horror."[51] Hence pleasurable fear (*Angst-Lust*) does not consist of two components that stand next to each other (like the two emotions horror and disgust in many horror scenes). Instead, pleasure is a quality of the emotion *itself*—its positive valence, as psychologists say. What is more, it might be misleading if we associate pleasure exclusively with words like happy, blissful, glad, joyful etc. The Geiger quote underscores that an emotion like cinematic fear can be experienced positively, even if the pleasure it yields does not make you straighforwardly happy, but comes across as somewhat mixed and with a slightly bitter flavor. Pleasurable fear is described more acurately as satisfying or gratifying rather than pure bliss, joy and delight.

This also helps to explain why we enjoy the moment of relief after the scene is over. If pleasurable fear was pure bliss, the relief could not stand out. A narrative of unmixed joy soon means utter boredom. It is the slightly more bitter—but still pleasurable—experience of horror, shock, dread and terror that makes the straightforwardly enjoyable moments of relief all the more noticeable. But this is obviously not to say that we enjoy relief alone; moments of cinematic fear are not a price to be paid but enable a very specific gratifying form of pleasure—one flavored with a grain of ambivalence.

The emotional fascination characteristic of pleasurable fear entails that our phenomenological distance from the filmic world decreases. I have indicated that the viewer experiences the phenomenological distance as vacillating between decreasing and growing. The first type of distance reduction is immersion proper—an experience particularly accentuated in the immersive environment of the multiplex theater. In cinematic horror we seem to be *pulled in*, because we show *interest* in the object, but also and foremost because we are *emotionally captivated*. We acknowledge this phenomenological movement towards the film in ordinary language when we ascribe the movie a 'magnetizing' potential or talk about being 'glued to the screen.' Cinematic horror, at first, draws us near.

However, the direction is reversed once we reach the tipping point where we consider it necessary to untangle ourselves from the film. This tipping point changes, of course, from viewer to viewer. Hence it is impossible to gauge the precise starting point beyond which something objectively or universally becomes unbearable. If it happens and we are overwhelmed and overly frightened by the horrific, we experience a second type of distance variation: a radical reduction in which the film seems to close in on, jump at or even attack us. This breakdown of the phenomenological distance—the opposite of immersion—happens precisely during those instances when we have turned away too late and have glimpsed and heard too much. The fact that the film is experienced as suddenly and powerfully *coming near* can be judged from the various *receding* activities described previously. During the most intense moments the viewer responds by raising the hands in front of the eyes or covering the ears as if to escape the overwhelming proximity and threat of the film. Hard-pressed by the film the viewer retreats and reacts with bodily defense reactions, thus putting a literal barrier between him or her and the film. These protective responses against the distance reduction of the film are attempts to renew the previous phenomenological distance. As such, they can lead to the biggest detachment possible: the viewer *extricates* him- or herself from the closeness of the movie by cutting the intertwinement with the filmic world. Even if this happens in most cases only briefly, the viewer leaves the film experience temporarily behind. Immersion makes way for extrication.

The pleasurable-fear experience is therefore characterized by a balancing act between the strong intertwinement of immersion and the loosened or even cut entanglement of extrication. When the viewer decides to watch a thriller or a horror movie, he or she turns into a sensation-seeker walking the tightrope of a *still*-pleasurable experience that could easily entail a plunge into the depth of an *already*-unpleasant experience. The pleasure would not be possible, however, if the balancing act did not include the very danger of stumbling into the abyss. Hence direct horror is dominated by the simultaneity of a strong curious and emotional fascination and the fear of being overwhelmed. We want to see it all—but not see *too much*. We wish to hear everything—yet not hear *too much*. We long for a strong emotional experience—but dread an experience that overwhelms. In short, we enjoy pleasurable fear, but shy away from displeasing fear. Direct horror can therefore imply a push-pull experience: quick back-and-forth movements between a strong engagement with the pleasurably dangerous filmic There and a receding into the safe shelter of the cinematic Here.

THE LIVED-BODY EXPERIENCE:
A DENSE FRIGHTENING MOMENT

No matter what the experiential differences between the two types of distance reduction might be, in *both* cases the viewer is strongly affected *bodily*. But how exactly do we experience the bodily stimulation of direct horror? So far I have talked predominantly about the relation between viewer and film in terms of distance variation, leaving out the bodily experience proper. The frightening confrontation with violence or monstrosity is, above all, a *wholesale* emotional captivation that has to be distinguished from more *localized* reactions such as nausea caused by cinematic disgust (which is focused around the stomach and/or the gorge) or crying in the face of a melodramatic scene (which converges foremost around the eyes). Our experiences of the lived-body have various shadings: sometimes as a fully integrated, close part of the self, at other times as a loosely attached, somewhat distanced part of the self. The less clearly it can be localized and the less qualitatively circumscribed it seems, the more embracing and encompassing it is. Think of extreme fear versus strong pain in your fingertip. The pain in the fingertip is certainly part of you, but it is also somewhat externalized. The (physiological) body that I *have*, not the (lived) body that I *am* is foregrounded. In contrast, fear colors the whole self with a different hue; hence the lived-body that I *am* pushes to the fore. Aurel Kolnai notes, "fear never singles out [. . .] particular spheres of interest in one's own self: for in every genuine case of fear it is somehow the *whole* self, or the very existence of the self, that is put into question [. . .] Even if fear be particularly weak because of the distance or uncertain effectiveness of what provokes it, still its intentional directedness always somehow 'permeates through' to the most ultimate and vital interests which appear to be endangered."[52]

This wholesale emotional captivation is characterized by a peculiar *constriction* of the viewer's lived-body caused precisely by the importunate threat of the film. According to Hermann Schmitz, the lived-body experience generally shifts on a continuum between *constriction* and *expansion*. For instance, the emotions of guilt and sorrow amount to a negative constrictive experience, whereas joy and yearning have strong expansive tendencies. Think of the phenomenological—not physical!—heaviness that pulls you down in sorrow or the strong feeling of guilt that leaves you little air to breathe. In joy, on the other hand, we have a tendency to jump into the air or embrace the whole world, and yearning reaches out for the spatial or temporal distance. Hence both are expansive.[53] What about fear? Just as disgust, it is located very much on the constrictive end of the spectrum. In the face of an act of violence or monstrous object the threatening film appears (overly) close phenomenologically: the viewer experiences the fright vis-à-vis the importunate, threatening object's proximity as a constriction of the lived-body. The etymology of the French, German and English words 'angoisse,' 'Angst' and 'anxious' retains this constrictive tendency. The Latin word 'angor' has the same roots as 'ango', which implies choking and suffocating.[54]

The notion of constriction will play a crucial role throughout this study: it describes a recurring, if differently shaded experience of *all* forms of cinematic fear discussed here. But constriction is not the whole story. Fear is also characterized by an expansive, if hampered *Away!*-tendency: an ultimately futile impulse to escape the lived-body's constriction. In order to understand what Schmitz means by this expansive *Away!*-tendency one has to grasp his distinction between *relative* and *absolute* location.[55] In fear, one can escape the *physical* body's *relative* location, that is, the subject's position in geometrical space vis-à-vis the threatening object. This is what we do when we look away or cover our ears: we leave the relative location. However, one cannot flee one's *absolute* location, i.e. the *lived*-body's phenomenological Here. It is precisely this absolute phenomenological location right here that we experience as constricted in moments of fear. We desperately want to escape our skin, as it were, by expanding *Away* somewhere, but cannot flee the lived-body's constriction. As a consequence, there is a pulsating *tension* between dominant constriction and attempted expansion—a characteristic experience not unlike the one that defines erotic lust. According to Schmitz, it is this pulsating game of lived-body constriction and expansion that can turn fear into a source of pleasure—if handled properly.

Since our bodies in tension are so intensely engaged by the threatening—and threateningly close—film, moments of horror stand out from the temporal flux of mundane life. What is usually lived transparently and implicitly becomes densely compressed—like a slow river that is suddenly caught by a wild and ferocious current. Horror has a decidedly temporal component that deeply underscores the present here and now. In the face of frightening violence or monstrosity, the body in tension is caught by the gravity of time. As Vivian Sobchack reminds us, it has often been noted that we tend "to feel this intense sense of presence, to feel most alive, when we are most at bodily (and psychic) risk. Faced with a present threat to our being, we have no time to think about past or future, but this could also be reversed: it is the past and future that have 'no time' because the extended 'now' excludes them as it encloses us. Thus, this sense of aliveness—of being just here, just now—emerges both from and as the simultaneous extension of our present and the heightening of our presence."[56]

SOMATIC EMPATHY: PAINFUL ACTS OF VIOLENCE

While this intense, engrossing bodily and temporal experience can be recuperated through phenomenological reflection, during the film it does not enter the viewer's *focal* awareness (even if it is much less *peripheral* than in real-life situations of danger). Yet cinematic horror often entails another form of bodily stimulation—one that is *restricted* to a limited corporeal area rather than being *fully* engrossing and is therefore able to force its way into awareness more centrally. I am talking about somatic empathy in its varieties of *sensation, affective* and *motor* mimicry.[57] Somatic empathy is a form of *Einfühlung* that describes a more or less automatic, but no more than *partial* parallelism between a character's and my own body's sensations, affects or motions. Think of the muscular urge to support a character who is untangling the cables of a ticking time bomb (motor mimicry); the itchiness experienced when looking at a character wearing coarse cotton on bare skin (sensation mimicry); the disgust one experiences upon seeing a fully grossed-out character waking up in a freezer full of putrefying body parts, as in the 2006 remake of *The Hills Have Eyes* (affective mimicry). Or take the impression that one is short of breath when a character drowns, gets strangled or has to fight against the breath-taking impact of lethal nerve gas, as in *Saw II* (2005). Having argued that the *frightening* aspect of cinematic horror does not depend on character engagement, I do not want to exclude this important form of empathy, a recurrent corollary of our confrontation with the horrific. However, somatic empathy does not demand strong character allegiance either. In fact, it works in connection with figures never encountered before in the film; even animals or cartoon characters can be objects of somatic empathy.

I have mentioned that the ontological distance allows us to become partly aware of our bodily experience. This is particularly true for cases like shock. But it also goes for somatic empathy, a particular carnal response that makes us feel ourselves feeling and thus enables a strong awareness-of-oneself as an embodied viewer. In horror movies and thrillers a typical form of somatic empathy is the vague and diffuse, yet intense sensation one feels while exposed to graphic moving-images of *pain*. A classic example is the dentist scene in *Marathon Man* (1976), in which Dr. Szell (Laurence Olivier) tortures Babe Levy (Dustin Hoffman) by drilling holes into his teeth. Or the moment in *Misery* (1990) when the mad aficionado Annie Wilkes (Kathy Bates) smashes the ankles of her beloved author Paul Sheldon (James Caan) with a sledgehammer. One could also take a drastic imagination evoked by the description of tubes inserted into a male character's genitals in *Seven*.

In these cases we obviously do not suffer from tooth-ache or a piercing pain in our ankles; nor do we feel a hellish anguish in our genitals. Insofar, the feeling is clearly reduced and changed. Still, one cannot deny that we experience a peculiar, intense foregrounding of the lived-body. In contrast to fear which overwhelms us completely and therefore cannot be localized directly, painful somatic empathy often affects more distinct *local regions* of the body and thus touches us merely partially. Even in cases in which somatic empathy cannot be pinpointed and seems to be spread out over the lived-body somewhat diffusely, it is less engrossing than fear. What is true for the spatial structure also counts for the temporal side. The wholesale emotional captivation of fearful cinematic horror is comparatively *gradual* and *continual*: the beginning and end are not clearly marked. The *abrupt* transformation of empathic pain, on the other hand, has a much more *episodic* structure. Similar to moments of shock, it stands out as a *discrete puncturing gestalt* with a clear beginning and end. The lived-body speaks up shortly, as it were, but does not keep its voice up for long. Moreover, since it is such an abrupt and reflex-like response somatic

Figure 3.3 Painful somatic empathy: Szell (Laurence Olivier) tortures Babe Levy (Dustin Hoffman) in *Marathon Man*.

empathy has a *compulsory* quality: we can hardly avoid it. This coercive aspect of empathic pain makes it so effective, yet it is also one of the reasons why some viewers despise it. While I have a certain freedom of avoidance in looking away from the monster, in abrupt cases of empathic pain I have to concede the initiative largely to the film.

Fear appears close to the self, overwhelms us completely, comes into being gradually and lasts. Painful somatic empathy, on the other hand, is a somewhat distanced, localized and abrupt feeling. These differences are mirrored in the psychological longevity. Fear can haunt us for hours and even weeks. The spectrum ranges from avoiding dark alleys on the way home to the abiding fear of swimming in the ocean (think of Spielberg's *Jaws*) or taking showers (a phobia sparked by Hitchcock's *Psycho*). Long-lasting effects are rare in connection to somatic empathy. Unlike dread and much like shock, somatic empathy tends to vanish quickly after the scene has ended. When we leave the theater, we might feel a bit unpleasant, but we usually recover quickly.

But how is somatic empathy possible in the first place? Precisely because I am in a position *different* from the character onscreen, the only thing left to balance this experiential disproportion is my own body. Vivian Sobchack explains how the viewer autonomously responds to the solicitation of the graphically violent scene: "my body's intentional trajectory, seeking a sensible object to fulfill this sensual solicitation, will reverse its direction to locate its partially frustrated sensual grasp on something more literally accessible. That more literally accessible sensual object is my own subjectively felt lived-body. Thus, 'on the rebound' from the screen—and *without a reflective thought*—I will *reflexively* turn toward my own carnal, sensual, and sensible being."[58] We experience and comprehend movies not just *cognitively* but with our entire *bodily* being—a body that is always informed by the history and carnal knowledge of our acculturated sensorium. Since the viewer is dependent on the personal *carnal knowledge* of the object and the pain it inflicts, *familiar* weapons and affected body parts tend to cause stronger somatic empathy. Hence knife cuts are more effective than gunshots, needles stabbed in the eye are more somatically painful than the sight and sound of a body torn apart by a bomb.[59] What is more, precisely because the former weapons are familiar, they enhance the likelihood of a collective response: while the great majority of viewers can draw on the carnal knowledge of a knife-cut, the spectators who were ripped apart by a bomb must, I gladly assume, be few and far between.

The reflexive turn towards the body in somatic empathy certainly depends on the primacy of seeing and hearing as the two primary cinematic senses. But when we go to the cinema we do not leave our culturally shaped senses of touch, smell, and taste at the entrance door just because the film privileges seeing and hearing. There might be a sense hierarchy, but the cinema uses dominant vision and hearing to speak comprehensibly to the other senses as well—or better: to the lived-body as a whole. The experiencing body sees and hears always *in cooperation* and *exchange* with other sensorial accesses to the world. A centralizing self always synthesizes the empirically discrete perceptions. Sobchack therefore describes the viewer as a cinesthetic subject—a portmanteau expression that combines the words cinema and synaesthetic. She notes that "even if the intentional objects of my experience at the movies are not wholly realized by me and are grasped in a sensual distribution that would be differently structured were I outside the theater, I nonetheless do have a *real* sensual experience that is not reducible either to the satisfaction of merely two of my senses or to sensual analogies and metaphors constructed only 'after the fact' through the cognitive operations of conscious thought."[60] Harking back to my examples of painful somatic empathy: despite the fact that my feeling of toothache or genital pain is clearly reduced and transformed, I still have a *partially* fulfilled sensory experience.

Obviously, filmmakers can manipulate the carnal intensity of somatic empathy. They simply need to optimize our sensual access of seeing and hearing so that the two senses can be cross-modally translated more easily. Think of the torture scene in *Marathon Man*: if it was shown in long shot with a distant soundtrack, we would barely feel anything. This is why the film literally brings us closer to the *pain*-ful site. In order to affect us deeply and painfully, close-ups and loud, horrifying sounds reduce the sensual and thus the phenomenological distance. Even if it is primarily an object of vision and not touch, the close-up nevertheless provokes a sense of the intimate and tangible.[61]

In this chapter I have dealt with *direct horror*, an aesthetic strategy that presents the fascinating and frightening violent event or monstrous object as directly as possible. But, as the next chapter will show, there is a type of horror that is not based on *perceptions* of sound-supported moving-images of violence or monstrosity but on *imaginations* of the horrific. I am talking about *suggested horror*. Often horrifying imaginations contribute just as much—or even more—to the effectiveness of frightening movies. Since considerable aesthetic as well as phenomenological differences exist, the two categories should not be lumped together.

4 Intimidating Imaginations
A Phenomenology of Suggested Horror

> [W]hatever you can imagine is far worse than what you can portray. The thing that really scares you in a movie is when suggestions are made to your mind, and then your mind does most of the work.
>
> (Stuart Gordon)[1]

> [O]nly that which gives free rein to the imagination is effective. The more we see, the more we must be able to imagine. And the more we add to our imaginations, the more we must think we see. [. . .] to present the utmost to the eye is to bind the wings of fancy.
>
> (Gotthold Ephraim Lessing)[2]

SUGGESTED HORROR: THE DEFINITION

- A woman has just delivered a baby. A doctor arrives on the scene. The worried mother asks the doctor whether her child is supposed to be "crying like this." The doctor takes the weeping baby, which is wrapped in a blanket and hence cannot be seen properly. He looks astonished, even frightened, and asks a woman standing next to him: "What happened during the delivery?" After receiving the response that everything was normal, he asks her anxiously: "Did you drop him?" And then, looking more terrified, in a crescendo of revelations, he conveys more information about the crying baby—which the viewer still cannot see: "Inform the ambulance that we have a situation . . . *(now addressing the mother)* I have never seen—*this*. It appears that your baby has sustained some fractions while inside your uterus. His arms and his legs are broken."
- A private detective questions a suspect who tells him the story of an extremely violent occult ceremony that took place in a hotel room. "[A] boy was bound naked on a rubber mat. There were complicated incantations and stuff in Latin and Greek. A pentacle was branded on his chest." While the music gradually intensifies, he continues by mentioning a man who was handed a dagger: "And he sliced the boy clean open. And he ate his heart. He cut it out so quickly, the heart was still beating when he wolfed it down."

- The female lieutenant of a spaceship believes that a contagious alien might be found inside the corpse of a young girl. She demands an autopsy. We see a tablet full of chirurgic scalpels, scissors and saws. A doctor puts on rubber gloves. We hear quiet sounds of cutting, while we see the doctors face in close-up looking downwards and offscreen towards the corpse he is working on. A cut follows: blood runs into a rinse, hands smear blood on rubber, blood on the doctor's rubber cloak. The doctor: "Everything is in place. There is no sign of infection." Still we haven't seen the girl's opened body. The lieutenant: "Chest! Open the chest." The doctor puts his bloody scalpel into a glass and grabs a huge saw. The lieutenant: "Be careful." A shot of the bloody saw is followed by a close-up of the commander's face and sounds of breaking bones. She flinches. The doctor puts the bloody saw away.

Taken from *Unbreakable* (2000), *Angel Heart* (1987) and *Alien 3* these scenes exemplify an aesthetic strategy I call 'suggested horror.' In contrast to direct horror's frightening perceptions of the horrific, suggested horror relies on *intimidating imaginations* of violence and/or a monster evoked through verbal descriptions, sound effects or partial, blocked and withheld vision. In other words, while in direct horror the viewer primarily perceives a visibly and aurally present, horrific cinematic object to which he or she responds emotionally, in most cases of suggested horror he or she visually concretizes through imagination a merely aurally present horrific object—and it is precisely this concrete and vividly visualized horrific object of imagination that scares the viewer. Unlike anticipatory forms of fear such as dread and terror, suggested horror is rooted in the present moment (a fact that connects it to direct horror and cinematic shock): At this very

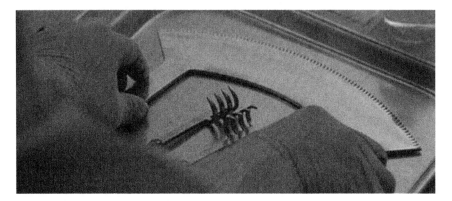

Figure 4.1 Suggested horror: *Alien 3*.

moment the viewer is afraid of his or her mental visualization of horrific events and/or monsters suggested by the film.

The frightening effect of the *Alien 3* example cited previously, for example, depends both on suggestive *moving-images* of sharp tools, blood, reaction shots of emotionally affected characters and evocative *sounds* of cutting, sawing and breaking bones as well as verbal descriptions of what goes on beyond the frame. What lacks, is full vision.[3] Hence in an attempt to imagine what he or she cannot fully perceive (due to a filmic omission) but is simultaneously strongly seduced to perceive (due to a filmic suggestion), the viewer compensates the visual lack with mental visualizations: his or her visual imagination fills in what has been left out.

During this process the field of consciousness is temporarily restructured: While in most instances of film reception imagination *supports* the perception of 'material' moving-images and sounds, the imaginative act claims a more prominent role in suggested horror. When I follow a moment of direct horror—say, a victim being tortured in a movie like *Hostel*—what I *perceive* visually and aurally is the source of fear. I do not need to *imagine* visually and aurally. Hence my visual and aural imagination is mostly out of play (even if other parts of the imagination are still involved). In cases of suggested horror, on the other hand, I perceive *and* imagine visually at the same time: I see and hear suggestive moving-images and sounds *and* visually imagine concrete horrific objects or events. One could talk about an experience of 'mental superimposition': visual perception *and* visual imagination are layered on top of each other so that both simultaneously become conscious, albeit mostly pre-reflective parts of the film experience. Since imagination is necessarily involved when we watch a movie, the terms 'visual imagination' or 'mental visualization' describe a *specific* kind of film experience in which the act of imagining becomes more conspicuous. Imagining moves from the periphery into the center of our field of consciousness.

Suggested horror is a prime instance of what Mirjam Schaub calls the cinema of invisibility (*Kino der Unsichtbarkeit*). It represents an aesthetics that cuts down the weight of the visible and favors blocked or withheld vision realized through strategic employment of camera position, mise-en-scène or montage. It is an approach to cinema that often underscores the importance of the *acoustic off* for the *visual on* and thus foregrounds sound as a powerful instrument of directing attention and structuring imagination. Since the viewer does not observe from a secret vantage point with perfect vision, but often suffers from visual lack, suggested horror is also a good case against overblown theories considering spectatorship as voyeurism. As a specific kind of filmmaking it stands in opposition to the full vision epitomized by the *cinema of visibility's* direct horror. Of course, we cannot conceive of these two heuristic concepts as pure. Direct and suggested horror—the visible and the invisible, full vision and withheld vision—mark tendencies or extreme points on a continuum. How do we categorize a shot, for instance, that presents a brutal stabbing behind a semi-transparent shower curtain? Is it still suggestive or already direct? There is no clear-cut borderline separating what in reality fades into each other. In fact, necessarily so: in the movie theater (just as elsewhere) the visible and the invisible are bound in a complicated, non-static relationship. Whenever there is something visible on the screen, its opaqueness blocks something else. This process of discovering and disclosing remains interminable, because we cannot see the other thing inside or behind it.[4] Still, I believe that my heuristic concepts help to tell apart two approaches to cinematic horror: one relies on visual *perceptions*, whereas the other thrives on visual *imaginations*.

OMITTING AND SUGGESTING

From Roman Ingarden's spots of indeterminacy (*Unbestimmtheitsstellen*) to Wolfgang Iser's blanks (*Leerstellen*) phenomenology-inflected aesthetics has long been interested in how the recipient is actively involved in the dialectics of hiding and presenting. If something is supposed to suggest, other parts must be omitted. If something is omitted, we need suggestive parts—otherwise we would neither perceive nor imagine at all. In suggested horror the viewer completes in imagination what is incomplete in visual perception. Modifying Marshall McLuhan's distinction between hot and cool media, one could call direct horror the *hot* and suggested horror the *cool* forms of cinematic horror: the former needs barely any completion, while the latter depends strongly on the viewer's filling-in.[5] Without this crucial activity the aesthetic object would be shot through with omissions and left partially unrealized. But obviously the viewer does not fill in *everything* left out—what a futile, endless activity would this be? There is a literally infinite amount of information that we could add to the film. What I am referring to, are those parts that the object seduces or even forces the viewer to visualize. Only if the film gives a strong-enough incentive, a vivid visual imagination comes into play. Hence mental visualizations are a form of bounded imagination; they are an implicit part of the film's aesthetic structure.

But what are the reasons for bringing into play the dialectics of omission and suggestion rather than showing everything directly? First, there are political or legal grounds. Where graphic depictions of violence or sexuality are taboo or legally prohibited, strategies of visual imagination enable an ersatz presentification of the forbidden. While the former always rely on the perception of a present object, the constitutive precondition of the latter is precisely something *absent* that comes to life only as an imaginary object.[6] As such they can help to circumvent censorship. Second, there might be economic reasons. Since the filmmaker does not *show* certain things or actions but merely *evokes* them, he or she can address a larger audience otherwise restricted by censorship or age limit. And he can save parts of the budget otherwise spent on an expensive set design.

However, with few taboos remaining, the problem nowadays often boils down to aesthetic choice. What was a legally necessary—or at least financially advisable—strategy during the Production Code era, is an aesthetic question today. This goes, first of all, for the aesthetic *value* of a given film. Often, suggestive filmmakers are ranked higher in critical esteem than those trying to show everything—a fact that is evident in the normatively charged question of 'passive' versus 'active' media reception (e.g. in McLuhan's distinction between *hot* and *cool* media). Those who show everything are derided as proponents of a sensationalist cinema of effects. Since the question of value is a matter of aesthetic preferences (and therefore a matter of critical power), I will not pursue it any further.[7] Yet the question "To show or not to show?" also pertains to *experiential differences*. Drawing on phenomenological description, I will formulate a hypothesis why proponents of suggestive horror could be right about its superior effectiveness (compared to direct horror). Moreover, at the end of the chapter I will present a number of typical strategies how films manage to evoke horrifying imaginations by visually and aurally seducing the viewer to imagine vividly. Since I am interested in horrifying imaginations *in the face of which* we are frightened, I will describe those imaginations that are characterized by a vivid mental visualization rather than a vague imaginative floating. However, even though the word group 'imagination' has a visual bias, it is important to remember that it includes the imaginative presentation of other senses as well. As we have seen, somatic empathy can be an important way of imagining painful feelings. Or consider the cinematic emotion of disgust: it often depends on conjuring an imagination of smell. Here I will restrict myself to strong cases of imaginative *visualization*.

IMAGINING VS. PERCEIVING

The film experience is defined by *the primacy of perception*. In fact, the film experience comes to a halt when imagination occurs *without* the simultaneity of perception: if imagination takes over entirely and encumbers perception, the aesthetic object vanishes. If we sit in the movie theater and pretend to follow the film but instead imagine ourselves in a far-away place, we are not part of the film experience anymore. Imagination is subsequent to and contingent upon the perception of the aesthetic object. Edward Casey puts it nicely when he writes: "Perception continues throughout aesthetic experience as a *basso continuo* onto which the melody line of imagination may be subtly and nonirrevocably superimposed."[8]

In what ways does imagination differ from perception? There are three main differences. First, *ephemerality*: an imagined object is not as stable and therefore does not remain present to us in the same persistent manner as an object of perception. An imagined object cannot sustain the imaginer's mental look indefinitely. It tends to fade rapidly from view. Plus, in the moment of apprehension it has an uneven, undulating character.[9] Second, *unexplorability*: in contrast to perception, imagined objects do not open themselves for *exploration* (even if they are certainly open for *reflection*). The imaginative presentation, and thus its specific content, is given all at once. But something that is given all at once lacks concealed, still-to-be-disclosed aspects. Thus it renders exploration superfluous.[10] Third, *indeterminacy*: the imagined object is decidedly less specific in detail. The materials that influence and contribute to imagination—perception, knowledge, memory etc.—'degrade.' As a consequence, imagination is characterized by an intrinsic sketchiness and visual poverty. Edward Casey elaborates: "An imagined object does not present itself as having the sort of strictly interior depth that is the basis for the palpability and plenitude of perceived objects. Lacking any sense of inherent mass or solidity and thus any bona fide lateral or rear surfaces, the imagined object is constrained to appear in a somewhat flattened and fore-shortened manner and as situated in a shallow, quasi-planar space."[11] This aspect is particularly vital for our distinction of direct horror: direct horror is, by definition, direct, in your face and strongly determined. It strives to keep the degree of imagination at the lowest possible level and rather presents its content as minutely, explicitly and forcefully as possible.

FORCED AND CONSTRAINED IMAGINATIONS

So far this account did not cast an overly positive light on imagination. Why do some filmmakers and most critics prefer it then? It might have to do with the degree of will and control the viewer has over his or her imagination. But is this true in case of suggested horror? In everyday life imagining is a mental act that we can enter into and terminate easily and without specific efforts. We either do it involuntarily and spontaneously *or* deliberately and in a controlled way. In the film experience the situation is somewhat different. Here, imagining occurs almost always spontaneously, guided and constrained by the film. We do not just imagine *anything*, but the film offers us a limited range of possibilities. This range—and thus the degree of control—varies according to the filmic strategies. In the case of suggested horror the power of suggestive images and sounds often initiates such a strong form of imagination that it's almost impossible to control. The degree of control over what is imagined appears almost just as low as the degree over what is perceived. To put it bluntly: often we cannot *not* imagine. If I tell you *not* to imagine a red Ferrari, the result will almost certainly be the opposite: the red Ferrari will turn up despite the explicit order not to. The same applies in the case of frightening movies. When we follow the verbal account of a gruesome murder taking place offscreen and hear accompanying screams of a tortured man, we can't 'overwrite' the ensuing imagination by imagining the victim playing soccer. And when a movie presents shadows on a wall suggesting a brutal rape, we can hardly imagine an idyllic, sunshiny scene. Nor would it be easy (in both cases) to simply *perceive* the images and sounds and repress imagination altogether. In many other cases one remains capable of expunging the persistent presentation by allowing oneself to become *distracted*. This escape exit is partly blocked precisely by the movie theater's aim to eliminate most forms of distraction.

Hence imagination is so easily triggered that in certain situations it is more difficult to fail than to succeed in imagining. Imagination appears so effortless that the imaginer does not consider him- or herself *actively* contributing to it. Sartre exaggerates when he asserts that in perception the actual representative element corresponds to a *passivity* of consciousness, whereas in imagination that element is "the product of a conscious *activity*, is shot through with a flow of creative *will*."[12] In many instances of the film experience the imaginer does not play a *conscious* role in bringing about the imaginative presentations. It would be a grave mistake to understand the kind of *imagination* I am talking about as synonymous with *imaginativeness* with its connotations of creativity and originality. Unlike Ingarden and Iser's *literary* concepts (tacitly connoting creativity), *filmic* omissions often have a forced character that leaves the viewer helplessly 'facing' the imagined object.[13]

Nevertheless, the fact that some people prefer imagination to perception can not only be inferred from critical writings and the strategies of actual films, but also from instances in which we actively switch to *self*-suggestion. This is precisely the case when we are not *able* to (or do not *want* to) confront the perceived images themselves. We look away or raise our hands in front of our eyes, relying on aural perception and thus creating our *own* form of suggestion. This points to the opposite of our fascination with violence and the monster in direct horror: a pleasure in *not seeing*. Delayed, blocked or partial vision is thus a central strategy of suggested horror.[14] Dennis Giles recounts an anecdote from his student days when his lover irritated him by her behavior during a horror film: "During the most terrifying scenes she would put her hands over her eyes. 'I can't watch it,' she would say; then, 'tell me what's happening!'"[15] The images were apparently too much for her; she couldn't bear the *visible* but wanted to rely on the *audible*. Sometimes, however, she would peek through her fingers to achieve a *partial* vision. She created her own game of seeing and not-seeing, of suggestion and imagination.

The imagined object exists only while we imagine it. It is here that we find its creative character: in the act of imagining consciousness creates something that is not existent or exists elsewhere and that is so fully worked out that it contains describable qualities. Hence the viewer *is* in fact creative in a narrow sense of the word; however not in the larger sense of imaginativeness that Romanticism would attribute to the recipient. Being in the presence of the imagined object can, in turn, entail that we are further removed from our here-and-now than in mere perceptual horror. We still follow the action on screen, but we also devote our consciousness to the imagined object. Robert Sokolowski calls it "a displacement of the self," a self established in the interplay between the here-and-now of perception and the nowhere-and-nowhen of imagination.[16] As a consequence, scenes that engage us not only via perception but also demand an imaginative involvement have a strong immersive tendency: we feel 'taken in' by the movie since we are both captivated perceptually *and* imaginatively.

Moreover, there are differences in what one could call the *phenomenological perspective* towards both the perceived and the imagined object. In perception the occurring situation takes place *outside* of the self as its observer. It is located *externally*. This is true for the film experience as well: even if the viewer is involved in a deeply immersive perception, he or she still looks from the outside upon the "viewed-view" (Sobchack, 1992) of the film. But the perception of the film is also different insofar as the spectator's "viewing-view" perceives the film's "viewed-view" as an *intermediary*. In imagination there is no intermediary. The situation takes place in a *spatial limbo* that is felt to be neither *external* nor *internal* to the imaginer—a decisively different experience. The different phenomenological perspective has ramifications for our ability to keep the filmic threat at bay. Given the fact that we can far more quickly shut our eyes than cover our ears, suggested horror (evoked through sound) is harder to avoid: it takes longer to distance oneself from a frightening imagination than from a horrifying perception. What is more, suggested horror does not leave the exit strategy of looking *at* the movie and its technological effects, but forces the viewer into a confrontation with mental visualizations of the horrific. Furthermore, due to the externality and exactitude of perceptions the frightening aspect of direct horror quickly wears out. This is why scenes of direct horror are often kept relatively short (particularly if compared with scenes of dread or terror). As Dennis Giles argues, "The viewer 'knows' that the more he/she stares, the more the [horror] will dissipate—to the extent that the image of full horror will be revealed (un-veiled) as more constructed, more artificial, more a fantasy, more a fiction than the fiction which prepares and exhibits it. To look the horror in the face for very long robs it of its power."[17] It seems as if to see means to possess and therefore to be acquainted with. The metaphor of 'enlightenment' implies a bringing to light of what remains in darkness. The viewer facing violence and monstrosity *directly*, after a while becomes 'enlightened': he or she stops fearing what was once unseen. Hence in the essential poverty and elusiveness of the mental visualization might reside its long-lasting horrifying potential. The weakness turns into an advantage.

Closely related to the different phenomenological perspectives is the question of *intersubjectivity*. Describing a scene in which he and his friend Paul are looking together at a landscape, Maurice Merleau-Ponty notes: "Paul and I 'together' see this landscape, we are jointly present to it, it is the same for both of us, not only as an intelligible significance, but as a certain accent of the world's style."[18] By extension, the viewers in the movie theater co-perceive the film 'together': there is hardly a disagreement in terms of what can be seen and heard on the screen. Moreover, our observations of the *perceptible* images can be checked by viewing the film again. On the other hand, there is no such thing as co-imagining in any strict sense. Imagining always has a first-person character.[19] It tends to be considered as *mine*—my individual imagination. Consequently, the perceived object is out there, acquiring a rather objective character for us, whereas my own imagined object occurs neither externally nor internally and therefore leans more strongly towards the subjective side.

Paradoxically, this individualizing aspect of imagining helps to harmonize the viewers' otherwise dissimilar responses. In direct horror there might be little disagreement in terms of what can be objectively *seen* or *heard*, but there are certainly discrepancies among the audience in regard to the subjective *emotional* experience. In suggestive horror this can be quite different. In order to illuminate this point I would like to refer in length to an interview with Fritz Lang, in which the director describes how in *M—Eine Stadt sucht einen Mörder* (1931) he handled the presentation of the horrifying crimes of the child murderer (Peter Lorre): "If I could show what is most horrible for *me*, it may not be horrible for somebody else. *Everybody* in the audience—even the one who doesn't *dare* allow himself to understand what really happened to that poor child—has a horrible feeling that runs cold over his back [. . .] because everybody *imagines* the most horrible thing that could happen to her. And that is something I could not have achieved by showing only one possibility—say, that he tears open the child, cuts her open. Now, in this way, I force the audience to become a collaborator of mine; by *suggesting* something I achieve a greater impression, a greater involvement than showing it."[20] Lang exploits the seeming disadvantage that every viewer imagines the scene idiosyncratically. This strategy secures a way to lead the audience to the desired goal: make them imagine the worst horror. The harmonizing effect can be lost in direct horror, precisely because everybody sees and hears the same thing but might respond differently. This is no problem for the collective experience unless these discrepancies become obvious. I attended a screening of David Cronenberg's *The Brood* (1979) in Los Angeles once, in which these incongruities became annoyingly clear: while I was truly frightened by the film's direct horror, some viewers found it amusing if not hilarious (at least, they pretended to do).

Are phenomenological perspective and intersubjectivity the answer to the question why many people consider movies relying on suggestion more horrifying than those employing direct horror? Could it be that the spatial limbo of imagination is phenomenologically *closer* to the self than the externality of perception? Does the vagueness and elusiveness of the mental visualization make it more enduring in terms of fright? Plus: Shall we assume that the *subjective-individualizing* tendency of imagination affects us deeper than the more *objective-collectivizing* characteristic of perception that we can share with others? Tentatively answering in the affirmative, I want to leave these propositions as hypotheses.

FILMIC STRATEGIES OF SUGGESTED HORROR

In the remaining part of this chapter I will introduce examples of how horror films and thrillers manage to address the viewer's visual imagination in frightening ways and thus become the source of fearful pleasure. Even if this list is by no means exhaustive, it tries to cover some of the most effective strategies. In order to illuminate what kind of mental visualizations these movies evoke, I will rely on personal experience. Note, however, that by performing ekphrases of my own visualizations I do not imply that every viewer will experience these scenes equally. My descriptions merely serve as illustrations! The examples will, moreover, afford the chance to address some further specificities of imagination: among other things its synthesizing activity, the varying 'point-of-views' one assumes towards one's own imaginations; the modalities in which the mental visualization occurs; the way music and sound evoke the imagination of space etc. As we shall see, the dialectics of hiding and showing depends on an intricate interweaving of visual and aural cues.

This certainly goes for the first strategy that I want to address: *verbal accounts*. Verbal accounts can be distinguished according to two criteria: a) their *temporality*, and b) their *degree of explicitness*.[21] In terms of temporality a character can either give a verbal description of what *is* concealed and/or is happening at this very moment; using a term from drama theory I call it *teichoscopy* (recall the scene from *Unbreakable* described at the beginning). Or the character might recount what *was* concealed and/or has happened in the past; in drama theory this is called *messenger's report* (remember the scene from *Angel Heart* mentioned at the beginning). To some, this dramaturgical technique might sound overly 'literary.' This is not the case. There is always more involved than mere verbal accounts. First, the character's *voice* and his *intonation* add important cues to our imagination (which distinguishes the account from a literary *text*). Second, the facial expressions of the characters *reporting* as well as *listening* give the scene a dimension beyond the literary.

In order to exemplify *teichoscopy* I would like to draw on a simple, but effective example from *Halloween*. It illustrates how a short, suggestive dialogue about something omitted from the visual space onscreen can trigger the viewer's imagination. It also underscores my rather loose application of the term *teichoscopy* since the two characters involved do not give a *direct* description but hint to the concealed object *indirectly* via dialogue. In this scene the psychiatrist Dr. Loomis (Donald Pleasance) and Sheriff Brackett

(Charles Cyphers) enter a rundown house at night in order to look for the movie's monster, Michael Myers, when something catches their attention—something we never get to see. "Look!" the policeman says. "What?" the psychiatrist replies.—"What *is* that?"—"It's a dog." The two man approach the camera, looking worriedly offscreen towards the undisclosed dog. "It's still warm," the policeman remarks. "He got hungry," Loomis says dryly, referring to his runaway-patient Michael Myers. The sheriff: "Could have been a skunk."—"*Could* have."–"Come on. A man wouldn't do *that*."—"This isn't a *man*." Since the whole scene omits the visual depiction of the dead, disfigured dog, we are strongly seduced to *imagine* it. In *my* imagination a bloody, heavily wounded animal showed up, lying in front of a window, opposite of the two men. To be sure, the mental visualization of the dog was not present right away but came into being only gradually, along with the progression of the revealing dialogue. The viewer's curiosity and his or her willingness to imagine are set in motion not only by the verbal description, but also the intonation and the worried looks.

A similar thing can be said about my example for a *messenger's report* taken from an excruciating scene in the movie *Seven*. Here it is not only the verbal account, but also the messenger's utterly terrified, traumatized, pale looks, his unstable, sobbing voice, the facial expressions of the questioning detective William Somerset and, in particular, a *photo* that we are finally shown after it has been withheld from view in a previous scene. On this photo a horrifying strap-on penis can be seen. It contains a long knife instead of a dildo. From the unfolding of the plot we know that a prostitute has become the serial killers fourth victim. These details are conjoined and come to life, so to speak, through the messenger (Leland Orser), a suitor in police custody. His highly suggestive report helps to fill in the final omissions and enables a horrifying imagination of the murder. "Who tied her down, you or him?" the detective asks. And the messenger reports: "He had a gun, and he made it happen. He made me do it. He put that thing on me. Then he made me wear it [referring to the serrated strap-on]. Then he told me to fuck her. And I did. I fucked her! Oh god, oh god, oh god! He had a gun in my mouth. The fucking gun was in my throat."

This example underscores two things. First, an *actual* non-filmic image (the photo) is used as a clue for a visual *mental* imagination—a strategy that is both popular and effective. Second, the scene highlights the *synthetic act* taking place in imagining. We have a photo and a verbal description, and in an act of synthesis both are put together. To be more precise, the *inanimate* object of the photo is removed, as it were, from the picture and inserted into a mental scene *in motion*. At least in my mental visualization I 'saw' the act itself appended to the messenger reporting: the suitor, forced by the armed serial killer, raping the prostitute with the lethal strap-on. What makes this scene—and messenger's reports in general—even more horrifying is the fact that it took place in the past: nothing can change the course of events anymore. The narrative determinacy evokes a dreadful desperation.

Verbal accounts can be distinguished not only in terms of temporality, however, but also vary according to the *degree of explicitness*. A character can tell what happened in a single, detailed report. In this case the degree of explicitness is high—as when Detective Somerset in *Seven* tells his boss a cruel event from the night before: "A guy's out walking his dog. Gets attacked. His watch is taken, his wallet . . . While he's lying there on the sidewalk helpless, his attacker stabs him in both eyes." The aspects of the event can also be merely suggested or implied. For instance, when Detective Mills studies the crime report of the second victim (greed) which states "Victim forced to mutilate himself" and we subsequently see the barely recognizable photo of a naked man covered with blood. In this case the degree of explicitness is lower. The lowest point of explicitness is reached when the events of the past are not told but implied by the changing dramatic situation or by some vague visual indications. When in *Henry—Portrait of a Serial Killer* the psychopathic title character (Michael Rooker) gives a ride to a female hitchhiker with a guitar case in her hand and later brings the guitar case home, we know—and might vaguely imagine—that he has murdered her just as brutally as the other victims that we were shown before. The three examples decrease in explicitness and therefore also in terms of their vivid visualization.

The scenes previously described depend strongly on verbal accounts. Obviously there are alternatives that do *without* teichoscopies or messenger's reports. One strategy is the suggestive use of voices and sounds in acousmatically imaginative and generative films like *The Blair Witch Project*: It is night when Heather (Heather Donahue) and Mike (Michael Williams), the two remaining protagonists, hear screams from somewhere in the pitch-black depth of the woods. The screams seem to come from Josh (Joshua Leonard), a friend who disappeared the night before. The camera reveals nothing but blackness, thus leaving much room for paying attention to the scene's audible dimension. Apart from Josh's screams, we can hear Heather and Mike's reactions: their nervous rustling, fast breathing, trembling voices. The horrifying screams, on the other hand, indicate pain, injury, even torture. Because there is no clue as to who kidnapped Josh—a group of local lunatics or the supernatural title figure—the viewer is left without clear guidance what to imagine *around* Josh. Rather than skipping imagining altogether, I visualized various close-ups of Josh screaming in pain. These mental visualizations were rather hazy and instable. Nevertheless, they resulted from the suggestive use of sound. Sobchack argues: "what is invisible or 'absent' in *vision* might be *audible* or 'present' in perception to inform the act and significance of seeing. Thus, what is concretely 'sensed' as significant by the embodied subject may be invisible *in* vision or, as well, *to* vision but is still available to perception—of which vision is only a single modality (one synaesthetically informed and synthesized with all one's perceptual modes of access to the world)."[22]

The fact that the various examples so far stressed *sound* (verbal accounts, voices, noise) does not imply that *images* cannot be highly evocative themselves. Think of scenes in which the image is suggestively obscured by fog, smoke, rain, the shadows of chiaroscuro lighting or *veiled* in some other way. It can also be evocatively *blurred* by overexposure of the filmstrip. Or one might think of a staging-in-depth strategy with the suggestive part remaining unfocused. Moreover, visual access might also be partially *blocked* by various means: props or characters standing in the way, or the attacked person him- or herself might be positioned between our view and the horrific act. When Billy Loomis (Skeet Ulrich) is—supposedly—killed in *Scream*, we cannot *actually* see him being stabbed in the stomach, because he stands with his back towards us. We have to imagine the horror that occurred due to the stabbing, the sounds of the knife entering flesh, Billy's screams and the reaction shots of horrified Sidney (Neve Campbell). Another way of blocking the visual access is the (literally) *masked* view, its most famous example presumably being the beginning of *Halloween*. In a point-of-view shot of young Michael Myers we follow him stabbing his older sister. Since he is wearing a mask, however, our visual access is hampered: 'looking through' the two eyeholes of the mask, most of the murder is hidden from our view. We see the up-and-down movement of the knife, but we cannot see it penetrating the girl's body—a lack that we *have to* (and, most likely, *do*) compensate imaginatively until we eventually see the blood-splattered girl falling to the floor.

Another image-based way of suggestion can be found in what could be called the *cut-away*. It is a classic type of suggestion that gives strong hints as to the horrific, but cuts away right in time to a different shot, thus concealing the violence proper. A simple, but effective moment takes place at the beginning of *Scream*: The masked murderer has already stabbed the first female victim; now he sits on top of the wounded girl (Drew Barrymore) in order to finish her off once and for all. We see his hand holding the bloody knife against the dark sky. Cut to the girl lying on the veranda floor, her neck and pullover covered with blood. She looks at the stalker and passively awaits her death. Cut back to the knife. The murder weapon rapidly moves downward and out of the frame, accompanied by a crescendo of music and an aggressive male voice. Once the knife has left the frame, however, the crucial 'cut away' takes place. Rather than showing the stabbing, the film moves to a different setting (the father looking for the girl inside the house) and relies on the viewer imaginatively continuing the killer's arm movement. The suggestive *sounds* of a knife entering human flesh, which are blended *with* and carry shortly *into* the images of the next shot are obviously of great help. Whenever I watch this scene I have the *mental* imagination of the murder briefly layered on top of the *actual* image of the father looking for the girl. My rather transparent, not overly detailed imagination is added to the perception of the next scene.

Yet another type of suggestion employs a *temporal bifurcation of sound and image*. This is to say, the images seen and the sounds heard occupy two different places in time. At the beginning of *Henry—Portrait of a Serial Killer* we see two liquor store clerks lying dead on the counter and the floor respectively. While the camera slowly moves away revealing their fatal, bloody wounds, the soundtrack offers an acoustic flashback of various gunshots, a shocked, frightened female voice, a man laughing and screaming aggressively "Shut up!". Slightly later in the film the camera shows a naked female corpse lying in a river, while we hear cloth being torn apart, the frantic screams of a woman, a gunshot. These *acoustic* flashbacks illuminate the *images* by simultaneously presenting us an aural account of what happened to the victims. Thus they guide our imagination: if the images were seen without aural comment, our imagination would ramble around. By adding the dimension of sound from the past, the film offers a straightforward way to mentally imagine the murderous scenes while simultaneously watching the images onscreen. We should not ignore, moreover, that both scenes are accompanied by an eerie, hollow crescendo of electronic music. The *perception* of music opens a phenomenological (not geometrical!) space in which the viewer is placed, thus influencing the *imagination* of the scene.[23] The imagination of the murder is not only determined by the sounds of the victims but also the phenomenological space of music.

What is the advantage of the acoustic flashback? The images of the victims in *Henry* might be accompanied by a narrator's voice-over recounting the scene as a messenger's report. The narrator, for instance a detective, would tell the scene in retrospect. Both images and sound would be located on the *same* level of time, even if the words described the past. However, since the narrator's voice would *re*-count the past from a third-person perspective, it would be somewhat *re*-moved. The acoustic flashback takes us back in the midst of the scene, even if we visually stay bound in its aftermath. We are suspended between the image-present and the sound-past. This allows for a more immediate and forceful experience of horrific imagination while at the same time avoiding a straightforward visualization of violence.

How an imagined object or event is given to the imaginer's consciousness is highly variable. One can distinguish at least three modalities of how the imaginative presentation appears. First of all, *clarity*: the imagined object or event ranges on a scale from unambiguously clear and fully discernible to dimness and barely recognizable. Second, *directness*: the object or event can be presented straightforwardly—as if confronting the imaginer directly—or somewhat remote. Third, *mobility*: does the imagined object come across as a static, frozen image or as a mobile scene in motion? I will discuss these modalities while introducing another suggestive strategy: the *conspicuous omission*. In *The Silence of the Lambs* the psychiatrist Dr. Chilton (Anthony Heald) prepares agent Clarice Starling (Jodie Foster) for her first encounter with the extremely dangerous serial killer Hannibal Lecter (Anthony Hopkins). While descending into the basement where Lecter is imprisoned, Chilton recounts a horrendous event: "On the afternoon of July 8, 1981 he complained of chest pains and was taken to the dispensary. His mouthpiece and restraints were removed for an EKG. When the nurse leaned over him, he did this to her . . . ." At this point Chilton produces a photo from his pocket and shows it to Clarice. While Clarice, in close-up, holds the photo in front of her and studies this—presumably— horrifying depiction never exposed to the viewer, we hear Chilton go on with his messenger's report: "The doctors managed to reset her jaw, more or less. Saved one of her eyes. . . . His pulse never got over 85—even when he ate her tongue."

Several mentionable things happened when I watched this scene. While the film presents us both Clarice studying the photo *onscreen* and Chilton recounting the events *offscreen*, it grants no visual access to the picture: only the *blank* backside of the photo can be seen. However, since Chilton introduces it so prominently, the photo almost begs for being imagined. As a conspicuous omission the photo is withheld precisely in order to stimulate a mental visualizing of the unseen—which I vividly did. I started with an visualization of the distorted jaw and, as Chilton progresses, added the upper part of the face with one healthy and one monstrously disfigured eye. My imagination reached a high degree of *clarity*, which is remarkable insofar as Chilton's report is rather sketchy. What might have been helpful is the fact that not much else happens in this scene. Hence my consciousness was not strongly occupied by perceptual obligations but could freely devote itself to imagining the photo. What is more, my imagination would not 'blow up' the imagination of the disfigured face to cover the full screen, as it were; nor would it take me in close proximity to the nurse. Rather I imagined the nurse's face on a small photo comparable to the one Clarice holds in her hand. Thus it was not only limited in scope, but in terms of *directness* it also came across as somewhat removed. Significantly, the whole scene is drowned in red light, which adds the aspect of color. Not surprisingly, my imagination of the photo was also tinted in red. This redness might be seen as a catalyst for the visualization of the blood and the wounds figuring so prominently in this scene. My mental photograph lasted only a short time because the scene progresses briefly thereafter. In fact, my imagination fluently switched from an *imagination-in-motion* of the narrated act (Hannibal taken to the EKG and the nurse leaning over him) to a *static* visualization of the withheld photo freezing the flow of mental imagination (the nurse's disfigured face), back to an *imagination-in-motion* (Hannibal eating her tongue). The modality of the imagined object in terms of *mobility* proved to be rather fluid.

The fact that I imagined the nurse in a photo underscores how the film influences not only the content, the color and the vividness of the mental visualization, but also has an effect on the form and the size we seem to 'see' it in. Moreover, it also affects our imaginary point-of-view, i.e. the particular point in imagined space from which we seem to observe the imagined object. I 'saw' the photo of the nurse from a similar angle as Clarice would, just as I 'observed' the murder in *Scream* more or less from the killer's point-of-view. Hence in both cases my imaginary point-of-view was bound to a *character*. This is not always the case, however. I 'followed' the murders in *Henry—Portrait of a Serial Killer* from a position similar to the *camera's*, thus assuming a third-person perspective.

So far I have only briefly mentioned the materials synthetically fused in imagining. I want to get a little more specific now by bringing into play a variant of imagining that occurs when *perceptual* cues laid out earlier in the film are reactivated and used *imaginatively* by a gradual feeding of more verbal information. The film lays the perceptual groundwork early on, so to speak, and then uses it little by little to erect various imaginations on top of it. A fine example can be found in *Seven* in connection with the year-long torture of the sloth victim. First, we see the room in which the victim, named Victor, *presently* lies. It is a dark, dirty room with medical instruments lying on a nightstand. We see the body of Victor revealed under a blanket: a putrefying quasi-corpse strapped to his mattress and wearing torn rags of cloth; one hand must have been cut from his arm; a disgusting smell fills the room.

At this point we do not know what happened to him. The horrifying aspects of this scene rely mostly on what we *perceive*. A little later in the film, however, a doctor feeds our imagination by providing us with grim details of what occurred in that room *in the past*. In his messenger's report we get to know what Victor had to endure: he was lying immobile in his bed for a whole year, causing the spine muscles to deteriorate. He was fed drugs and antibiotics in order to prevent the bedsores from infecting. He chewed off his own tongue. Finally, the doctor states a devastating assessment: "he's experienced about as much pain and suffering of anyone I've encountered, give or take." As if this was not enough, Detective Somerset gives us even more verbal information about John Doe's torture methods later in the film. Hearing that Doe severed Victor's hand to use his fingerprints and inserted tubes into the victim's genitals once again revives and further illuminates the imagination of the torture scene. Obviously, both the doctor's and the detective's verbal accounts could have set off our imagination all by themselves. Since we have *perceived* the disgusting victim and his dilapidated apartment earlier, the imagination is much more bound and restricted: the spot of indeterminacy, to use Ingarden's term, is rather tight. On the other hand, bringing in our *memory* of the crime scene and synthetically fusing it with the messenger's report, makes the imagination much more vivid and colorful. Whenever I hear the verbal accounts I am taken back into Victor's room and mentally visualize John Doe torturing his victim. This example grants us a first glimpse at how imagining as a synthetic act is dependent on and draws on other material: perceptions, memories, dreams etc.

Let me further illuminate this 'parasitic' activity by drawing attention to the end of *Rosemary's Baby*. I use this example also because it allows me to discuss how films engage us in mentally picturing the concealed *monster*. In this scene Rosemary (Mia Farrow) slowly approaches her baby's black cradle. Until now she has not seen the baby. Neither have we, the viewers. We have *heard* it scream, but we have not *seen* it—and, in fact, we won't see the baby, except in our imagination. The scene, which is completely quiet except for the monotonous tick-tock of a clock somewhere in the room, functions like an effective *dread* scene initially: we scan the immediate temporal horizon for a sudden shocking interruption or an overwhelming revelation of something horrific. However, dread gradually blends into *horror* when Rosemary slowly pulls away the cradle's curtain and looks at the baby, the film deliberately concealing the child from our view. Rosemary's eyes open widely. She raises her left hand in front of her mouth and looks around horrified. Music swells, with the strings imitating female screams. At this point I was visualizing the scenario only vaguely (if at all), since the film did not channel my imagination clearly enough.

This changed step by step. First, when Rosemary asks "What have you done to its *eyes*?" and then, more clearly, when her neighbor Roman Castavet (Sidney Blackmer) responds: "He has his *father's* eyes." Hearing these words, I was immediately led back to an earlier scene in which Satan raped Rosemary and in which we could get a glimpse of the devil's frightening, orange-colored eyes. Since the film strongly leads us to believe that Rosemary gave birth to the devil's son, the film triggered a vivid imagination based on my *memory* of Satan's eyes from earlier in the film and my *knowledge* of babies in general: a visual imagination composed of a baby's face with devilish orange-colored eyes similar, but not identical to the ones

Figure 4.2 Imagining Satan's son: Rosemary (Mia Farrow) in *Rosemary's Baby*.

remembered came to mind. Again, the act of synthesis in imagining can be seen at work here: two different mental acts—remembering and thinking—were fused in into a third one—imagining—and thus came up with a synthesized imagination of the devil's son.

This imagination was revived (albeit less vividly) when, a little later into the scene, the neighbor confirms our suspicion that Satan is the baby's father and, still later, the film presents the devil's eyes once again, this time superimposed on Rosemary's face. Moreover, the imagination of the devil's son was extended to his extremities when two women ask Rosemary to go look at his hands and feet. For a brief moment I was visualizing a baby with brown, disgusting, disfigured hands, *similar* to, but *smaller* than the devil's hands seen in the aforementioned rape scene. The rape scene did not contain a depiction of the devil's feet, however. Hence my imagination had to draw on different mental material. What popped up in my imagination were two club feet akin to the ones that I saw as a child in the popular German picture book *Hans Wundersam*. Hence my visual imagination in this scene availed itself of *two* different memories: of an earlier moment in the film and of a depiction that I had often seen as a child. We have to be cautious, however, not to mistake the memories that *contribute* to imagining (or, if you will, that imagination parasitically *draws on*) with the mental state of memory itself. When I was visualizing the devil's son, my consciousness was not in a state of memory. Instead, my consciousness presented to itself the devil's son in *imagination*—an imagination to which memory had contributed its specific share.

Interestingly, before I re-watched the film recently, I was sure that it contains actual *images* of Satan's son. Obviously, I was astonished when not a single image could be found throughout the film. My memory had mistaken my previous visual *imagination* of Satan's son as a visual *perception*! In his autobiography, Roman Polanski mentions that this happened to many viewers.[24] A similar case is the ear-slicing scene in Quentin Tarantino's *Reservoir Dogs*. We never get to see Mr. Blonde (Michael Madsen) cut the ear of policeman Marvin Nash (Kirk Baltz). Nevertheless, many viewers believe they have seen it. Annette Hill ascribes this misperception to the strong build-up—an argument that can also count for the misperception in *Rosemary's Baby*.[25] One viewer of *Reservoir Dogs*, in fact, admitted: "I guess I thought I saw more because I was looking at it through my fingers."[26] Harking back to what Dennis Giles said about the pleasure of partial vision: the example of this viewer's imagination-as-perception-through-blocking is another striking proof for the power of suggested horror.

Chapters 3 and 4 have not only presented my definitions of direct and suggested horror as fearful, engrossing, potentially overwhelming corporeal confrontations with sound-supported moving-images and imaginations of evil acts of violence or a threatening monster, but also characterized them as balancing acts between the corporeally pleasing pull towards the frightening object of fascination and the threatening push away from the fascinating object of fright. Along the way I introduced a number of crucial concepts and distinctions that will recur in the next chapters: ontological vs. phenomenological distance, immersion vs. extrication, lived-body constriction and somatic empathy. Based on the observation that seeing and hearing have pathic quality affecting us even if we look at an irreal event such as a movie, I argued that horror films and thrillers can pose a real threat not based on an illusion of reality but rather on the vividness and impressiveness with which sound-supported moving-images present—bring to appearance—the disproportionally immoral and disturbingly brutal acts of violence or monstrosity. Finally, I spent a considerable amount of time describing the aesthetics and phenomenology of a largely neglected field, namely mental visualizations evoked through filmic omissions and suggestions. The next chapter will deal with the cinematic shock—a despised aesthetic strategy recurring time and again in horror films and thrillers. Like horror it plays a crucial role for the anticipatory fear of dread, the aesthetic strategy I will discuss in Chapter 6.

5 Startling Scares
A Phenomenology of Cinematic Shock

> *Every now and then in a horror movie, you like to give the audience a sizable jump. Something that will just make them leap out of their seats for a moment: the 'Boo!' effect. It's not a terribly sophisticated thing to do to an audience, but it keeps them on their toes.*
>
> (Clive Barker)[1]

> *I nearly screamed. The hairs stood up on the back of my neck, and I felt thrilled that a film could still have that effect on me.*
>
> (Scott Reynolds on a shock scene in *Seven*)[2]

CINEMATIC SHOCK: THE DEFINITION

- Walking his bicycle, a young boy quietly crosses a street, when he loses a stack of baseball cards. Trying to pick them up, he is suddenly run over by an unexpected car, which enters the frame with a bursting sound that disrupts the preceding quietude.
- A young mother, terrorized by frightening phone calls from a psychopathic killer, hears the phone ring. She picks up the receiver. It's the psychopath. The woman looks frightened, but nevertheless talks to the killer, when completely out of the blue a huge tongue shoots out of the receiver and starts to lick her face, accompanied by a slimy, disgusting sound and the women's terrified scream.
- Three astronauts roam through the dark, quiet, tunnel-like compartment of their spacecraft. They search for an unknown, possibly threatening entity inhabiting the spaceship. When their electronic equipment indicates something alive behind a metal door, they prepare a weapon and a net. They cautiously open the door, when all of a sudden an aggressive cat confronts them with a piercing shriek.

Taken from *Jacob's Ladder*, *New Nightmare* and *Alien* (1979) these examples demonstrate three filmic moments culminating in what psychologists identify as *startle* and what I will call—due to greater precision in terms of intensity and onomatopoeia—*cinematic shock*. The cinematic shock is a brief, highly compressed type of fear. It responds to a threatening object or event that ruptures the situation suddenly and unexpectedly.

Figure 5.1 Cinematic shock: *Alien*.

The goal of this chapter is to describe the aesthetic strategies designed to create the shocking experience as well as the startling phenomenological experience aimed at by the aesthetic strategies—in other words: the formal as well as the experiential side.

But is 'startle' an emotion at all? While some scholars would categorize it as a physiological reflex that prepares and subsequently turns into an emotion, others call it an emotion and consider it fear-like.[3] I regard it as a variant of fear, because just like other types of fear it responds to an object registered as *threatening*. In contrast to other types of fear, however, it is an extremely brief, highly compressed response to a sudden, unexpected, rupturing threat. Depending on whether this short-lived threat turns out to be a more longstanding danger or not, shock may quickly be replaced by another type of fear (like horror) or by joy or anger at the end of the emotional episode. While the brevity of shock distinguishes it from other types of suspenseful fear like dread and terror, its short duration is not an argument to exclude it from the ranks of cinematic fear.

Admittedly, shock bears almost as much resemblance to surprise as it does to fear. The categorical borders are somewhat fuzzy here. Nevertheless I consider shock a type of fear rather than surprise, even though shock and surprise share unexpectedness as a characteristic of their intentional objects. My argument is that not every type of surprise is startling, let alone fearful, whereas in every instance of shock we are frightened (if only very briefly). In other words, while not in every case of surprise we respond to something threatening, in every instance of shock we do. Although I will frequently talk about a shock 'taking us by surprise,' I consider it surprising first and foremost in the sense of startling. Hence shock is not a subcategory of surprise proper.

In its simplest forms cinematic shock is a non-propositional form of intentionality: We are startled *at* the sudden increase of loudness or *at* the abrupt and rapid approach of a visual object (as in the 3-D shock). But we do not have a genuinely cognitive thought or belief about the object. Hence we respond in an automatic way—at least in the beginning, before the more culturally informed part sets in. In its most primitive form shock is a non-cognitive form of appraisal: We automatically and without a thought appraise the situation as dangerous. Even though these simple types of shock do not involve any cognitive *judgment* or *evaluation* in any strong sense, it is nevertheless a way in which the body registers a situation as threatening.[4] One could argue that the frightened body takes over and leaves us little control. However, there are also instances of cinematic shock that are more complex—what I will identify as the 'unexpected identity shock' is a case in point. Hence we could open up a continuum ranging from simple, almost reflex-like forms of shock to instances that involve judgment and cognition.

To be sure, scary movies are not *obliged* to integrate moments of shock. Early horror films like *Dracula* (1931) did not try to shock the audience at all and nevertheless were considered scary. More recent, highly effective films without such scare tactics are *The Silence of the Lambs* and *The Blair Witch Project*. Scary movies *can* do without cinematic shocks, but in reality they rarely ever do. And even European arthouse directors like Catherine Breillat and Bruno Dumont use this potent aesthetic device at the end of their movies *À ma soeur* (2001) and *Twentynine Palms* (2003) respectively. However, despite its wide usage the cinematic shock does not have a good reputation at all. This goes especially for critics who often loathe cinematic shocks with a vengeance. David Denby might serve as a stand-in for a legion of other critics likewise denouncing the "hackneyed 'Boo!'": "As a moviegoer, I'm more easily and unhappily scared than a nun; I hate things jumping out of the dark—the cheap, arbitrary terror tactics of generations of ruthless directors."[5] Interestingly, cinematic shocks also have a low status among the directors who employ them most efficiently. It seems as if shocking the audience is achieved almost *too* easily. That's why Clive Barker, director of *Hellraiser*, calls them "cheap boos."[6] And John Carpenter, creator of *Halloween*, talks about "cheeseball trick[s]."[7]

In fact, cinematic shocks are so 'cheap,' produced with so little prior effort in creating fear, that even comedies and parodies employ them effectively. John Landis' vampire comedy *Innocent Blood* (1992) and the postmodern parody of postmodern parodies, *Scary Movie* (2000), might both serve as examples. Nevertheless, there are differences. The mild startles in *Scary Movie* bear only slight resemblance to such extreme shocks as the endings of *Friday the 13th* (1980) and *Klute* (1971). And while some filmmakers use cinematic shocks heavy-handedly and with little impact, others employ them elegantly and in efficient ways. One might therefore justifiably ask whether they are really that 'cheap.' The first purpose of this chapter is to analyze how cinematic shocks *work*. Since the literature on cinematic shocks is scarce, the discussion of the formal elements will introduce a range of new names and concepts.

The fact that, despite their derisive rhetoric, even sophisticated experts of horror like Barker and Carpenter do not refrain from using cinematic 'Boos!' begs for a second set of questions. If these directors consider them inferior why do they use them at all? What purpose does the effect have? And what viewing experience does it enable? As Robert Baird puts it, "The profits of this cheap trick apparently exceed the cost of any critical tax levied against it."[8] In the last part of the chapter I get to the core of the cinematic shock experience by describing it phenomenologically. Part of the reason for doing this is an incentive to redeem the cinematic shock from its abysmal reputation. Without it, I argue, thrillers and horror films would have a much harder time to achieve one of their most significant pleasures: raising awareness of the collective cinematic experience. In his own attempt to underscore the value of cinematic shocks Baird argued for their capacity "to prove to us, in the very maw of virtual death, how very much alive we are. Much like the genres they are found in, startles engage our primitive psychophysiologies, and, for an hour or so, mock and remember mortality."[9] This argument is well-taken since it ties in nicely with my thesis about bodily stimulation. However, it relies exclusively on the *individual film* experience and does not situate the viewers inside the theatrical surroundings. I will come up with a different answer taking into account the social element of the *cinematic* experience as well.

SIX TYPES OF SHOCK: AN INVENTORY OF STARTLING MOMENTS

This chapter tries to fill a conspicuous void. Apart from Robert Baird's groundbreaking but ultimately incomplete study and David Scott Diffrient's insightful but overly impressionistic essay there is barely anything written on this frequent effect.[10] The scarcity of literature is inversely proportional to the wide usage of cinematic shocks. In his study of over 100 American horror films and thrillers from the 1930s to 2000 Baird found not only formal refinement but also increased usage.[11] If one wanted to classify cinematic shocks, one could identify at least *six* recurrent types. The following short overview does not claim to be exhaustive, nor does it pretend that these types are pure. Because their defining characteristics are of different orders, the various entries can overlap.

First, there is the *fake* shock: the viewer is shocked even though the source of startle turns out to be bogus. The shock neither comes from a real threat to the character nor does it contain horrifying elements for the viewer. This variant is the most superfluous if we look at it from the perspective of narrative progress. The scene from *Alien* mentioned at the beginning is an overly clichéd example: a cat jumping out of the dark. Or take *Evil Dead*: the terrified protagonist Ashly (Bruce Campbell) descends into the spooky basement of a log cabin in the woods. He looks to the right, but slowly moves to the left, when all of a sudden his friend Scotty (Richard DeManincor) enters the frame from the left and cries "Boo!" Ashly startles, while Scotty is amused and laughs wildly. The second type is the *return-of-the-dead* shock in which the dead villain, who is not quite dead, rises again. At the end of *Sleeping with the Enemy*, for instance, Laura Burney (Julia Roberts) has overcome and shot her ultra-jealous, psychopathic husband Martin (Patrick Bergin). The camera slowly pans away, suggesting a closing shot of the crying Laura in front of Martin's seemingly dead body. Plot, camera movement, editing and music suggest that the film is over. After another cut we see the crying Laura tightly framed, when suddenly from the lower edge Martins's bloody arm swiftly enters the frame in order to grab her. The unexpected frame intrusion is accompanied by a loud, sharp orchestral sound and Laura's startled scream.

Third, the *3-D* shock, which mimics one of the most characteristic elements of 3-D movies: scenes in which something jumps, flies or is thrown towards the camera as if to bridge the ontological gap between filmic There and cinematic Here. In *Mimic* (1997) a scene takes place in the dark tunnel system of the New York subway. The male protagonists endeavor to rescue the heroine, Dr. Susan Tyler (Mira Sorvino), from the deadly giant bugs that inhabit this space. When frantically trying to pull her through an opening in the ground, the policeman Leonard (Charles S. Dutton) accidentally kicks a lamp down the opening. Following a cut, we see the lamp falling into the dark depths of a seemingly endless space underground, from which one of the giant bugs suddenly jumps forward. The bug moves so fast and eventually becomes so big that after the negligible duration of 17 frames the whole screen is filled by the animal's body. Since the impression of enhanced three-dimensionality is aimed directly at the *viewer*, this type of shock is least dependent on character involvement. It makes evident that character presence is—contra Baird—ultimately not a precondition for the cinematic shock.[12] Fourth, the *horror* shock, which is based on the abrupt revelation of the monster or an act of violence. In *Raising Cain* a scared man (John Lithgow) enters a dark bedroom, where we strongly expect something to happen. We see the man's hand in close-up trying to switch on the light, when his wife's hand suddenly enters the frame from below and cuts his wrist swiftly with a razor blade. There are almost no sound effects; we only hear the disturbing cut of the knife. The revelation often takes the form of a sudden and quick 'rising of the curtain': at the top of its lungs the film screams "Boo!" and "Voilà!" at the same time.

Fifth, the *behind-the-back* shock. In a scene filled with dread a frightened character—his or her eyes continuously and almost stubbornly directed ahead—moves backwards and runs into a threat. Or: a *reflection* in a mirror or on the surface of a lake suddenly reveals a villain or a fake threat looming at the back of a character. Towards the end of *Deep Rising*, for instance, the protagonist Trillian St. James (Famke Janssen) tries to escape from the mad captain (Anthony Heald). She sneaks backwards to the left while looking ahead to the right. Panning leftward with her, the camera gradually moves in on her, framing her more tightly, leaving little space behind her vulnerably exposed back and the left edge of the frame. When she eventually bumps into the menacing captain, her turning around is accompanied by a scream and a sudden sound effect.

Sixth, the *unexpected-identity* shock: this variant takes us by surprise because the identity of a character suddenly and shockingly turns out to be less stable than expected. Either we are faced with an inversion of *gender*: usually a man dressed as a woman, but sometimes a woman instead of a man. Or an undermining of the character's *ontological status* takes place: a person assumed to be alive turns out to be dead or a lifeless dummy. A fine example can be found in Martin Scosese's *Cape Fear*. The private-eye Claude Kersek (Joe Don Baker), hired to protect the Bowden family from the psychopathic stalker Max Cady (Robert De Niro), has set up a trap. He tries to lure Cady into the Bowden house, in order to finish him off legally on the basis of trespassing. Following an intense scene in which Cady apparently tried to enter the house, Kersek eventually considers the threat as bogus. He walks into the kitchen, sits down and pours himself a drink, all the while talking to the nice Hispanic maid who stands behind him. During this scene we have seen the maid only from behind, but when she turns around in a strangely machine-like way, we shockingly realize that it is Cady in disguise.

The unexpected-identity shock is clearly the most sophisticated version of cinematic shock. It relies on a more or less complicated dialectics of suggesting and showing. The filmmakers have to expose enough for us to understand the scene, but not too much so we don't guess the surprise in advance. In many cases it has reverberations for the narrative past *as well as* the future. In *Cape Fear* part of the shock results from our knowledge that Cady must have cold-bloodedly killed the servant in the *close* past and

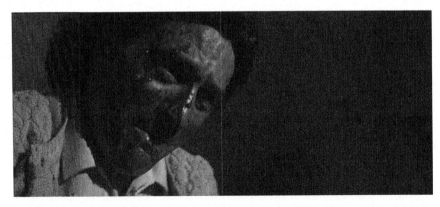

Figure 5.2 Unexpected Identity: Max Cady (Robert De Niro) dressed as a woman in *Cape Fear*.

that he will attack the private eye in the *immediate* future. A similar thing can be said about the end of *Psycho*. From the mother's less-than-alive status we conclude that something unusual, maybe even horrifying, must have happened to her in the *distant* past and that she cannot be the murderer. Hence the killer is still around posing a threat to Lila in the *near or distant* future—in fact, Norman (Anthony Perkins), the killer, will enter the scene shortly thereafter in female disguise. In comparison to the fake shock and the 3-D shock, the narrative function of the unexpected-identity shock therefore goes beyond pure spectacle.

ESSENTIAL ELEMENTS OF SHOCK: RAPID MOVEMENT AND INCREASE IN VOLUME

Cinematic shocks depend on one of two formal elements: a) an *abrupt and rapid visual change*, and b) a *sudden and stabbing increase of loudness*. One of these elements *must* occur.

Abrupt and Rapid Visual Change

What I mean by 'abrupt and rapid visual change' is first and foremost a fast, unforeseen movement *within a shot* or a rapid movement *from one shot to another* initiated by a sudden cut.[13] In many cases filmmakers do not rely on visual *changes* alone but add visual *acceleration*. This might occur through accelerated movement within a shot (accelerated mise-en-scène) or through cutting (accelerated editing). Often rapid editing and accelerated mise-en-scène are combined. This can lead to a strong pictorial disorientation. Hence what in the following discussion is separated analytically often occurs in combination. Generally speaking, *how* the visual change occurs is less important than its unexpectedness and its speed: in order to be effective, the visual change has to be abrupt and rapid. As Robert Baird points out, startle effects are rendered impotent when sufficiently slowed.[14]

The Shock Cut

The most obvious case of abrupt and rapid visual movement from one shot to another is the 'shock cut.' In this case the movement results from the visual discrepancy between shot 1 and shot 2. Moreover, the visual movement is often underscored by a strong contrast in shot duration resulting in accelerated editing. While shot 1 is comparatively long (sometimes twenty seconds or longer), shot 2 marks the prelude of a veritable storm of two, three or more quick shots (sometimes consisting of 12 frames and less).

This rapid alternation may—but does not have to—involve *three* typical forms of shots: 'shock shot,' 'reaction shot' and 'revelation shot.' The 'shock shot' includes the shock proper. The 'reaction shot' depicts the response of the character. As a way of quick information it helps to clarify whether the shocking source is dangerous or not: if the character looks relieved, we immediately know that the threat was either fake or meant mockingly. Moreover, it gives the viewer a possibility to empathize. Even if empathy is not necessary, many filmmakers rely on it since it enforces the viewer's relatedness to the character. In addition, the quick movement of the startled character supplies another visual acceleration. As the last category, the 'revelation shot' discloses the source of shock. Just like the reaction shot, it shows us whether the source of shock is dangerous (an alien, a serial killer) or harmless (a cat, a mocking friend). At this point a scene that began as dread and has culminated in a cinematic shock often turns into a scene of *horror* confronting us with something frightening.

A typical cinematic shock might first shock us by way of an unidentified source, then cut to a character response, and, finally, a third shot reveals the source of shock. However, the three types of shot are not present in every case. Nor do shock, reaction and revelation shot have to be separated. In fact, in many cases two or even all the elements are included in a single shot (either simultaneously *or* successively by way of camera movement, frame intrusion, prop movement etc.). For instance, scenes in which the monster suddenly bursts into the frame fuse shock and revelation. Or, scenes in which a character is startled by a sudden frame intrusion combine shock and reaction. Any permutation is imaginable.

What might be the advantage of dispersing shock, reaction and revelation over different shots? First, employing a series of shots enables an *acceleration* of the visual. Second, it also allows for a *protraction* of the scene. Since screen duration exceeds story duration the filmmaker can put a special emphasis—which, in turn, might deepen the shock reverberations. The most striking examples of protraction occur in relation to reaction shots. In numerous cases the reaction shot does *not* proceed from the exact point where the previous shot has ended (this would imply losing a fraction of the character's reaction). Instead, the film *jumps back* to reveal the split second of astonishment and shock *in its entirety*. The result is an overlap of time between the shock shot and the reaction shot that enables the protraction of an otherwise very short phenomenon. In the most obvious case—a shock scene in *Deep Blue Sea,* in which one of the main characters (Samuel L. Jackson) is suddenly attacked and eaten by a shark—I found this temporal overlap added 2 seconds.

Frame Intrusion from Off-Screen Space

An abrupt and rapid visual change can also happen *without* editing. Two alternatives exist: the rapid visual movement takes place through an object visible *within* the frame (i.e. inside screen space) or by way of an unseen object *intruding* the frame (i.e. from offscreen space).[15] Since many film critics and lay viewers consider the abrupt and rapid frame intrusion from offscreen space more paradigmatic, let us look at it first. Following Noël Burch's definition, frame intrusion can happen a) through entering from the space *outside* the frame, or b) through entering from the space *behind the set* or *hidden behind an object within the frame*. If something enters from *outside* screen space this usually takes place via the four edges of the frame: left, right, above and below; but it can also come from what we perceive as the space 'behind the camera.' Interestingly, Burch claims that films rarely bring the upper and lower segments of the frame into play.[16] This assumption is incorrect when it comes to the cinematic shock. There are numerous examples of frame intrusion from the upper or lower edge of the frame. In *Deep Rising*, for instance, cables fall from the ceiling, enter the frame from above, and (fake) shock both character and audience.

Since movement has to be abrupt and rapid, the most potent frame intrusions happen very quickly. This is the case in a typical dread scene in *The Dark Half* (1993). A woman (Rutanya Alda), already established as a potential victim, walks through a quiet, abandoned hallway towards her apartment, when her door opens itself uncannily. Cut to a tightly framed shot showing her room. All of a sudden the frame is penetrated by an extremely fast movement of an arm coming from the right, attacking the woman. In this scene the frame intrusion can happen fast enough because the framing is tight. On the other hand, the framing must not be too tight so that we are still able to perceive the intrusion clearly; otherwise the effect falls flat.

For an illustration of an *intrusion from behind the set* we might draw on *Evil Dead*. In one scene the main protagonist Ashly (Bruce Campbell) rests with his back against the wooden door of the log cabin, when suddenly the hands of a zombie break through the wood (i.e. from behind the stage) and start to choke him. An example for a startling effect based on an intrusion of screen space from something hidden *behind an object inside the frame* can be drawn from John Landis' horror comedy *Innocent Blood*. Tracking the female vampire Marie (Anne Parillaud) undercover agent Gennaro (Anthony LaPaglia) discovers blood on a snowy rooftop, the traces of which lead towards a chimney. When the camera focuses on the chimney, the vampire suddenly jumps up from behind it with a roaring scream.

Movement within Onscreen Space

The last possibility of abrupt and rapid visual movement is the one most often ignored. If film critics talk about cinematic shocks at all, they generally refer to shock cuts and frame intrusions. Sudden movements *within onscreen space* are rarely mentioned. In *Evil Dead* there is a scene in which the protagonists sit around the dinner table of their log cabin in the woods. The shot in question is composed of a female character in the right foreground, while in the background there is a living room with a door in the floor leading to an ominous cellar. I assume that in this scene most viewers direct their attention to the girl who is in sharp focus, while the background remains unacknowledged. This changes when we are taken aback because the cellar door abruptly, rapidly and unexpectedly springs open. Other examples based on an abrupt and rapid movement *within* the frame include those shocking scenes in which something is hurled or jumps towards the camera and thus seemingly in our direction—what I have identified as the '3-D shock.' In all cases the movement has to be extremely fast; otherwise a clearly visible object cannot shock us.

Note that the movement *within onscreen space* is not identical with an intrusion of the frame *from behind an onscreen object*. While in the former case the moving object is *visible* from the beginning, in the latter case the object is *hidden*. Admittedly, there are borderline cases. What about those parts of the frame that are buried in darkness? Do they belong to onscreen or offscreen space? In genres that thrive on scenes taking place at night or inside dark interiors it is not uncommon that a character or an object suddenly moves out of the dark. In any case, if the cinematic shock relies on movements *within onscreen space* or *out of the dark*, the director has to be able to stage in depth. David Bordwell has repeatedly argued that contemporary directors have neglected if not forgotten the art of staging in depth. Instead, they prefer a cinema based on editing.[17] As some of my examples indicate, Bordwell's argument is too sweeping. Even if shock effects are often based on frantic editing, there are numerous cases that depend on staging in depth.

Scare Chords: The Sudden and Stabbing Increase of Loudness

Ultimately the more significant component of cinematic shock is the sudden, stabbing increase of *loudness*. This strategy is often referred to as the 'stinger' or 'sting'—director Sam Raimi also talks about "scare chords."[18] While the aesthetic strategy of direct cinematic horror relies predominantly on sound-supported moving-images, the cinematic shock is primarily dependent on image-supported sounds.

Scare chords consist of three elements: suddenness, stabbing shortness and, most importantly, increase in volume. Generally speaking, the shock is most efficient if the *discrepancy* between the relative quietude *before* and the relative loudness *during* the shock is high. In order to maximize the discrepancy in volume filmmakers sometimes completely suspend sound before the shock, whether speech, music or noise. According to Michel Chion's definition 'suspension' occurs when a sound naturally expected from a situation (and heard at first) becomes suppressed and vanishes.[19] The scene from *Jacob's Ladder* described at the beginning in which the protagonist's son Gabe (Macaulay Culkin) is run down by a car is a case in point.[20] But even if the use of suspension before the shock often enhances the effect, it is not mandatory. Most scenes preceding cinematic shocks contain some sort of brooding, apprehensive music. The fact that these scenes are often equally effective underscores the significance of the *contrast* between a relatively *loud* sound bursting into a relatively *quiet* scene. In gestalt theoretical terms: a figure that stands off perceptibly from a ground.

Sometimes cinematic shocks are prepared by a *crescendo* of music or noise that culminates in a short sound stab. During those scenes we are cued to believe that the threat is fast approaching and ever-more imminent—which stimulates our fear of shock or horror. However, the crescendo version has a disadvantage: shocks are felt more effectively if introduced by a *sudden*, unprepared increase of volume.

But the shock caused by sound does not only result from an increase in *volume*, but also from a contrast in terms of *other* acoustic properties. The sound before the shock usually consists of extended, regular, even monotonous non-diegetic music or atmospheric, ambient diegetic noise (such as raindrops, crickets or ventilating fans). The shock itself results from the sudden stab of a short sound. This sound can either be diegetic (e.g., a loud scream) or non-diegetic (e.g., orchestral music or sound effects). Often, both occur at the same time, layered on top of each other. Moreover, the effect can be enhanced by a sound that is not only comparatively loud but also unpleasant or eerie: deep, guttural male voices; sharp female screams; shrill, shrieking violins; high-pitched telephone rings; sound effects suggesting breaking glass etc.

Shocks ignoring the effectiveness of the volume contrast are few and far between. On the other hand, there are numerous cinematic shocks that work without *visual* contrasts. Where, then, does this higher efficiency of the increase in volume compared to the visual contrast come from? There are two reasons. First: differences in the speed of perception. The ear analyzes, processes and synthesizes faster than the eye. While the eye must explore in space as well as follow along in time and hence has more to take in all at once, the ear can isolate a detail and follow this point or line in time alone.[21] John Dewey points out: "Sounds *come* from outside the body, but sound itself is near, intimate; it is an excitation of the organism; we feel the clash of vibrations throughout our whole body . . . It is sounds that make us jump."[22]

Second: auditory perception intrudes awareness not only faster but also more inexorably than visual phenomena. Since we cannot shut our ears quickly, we have less control over the attempted auditory intrusion. What the philosopher Hans Jonas calls the *simultaneous coordinated manifold of objects* in seeing is not available in hearing, which is governed by a *succession* of impressions.[23] As we have seen in the chapter on direct horror, one strategy to avoid the impact of the horrifying image is to *escape* it by looking away or switching into the mode of aesthetic appreciation (rather than immersion). Because of the *simultaneity* of innumerable percepts in *sight*, I can let my gaze wander and look at the exit sign or appreciate the formal characteristics of violence. But how can I escape the impact of sound? I cannot simply hear *away* nor can I let my sense of hearing *wander*. The sudden burst of sound has penetrated me long before I have covered my ears. As

Jonas notes: "In hearing, the percipient is at the mercy of environmental action, which intrudes upon his sensibility without his asking and by mere intensity decides for him which of several qualities distinguishable at the moment is to be the dominant impression. The strongest sound might not be the vitally most important one in a situation, but it simply seizes the attention among the competing ones. Against this the freedom of selective attention is extremely limited."[24] Similar to painful somatic empathy, the coercive aspect makes the cinematic shock so effective but also despised: while I have a certain freedom of selection in direct, present effects like horror (let alone in indirect, anticipatory ones like dread and terror), the cinematic shock puts me in a passive position by conceding the initiative to the film.

Cinematic shocks are most effective if a sudden visual contrast and an abrupt increase in loudness *coincide*. This is not only the case because both elements are added up, but also due to the supportive function of sound that turns the combination into a more clearly perceptible gestalt. The improvement of sound mentioned in the multiplex chapter allowed for a better perception of ever-more rapid visual movements. It made possible yet another turn of the screw in terms of shocking visual change.

HOW TO INTENSIFY CINEMATIC SHOCKS

There are various ways how filmmakers can intensify cinematic shocks. Judging from the previous discussion, the use of stronger, more stabbing increases in volume combined with more rapid visual changes would seem to be the most readily available (and, if you want, 'cheapest') one. If the purely formal analysis of the "Essential Elements of Shock" section was sometimes inclined towards such a simple cause-and-effect argument, the following discussion will show that the matter is more complicated. Gradually moving into a phenomenological direction I will demonstrate that the film cannot simply snap its fingers in order to shock the passive viewer. There is simply no one-way causality between an objective physical stimulus and its response. Think of two sounds that are equally loud, but have very different effects if put against a silent or a noisy background. Gestalt theory has long taught us that we perceive *relations*—the *difference of a figure on a ground*—not isolated elements. The allegedly isolated element (the physical stimulus of the sound) is always part of relations that form a gestalt (the sound against its backdrop).

The cinematic shock always relies on a minimum of viewer intertwinement with the filmic world—an intertwinement that needs to be established first. This becomes obvious when we look at those strategies that most effectively and elegantly intensify shocks: disrupted relief, deliberate distraction and the depiction of forceful objects. They function effectively precisely because they keep us entangled with the filmic world. Just like the various *types* of cinematic shock, these *strategies of intensification* are not exclusive, but can be combined. The three intensification strategies have a second function, however. By far not everybody has the same shock threshold. Some viewers are prone to easy startles; others must be provoked with strong shock attacks. The intensification strategies help (even if they do not guarantee) to homogenize the audience response, thus supporting the pleasure of collectivity.

Disrupted Relief

The *disrupted relief* strategy occurs when we are falsely led to believe that a dangerous situation has been positively solved. Since the threats of shock or horror have deceptively disappeared, the film lures us into a position of *non*-expectation. We relax and forget the offscreen threat. Precisely at this moment, the unexpected sting of shock penetrates. Often, apparent happy endings, promising relief from an accumulation of dread, terror, shock and horror sequences that took place before, are used to this effect. The viewer finally expects some quietude and relaxation. Erroneously so. A great example can be found at the end of *Friday the 13th*, probably the biggest shock I have ever experienced. The extended carnage of the preceding night finally seems to be over. The darkness has made way for daylight. The psychopathic slasher Mrs. Voorhees (Betsy Palmer) got killed. And Alice (Adrienne King), the surviving last victim, awakes in a canoe in the middle of a lake in a tranquil natural environment. The soundtrack offers relaxing, almost sentimental music. At the lakeshore the police arrive, promising the protection of official authority. Alice puts her hand into the water, when all of a sudden monstrous Jason Voorhees (Ari Lehman), a dead figure

Figure 5.3 Disrupted relief: Jason (Ari Lehman) attacks Alice (Adrienne King) in *Friday the 13th*.

mentioned but never encountered before, jumps out of the lake and grabs her from behind.

Or consider this sequence from *Malice*. College professor Andy Safian (Bill Pullman) intrudes the caretaker's (Tobin Bell) room in the basement of a university building and pokes around in his belongings. When the caretaker suddenly stands behind him, Andy and the viewers are heavily startled. Andy apologizes; the caretaker accepts. In turn he tells a story about his dead mother that almost awakes feelings of compassion. The tension between the two seems resolved. Relieved and a little ashamed, Andy walks out of the room. He believes that everything is fine and the caretaker does not nurse a grudge. There are no clues that the caretaker might attack from behind. But this is exactly what happens: accompanied by a sudden scream and a burst of non-diegetic sound, the caretaker throws himself towards Andy.

Why is the disrupted relief strategy so powerful? Its impact relies on the strong *discrepancy* between the viewer's relaxed, *expanded* position in the moment of relief and the startled, *constricted* position in the moment of shock. The shocked lived body's constriction is felt all the more powerful precisely because it contrasts with the preceding bodily expansion. The lived-body's effort to bridge the gap between two opposed somatic extremes makes the strategy of disrupted relief quite effective. (If this still sounds slightly opaque, it will become more accessible after the following extended phenomenological discussion)

Sometimes directors take this principle yet another step further and add a second *specific* relief to the first *general* relief. The ending of *Poltergeist* (1982) might serve as a case in point. After a long, very loud and intense battle the poltergeist seems to be defeated and the family is happily reunited at the end of the film (general relief). Cut to a scene in the boy's bedroom at bedtime. Before finally putting himself to sleep, the boy checks underneath his bed if there is another hostile intruder. We are led to believe that something might be there, but the boy finds nothing (specific relief). When he moves upwards from below his mattress, the camera tilts with him and suddenly reveals an aggressive, brutal clown doll waiting behind him.

However efficient the disrupted relief strategy might be, there is a flipside to it: it sacrifices moments of dread, i.e. the fearful tension caused by the *anticipation* of shock and horror. If the viewer is successfully lured into a position of relief, he or she obviously does not expect anything bad to happen. Hence filmmakers have to decide: do they want to frighten the audience *and* shock them, taking into account that the startle is possibly less powerful than in cases of disrupted relief? Or do they leave out dread and put emphasis solely on the cinematic shock? As a preliminary conclusion we might say that shocks are experienced as particularly effective when the discrepancy between *anticipation* and *shock* is high. Unprepared, we are all the more vulnerable to the shocking attack. But how, then, do we explain that some of the most startling effects occur during scenes in which we *have* strong expectations of an imminent threat?

Deliberate Distraction

The answer is: by deliberately *distracting* our expectation. This potent shock strategy takes us aback not by lulling us into a false sense of security but by leading our attention in the wrong direction—figuratively, but also literally. An advantage of this *deliberate distraction* strategy is the fact that it does not have to sacrifice moments of fear. Quite to the contrary, it most often goes hand in hand with scenes of dread. In contrast to the disrupted relief strategy, we usually *expect* something and are consequently highly alarmed—even if our alarm is misled. Often this intensification strategy relies on frame *intrusion*. But the filmmaker can also deliberately distract us from something hidden *within* the frame. Thus clever depth staging can become an effective means of shock. I have mentioned a scene from *Evil Dead*, in which the opening of a cellar door in the background can take us by surprise precisely because we direct our attention to the woman in the front. There are two important means of distraction. First, the *character*: through posture, gestures, verbal announcements and eye-line the character is able to lead the viewer's attention to specific onscreen and offscreen parts. However, the character alone does not guarantee distraction. Think of the behind-the-back shock: the backwards moving character looks *ahead* into onscreen or offscreen space—nevertheless we concentrate on something coming from *behind*. In this case, the scene's convention trumps the character's posture and eye-line. This is where the second means of distraction, *offscreen sound*, comes into play: a salient sound whose source is not seen onscreen can raise our awareness of the space beyond the four edges of the frame. In both cases the distraction relies on *spatial* disorientation. The film leads the viewer to concentrate on parts of onscreen and offscreen space where the shock is precisely *not* initiated. But this spatial distraction also has a *temporal* component. Since we concentrate on something still *in the act* of approaching, we expect the shocking moment to take place *later* in time—which is, again, a mistake.

Deliberate distractions work also in a slightly different manner. A highly effective strategy is placing the shock while *verbal interactions* between characters absorb our attention. In this case there is no anticipatory dread involved and we expect nothing shocking or horrifying. Similar to the disrupted relief strategy, the shock hits us wholly unprepared. Take this example from *I Know What You Did Last Summer*: the two protagonists Julie James (Jennifer Love Hewitt) and Helen Shivers (Sarah Michelle Gellar) sit in Julie's parked car and discuss how their (supposed) murder has affected the lives of many people. The scene is very earnest and quiet. All of a sudden, a weird woman (Anne Heche) unexpectedly enters the frame from the left and bangs against their window. We are deeply involved in following the characters. Our attention is absorbed by the content of their speech and their emotionality, distracting us from the onslaught of shock.

Forceful Objects

Some of the most intense cinematic shocks occur when something *massive and forceful*—mostly a threatening killer or monster, but it can also be a non-living object—bursts through *solid material*—in most cases shattering glass, but sometimes wood or concrete—in order to confront a character. Let me illustrate this strategy by referring to the ending of *I Know What You Did Last Summer*. About to take a shower, Julie James finds a disturbing note written on the shower's glass door, indicating that the killer must still be around. Cut to a point-of-view shot of Julie looking at the door, when suddenly the killer with a loud noise forcefully bursts through the glass and towards her and the camera.

If the threatening character simply intruded the frame from behind the scene without shattering any material, the shock would be decidedly less intense. Why do we experience it so powerfully? The intensity cannot be explained away by referring to the *higher volumes* of the sound effects 'allowed for' by the shattered material. In case of forceful objects shattering solid materials there is an intensity surplus we do not find in scenes that rely solely on strong volume contrasts. Furthermore, the strong impact cannot rely solely on the *threat* posed by the forceful attacker. It certainly plays a role that the killer is *dangerous*. But is it crucial for the—initial—forcefulness of the shock? I don't think so. Our conclusion whether the attacker means danger or not is a judgment *after* the fact: only after we were shocked do we evaluate the danger of the attacking object. The outcome of our cognitive judgment can either prolong the shock or cut it short. However, our initial shock reaction does not depend on reflection, but reacts *pre-reflectively* to something else. The question is: to what?

The intensification of the shock effect relies on our phenomenological experience of living and non-living external objects suddenly displaying massive *force*. The term 'force' is used here in the sense of such phrases as 'a stone hit me with considerable force' or 'a car struck the tree with great force.' As a synonym one could also use the word 'impact.'[25] A *penetrating* object carries force and a *bursting or exploding* object (glass, wood, concrete) carries it on. In order to experience the display of force as a cinematic shock we do not necessarily need the *simultaneity* of a 'penetrating object' and a 'bursting or exploding object.' The same effect, if certainly with less impact, works *without* a bursting object that carries on force. Think of a scene in which someone strongly and unexpectedly hammers against a window (as in *Mimic*) or a loose brick falls from the ceiling and crashes onto a table (as in *The Fog*, 1980).

But how should it be possible at all that we, as viewers, ascribe impact to *objects*? And, what is more, why should we be able to *feel* this force? Usually this kind of argument is wiped away by calling it a blatant case of anthropomorphism. Following Herbert Spiegelberg's phenomenology of force I would claim that this accusation ignores the continuity *between* and intertwining *of* man and nature. Spiegelberg notes: "The charge of 'anthropomorphism' seems to imply that man (*anthropos*) has nothing in common with non-human nature and that any common shape (*morphe*) which we may find in nature must have been illegitimately projected upon it from the observation of the human original."[26] This is not the case. Spiegelberg's argument is complex but convincing, it deserves extended quoting: "There are times when we have good reasons for extrapolating from the experience of forces within our own body to such forces in foreign bodies beyond its range. Such an extrapolation may be buttressed by the consideration of cases where forces are transmitted from one part of our body to another part, and where we experience the forces in both these parts, for instance when one member exerts and the other undergoes such force, or vice versa. Such cases would seem to justify an inference by analogy to the effect that forces are present even where the other member of such a relationship is no longer our own body but some foreign or inanimate object. Moreover, insofar as this first extrapolation can be justified, there would seem to be no basic objection to a final extrapolation to cases where our body and its forces are no longer involved, i.e., to the interaction between inanimate bodies."[27]

Vivian Sobchack calls this experience "interobjectivity."[28] It describes our ability to recognize, care for and feel with material objects external to ourselves, based on the recognition, caring for and feeling with our *own* material being. We derive the ability of interobjectivity from moments in which we are ourselves subjected to the *will of others* or the *action of intentionless external forces*: passive moments in which we experience the irrelevance of our subjective will and in which we are constituted and treated as material objects. Her examples comprise the experience of tornadoes and earthquakes, of illness and torture. Our ability to be interobjectively related originates not only in a *passive* suffering, but also in an *active* devotion to objects. Taking an example from Walter Benjamin, Sobchack refers to the playing child's 'mimetic faculty' for not only acting as the shopkeeper or teacher, but also as the windmill and the train. Hence *passive suffering* and *active devotion* to the world of objects are the two components of the intimate and dual relationship we have with materiality. They are the very empathy and sympathy that we as subjective bodies feel towards material objects.

This relatedness to material objects is experienced in a wide and graded range, varying in the ratio of involvement and the degree to which it becomes explicit to consciousness. Sobchack asks how proportionally subjective and for-itself is the object: obviously there is a difference in kicking the tire of one's car, giving a boat a proper name, and believing in the subjective agency of a magic charm.[29] It is somewhere within this wide and graded range of subjectively experienced reversibility with objects where the possibility is located that allows us to experience the impact of a football destroying a window in the real world as well as a character crashing through a glass door in the filmic world.

However, in order to render effectively the material force and the forceful material as the basis for an intensification of shock, filmmakers cannot rely on coincidence but have to draw on well-tried strategies. First, there is the *choice of props*. The reason why films use glass as the material-to-be-shattered has to do with the characteristic 'explosion' of this otherwise solid material: the sudden and extremely rapid burst of glass splinters is able to visualize the carrying on of force more effectively than materials like wood or concrete. Second, there is the *size of the props*: a rock breaking through a window makes the object's materiality more tangible than a pebble. The size of the props goes hand in hand with a third choice: the *frame distance*. The biggest object breaking through a window is robbed its effectiveness if shown in a panorama shot. In turn, a close-up of two colliding objects renders them more concrete and tactile than a long shot. Moreover, frame distance is often correlated with *sound volume*: the louder the sound the closer we consider its source and vice versa.

This brings us to a second complex of aesthetic strategies. Apart from the visual side, the use of sound—and particularly the choice of *noise*—supports the rendering of the materiality of objects. As Michel Chion notes, "Noises are reintroducing an acute feeling of the materiality of things and beings, and they herald a sensory cinema..."[30] According to Chion, it was the horror film that functioned as a motor for the renewal of the senses in film—a tendency set in motion by directors like Raimi, Philip Kauffman or David Cronenberg and propelled by the action movies of the *Die Hard* (1988) category. "In these movies matter—glass, fire, metal, water, tar—resists, surges, lives, explodes in infinite variations, with an eloquence in which we can recognize the invigorating influence of sound on the overall vocabulary of modern-day film language," he writes.[31] In our case it is the noise of shattering glass that adds an aural dimension to its visual representation and thus helps rendering the weight, speed, impact and resistance of the crash between object and object. In scenes of cinematic shock the visual and the aural dimension coincide in what Chion calls the point of synchronization: the punctual and abrupt coincidence of sound and visible impact.[32]

The forceful materiality of objects makes itself felt in all kinds of viewing environments, but it develops its full potential first and foremost in the *multichannel* surroundings of the multiplex. There are two reasons. First, the effect is reinforced by "offscreen trash," a phenomenon that occurs when a loud event takes place visually in the *middle* of the screen, but participatory sounds are heard in the *lateral* and *surround* speakers. In what sounds like a poetic description of interobjective empathy and sympathy

Chion claims that surrounding offscreen trash is able to give "an almost *physical existence* to objects at the very moment they are dying."[33] The second advantage of the multiplex has to do with *sound volume* and *acoustic pressure*. Since a loud crash has more impact than a silent one, other viewing surroundings have a hard time competing with the improved sound systems of the multiplex. Moreover, as we have seen, digital sound tracks permit acoustic pressure that is ten times as high as its analogue equivalent and can be boosted up to a level close to the human pain threshold. Last but not least, multiplex sound systems are powerful enough to move a significant amount of air that literally hits the spectator. Hence horror films and thrillers belong to those genres in which visuals and noises cooperate particularly well in creating a sensory cinema that often shockingly makes us sense the materiality and the forcefulness of the object.

This extended discussion has revealed something we know from extra-cinematic experiences of startle: in order to intensify cinematic shocks filmmakers better take us by surprise. This is most obvious in 'disrupted relief' cases, which make us believe that the threat has disappeared. But even when we consciously expect and, in fact, know that something is going to happen, shocks can effectively be established. Familiarity with genre conventions may help to raise our expectations but cannot avert the response when we anticipate something differently. This is the case in 'deliberate distractions.' Here we *do* expect something, but from a *different place* and *later in time*. It is as if we erect a bulwark but the film avoids it and attacks from behind. And even if we know the exact place and time, we can be surprised if the shock effect is stronger than anticipated (here the 'forceful objects' strategy comes into play). The affective strength surprises us—otherwise we would not be shocked in the first place. Hence the surprising element of shock comes in three forms. First, we do not expect it at all. Second, we expect it, but somewhere else or at a different time. Third, we expect it less powerfully.

PHENOMENOLOGY (I): THE TRANSFORMED INTERRELATION OF VIEWER AND FILM

While deeply-felt dread and terror are hard to establish, cinematic shocks can be achieved quite easily: the atmosphere precluding the startling moment is set up quickly and quite independently of the film's overall mood. Nevertheless, cinematic shocks depend on an important precondition: the viewer's *thorough-enough* attentional intertwinement with the filmic world. How strongly the cinematic shock depends on this precondition can be judged from a series of *negative* cases. A viewer entering the theater seconds before the intended shock will hardly be affected. Or think of someone concentrating on a cell phone display—his or her reaction will be much weaker. Last but not least, there are forms of distraction resulting from the film rather than the viewer—for instance if the projection breaks down shortly before the startling moment and resumes only after an interval that cut off our relation with the filmic world. Again, the effect will evaporate. Quite the opposite happens when there *is* a minimum of intertwinement. This is clearly the case in anticipatory scenes of dread preceding the actual shock. During these highly immersive moments the viewer seems to be glued to the screen. The *cinematic* experience is almost wholly dominated by the *film* experience. Absorbed by our interaction with the movie, we barely pay attention to anything happening around us. The intensity of the moment is defined by stillness—both inside the auditorium as well as in terms of our corporeal mobility. The cinematic shock unsettles this relationship between viewer and movie.

Often initiated by a *shock-cut*, the cinematic shock abruptly 'cuts' our merger with the onscreen world. Deep immersion ends. Suddenly the phenomenological distance between film and viewer, between aesthetic object and aesthetic perceiver, disappears. In contrast to the seeming forward movement in preceding moments of dread in which the viewer deeply immerses him- or herself in the filmic world, the direction of movement in shock is suddenly reversed. This abrupt vanishing of the phenomenological distance disrupts the viewer's perceptual flow so fast and unexpectedly (even if in most cases not wholly unforeseen) that he or she cannot raise the hands, shut the eyes or cover the ears as a means of defense in time. What works as a preparatory self-defense against images and sounds of violence and monstrosity by definition comes *too* late in moments of shock.

As a consequence, the extreme proximity of the aesthetic object cannot be averted: the startle effect implies a temporary *emptiness* of consciousness.[34] One could call it a microsecond-*un*-consciousness: the shock 'scares the audience witless' or manages to 'scare the daylights out of the viewers' for a brief period of time. At the speed of light and sound, the film pushes forward, forces on and closes in on the viewer who literally retreats, resiles, recoils in a very real sense. Its disruptive character can be judged from the typical blinking response—the immediate closing of the eyes—that a number of behavioral observations from the third-person perspective have documented. An even more observable, three-dimensional prove is the jump. If the shock makes you jump out of your seat, you are forced to loosen your tight position, your clenched fists, your grabbing the armrest. You are literally 'un-settled.' The film shakes the bodily foundations and changes the viewing position *more* than just metaphorically. In the 'hold' of and 'captivated' by the movie, we are suddenly 'taken by surprise' (or, maybe more appropriately, 'taken aback') by a 'jumpy' scene and almost completely thrust out of the immersive experience in the filmic There back into a momentary awareness of our cinematic Here. During the shock and its short aftermath the *film* experience does not exit but is, as it were, relegated to the fringe of our attention's limelight. And even if we do not lose touch with the film completely, after a shocking scene it takes a moment to get back into the deeply immersed state experienced before. Instead other aspects of our *cinematic* experience climb the center stage of awareness.

PHENOMENOLOGY (II): THE SUBJECTIVE EXPERIENCE OF CINEMATIC SHOCK

The Lived-Body Experience

During moments of immersion, my *self*-consciousness is reduced to a minimum: I am lost almost wholly in the filmic world. I do not notice much of my surroundings nor do I self-consciously attend to my own body. When the shock bursts into the scene, however, not only my relation to the film as the intended object changes; it is also the experience of my lived-body that undergoes a quick and sudden metamorphosis. While there might be a microsecond of unconsciousness, the body subsequently returns with a vengeance and briefly dominates consciousness. The literally un-settling effect of the cinematic shock is nicely captured by the German word *Entsetzen*, describing a horrified response, but literally implying a dislocation: the *entsetzte* viewer is dislocated; temporarily leaving the center of the self, the viewer is able to reflect on him- or herself from an eccentric position.[35] Here we can sense the advantage of aesthetic experience. In cinematic shock the phenomenological distance breaks down for a microsecond—but then quickly jumps back into place. In fact, it has already been restored when the overwhelmed viewer self-consciously recognizes the affective effectiveness the cinematic shock has had. But this self-awareness is possible only because the *ontological* distance has existed throughout. Otherwise the viewer would be involved wholly in the practical side of life. If someone is afraid of thunderstorms, a shocking thunder does not enable self-awareness: the individual would grapple with fright and a search for shelter or mental support rather than being consciously aware of his or her lived-body.

As a figure-ground correlation, the shocking scene is most effective when it stands out most clearly from its background, when it is most distinctively experienced as a gestalt. This is especially true when it is supported by a forceful, digitally enhanced noise so *loud* and *stabbing* that it penetrates our body like a knife. Robert Baird appositely talks about an "affective punctuation"—a *subjectively* felt exclamation mark that *objectively* measured might last between three-tenths of a second to a couple of seconds.[36] Even if in the majority of cases being 'cut off' from the intertwinement with the filmic world does not result in physical *pain* of our *physiological* body, the startle clearly 'cuts' into the flesh of our *phenomenological* lived-body.

In order to explore this experience more thoroughly, I will again rely on Hermann Schmitz' compelling phenomenology of the lived-body. As we have seen, Schmitz argues that the lived-body experience shifts on a highly nuanced continuum between *constriction* and *expansion*. Constriction and expansion are never reached in their entirety though. Consciousness puts its lights out, as it were, before we arrive at either pure constriction or pure expansion.[37] For instance, before expansion reaches its peak, we fall asleep; and prior to the climax of constriction, we pass out. As we have seen, startle is one of those instances in which we, however briefly, lose consciousness because it is too constrictive. Other examples are sudden pangs or panic attacks. Since their entirety is never reached, constriction and expansion usually stand in contending opposition. If constriction dominates, we experience *tension*. If expansion prevails, we feel *swelling*. This struggle can either occur simultaneously—then we experience it as bodily *intensity*. Or it can take place successively—Schmitz calls this experience bodily *rhythm*. Voluptuousness with its characteristic heavy rhythmical breathing is an example for the alternating prevalence of expansion over constriction and vice versa.

Another perfect case in point, illustrating a rhythmic succession of radical constriction and expansion, is precisely the startle reaction. At first, it involves a radical constriction that can lead to as much as a temporary unconsciousness. For a brief moment our usual "unfolded present" shrinks to a "primitive present," as Schmitz calls it. Just like sudden pangs, extreme forms of shame, or states of panic the *constricting suddenness* of startle implies a temporary withdrawal to the first poles of our five bipolar markers of orientation: the *Here* (as opposed to Vastness), the *Now* (as opposed to Duration), *Being* (as opposed to Not-Being), *Identity* (as opposed to Difference) and the *Self* (as opposed to the Other).[38] Consider the temporal aspect of shock: the time experience prior to the startling moment is dominated by a temporal *flow*. This could mean the loose and extended flow of time characteristic of unremarkable scenes. Or it could imply the dense, forward-leaning time experience of a terror or dread scene in which we heavily anticipate the outcome and therefore experience the temporal flow prominently. In either case the shock marks a strong caesura: a gestalt standing out. The durational flow seems to come to a halt, and extended time suddenly shrinks to a very dense and pointed Now.

Since this radical constriction would be an unbearable state, however, it is immediately followed by expansion. At this point the reason why we experience the 'disrupted relief' strategy as particularly effective becomes more obvious. It involves a rapid back-and forth movement between opposed poles of the lived-body: a state of relaxed bodily expansion in the moment of relief is followed by the short constriction and the subsequent expansion of shock. The lived-body has to bridge two gaps: from expansion to constriction and from constriction to expansion. These discrepancies allow for a powerful corporeal experience.

The subjective *phenomenological* expansion finds an equivalent expression in some objective *physiological* reactions. These physiological reactions not only reveal a similar *expansive* tendency but can also make their way into consciousness. I have mentioned the reflex-like bodily *jump*, visualizing a literal three-dimensional expansion into the space of the movie theater. Another very common reaction is the hair that will *stand up* and the goose pimples that manifest the expansive *swelling* of the skin. Moreover, the shock experience seems to literally set the surface of our body into *motion*: it makes our skin *crawl*; it gives us the *creeps*; it sends a *shiver* down our spines. And then there is the heart that beats so heavily as if to *break out* of the constricted body. Needless to say that these expansive physiological reactions do not in every case take place objectively let alone make their way into subjective consciousness. But *some* of them do in most cases.

Last but not least, I have to mention the scream. Almost reflex-like it *frees its way out* into the open by way of the viewer's mouth. Unlike inward-directed weeping but similar to outward-directed laughing the scream implies a sudden, eruptive opening: the inner constriction expands audibly into the world. Clearly, not everyone in the theater screams. While some viewers articulate their reactions in an expressive, public way, others experience the cinematic shock privately. Moreover, while male screamers are few and far between, American women often react more expressively. How can we reconcile these facts with the common assumption that the startle reaction is hardwired? Robert Baird makes perfectly clear that cinematic shocks are more intricate than simple reflexes like the knee jerk: the shock is *almost* reflex-like. While it is true that the startle reaction consists of an initial rapid *involuntary* phase, there is also a second phase which falls under some degree of *voluntary control*.[39] At this juncture nurture takes over from nature. As Baird puts it, "startle is at once genetically hard-wired, socially constructed, and personally expressed."[40] While some physiological manifestations seem unmistakably hardwired—notably the accelerated heartbeat and the hair standing up—others like the scream are culturally shaped. Hence we must acknowledge that in screaming there is more active 'doing' than passive 'being done by.' This causes us to question what its purpose might be: what do we gain from screaming?

First, the outward-directed character of the scream helps to overcome constriction by pushing, so to speak, the shocking object back and re-creating a relieving distance by literally screaming it away. Second, following Helmuth Plessner one could argue that the scream is a form of self-confirmation and self-verification.[41] Breaking free from the constriction of shock, we expand outwardly not just by responding passively but by *actively* and *literally* giving voice to our reaction. As a powerful embodied expression of a powerful lived-body experience, the scream seems adequate. Hearing ourselves scream in response to a cinematic shock helps to reassure us in the face of a startling interruption, because the scream can draw us even further away from the state of frightening re-immersion. It can prolong the self-recognizing bodily reaction that grounds us in the cinematic Here.

The result of this phenomenological as well as physiological constriction and expansion is, first and foremost, a shift in consciousness from the film to our own lived bodies. Undergoing a corporeal metamorphosis our otherwise "backgrounded" bodies enter the foreground of awareness.[42] The absent body, like an epiphany, 'comes to mind' and is felt as a tangible presence. In contrast to *gradually approaching* affective states like melodramatic tears or cinematic dread, the shocked body bursts *abruptly* and *forcefully* into consciousness. Similar to comedic laughter, the scream asserts the experience audibly. Taking away the control over the body, this experience of powerlessness causes uneasiness among some viewers, especially those who should remain in control due to professional reasons; critics in particular. Many viewers, on the other hand, experience the foregrounding of the body as both self-affirmative and pleasurable. The cinematic shock is self-affirmative, because it enables a heightened experience of presence.

The Social Experience

Sean S. Cunningham—director of *Friday, the 13th*, a film full of intense cinematic shocks—maintains: "If you see a horror film in an empty theater, it's just ugly and grim; there's no fun. But if you go with four hundred kids laughing and screaming, it's a different experience."[43] The cinematic shock raises awareness of our own bodies, but it often (if not always) directs attention towards our social co-presences in the auditorium as well. Personal and collective awareness are intricately interwoven. On the one hand, it is precisely because our bodily reaction is both *strongly felt* and experienced as *inevitable* that cinematic shocks are able to foster an intersubjective understanding of affective equality: because we can hardly avoid the shock reaction, we can tacitly assume that this goes for the rest of the audience as well. And even if this heightened state of intersubjectivity does not necessarily enter our awareness, it often does by way of another particular form of response: it is the *scream* as the most clearly perceptible response that binds together the *individual bodily* with the *collective social* experience. This corporeal reaction—either practiced personally or perceived indirectly as a response of others—is literally crying out loud into the auditorium that at this very moment we have similar experiences. In the most intense cases screaming together and being aware of this common responding can create what I call a 'collective body.' On the other hand, the personal awareness might also be influenced by the collective response. The psychologist Daniel Stern underscores the importance of social confirmation for one's own awareness: "We become aware of our own internal states as we discover that others have them."[44]

But why scream? Why not utter a sentence like 'Wow, this is shocking!'? Erving Goffman notes that expressive messages must often preserve the fiction that they are uncalculated, spontaneous, and involuntary.[45] 'My experience was so shocking that only an uncalculated, spontaneous, involuntary response like the scream seems appropriate'—this is what the shocked screamer expresses and what a lengthy sentence could not. If this explanation seems implausible, it might sound more convincing if we think about the ashamed laughter that often follows *isolated* screams. A screamer who stands out by screaming while others don't is suddenly reminded of the social interrelations inside the auditorium: he or she feels shamefully singled out because the overly obvious need for a reassuring scream puts him or her in stark opposition to the rest of the audience. By screaming one admits one's own weakness. As if trying to transform the situation and intending to take the incriminating scream back, he or she tries to cover it up with laughter, signaling as it were: 'I know that my scream was ridiculous! But, please, don't think that I am a coward who needs the reassurance of the scream!' Quite appositely, Daniel Stern calls this state of social disorientation in which one's place or position in a group is thrown into question "intersubjective anxiety."[46] In shameful situations a return into the imaginary or actual embrace of the community is crucial for the emotion to disappear.[47] The isolated screamer who stands out begs for reintegration by sending the humble signal of ashamed and insecure laughter. How much more susceptible to shame would the viewer be if he or she had cried a whole sentence? The scream is a less exposing way of self-confirmation. The fact that the screamer has risked to be ashamed *at all*, no matter how safeguarded, underscores the self-confirming value of screaming.

Obviously the laughing cover-up strategy is not necessary if many people scream simultaneously. In this case the viewer does not consider his possibly shameful scream an act of *isolated* self-confirmation but recognizes it as a legitimate part of a *common* response. Since one is already part of a group, a reintegration is not necessary. Isabel Cristina Pinedo therefore reminds us that by way of a collective response screaming acquires a *second* reassuring aspect.[48] It is not only self-confirming when we hear *ourselves* scream, but also when we hear *others* make their reactions publicly available: hearing their screams can pull us away from the fearful filmic experience and transpose us into the cinematic Here. Moreover, in moments of collective screaming the taken-for-granted background of our cinematic experience suddenly comes to the fore. What before was tacitly acknowledged, now enters awareness: the fact that we are not alone and that others experience similarly. As we know from other instances of everyday life, *sharing* an experience of something fearful and shocking can have a relieving effect.

In extraordinary cases this effect can lead up not just to reassurance but to a specific pleasurable experience that I call the 'collective body' and that Hermann Schmitz dubs "solidary incorporation" (*solidarische Einleibung*). Schmitz describes the phenomenon as a spontaneous formation of a comprehensive *quasi*-lived-body.[49] This quasi-lived-body results from a cooperative fusion of well-attuned and synchronized lived-bodies co-acting without thinking distance but with a shared focus. His examples comprise common singing in a choir, clapping, playing in an orchestra, sawing or rowing. Even more to the point might be the collective shout of the soccer stadium after the favored team has scored. In contrast to Schmitz' twin concept of *antagonistic* incorporation, solidary incorporation contains no domination or suppression among the various partners. In these moments the feeling of collectivity is not backgrounded, but stands out. It is literally *ecstatic* in the sense of the Greek word *ekstasis* for 'standing out' (*ek* 'out' + *histanai* 'to place, cause to stand'). A distinct feeling of collectivity is created. For a short period of time the social fragmentation, the feelings of isolation, and the contradictions, differences and struggles of everyday life are forgotten and buried under a heap of pleasurable equality and integration.[50]

To be sure, the collective-body experience does not follow from every moment of shock. And obviously in cases it does result, not everybody experiences it, let alone experiences it *identically*. The preconditions for the collective-body experience are best when the shocking scene is intense (which encourages a *uniform reaction*) and when the screaming crowd is sufficiently big and densely seated (which enforces the *fusion* of the individual viewers). As we have seen, screaming belongs to the culturally shaped side of the startle reaction. Hence in order for the collective screaming to take place, the viewers have to *actively* engage in it. Among—at least minimally—experienced horror audiences this is precisely the case. They share a tacit knowledge that only actively *doing* the scream can produce the pleasurable experience of being part of a collective body (even if this is often left to female spectators). In fact, in the eyes of those who scream, the ones who remain completely silent might carry an air of deliberate unwillingness and therefore be regarded as killjoys. Quiet viewers potentially embarrass those who scream, leaving them unaccompanied. As Goffman reminds us, "silence, coming from a person in a situation where participants are obliged to be busily engaged [. . .], can itself be a noisy thing, loudly expressing that the individual is not properly involved and attuned to the gathering."[51] Undeniably, this is a more valid description for refused laughter in the face of a funny comedy. But complete silence vis-à-vis a shocking horror movie can create a feeling of being in the wrong place as well. The difference is: while solitary laughter merely makes one feel left alone, a sole screamer is inclined to feel shamefully standing out.

The *reassuring* aspects of screaming mentioned before are certainly part of the explanation why we actively engage in it *individually*. But as the discussion of the collective-body experience indicates, there is a more *social* element involved. Screaming can also imply reaching out to and fusing with others. Since inside a dark auditorium with everyone looking in the same direction, personal interaction cannot be based on the minute facets of facial expression and bodily posture, one has to employ the most obvious means of communication: the voice. Again, we might ask: why screaming and not uttering a full-fledged sentence? If we presume a certain *active* (albeit tacit) willingness to make possible a collective experience, individual sentences would be counterproductive. Sentences simply cannot be synchronized as easily as primitive screams. Unlike singing in a choir or chanting songs in a stadium, collective reactions in the movie theater are not actively coordinated and must therefore rely on the most primitive non-verbal expressions: laughing or screaming. Only thus, the collective body as a peculiar intersubjective experience becomes possible.

Because startle is such a hardwired, universal reaction, the *cinematic* shock can be achieved easier than any other affective response at the movies. Not even male arousal in the face of pornographic images can compete with shocks; nor can the disgust of confrontations with slimy, putrefying monsters. If we describe film as a medium that oscillates between cognition and emotion, between a meaning-dimension and a presence-dimension—moments of cinematic shock mark an extreme. Critics who can't help their somatic responses often greet shocks with strong suspicion. They defy the lack of phenomenological distance and the sense of over-involvement. They reject the irresistible, homogenizing power that the movie wields over them (since the power to shock *is* power after all). Obviously, these critics prefer an *idiosyncratic* reaction to a *uniform* response, missing the potentially pleasurable aspect of being shocked alike and together. This goes hand in hand with the belief that effects drawing on biologically determined reactions do not carry aesthetic value: aesthetic strategies that work similarly in real-life situations cannot be judged artistic. This negative attitude led critics to ignore what occupied us in this chapter: the vast differences in type and intensification strategies as well as their phenomenological experience. Harking back to the remarks of Clive Barker and John Carpenter, we can now understand why these directors feel the need to mock their own use of shocks. Acknowledging the futility to defend shocks on aesthetic grounds (or, at least, on what traditional aesthetics would judge as *valuable*), they miss its pleasurable potential. And even if they intuitively grasp the purposefulness of this 'cheap' aesthetic strategy, they lack proper counterarguments, raising their arms in defense.

The preceding phenomenological analysis has shown that the cinematic shock is characterized by a series of quick transitions. It often moves from an individualized, immersive experience (shortly before the shock) to a peak of individualized, non-immersive lived-body experience (during the shock) to an experience of the audience's collectivity (shortly after the shock)—before we subsequently delve back full circle into a state of re-immersion. Films relying on cinematic shocks set into motion a back-and-forth movement between cinematic Here and filmic There, between brief moments of shock and more extended periods of immersion, between a foregrounded and a backgrounded awareness of the collective viewing situation. The *number* of shocks and their *intensity* determine the nature of the back-and-forth movement. A film with few mild shocks will not initiate a strong amplitude, whereas a movie with many intensive shocks will tend away from an individualized immersive towards a collective experience shot through with moments of extrication. Hence strong experiential differences exist between a movie that aims primarily at cinematic shocks (like *I Know What You Did Last Summer*) and a film dominated by dread (like *The Silence of the Lambs*). What this oft-mentioned anticipatory emotion of dread means precisely, will now occupy us in the next chapter.

6 Anxious Anticipations
A Phenomenology of Cinematic Dread

> *To make any thing very terrible, obscurity seems in general to be necessary. When we know the full extent of any danger, when we can accustom our eyes to it, a great deal of the apprehension vanishes.*
>
> (Edmund Burke)[1]

> *No matter how horrible something is, once you've seen it you feel better. So it's the anticipation of the horrible that really scares you.*
>
> (Stuart Gordon)[2]

CINEMATIC DREAD: THE DEFINITION

- It is night outside, when a middle-aged private detective sneaks into a dark old house off the beaten track somewhere in the Californian countryside. In contrast to the detective the viewer thinks that this is the home of a knife-wielding, murderous old lady. The man slowly and cautiously climbs a flight of stairs, venturing deeper into the eerie place. Apart from quiet string music barely anything can be heard, when upstairs a door slowly opens, confirming the presence of extreme danger. The detective, however, moves on unsuspecting.
- After an erotic encounter with a perfect stranger, a sorrowful, distraught woman realizes on her way home that she has left her wedding ring in the man's apartment. She returns, but unlike the viewer she is unaware of a psychopathic killer waiting for her somewhere in the quiet, deserted apartment building. The distressed woman takes the elevator, which slowly climbs to the seventh floor.
- A petite, young, inexperienced FBI agent enters the house of a dangerous serial killer without knowing the man's identity. When it begins to dawn on her who the man is, she attempts to arrest him, but the psychopath escapes into the cellar of his dirty, unsettling house. The determined but extremely frightened agent slowly and very warily tries to trace him, descending into the labyrinthine basement with her cocked gun, not knowing where to look for the armed killer. She breathes heavily and looks around scared when she passes through narrow corridors and opens doors that seem to lead yet deeper into the complex structure and further away from the outside world.

Figure 6.1 Cinematic dread: *The Silence of the Lambs*.

Taken from *Psycho*, *Dressed to Kill* (1980) and *The Silence of the Lambs* these scenes exemplify a highly conventionalized aesthetic strategy that I call 'cinematic dread.' In terms of narrative content the paradigm case of dread presents a vulnerable character slowly and quietly entering a dark, forsaken place harboring a threat. Call this the alone-in-the-dark scenario. While the character might be informed about the threat or not (and hence behave either terrified or ignorant), it is highly probable that she will confront it anytime soon—even if the outcome is still uncertain. Although we, as viewers, often have at least some information about the danger, the exact nature of the threat remains open. Yet for various reasons—ranging from genre experience to internal narrative cues—we expect that the scene will end with the bursting effect of shock and/or a potentially overwhelming moment of horror. In formal terms dread scenes mirror the fact that the character moves through the dangerous space either with almost paralyzing fear or without any knowledge at all. In both cases there is no need for formal agitation, and hence (intense) stillness and slowness dominate: few camera movements, comparatively long shots, little movement within the mise-en-scène and an unobtrusive soundtrack. Dread is an intense, but quiet anticipatory type of cinematic fear in which we both feel *for the endangered character* and fearfully expect a threatening outcome that promises to be shocking and/or horrifying *to us*. Dread lasts until it gives way to shock or horror or disappears otherwise, but it does not include those other effects.[3]

The characteristics of dread clearly set it apart from horror. First, dread and horror have different *temporal structures*. While both types of fear are felt at the present moment, dread points toward the future, whereas horror focuses on the now.[4] In an anticipatory type of fear like dread we expect something threatening to happen anytime soon. We feel afraid of a prospecting, largely unknown and sometimes even amorphous danger. In a present-oriented type of fear like horror we are afraid literally 'in the face of' the overwhelming sound-evoked moving-images and imaginations. It is precisely the Hereness and Nowness of the monstrous or violent in-your-face moving-images and imaginations that constitute the source of horror. Let me illustrate this difference with an apocryphal mini-story that can serve as a figurative stand-in for frightening scenes in general: "The last man on earth sat reading in his library. Something knocked at the door."[5] In this allegorical story the *closed* door represents the state of dread: the viewer expects that something will happen and consequently anticipates the revelation of a threat that could turn out to be utterly shocking or horrific. The *open* door, on the other hand, represents the state of horror: dread disappears when the viewer is confronted with the presentation or imagination of the horrific.

Second, dread and horror can also be set apart in terms of *intentionality*. As indicated in the introduction, our common understanding of intentionality can be advanced, if we take into account a suggestion by Hermann Schmitz. Schmitz illustrates what he has in mind with the following example: When we go to the dentist, our fear is directed toward the dentist and his drill. But is this really what we are afraid of? *Actually*, Schmitz says, we are afraid of the pain that expects us. However, the dentist and the drill as the immediate objects of fear push the anticipation of pain into the background. Hence the intentionality of fear is split.[6] The first part—the dentist and his drill—Schmitz terms 'concentration section' (*Verdichtungsbereich*): It is here that fear condenses, as it were; it is the center of attention. The second part—the anticipation of pain—he dubs 'anchoring point' (*Verankerungspunkt*): It is this part of the intentional object where the emotion is causally anchored. The anchoring point remains mostly present as a background assumption and rarely becomes foregrounded. While this aspect might sound as if it was negligible, quite the opposite is the case: the anchoring point dominates the character of the respective type of fear and feeds it.

Now, someone might object that when we face an aggressive dog, the intentional object is similarly split and there is no difference to the dentist scenario: We are actually not afraid of the dog, but the pain that it might inflict upon us. This objection sounds wrong to me. While the dentist and the drill do *not* intentionally threaten us (and are therefore somehow distanced from the cause of fear, namely potential pain), the dog *does* actively threaten us (and is therefore closely intertwined with our potential physical pain). Hence in the former case it makes sense to separate concentration section and anchoring point, whereas in the latter case it doesn't.

Schmitz' distinction has important ramifications for our current discussion. In some types of cinematic fear (like dread) the intentional object—the object or event that we are afraid *of*—is less coherent and more complex than in others (such as horror). In cases like horror (and shock, as we have seen) the intentional object is not split but given all at once. The violent and monstrous moving-images are comparable to the aggressive dog: they actively threaten us *hic et nunc*. Concentration section and anchoring point match: In horror we are intentionally directed toward horrific moving-images or imaginations of violence and the monster. In cases like dread (and terror, as we shall see) the intentional object is split—or, rather, two different aspects simultaneously acquire different roles as part of the intentional object. On the one hand, the viewer fears *for the character*: He is afraid that in *The Silence of the Lambs* serial killer Jame Gumb will harm FBI agent Clarice Starling or that in *Psycho* private detective Arbogast (Martin Balsam) will become the next victim of the knife-wielding old lady. This is the viewer's focal center of attention (the concentration section). On the other hand, the spectator fearfully anticipates the confrontation with two potentially overwhelming emotional states that usually follow in the wake of dread scenes—shock and horror—and therefore fears *for him- or herself*. For various reasons I will explore, the viewer strongly expects the old lady to appear suddenly out of nowhere (shock) and brutally stab the private eye (horror). This is the viewer's background assumption that dominates the character of dread and feeds it (the anchoring point).

Schmitz argues that in cases with split intentional object, the concentration section tends to push the anchoring point into the background. This insight is extremely valuable, because it helps to explain why film scholarly attention has focused primarily on character engagement when it comes to emotions—and why fear for oneself was often overlooked. Carl Plantinga, for instance, argues that during the dread scene in *The Silence of the Lambs* the viewer does not fear that Buffalo Bill will kill the spectator but that he will kill Clarice Starling. This is correct. But then he goes on, "Thus my fear is for her rather than for myself."[7] This seems insufficient to me. The viewer is not only afraid for Clarice, but also fears for him- or herself. After all, it is the viewer who has to face cinematic shock and horror. Thus my account diminishes the importance of other-focused responses hitherto often deemed *fully* responsible for fearful emotions at the movies.[8] This move yields two advantages. First, the analysis becomes less monolithic since we do not fully depend on the explanatory value of sympathy and empathy. Second, heading in this direction might answer the intriguing question why we are afraid even when unpleasant characters are involved.

Fear for the character and fear of my own confrontation with shock and horror are the two thoroughly intertwined parts of the split intentional object in dread. Now, if in dread I fearfully anticipate horror, the intensification strategies for horror must also help to intensify dread. In other words, if horror can be intensified by strong character allegiance, along with exceptional immorality and brutality (as argued in Chapter 3), the same must be true for dread. Since the viewer's fear is dominated and fed by the anchoring point, changing it must have important reverberations for the concentration section. Hence if the film manages to intensify our fear of the potential moments of horror and shock arising at the end of the scene (the anchoring point of dread), we are also more afraid for the threatened characters (the concentration section of dread). A likeable character I strongly care for (like Clarice) raises the stakes in terms of dread, because I fear the horror that I had to confront if she were killed in an unusually immoral and brutal way. A less sympathetic character (like private detective Arbogast) still evokes dread, but the horror of his death is not something I fear as much as Clarice's harm.

As the two examples make clear, the amount of information the characters possess about their danger can diverge. While Clarice knows that she is endangered, Arbogast is ignorant of the threat awaiting him. In Clarice's case we can empathize and share her dread (fear *with* her), whereas in Arbogast's case we can only sympathize (fear *for* him). Thus the *Psycho* example shows that empathic fear-with-the-character is not a necessary condition for dread. It is merely effective icing on the cake. The essential prerequisite is that *we* strongly expect that something will happen—and therefore fear for the character and ourselves.

But what is it actually that we think we know? Genre experience, narrative cues, atmospheric elements etc. tell us that the character is strongly endangered and that the scene will—most likely—end with horror, shock or both. However, and this will prove to be an important difference to terror, the degree of *our* information (not the character's!) is only moderately high. Although we know that Jame Gumb is hidden somewhere in his cellar, we do not know when and how exactly—and if at all—he will harm Clarice. Will he jump around the corner in two seconds or two minutes? Will he attack with his gun, a sledgehammer or something far more vicious? In other examples of dread we know even less about the precise source of danger. But if the exact threat is largely uncertain and sometimes even amorphous, we cannot be sure about the kinds of shock and horror that await us either. The horizon of expectation widens. In those cases in which the film leads us to expect an *enormous* but at the same time *not very specific* threat looming somewhere and closing in gradually, the scene is prepared for the perfect conditions of dread, according to Edmund Burke: "To make any thing very terrible, obscurity seems in general to be necessary. When we know the full extent of any danger, [. . .] a great deal of the apprehension vanishes."

Burke's quote underscores the idea that an obscure and amorphous threat cannot be controlled by reason, whereas something visible becomes manageable. In a state of dread we never know if the danger might not potentially exceed our psychic means of self-protection—precisely because we cannot perceive it and thus mentally categorize it yet. Thus our epistemic deficit in dread scenes creates an expectation of the worst: the unknown, potentially enormous horror that might await us at the end of the scene is particularly terrifying because the threat is only hinted at but not clearly spelled out. The as-yet unimaginable horror might overwhelm our rational selves. (Note that this fear of the unseen does not evoke a form of visualizing imagination, as in the case of suggested horror. I will elaborate on the non-visualizing anticipation of dread.) Conversely, the longer we perceive the horrifying moving-images, the easier we can categorize them and the less threatening they become. This is why splatter films often tend toward parody or the grotesque.

During intense moments of dread the viewer is deeply immersed in the filmic world and the phenomenological distance is—once again—reduced. However, unlike in shock the viewer is not 'approached' by the film, but seems to 'advance' towards the filmic world. Dread presumably enables the strongest form of immersion in all cinema. First, because of *spatial* immersion: even though visual access is often strongly restricted, there is almost always movement *into* or *through* space, as when a character walks into a house or through a cellar. The filmic space thus develops a kind of undertow, 'sucking' the viewer in. Moreover, since these scenes often take place in the dark, the diegetic darkness spills over into the auditorium, making the boundary between filmic world and reality more permissible. As Richard Dyer notes about *Seven*, a particularly dark movie: "Seen in ideal conditions (a silver print [which provides rich blacks and desaturated colors J.H.] in a properly darkened auditorium), it should be impossible to discern the contours of the screen, the film's darkness reaching out to embrace us."[9] Second, due to *temporal* immersion: dread scenes are much more extended than scenes of shock or horror. Since the viewer cautiously scans the temporal horizon for potential ruptures, the scene becomes highly teleological, thus thickening inner-time experience. Third, as a result of *emotional* immersion: since we expect something frightening coming up, we are glued to the screen and captivated emotionally in anticipatory fear. Consequently, movies that rely predominantly on dread will, as a whole, be more immersive than those that first and foremost make use of aesthetic strategies like horror or shock.

Anticipatory types of fear are currently included in the larger category of suspense, a category that *can* but *does not need to* involve fear. Deborah Knight and George McKnight, for instance, define: "Suspense relies upon the audience's strong sense of uncertainty about how events will play out. This focused uncertainty allows the audience to imagine different possible outcomes that could impact positively or negatively on the characters. And the audience has to care which outcome obtains. The requirement of keen audience interest is why suspense is often associated with notions such as hope and fear."[10] On the face of it, there seems to be no major difference between their conception of suspense and my understanding of dread. Since I am particularly interested in the *viewer's* affective experience, however, a distinction between dread and the larger category of suspense precisely on these grounds seems not only defensible but mandatory. Downplaying the narrative side in favor of formal as well as experiential aspects will allow me to introduce this separate category.

Richard Allen mentions that suspense involves "the generation of a state of anxious uncertainty about what happens next."[11] I will show that "anxious uncertainty about what happens next" is only a necessary but not a sufficient condition for both dread and terror—two *frightening* versions of suspense—since both are experienced very differently. Dread's paradigm case is the alone-in-the-dark scenario—terror is best exemplified by chase-and-escape scenes. In dread the exact nature of the threat to the characters is still uncertain for me—in terror I know the nature of the threat, because I can perceive its approach. In dread I cannot judge the temporal advent of horror and shock (even if I expect it anytime soon)—in terror I can perceive how the threat closes in gradually and therefore approximate the time of horror's arrival. Dread is almost unmoving, quiet and slow—suspense is hectic, loud and fast. Dread creates an intense fearful stillness in which we hardly dare to breathe—terror evokes anxious agitation and inner acceleration. In dread we fear shock and a rather undetermined form of horror—in terror we are afraid of a fairly determined form of horror (but no shock!). In dread we are bound to our seats—in terror we sit on the edge of our seat. Describing these formal as well as experiential differences will be at the heart of this and the following chapter.

EXPECTING THE WORST: IN ANTICIPATION OF SHOCK AND HORROR

Expectation belongs to the crucial elements of cinematic dread. However, expectation does not mean certainty. We strongly expect *something* but never know what will happen precisely and if it will happen at all. One could therefore talk about *unknowing knowingness*. Expectations can be a cause for frustration when the viewer anticipates the wrong outcome or expects too much. But they are also the source from which variation and parody can spring. More than many other genres, horror movies and thrillers presuppose and play self-consciously with audience expectations. As we have seen, some of the most effective shock scenes occur when we anticipate something, but are fooled in the wrong direction temporally or spatially. The postmodern slasher films of the 1990s have pushed this envelope to an extreme. In a movie such as *Scream* tension not only derives from genre clichés—as when Casey Becker (Drew Barrymore) withdraws backwards out of the room, her back unprotected, and the knowledgeable audience expects the killer to attack her from behind. But the characters also comment on those clichés, as when Randy Meeks watches the movie *Halloween* on television and warns the Jamie-Lee-Curtis character on the TV screen: "Jamie, look behind you! Look behind you. Turn around. Behind you!" This scene is, of course, doubly ironic, since Randy—played by the actor *Jamie* (!) Kennedy—is about to be attacked by a killer himself.

But how come we expect something specific to happen in a movie that we haven't seen? Why is it obvious to us that a scene in which a woman rummages alone through a dilapidated house or a dark tunnel will—most likely—lead to shock or horror? As mentioned, we never approach a film completely uninformed but always with a certain horizon of expectations, shaped by the title (*Tales of Terror*, 1962), various forms of discourse (reviews, commercials, word-of-mouth etc.) and genre experience. Drawing on our emotional and sensation memories, we know from previous encounters with these genres that something frightening will occur and that the specific aesthetic strategy of dread will probably be part of this experience. But even if we came to the film wholly uninformed and with no genre experience, it is likely that we would anxiously anticipate the outcome of a dread scene. The film lies out explicit and implicit cognitive cues and also creates an atmosphere that is phenomenologically favorable to dread.

EXPLICIT CUES: NARRATIVE FOREWARNING AND VERBAL FORESHADOWING

Narrative Forewarning

Before a dread scene begins we are often informed directly through the development of the plot that something shocking or horrific will take place. The film has scattered advance references to events that will occur later in the story. These pre-information is called *cataphora*, which in most cases comes in form of a potential *danger* to the characters: the 'not yet' of a catastrophe or injury.[12] In *Alien 3* we know from previous scenes that the alien is roaming the prison on planet Fiorina 161 where Lieutenant Ripley (Sigourney Weaver) has landed, because a dog has been attacked by the alien. When a character discovers the dog in a dark hole inside the prison wall, it is a sure sign that something is imminently going to happen. This is all the more obvious, since the filmmakers have used a second form of narrative forewarning a little earlier in the film when the same character came across a slimy mass: the inclusion of a *mysterious object* or *inexplicable, ominous occurrence*. Last but not least, the scene plays with the anticipatory element of *repetition*, since it mirrors the killing of the dog. Similar, albeit slightly varying, events assume special significance, since repetitions brings to mind something that happened earlier. They provide extra information for interpreting events.[13] The narrative structures of serial killer movies (*Copycat*), slasher films (*Friday, the 13th*) and monster movies (*Alien*) in particular depend on the repetitive seriality of killing: the (in-)famous body count.

Verbal Foreshadowing

Before the dread scene begins, expectation has usually been raised by an explicit cueing strategy that I call *verbal foreshadowing*. Verbal foreshadowing can be distinguished according to two criteria. First, there are various grades of *communicative specificity*: the foreshadowing can range from rather vague to quite precise. Second, it can be differentiated according to its *temporal proximity* to the scene: the foreshadowing might occur early on in the film and distant from the dread scene; or it can be placed immediately prior to it. Often, the farer away the less specific and the closer to the scene the more precise it is.

Removed and unspecific verbal foreshadowing includes simple assertions like Detective Somerset's "This is beginning," announcing the serial character of the first murder in *Seven*. Or his "This isn't gonna have a happy ending." A more precise statement would be Somerset's comment on the first two murders: "There are seven deadly sins, Captain. Gluttony, greed, sloth, wrath, pride, lust and envy. Seven. . . . You can expect five more of these." This form of foreshadowing can be grouped as *rules* and *laws* valid within the filmic world. A similar form of verbal foreshadowing are *taboos* and *bans*: Since disregarding taboos and bans is such a common element of narratives, the viewer can always anticipate precisely the breaking of the rules as well as the ensuing consequences.[14]

While these examples of foreshadowing from near the beginning of the film are rather unspecific, the closer we get to the point of dread the more precise the information becomes. On the way to a serial killer suspect named Victor Detectives Mills and Somerset discuss if they had ever taken a bullet before—a premonitory warning that this might happen during the following encounter with Victor. The dialogue is placed strategically in order to arouse our expectations. Even closer to the scene and more specific is overt verbal information about the dangers a character is about to be confronted with. Such explicit information magnifies the threat, raises our expectations and enhances dread.

IMPLICIT CUES: DELIBERATE DISREGARD OF VISIBILITY AND TEMPORAL ECONOMY

Even minimally experienced viewers are intuitively familiar with Hollywood story-telling principles. In scenes of dread two of the most important principles—maximum visibility and temporal economy—are conspicuously inoperative. As a consequence, their absence works as an *implicit* cue. Even if less obvious and explicit than the previous examples, implicit cues effortlessly and pre-reflectively arouse the viewers' expectations.

Disregarding the Principle of Maximum Visibility: An Obstructed View

Hollywood movies characteristically grant us the best view. Through cinematography, editing, sound and mise-en-scène (figures, lighting, setting etc.) the spectator is put in a position to oversee and overhear the action from a succession of ideal viewpoints.[15] In scenes of dread this principle of maximum visibility is out of order; the spatial omnipresence of narration is restricted. In fact, the narration deliberately confines itself to a position that goes as far as minimum visibility. Consequently, it frustrates scopophilia and thus titillates the desire to see more. This stands in opposition to common practices in other Hollywood genres. As Richard Maltby informs us, "Hollywood space rewards us for looking at it by constantly addressing and satisfying our expectations in looking. We can take pleasure in looking simply because, in the benevolent space of a Hollywood movie, we repeatedly see what we want to look at."[16] Since withholding spatial information and frustrating our desire to see is unusal, we know that it must be done purposefully. Again, we are cued to expect something negative. Scenes of dread turn the generally safe (or benevolent) space of Hollywood movies into unsafe space, in which the viewer feels insecure.[17] As a consequence, time becomes accentuated: "Duration is energized by invisibility, by the inability to see all," in Mary Ann Doane's words.[18] But how exactly does the film manage to obstruct the viewer's visual access?

Cinematography: The camera knows several ways to minimize the viewer's access to onscreen space. First of all, it can refrain from revealing the setting as a whole by offering *no establishing shot.* According to the common editing pattern the space of a scene is introduced by an orienting shot and then broken down analytically into smaller units. Classical narration of space therefore aims at orientation.[19] This is what dread scenes try to avoid. Precisely because the ensuing events are supposed to remain indistinct, the space entered by the character must stay unclear as well. This strategy is supported by *tight framing.* The camera does not grant a sweeping vista, but remains close to the object. The camera tightly frames, say, Clarice Starling's face, withholding what she sees and consequently creating a longing for her vision. When the camera eventually gives in and grants us Clarice's point of view (either as a subjective POV shot or a slightly more wide-ranging over-the-shoulder shot), the relief is short-lived: the restricted field of vision immediately turns the situation 180 degrees around—we are curious about what takes place *behind* her. The specifically filmic dialectics of camera movement and editing are fully at work here: once something is shown, something else is necessarily hidden.

The tighter the framing the more weight is put on offscreen space. This becomes particularly obvious through the disconcerting technique of a camera slowly tracking back and revealing the presence of an unexpected character. This strategy assures that we remain aware of the limitations of any perspective.[20] More than usual, a disparity exists between what we actually see and what might potentially be visible. This discrepancy can also be underlined by the use of anticipatory composition.[21] In this case the camera deliberately leaves onscreen space empty. Since in dread scenes the unbalanced composition cues us to expect the space left free to be filled by the killer or the monster, we are reminded of what we do not see. This strategy does not so much restrict our visual access than tell us again how constrained it already *is*.

Obviously, one important goal of restricting visual access is hiding the threat. Dennis Giles talks about *anticipatory vision* that shows little or nothing of the true object of dread: "The viewer senses a terrible presence in the articulation of imagery, but the images themselves display only an *absence* of the terrible object, or the possibility that it may become visible."[22] If the monster or killer is present at all in a dread scene, he or she is rarely shown in plain sight. We perceive the monstrous threat from behind or hiding in the shade. We glimpse parts of the body that do not reveal the killer's identity (often hands or feet). Or we assume his or her point of view. A specific case of obstructed vision derives from those threatening point of view shots that Dennis Giles has dubbed *prowling camera*.[23] In *Jennifer Eight*—just as in *Halloween*, *Sleeping With the Enemy* and countless other examples—we find a sudden cut to a somewhat blurred, shaky, handheld-camera view gazing from outside through a window into a house. Through conventionalized use we have learned to interpret this voyeuristic camera position as a point of view shot. Since the point/object shot (the view of what the character sees, in Edward Branigan's terminology) is *not* preceded or followed by a point/glance shot (the shot of the character's face), full vision is, again, obstructed and the principle of maximum visibility violated.[24] The prowling camera following the policeman (Andy Garcia) and his blind witness (Uma Thurman) signals the observing presence of someone the characters are *not aware of* and we, the viewers, *cannot identify*. The withheld identity of the subject whose vision is represented contains a creepy element: we are forced to see with the 'eyes' of a strange subject that cannot be categorized.

This shift from a disembodied, narrative camera to a character's point of view is immediately felt and conventionally ascribed to a menace. Hence the scene prepares us that something dangerous might happen anytime soon—to the character *and* to us. But even if the prowling camera scene remains a fake threat that logically cannot be ascribed to the killer, the dreadful incident is unsafely stored in the viewer's narrative memory: the principle of linear causality suggests that this scene must have a consequence. As Maltby laconically puts it, "In Hollywood, bombs are not planted in order to be forgotten."[25]

Editing: One of the most forceful pointers beyond the frame is the character's look. Threatened characters often stare nervously into offscreen space, thus drawing attention to the space we *cannot* but urgently *want* to see because we expect something important to take place there. In regular scenes this does not pose a problem: when a character looks offscreen, the following shot reveals what the character perceives (eyeline matching). Dread scenes often refrain from matching the eyeline—or at least protract it deliberately. In the chapter on direct horror, I have discussed the tendency of horror movies to turn around the logical cause-and-effect sequence of storytelling. Showing the reaction shot first and revealing the cause only after a terrifying span of time is exactly a case of delayed eyeline matching. But the problem also works the other way around: often we glimpse something important the character cannot realize, for instance someone approaching from behind. In this case the discrepancy between what we perceive and what the character observes does not create a longing for the character's additional knowledge, but makes us want to share our surplus of information with the character. The scene from *Scream*, in which Randy warns the Jamie-Lee-Curtis character, is a case in point.

Sound: Another strategy to underscore the significance of offscreen space and our restricted access to it is the use of sound. A character can verbally refer to something offscreen. Or sound can enter from offscreen via music, noise and speech. In fact, since in dread scenes very little can be seen *within* the frame, sound sources are in all likelihood located *outside* of it. If an active sound like approaching footsteps, a creaking door, or a monstrous scream comes from offscreen space, it automatically draws attention to itself—particularly in relatively quiet scenes of dread that cue us to anticipate a threat.[26] Michel Chion argues that we generally do not ask: Where *is* the sound? A sound 'is' in the air or, better, pathically felt as a perception. We rather tend to ask: Where does the sound *come from*? "The problem of localizing a sound therefore most often translates as the problem of locating its source," he writes.[27] Locating the source of sound sets our expectation into motion. We want the offscreen sound to be placed squarely within the image, so that sound and image match. If the source of sound is not revealed, a similar effect as in the case of the denied eyeline match entails. Since a character is present in most cases, one could talk about a *denied earline-match*.

Interestingly, expectations can also be cued by the opposite of sound, namely silence. Since silence in the sound film is something unusual, it stands out as a void that we expect to be filled—in scenes of dread usually by a shocking, rupturing sound. Ironically, films often use sound as a synonym of silence. Think of distant birdcalls, chirping crickets, ticking clocks or dripping faucets, but also reverberations added to isolated sounds (for instance, footsteps in a street). Another popular means to indicate silence as well as a character's nervousness is the use of a thumping heart in a subjective point of audition. These synonyms of silence can have the same effect as silence itself: they raise our expectation that the silence might soon be shattered. Last but not least, filmmakers can cue us to expect something negative by suspension: It occurs when a sound first heard is either insidiously or suddenly suppressed. The spectator might not consciously realize it, but pre-reflectively feels the emptiness and starts to behold the image more actively and interrogatively. Think of those instances when crickets suddenly stop chirping.[28]

Mise-en-scène: The mise-en-scène restricts vision and enhances offscreen space in predominantly two ways: through lighting and the choice of setting. The majority of dread scenes takes place either in dark, gloomy interiors or outside at night. Shadows prevail and nothing more than the characters' flashlights illuminate the scenery. Dread scenes thus prefer lighting that holds back what's lying in wait. In regard to setting, one finds a strong preference for labyrinth-like places with winding corridors or a dizzying arrangement of rooms as in old castles, tunnel systems or cellars. In *The Astronaut's Wife* (1999), for instance, the main character Jillian Armacost (Charlize Theron) has to look for a safe deposit box in a labyrinthine space with no windows and narrow corridors that seem to lead nowhere. Often furniture, pillars, debris or other visual obstacles obstruct the view. Characters frequently have to cross barriers or need to climb through small holes. They approach corners or walls that are hard to observe. They have to open doors, windows or closets, sometimes revealing painstakingly slow what is hidden. Such transitional places arouse expectations, because they link to other spaces which hold their own threats and possibilities.[29]

Ignoring the Principle of Temporal Economy: A Narrative Surplus

Scenes of dread not only restrict visible space; they also imply a delay of the next piece of action. Hollywood cinema generally functions according to a tight temporal economy: it excises the irrelevant and focuses attention on the important parts. Avoiding dead time it shows us only what we need to see.[30] Hence one of its fundamental strategies of temporal organization is ellipsis. Moreover, Hollywood narratives follow a causal linearity: the rigorous chain of cause and effect implies that what is shown must yield a consequence. In scenes of dread these principles seem out of play. We have to follow activities that usually would not be integrated and seem to have no consequence. If Hitchcock's famously said that cinema is "life with the boring bits cut out," these scenes confront us precisely with what the characters might judge as the boring bits.[31] To be sure, Hollywood movies often depict mundane activities like eating dinner or walking down the street. However, these 'boring' scenes are filled with 'interesting' dialogue. In dread scenes dialogue is conspicuously absent, simply because the person we follow is most often alone. Hence in *Malice*, we track the protagonist (Bill Pullman) down into the storage room of his old university building, where he wants to pick up, of all things, a new bulb. In *Mimic*, the camera records in great detail how a lone woman leaves her office, unlocks her bike and drives into a dark alley. In *Basic Instinct*, a detective enters an empty office building alone in order to meet an informant: we see him waiting in the elevator which for no obvious reason stops at every floor.

These scenes are characterized by a *surplus of narrative information* as well as a *delay of outcome* (required by the cause-and-effect chain). The surplus is put in between the cause and the effect. It stretches the scene, implying what in narrative theory is called *retardation*. Because most of the film follows the rules of narrative efficiency and causal linearity, dread scenes stand out and raise suspicion. Often the longer the outcome is withheld, the more urgently we expect it to come. So when the film tracks a woman from the front-yard to the door of her house and then inside from the entry to the coat-hanger (as in *Sleeping with the Enemy*), we presuppose the rules of linear causality still in tact and infer that this scene cannot be inconsequential—otherwise we wouldn't see it.

Scenes of dread are therefore distinguished by a *lack* of spatial information, a *delay* of outcome as well as a *surplus* of narrative information. As a consequence, one could deem dread scenes as unnecessary for narrative progress: if story-telling was everything, one could easily replace them. The content happening *in* and the information produced *by* dread scenes might be passed on by a remembering character, a dialogue or a newspaper headline. Why do we accept—and, in fact, *expect*—these scenes as essential parts? If it is true that viewers seek a sense of motivation or logical justification—why does no one revolt against something so ostensibly purposeless in terms of straightforward narrative progress? Bordwell would say: because of generic motivation.[32] We accept dread scenes as part of horror movies and thrillers, because such scenes *conventionally* belong to these genres. But this argument begs the question since it cannot account for their existence in the first place. I would rather argue that scenes of dread are the condition *sine qua non* for a specific kind of *emotion*.

This takes us to the controversy about the primacy of story-telling or spectacle in Hollywood cinema. Bordwell has variously and forcefully argued for a narrative approach.[33] Richard Maltby, on the other hand, rejects the neo-formalist focus on story-telling. For him, Hollywood movies contain both straightforward story-telling *and* non-narrative spectacle as crucial, pleasurable elements: both elements are held in an essential tension, and the movie exists as a series of minor victories of one logic over the other.[34] Comedies with their gag scenes and set-piece routines or musicals with their extended song-and-dance numbers can serve as examples of 'spectacular' genres. Erotic movies like *Nine ½ Weeks* (1986) and *Wild Orchid* (1990)—or erotic thrillers like *Basic Instinct* and *Sliver*, for that matter—with their extended sex scenes work in similar ways. And the same goes for horror movies and thrillers. Jeffrey Sconce therefore maintains that horror fans do not expect compelling narratives but "episodes of spectacle punctuated by brief narrative links." The narrative in horror movies works as a form of window-dressing for the core attraction of these films: episodes of intense excitation.[35] Even if aesthetic strategies like horror or shock might contain a kernel of narrative, it is hardly disputable that they represent prime examples of spectacle. But what about dread?

Scenes of dread merge narrative and spectacle into what one could call *narrative spectacle*. The narrative does not completely stand still, as in many spectacular musical numbers, but most of the information conveyed is dispensable. Considering dread scenes as narrative spectacle enabling an emotional experience would explain why we accept—at least most of—their logical absurdities. Consider the aforementioned scene in *Basic Instinct* in which a detective enters an office building alone at night. Why should the killer bring the elevator to a halt at every floor? Does she want to annoy the detective before she finishes him off? Does she want to give the detective's colleague (Michael Douglas) waiting outside in a car more time to realize that something is wrong? Or think of an extended dread sequence in *Halloween*, in which Michael Myers sets out to kill a teenage girl in a garden cabin. Why should he wait in front of the cabin—in plain view for the viewer, but not the girl—and then disappear for no reason? And what is the point of shutting her in—which implies that *he* cannot get in anymore—if he simply wants to murder her? Asking these questions seems beside the point precisely because logical story-telling is *not* the predominant purpose of these scenes. The villain does not act according to logic but rather serves an audience-directed economy of fear. Contrary to what I have said previously, then, the viewer *does* get the best view of the action insofar as the emotional ends are concerned. The spectator is put in a succession of ideal viewpoints not in terms of full vision but in regard to optimal emotional effect. This is why he or she must *not* see everything.

The narrative spectacle of dread works more *cognitively* than horror and shock. Since dread scenes provide an overabundance of narrative information, retard the outcome and block visual access, the viewer is cued to categorize them as dread. Consequently, he or she formulates a specific hypothesis about their outcome—a cognitive activity which sets up and weighs the probabilities of forthcoming narrative events.[36] While the viewer's drive to anticipate narrative information is generally strong and ongoing, in scenes of dread this urge is even higher. What is more, since dread scenes put time between the formulation of the outcome-hypothesis and the fulfillment of expectations, the delay can have a peculiar effect: the withholding of knowledge can arouse keener interest.[37] Up to a certain tipping point the delayed outcome creates more and more interest. It attaches attention to the movie and draws us towards the filmic world because we eagerly wait for an answer.

This cognitive *interest* cannot account for our enormous emotional involvement, however. Here it becomes important that we know—or, at least, strongly expect—a negative ending. Against the backdrop of our horizon of expectations, the presentation of 'boring' activities makes us anticipate something *horrific* or *shocking*. Ironically, for *us* these sequences are quite the opposite of boring. Since our lived-bodies are affected directly, the anticipation of shock or horror rivets us even tighter to the screen. Obviously, cognitive interest and emotional involvement cannot be separated. We are strongly interested in the outcome of the scene, because this outcome might possibly be overwhelming. At the same time, we are afraid of the overwhelming outcome since we have formulated a hypothesis about what follows.

The fact that indirect cognitive inference and direct lived-body experience are entangled becomes particularly evident in music. Horror music works both through conscious and semi-conscious *conventions* as well as a *direct access* to the viewer's body bypassing learned structures.[38] While horror music can certainly *signify* an object or an idea, it also works beyond signification with a materiality immediately felt rather than inferred. It often attempts a direct engagement with the lived-body through the use of the very high—think of the stabbing strings in the shower murder in *Psycho*—or the very low like deep stingers or drones.[39] The leitmotif of Spielberg's *Jaws* not only *signifies* the shark, but the materiality of the deeply pitched strings *is* also a threatening presence itself.[40] The following section explores this experiential level more deeply by examining an important if neglected aspect of the movies: filmic atmospheres. The threatening aspect of dread scenes is also felt *directly* because the film draws on atmospheric elements that *correspond to* and *support* experiences that towards the end of this chapter will be identified as typical of the phenomenology of fear: constriction and isolation.

CONSTRICTING AND ISOLATING ATMOSPHERES: SETTING, WEATHER AND DAYTIME

"What is primary in creating true horror is the mood," horror author William F. Nolan says.[41] Often starting with the music and the typography of the opening credits, the cinema of fear establishes a specific atmosphere. Frequently described in popular criticism, the experience of atmospheres is rarely a topic in academic debates.[42] This is unfortunate since atmospheric elements play a crucial role in supporting and facilitating our emotions at the movies.[43]

Even if the ontological status of atmospheres seems elusive, their phenomenological existence can hardly be denied. In contrast to the natural sciences, the descriptive method of phenomenology does not need to measure and quantify atmospheres in order to accept them as real. The only criterion is whether they are irrefutably experienced. We experience a specific atmosphere when we leave a busy market place on a hot summer day and sneak into the solemn, cool interior of a church. Waking up in the morning, we are immediately enveloped by the bright atmosphere of a sunny spring day flooding through the window. Upon entering a library full of deeply concentrated people, we might be infected by the determined atmosphere prevailing. In ordinary language we acknowledge these phenomena by talking about elating, depressing, comfy, inviting, erotic, or dreadful atmospheres. These atmospheres are gushed out spatially, but cannot be pinpointed locally. They cloak and thus pre-reflectively affect and modify in very specific ways those who enter them.

In the realm of art specific atmospheres can be created. Maybe more than any other artform the movies are well equipped to evoke them. This is what location scouts, set designers, cinematographers, score composers etc. are hired for. Yet aesthetics has neglected not only the *experiential* but also the *production* side. As a consequence, practitioners know much more about producing atmospheres than academics. Filmmakers proof with stubborn success that evoking atmospheres is no esoteric hocus-pocus, but relies on the persistent use of specific settings, seasons, daytimes, types of weather, music etc.

Atmospheres are less intentional than emotions proper. They are 'in the air' and often function as the basso continuo for more straightforward emotions—in our case, goal-directed dread. While dread is temporally directed towards the outcome of the scene, atmospheres exist as diffuse emotive colorations of the lived-body without concrete object. The atmospheric elements singled out in the following suggest a viewing experience of *constriction* and *isolation*. As such, they are not a necessary condition for dread, but fear can thrive against their backdrop since the experiences they enable are concomitant to those of dread. Hence atmospheres of constriction and isolation do not create but *facilitate* and *enhance* dread and are therefore almost always part of it.

We have to bear in mind, however, that separating atmospheric *components* from the *whole*, contains the risk of distorting matters. Even if these analytical cuts are a necessary precondition for our discussion, the various experiential aspects of setting, weather, daytime, music etc. are always *part* of the whole—looking at them independently, alters the *effect* of the whole. A woman walking into a cellar at nighttime, a dark corridor, or a cut-off cabin in an autumnal forest may cause many things, but they do not necessarily result in dread. In a different context these atmospheric components can enable quite different experiences. It is the integrative fusion of a number of constricting and isolating *atmospheric* elements as the vague basso continuo and goal-oriented *narrative* elements into a single whole that constitutes the experience of dread. However, if we do not separate these elements, we will not be able to analyze how filmmakers *create* atmospheres of constriction and isolation. Even if the sum is always different from its parts and the assumption of a simple additive principle would be misleading, atmospheres are nonetheless constituted through specific components.

In the section on the multiplex cinema (Chapter 2) I have demonstrated how the *architectural* space influences the viewer's experience. What I have not looked at is the diegesis, the *filmic* space that opens up on the screen. How the atmospheric choice of setting, daytime, weather and season affects our experience might not be evident at first glance. Since phenomenology often works through description by negation, let us imagine an unlikely scenario. Think of a bright, sunshiny summer day in a tranquil, picturesque landscape. We hear birds singing and see white horses peacefully grazing in the distance. A group of virile young men sing and drink; they laugh happily; some of them play soccer. Why do horror films and thrillers rarely evoke such scenery?[44] The settings explored in the following evoke an atmosphere whose concomitant lived-body experience corresponds to, supports and intensifies the constrictive and isolated lived-body experience typical of fear. As a consequence, we often *feel* immediately that something is not right. Just as the *cinematic* space of the multiplex, then, the *filmic* space has important ramifications for the viewer's experience.

In *The Poetics of Space* Gaston Bachelard argues that we cannot reduce our experiences of space to its 'objective,' analyzable, geometric features: "A house that has been experienced is not an inert box. Inhabited space transcends geometrical space."[45] The same goes for the literary, painterly, cinematic spatial worlds. The act of viewing makes the diegetic space 'accessible' to us. We can 'dwell' in it. And just like the space that we inhabit *objectively*, the space opened up by the film can have strong reverberations: there is a correlation between the experience of the filmic space and our lived-body space (*Leibraum*). Corresponding to the setting onscreen, our *inner* space might expand into vastness, but it can also shrink until we feel tight and constricted. The endless prairie in *Dances with Wolves* (1990) might be an example of what Bachelard describes as "such joy in looking that [. . .] we experience an *extension* of our *inner* space."[46] Quite the opposite takes place in most houses, *the* topos of the horror genre.

The Constricted and Cut-Off Place

The fact that dread scenes take place predominantly *inside*—be it a house, an apartment or a cellar—indicates the tendency to confine filmic space and thus create a corresponding lived-body experience. The production designer of *Seven*, Arthur Max, describes: "The claustrophobia of the film is reflected by the physical elements of the rooms to a large degree: the heights of the ceilings in the interiors are meant to squeeze you physically and emotionally. The ceiling's bearing down on you, I think, is very disturbing—particularly when you are in an environment where you are always expecting to find something horrible lurking around the corner. If you entered a room with ample amounts of space, I don't think you would have felt the same degree of menace lurking in those rooms."[47] Often this tendency is reinforced once the scene approaches its climax. The character walks a narrow staircase, creeps through a tight corridor, crawls through a shaft. Sometimes she climbs under a bed, hides in a closet, or locks herself up in a small bathroom. The same walls and doors that initially promise to keep the killer out suddenly reverse their function once the killer is inside: the walls now hold the victim in.[48] The threat in-creases while the freedom of movement de-creases. These places signal that the character—and we, the viewers, with her—move deeper and deeper inside and are even more enclosed and constricted. This constricting experience can be enhanced through stuffy air, leaving the characters increasingly less oxygen to breathe.

In many cases the constriction is accompanied by an element of isolation. Early on the film makes clear that the scene of action is far from any help. In *The Haunting* the ancient manor is hidden behind thick walls and gates locked by heavy chains. It is explicitly stated that the next town is nine miles away. And the caretaker's wife warns: "There won't be anyone around if you need help." Numerous movies such as *Virus* or *Deep Rising* use the restricted space of a ship on the ocean cut off from help due to distance, bad weather or broken radio contact. The feeling of isolation goes first of all for the character who is almost always *alone*. And this is for good reason: it certainly makes a difference whether the character faces the threat entirely alone or surrounded by twenty supportive characters. So we are often prepared for a scene of dread, when a character stays behind alone. But the isolation not only goes for the characters, but is also true for the *viewer* immersed in the isolated filmic world.

The Labyrinth

A related, frightening topos common to horror films and thrillers is the labyrinth—either figuratively as in the bewildering arrangement of rooms in a huge museum (*The Relic*, 1997), the long corridors of an old manor (*The Haunting*) or a space ship (*Alien: Resurrection*), the dark, constricted tunnel system of the New York subway (*Mimic*) or the Vienna sewers (*The Third Man*, 1949), the endless corridors of the Pentagon (*No Way Out*, 1987), the disorienting arrangement of cabins and storage rooms on a ship (*I Know What You Did Last Summer*), the narrowness of a boiler room full of pipes and tubes (*A Nightmare On Elm Street*, 1984) or in form of a literal labyrinth (*The Shining*).[49] The labyrinth is disorienting and disturbing, because of its spatial complexity. Again, the labyrinth supports a feeling of no way out, of being cut off from the world, of isolation. Jan De Bont, the director of *The Haunting*, wanted the characters not only to be physically lost in the old manor of the film, but also to feel emotionally lost. He says: "It had to be oppressive in its scale," adding "to the feeling of suffocation and fear."[50] Often, the dense, constricting, labyrinth-like atmosphere is not only evoked visually, but also through dialogue passages. "We're like rats—rats in a maze," one of the characters complains in *The Haunting*. And in *The Shining* Wendy (Shelley Duvall), alluding to the Brothers Grimm fairy tale *Hansel and Gretel*, says: "This whole place is such an enormous maze. I feel like I'll have to leave a trail of breadcrumbs every time I come in."

The Descent

Reflecting on the verticality of the house, Gaston Bachelard contrasts the "rationality of the roof" with the "irrationality of the cellar," height with depth, lightness with darkness. For Bachelard, the cellar constitutes nothing less than "the *dark entity* of the house."[51] While the stairways to the attic always go upwards, we *descend* into the depths of the cellar on stairs leading *down*. This feeling is very much with us in countless scenes that show a character's descent into a cellar or a cave under ground. Good cases in point are Clarice descending into the depths of Jame Gumb's cellar and down to Hannibal Lecter's dungeon-like cell. What is more, when we enter a cellar vicariously as in a film, we feel, in Bachelard's words, "that the walls of the cellar are buried walls, that they are walls with a single casing, walls that have the entire earth behind them."[52] Walls, we might add, that admit no sound to the outside world. When Clarice climbs down the steps to Lecter's cell, she passes five barred metal doors that are shut behind her: as a consequence, this buried cellar removed form the world outside manages to further enhance our feelings of constriction and isolation. Arguably the most extensive use of the descent was made in Wes Craven's *A Nightmare On Elm Street*, in which the protagonist Nancy Thompson (Heather Langenkamp) walks and climbs down six (!) staircases and ladders—from her room on the first floor via the ground floor and three different cellars-under-the-cellar to the boiler room underneath it all.[53]

To be sure, the constricting experience of filmic space derives not only from settings like the cut-off house, the labyrinth or the cellar, but also from the viewer's visual and aural access to them. Hence the elements described before in terms of obstructed view have a function beyond a purely cognitive signal by supporting a specific experience. The small shot scales are particularly important here. One of the prime means of constriction is the close-up (which Dennis Giles appositely dubs the "choker" shot).[54] Apart from tight *framing* tight *composition* is another important, so far unmentioned factor: films like *What Lies Beneath*, *The Dark Half* or *Dark Water* recurrently use the frame-within-the-frame shot that compositionally encloses the characters.

Figure 6.2 A constricting experience: Frame-within-the-frame shot from *Dark Water*.

Summarizing, one could say that the constricted filmic space the viewer immerses him- or herself in is defined visually by *what* setting is shown *how*. This is not the whole story though. Obviously diegetic and non-diegetic noise and music play an important role as well. Sound is never simply additional to a scene. The oppressive atmosphere of the film *Seven* is not only due to its visual strategy, but also to the steady noise of cars, sirens, honks, subway trains, thunder ... Interestingly, a depressing atmosphere can also derive from *negative* sound—the deliberate absence of noise and music. "Even when you're on the exterior, you never hear a dog or even birds," sound specialist Scott Millan explains the strategy used for *Dark Water*.[55] And the filmmakers of *The Blair Witch Project* mention how they "deaden the woods more and more" by reducing the sounds of crickets and birds as each day goes on.[56]

What is true for diegetic sound also goes for *non*-diegetic music: it defines experience of space to a considerable degree. Perception of music places the viewer in a phenomenological (not geometrical) space. In music, spatially oriented terms like high, low, rounded, pointed, bright or dark have more than metaphorical meaning: they describe an experience. In the chapter on shock I have shown how the sudden blast of loud music—the 'stinger'—is experienced as a pointed stab. Similarly, the musical space of frightening films is often experienced as confining. Think of the aggressive, pressing rock music at the beginning of *Seven*. In dread scenes that rely on music we sometimes encounter the "tension ostinato, a loop of music that provides tension through cumulative effect" or its first cousin "the drone, where tension is built through anticipation," as K.J. Donnelly notes.[57] The *cumulative effects* of these musical strategies do not open up vast soundscapes, but can both be described as confining.

Endless Space

Even though filmic space in thrillers and horror films relies predominantly on constricted space, there are frightening films that take place in endless space. Prime examples are the desert horror of *The Hills Have Eyes* (1977) and its 2006 remake as well as the ocean movies *Jaws* and *Open Water* (2004). In films like *The Blair Witch Project* and *The Last Broadcast* (1998) a third exterior setting dominates the scene, namely the woods. The use of the woods as a dreadful place dates back at least to the German fairy tales of the Brothers Grimm. In the modern horror film it found its classic expression in *Evil Dead*, and more recently Eli Roth's *Cabin Fever* (2004) took advantage of the forest atmosphere. And even the commonly more urban thriller likes to go back to the woods—think of *The Vanishing* or *Kiss the Girls*.

Bachelard points out that the woods evoke something else besides what is offered for ready-to-hand objective expression: "What should be expressed is hidden grandeur, depth. [. . .] If one wants to 'experience the forest,' this is an excellent way of saying that one is in the presence of *immediate immensity*, of the immediate immensity of its depths."[58] In *The Blair Witch Project* it is precisely the sheer *endless* space of the forest that lies beneath the dreadful atmosphere of the film. This immensity is a specific immensity and very different from the one we experience in the prairie or under the blue afternoon sky. Why, then, is the immensity of the forest (as in *The Blair Witch Project*) frightening while the immensity of the prairie (as in *Dances with Wolves*) is not? In order to answer this question we have to keep in mind that immensity has little to do with geographical or mathematical data. While the blue sky is endlessly more endless than any forest could be, the experience inside the woods might cause deeper reverberations.

As Bachelard informs us about the feelings inside the forest: "We do not have to be long in the woods to experience the always rather anxious impression of 'going deeper and deeper' into a limitless world. Soon, if we do not know where we are *going*, we no longer know where we *are*."[59] In this respect it is quite fitting that the *actual* filmmakers of *The Blair Witch Project* talk about a road shown in the movie that "*descends* into the woods."[60] And one of the *fictive* filmmakers in the film says: "We're so damn deep in the woods." 'Descending into' and 'being deep inside' is where the experience of the forest originates. While the prairie gives you the feeling of standing *on top* and the sky creates an impression of being *under* their horizontal expansions, you are always *inside* the forest, enwrapped by its horizontal *and* vertical immensity. This is precisely the point of M. Night Shyamalan's *The Village* (2004). The threshold to the forest must not be crossed by any means: beyond it you are immediately *inside* the forest, enwrapped, as it were, by its frightening spell.

Moreover, the woods evoke a feeling of being cut off from the world. Hence in *The Last Broadcast* the narrator informs us that the protagonists ventured "into the loneliest of areas on a lonely cold day" and argues that "walking further and further into the woods virtually guaranteed a seclusion from civilization that would make the killing easier." Like the protagonists in *The Blair Witch Project* and *The Last Broadcast* the viewer can get lost in the deep immensity of the forest. 'Lost' is meant in both senses of the word here: in the sense of feeling left *alone* and being *isolated* from others and in the sense of being *disoriented*. Hence just as the labyrinth, the experience of the forest in *The Blair Witch Project* creates a feeling of 'no way out,' of being deep inside the unknown, of being *dis*-oriented.[61]

This impression is enhanced by the *invisibility* of the forest's deep and dark immensity, which propels our imagination of its expansion. The space of the forest prolongs endlessly, or so it seems, beyond the veil of treetrunks and leaves. In *The Blair Witch Project* this becomes particularly vital when the immensity of the forest is paired with the immensity of the night. In this respect one cannot overestimate the effect of the cheap Hi-8 video camera. Supported by nothing more than a small lamp on top and handicapped by its reduced depth focus (compared to the 16mm-footage also used in the film, but especially in comparison to a regular 35mm-camera), the video camera comes nowhere close to penetrate the depths of the woods. The only thing we can see is a dimly-lit web of twigs and branches in the immediate vicinity behind which the endless darkness of the woods opens up. Precisely because there is little depth focus, the immensity of the woods becomes even more graspable. Once again, our vision is constricted, even if the space itself seems to extend endlessly. This constricted vision enables a *depth* experience that we do not have in the prairie where vision can reach expansively out to the horizon.

The Blair Witch Project takes the intertwinement between viewer and film to an extreme. This goes especially for the recurrent night scenes in which we see nothing but blackness. Since the dark screen fails to illuminate the auditorium, the darkness of the filmic world enwraps the audience and thus correlates the worlds of the characters and the viewers. In one scene the scared characters wake up utterly frightened, because they hear the agonized voice of their friend Josh coming from somewhere distant in the woods. In this scene the screen is kept in complete darkness for 46 seconds. Just as the viewers in the middle of the multiplex Dolby Surround system, the characters are surrounded by terrifying noises. (Obviously, these effects are lost to a viewer who watches the film on a computer screen in bright daylight.)

The forest shares some characteristics with the immense depth of the ocean. The sea is a similar place of the unknown. Its immensity reaches much further than we can see, beyond an endless horizon. Most of it remains secretive and far away from civilization. Being alone out there can be a particularly isolating experience. I have mentioned the strategy to cut off ships and isolate the persons aboard through distance, bad weather or broken radio contact. Yet the sea knows other kinds of threat: the largely civilized woods in which we ramble are a tame place in comparison to the sea which can confront us with overwhelming natural forces and animal threats. Furthermore, in contrast to the forest the ocean has an immensity that not only reaches to the horizon, but extends deeply into the depth below us. It contains a dark world beneath its surface. When we swim, the greatest part of our body is literally immersed in an impenetrable immensity, while the eyes remain above the surface most of the time. In addition to this visual discrepancy, we are nakedly exposed to and surrounded by a habitat that is not natural to us. The movies *Jaws* and *Open Water* play quite efficiently with these dangers. The camera often reveals what is happening above and under water simultaneously, presenting more to us than the characters can know. Plus: when the danger approaches, the characters cannot run away but have to swim—an ultimately much slower technique. Last but not least, scenes taking place *under* water have their own specific effect: through somatic empathy one might feel short of air—again causing a feeling of lived-body constriction. A remarkable case in point is a scene in *Alien: Resurrection* in which a group of characters spend almost three minutes of *film* time (and even slightly more of *movie* time) swimming and fighting under water.[62]

Daytime, Season, Weather

Turning to daytime, season and weather, we immediately note a preference for the night, fall and fog or rain. The predilection for darkness is obvious. It is often right there in the title. Think of *Wait Until Dark* (1967), *Dark Water*, *Alone in the Dark* (2005) or *Hell Night* (1981), *Fright Night* (1985), *Nightwatch* and *Night of the Living Dead* (1968). The darkness of the night literally obscures identity and difference. The security derived from distinction vanishes. The sense of spatial expansion turns vague, remains without clearly defined intervals and distances. Darkness cloaks us like heavy cloth, imposing itself upon us. It affects not only our sense of vision but the lived body as a whole, oppressing and constricting us.[63] This is why Robert Musil talks about the "affective corporeality of the night."[64] Hence darkness functions not only as a cognitive cue that impairs visual access (as argued previously), but it affects the viewer's lived-body directly.

And if frightening scenes take place during the *day*, they rarely admit the expansive lived-body experience associated with vast landscapes, bright sunshine and a lively spring morning. *The Silence of the Lambs*, for example, starts in an autumnal forest with leaveless trees, a grey, foggy sky and an absence of lively colors. In movies like *Jennifer Eight*, *The Bone Collector* or *Seven* there is constant heavy rain falling from a clouded, grey, oppressive sky. Everything is wet. The characters wear rain-drenched trench coats and leather jackets—heavy second skins that envelop them and impede their movements and breathing. Compare this oppressive setting to a light summer day, where one literally feels *light* because no heavy boots and thick jackets interfere. Until the very last sequence *Seven* is dominated by the drabness of a depressing late autumn atmosphere: no green grass, no blossoming tree, no vista, only streets and concrete buildings. Its oppressiveness becomes particularly obvious when put in contrast to the expansive experience of the Western and its offspring, the road movie, with their sweeping vistas and vast, sun-flooded landscapes. These genres epitomize freedom—not only because of their unconventional characters, but also as a consequence of the viewer's expansive lived-body experience resulting from atmospheric elements.

Another atmospheric element so common in horror films and thrillers that it verges on the cliché is the thunderstorm that breaks loose at the most intense point of the film. *Cape Fear*, *Urban Legend* and *Final Analysis* come to mind. When all hell breaks loose, it changes the atmosphere inside the house. It is as if a second wall was added, a natural, stormy wall that makes it impossible to escape. The house besieged by a storm is confronted by the combined loudness of wind, rain and thunder. Moreover, the house adds its own uncanny noises: creaking doors, groaning stairways, banging windows. The house, often haunted before, seems to come fully alive now. Rather than protecting the people inside, it attacks its inmates. Doors slam shut, windows won't open, phone lines are dead, thus further isolating the occupants. One of the most overused elements is the house that withholds electricity. How many films have we seen in which a characters tries to switch on the light in vain? It is as if the house wanted to add its own element of darkness, restricted space and isolation.

A VULNERABLE STILLNESS: LAYING THE GROUND FOR THE SHOCKING FIGURE

Apart from explicit cues like narrative forewarning and verbal foreshadowing, implicit cues such as the disregard of the principles of temporal economy and maximum visibility, and the creation of a constricting and isolating atmosphere, there is a fourth factor contributing to the strong expectation in dread scenes: stillness. With stillness I do not simply mean silence, but the calming down of the film on various levels. First, there is little movement within the mise-en-scène. The characters grope, walk, crawl, and creep up slowly. Often, they remain in one place, shying away or hiding from the possible confrontation with the killer. Furthermore, the camera slows down considerably. If it moves at all, slow pans or tilts filmed from camera supports are preferred. Moreover, the editing pace decreases. Particularly in comparison to the utter bombardment of cuts in terror scenes (explored in the next chapter) the shot length in dread scenes is quite extended. Last but not least, there is the remarkable quietude of the scene. Very little is happening on the soundtrack, because the characters whisper or do not talk at all; in fact, they often hardly dare to breathe. If it exists at all, music and non-diegetic sound effects are backgrounded. Although I have mentioned the tension ostinato and the drone, in many dread scenes the music fades out completely—at least, shortly before the climax. Hence sound is often diegetic, coming from offscreen sources like dripping faucets or approaching steps. An apposite illustration is the most terrifying scene in *Marathon Man*. The Dustin Hoffman character Babe Levy lies in his bathtub, when kidnappers quietly enter his apartment. Apart from diegetic sound coming from the water in the bathtub and some groaning and whispering this dread scene is completely silent. When the scene eventually turns into a hectic terror sequence with Babe Levy trying to flee his followers, we can sense most clearly the conspicuous discrepancy between the utter stillness of *dread* and the ensuing frenzied chase-and-escape *terror*.

The use of stillness has an important ramification. It allows for a stronger discrepancy between what takes place at the moment and what could occur any time soon. As we have seen, cinematic shocks work through abrupt and rapid visual change as well as a sudden and stabbing increase of loudness. Obviously, these swift changes are more effective when put against a backdrop of stillness. This is the reason why a *gradual* increase in loudness and acceleration (for instance, a character starting to run) is often experienced as relieving: the discrepancy between the quiet present and the potential burst of shock is reduced. Here it is important to note that the stillness is not only part of the film, but defines the audience response as well. Dread scenes are characterized by deep silence inside the auditorium. The viewers hardly dare to breathe; one could hear a pin drop. In gestalt psychological terms, the stillness of both the filmic and the cinematic space is the ground from which the figures of shock and horror radically stand out and thus make us all the more vulnerable. The viewer senses this—and therefore anxiously anticipates the shocking or horrific outcome. This anxious anticipation of shock and horror is more significant than our cognitive interest in the outcome of the scene. Hence one could find a potential solution to what Noël Carroll calls the "paradox of suspense" here: We can watch a dread scene a second and third time and still be strongly captivated even though we know the outcome, precisely because reactions like shock and horror cannot be fully averted by the simple knowledge of their advent.[65]

Taking together all these cognitive cues and directly felt warnings, the viewer is in a highly knowledgeable position, even in cases where a threat has not been unambiguously announced. As a consequence, an implicit (sometimes even explicit) wish to warn the characters arises. We want to tell them not to go into the empty house, not to linger in the dark alley, not to descend into the basement. Dread scenes often evoke a "Don't go there!" response.

ENGAGING CHARACTERS: THE ROLE OF EMPATHY AND SYMPATHY

A fifth factor looming large in creating fearful expectations is our engagement with characters. The significance of character engagement was alluded to occasionally, and in the passages on painful somatic empathy (in Chapter 3) I addressed it more explicitly. Even if this study is an attempt to get away from a *purely* character-centered theory of response, this is clearly not to suggest that my account could do without the notions of empathy and sympathy.

Empathy

Empathizing with a character in a dread scene creates a heightened awareness of an impending threat and thus puts another layer on top of our anticipatory fear precisely because this character is often afraid to expect something *him-* or *herself*. To put it differently, the viewer fearfully anticipates because he or she empathizes with someone who fearfully anticipates. Think of Clarice Starling descending into the basement of serial killer Jame

Gumb. Her eyes are wide open, scanning frantically the surroundings or staring ahead in frightened attention. Her face is distorted, with an anxious look. She trembles and moves slowly, step by careful step, clutching the gun she holds in front of her. Her body is tense, while she advances half determined, half reluctantly. Sometimes her movements become nervous, even frenzied. Sweat gradually gathers on her face. She breathes unnaturally, at times exhaling heavily and rapidly, at other times withholding her breath. When she talks to the kidnapped woman, she almost screams, her strained voice revealing intense fear. Thanks to Jodie Foster's brilliant performance and guided by the degree of alert on her face (particularly eyes, eye brows and mouth), the frightened body postures and movements, the unnatural breathing as well as the apprehensive vocal expressions and tones, the viewer is not only cognitively cued into a state of expectation (thus *understanding* the threat), but he or she also emotionally empathizes *with* the character (thus *feeling* the threat). Needless to say, I do not take over Clarice's emotions and affects *identically*. Fear of a *real* killer and fear of a *filmic* killer are clearly of a different type. It is enough that the emotions are *congruent*. Moreover, empathizing deeply depends on preconditions such as adequate duration of attention on the character and a sympathetic allegiance with him or her. In other words, empathy is facilitated by a character like Clarice that we relate to and like.[66]

Two forms of empathy come into play: somatic and imaginative. Both are intermingled in the film experience, supporting and reinforcing each other. And both can be separated only heuristically, creating a continuum from a more cognitive to a more autonomous response. First, there is *imaginative* empathy (in Murray Smith's terminology also known as "emotional simulation"). The viewer imaginatively takes over the perspective of the character, as it were imagining it from inside, in order to feel him- or herself what the character feels at this moment. This form of empathy contains a cognitive component, because the viewer has to judge how significant the object or situation is for the character. The gaps, with which the depiction of the character is necessarily shot through, need to be filled. Hence, like Clarice, the viewer evaluates the situation as highly dangerous. Like her, he or she wonders apprehensively where the serial killer might hide in his labyrinth-like cellar. Like her, he or she reevaluates the danger as even more frightening when stumbling upon a disfigured corpse in a grimy bathtub. Like her, he or she asks anxiously what might be behind the various doors. And like her, he or she speculates why the lights go out all of a sudden and what this might mean for the immediate future. Not every empathic scene works identically though: "emotional simulation takes on a larger role as a mechanism of discovery the more underdetermined the narrative representation," Murray Smith informs us.[67] Scenes of dread in mainstream Hollywood movies challenge the viewer's ability for *imaginative* empathy only moderately, since strong redundancy is produced by another form of empathy: the *somatic* one.

182 *Cinematic Emotion in Horror Films and Thrillers*

In comparison to its imaginative counterpart, somatic empathy functions on a more basic level. And while imaginative empathy is somewhat controllable, granting the viewer a certain leeway to terminate the process of empathizing with an unsympathetic character, pre-cognitive somatic empathy is hardly avoidable. As indicated in Chapter 3, somatic empathy comes in three forms: *sensation*, *motor* and *affective* mimicry. In sensation mimicry I involuntarily and without reflection replicate a similar sensation as the character onscreen: a slimy parasite entering his ear, a hot needle being pierced in her eye.

A similar thing is true for motor mimicry. In motor mimicry, we mimic the muscular actions of someone we are observing—think of someone running or throwing a baseball. If we follow the action closely and have a strong interest in its outcome, we might tense up, imitating the muscular control of the runner or player. Motor mimicry is therefore a weak or partial simulation of someone else's physical motion.[68] I have mentioned the urge to help a character untangle the cables of a ticking time bomb. Another famous example comes from Hitchcock's *Strangers on a Train* (1951), in which the murderer Bruno Anthony (Robert Walker) loses a lighter in a storm drain and desperately tries to recover it by reaching down through the iron bars, gradually getting closer, involving the viewer in frenzied motor mimicry.

In dread scenes motor mimicry implies the 'inner' mimicking of fearful body postures, slow motions and tense breathing—all of this contributing

Figure 6.3 Motor mimicry: Bruno Anthony (Robert Walker) tries to recover his lighter in *Strangers on a Train*.

to the viewer's own lived-body constriction. In contrast to the rushing and running characters in terror scenes (see Chapter 7), in dread there are little 'inner motions' precisely because there is so little 'outer motion' to be mimicked. While motor mimicry might not always enter our awareness, it often *does* manage to do so. Think of the stillness of the dread scene experientially mirrored by the literally breathless viewer—whence the experience of being 'bound to the seat' or 'captivated.' As a consequence, there is a strong discrepancy between what the character does (and we involuntarily mimic) and what we would *like* him or her to do, namely run away as fast as possible so that our hampered urge towards motion (resulting in constriction) is satisfied. When the character in fact starts to run, we feel relief.

Closely related to the inner replication of sensation and physical motion is *affective* mimicry, the phenomenon whereby we—pre-cognitively—mimic an emotion or affect expressed by someone else.[69] Since scenes of dread often rely on close-ups the prime access to the character's affective state is the face. Unlike the more imaginative form of empathy, Clarice's facial expression of extreme anticipatory fear affects us directly, pre-cognitively through emotional contagion. How is this possible? Mimicking Clarice's facial expression we participate in her fear via facial feedback without recourse to the more elaborate operations of imaginative empathy. Carl Plantinga explains: "our subjective emotions are influenced by facial feedback, such that the one who mimics a facial expression actually catches the emotions of the one mimicked. According to the facial feedback hypothesis, our facial expressions provide us with proprioceptive feedback which at most determines and at the least influences our emotional experience. [. . .] If I mimic a fearful face, it may actually make me fearful or increase my feeling of suspense."[70] Even if the mimicry of facial muscles is often invisible, at least a *partial* replication can be established *ex negativo*: When we follow a frightening scene, we do not smile joyfully, grin ironically or make a sad face but assume a tight expression similar (if not identical) to the fearful character.

Sympathy

In sympathy we do not share a congruent emotion, affect or sensation *with* the character (as in empathy), but feel *for* the character. Empathy and sympathy are not exclusive: we can be concerned for a character while also feeling with him or her. Unlike empathy, sympathy *itself* cannot create anticipation, because it depends on a narrative information surplus that enables anticipatory fear in the first place. But a strong sympathetic character allegiance often makes empathy more likely. And it raises the stakes the viewer invests in the character, thus *enhancing* the anticipatory fear for the character. According to Murray Smith, the "structure of sympathy" depends on three variables: recognition, alignment and allegiance. First, the viewer needs to *recognize* the character as an individuated and continuous agent.[71] This is unproblematic in mainstream dread scenes and can therefore be presupposed. Second, the viewer must be *aligned* to the characters by gaining access to their actions and what they know and feel. Differences arise in terms of how strongly the narration is attached to a given character and the degree of access to his or her subjectivity. Third, the viewer cannot avoid an emotional evaluation of the characters and therefore building an *allegiance*, ranging on a continuum from strong sympathy to passionate antipathy: the stronger the sympathetic allegiance the more we feel for the character. Note, however, that even if strong alignment in most cases leads to strong sympathetic allegiance, this is not automatically so. Sometimes we are aligned with characters that we find ambivalent if not repugnant. Smith explains: "To become allied with a character, the spectator must evaluate the character as representing a [. . .] desirable (or at least preferable) set of traits, in relation to other characters within the fiction. On the basis of this evaluation, the spectator adopts an attitude of sympathy (or, in the case of a negative evaluation, antipathy) towards the character, and responds emotionally in an apposite way to situations in which this character is placed."[72]

Most truly effective dread scenes rely on a strong sympathetic character allegiance. The reason why the final confrontation between Clarice and Jame Gumb in *The Silence of the Lambs* is so powerful certainly has to do with our strong allegiance to the young FBI agent (as well as our antipathy towards the serial killer). Once we arrive at the scene the film has not only devoted much time to her as the protagonist (thus establishing a strong *alignment*); the narration has also provided us with an unusual amount of information revealing the "desirable set of traits" that Smith talks about (thus creating a strong *allegiance*). Clarice is a young, good-looking, vigorous and bright woman with whom viewers share a similar cultural background. She is honest, open, and direct, despite her trauma resulting from the premature death of her parents and the subsequent childhood as an orphan living with loveless relatives. She has an unusual ability (and willingness!) to empathize with the *victims* rather than the perpetrators, a feature that reveals her sensitivity and caring. And she is eager and ambitious, following the laudable goal to overcome the disadvantages of being a woman from poor, backwoods origins. "One generation away from poor white trash," as Lecter puts it, she tries to climb the social ladder and gain recognition by becoming a successful agent. The FBI is, of course, a very masculine environment. Hence we side with her also because her superior Jack Crawford (Scott Glenn) takes advantage of her as a female bait; because she is being hit on by lecherous Dr. Chilton who torpedoes her efforts after she has rejected his approaches; because a psychiatric patient throws semen into her face and makes disgusting remarks; because Lecter sneers at her simple origins as well as her mediocre taste in perfume and clothing . . . In short, in order to make it in a socially stratified, patriarchal world, Clarice has to overcome gender and social obstacles—a difficulty to which many viewers can relate in one way or another. Moreover, our investment in a filmic figure often rests not only on the *character*, but also on the main *star* impersonating the character. In her first role after winning an Oscar for *The Accused* (1988) Jodie Foster was both a star and a serious, successful actress.

Furthermore, our concern for a character grows if he—but more often *she*—is vulnerable. This is the reason, why dread scenes abound in lonely, fragile, defenseless female characters. Before she faces Buffalo Bill in the final scene, the movie has underscored Clarice Starling's small height, her psychological trauma and her status as a rookie.[73] Often characters are barely clad, exposing their flesh and enhancing their vulnerability. Think of the shower scenes with isolated female characters in *Psycho*, *Dressed to Kill* or *I Know What You Did Last Summer*, the terrifying bathroom situations in *Fatal Attraction* or *Jennifer Eight* or the swimming scenes in *Jaws* and *Open Water*. Frequently, the vulnerability of the character is heightened by a psychological or physical handicap: he or she is blind (*Wait Until Dark*, *Jennifer Eight*, *Blink* [1994]), bound to a wheelchair (*The Texas Chainsaw Massacre*, *Alien: Resurrection*) or suffers from trauma (*The Haunting*, *Copycat*). In contrast, a strong male character of the Arnold-Schwarzenegger-type carrying a weapon and clad in protective clothing would not create the same amount of dread.

Again, sympathy shows how closely related other-focused and ego-centered responses are. As mentioned before, the strong sympathetic allegiance in general and the character's vulnerability in particular also raise the personal stakes for the *spectator*. The prospect that my strong allegiance might be cut any time soon by the character's decease enhances anticipatory dread, because I fear not only *for* the character but also apprehend my *own* loss. Consider Robin Wood's devastated remark about the sudden death of Marion Crane (Janet Leigh) in *Psycho*: "It is not merely its incomparable physical impact that makes the shower bath murder probably the most horrific incident in any fiction film. [. . .] Never—not even in *Vertigo* [1958]—has identification been broken off so brutally. At the time, so engrossed are we in Marion, so secure in her potential salvation, that we can scarcely believe it is happening; when it is over, and she is dead, we are left shocked, with nothing to cling to, the apparent center of the film entirely dissolved."[74] The protagonist is important to us, because he is cool like the Samuel L. Jackson character in *Deep Blue Sea*, because she is sexy like the Drew Barrymore figure in *Scream* or because she is played by a star that I admire like Janet Leigh in *Psycho*. When these characters get killed early on and rather unexpectedly in their respective films, it implies that I suddenly lack the *pleasure* and *spectacle* of the admirable, the nice, the cool character or the attractive, congenial actress. If we look at it from the opposite perspective, this personal loss helps to explain why slasher films with their high 'body count' often avoid strong character allegiances and do not contain stars: precisely because the pleasure of these films heavily relies on horror and shock rather than dread the destroyed allegiance to character or star would imply too much displeasure. The more vulnerable the character the more probable it is that we have to face the *personal* horror of gruesome moving-images (or imaginations). And the stronger our character allegiance the greater the horror we would have to face if he or she were killed.

THE SENSE OF AN ENDING: A DENSE AND PROTRACTED TEMPORAL EXPERIENCE

The chapter on direct horror has shown that we oscillate between fascination and fear, between intellectual interest and emotional captivation, between the pleasure and displeasure of fear. A similar description is valid for dread. On the one hand, the film carefully tries to stir our anticipation by revealing just enough to engage our fascination for what will follow, but not too much so that our hunger for knowing and seeing would be satisfied. The *restricted vision* and the *slowness* of the extended scene titillate our will to know. They relegate beyond the fringe what *is* and postpone the outcome of what *will be*. But apart from this curious fascination we are afraid of something largely unknown and amorphous that is yet to come and that might overwhelm us: the moment of shock that bursts into the vulnerable stillness of the dread scene or the devastating potentiality of an unknown, possibly never before encountered horror. From Edmund Burke to Stuart Gordon and Will H. Rockett a long tradition of theorists and artists has argued that the diffuse potentiality of *unknown* horror is ultimately more frightening than straight-out *perceptible* horror. Underlying their argument is the belief that something we can see is manageable, whereas unseen horror cannot be controlled.[75] In other words, the epistemic deficit of unknown horror suggests something far worse than what can be shown in a film, because something that can be shown is at least within the realm of what we can grasp. Dread scenes force us precisely in a position *away* from visual access as an effective means of mastery. Hence our urge to see also derives from the implicit wish to get into a position of control through visual access.

This epistemic deficit is also true for scenes in which we seem to be familiar with the threat. Take the showdown of *The Silence of the Lambs*. On the one hand, we certainly know that it is the serial killer Jame Gumb who hides in his cellar and poses a threat to Clarice. On the other hand, we obviously do not know the *exact* nature of her—and our—danger. Maybe the killer escapes through a backdoor. Maybe he slowly enters the scene and threatens Clarice with his gun. Maybe he suddenly and aggressively jumps around the corner with an axe in his hand and hammers it into Clarice's head. Or maybe something as yet unimaginably evil and shocking occurs. The fact that Jame Gumb was established as the threat changes our epistemic deficit of unknown horror only minimally, if at all.

As in the case of horror, both fascination *and* fear are present in dread—this time in their anticipatory variety. Will Rockett calls it the "moth-and-flame effect."[76] One senses the danger of being negatively overwhelmed, but is drawn to it out of curios fascination and the present experience of a bodily stimulation. Dread scenes are characterized by expectation and ignorance, curious impatience and the wish to be spared, desire to see it all and the fear of being overwhelmed. Just like horror, cinematic dread is not an experience of fear pure and simple, but a specific form of *Angst-Lust* that derives from the *potentiality* of being overwhelmed negatively. If the phenomenological distance vanishes and the fearful aspect becomes unbearable, however, we have to disentangle ourselves from the film—otherwise the pleasurable thrilling experience would be replaced by displeasure.

Precisely because we are so attentive and expect something to happen any time soon, dread scenes mark the opposite of the characteristic open-endedness of mere succession: they are highly teleological since they push towards the goal of the shocking or horrific outcome. This teleological element is so strong that we often experience the scene as unfulfilled when it stops without the expected ending. In other words, because dread is an anticipatory form of fear that is felt *until* the very moment it gives way to shock or horror (or disappears otherwise), it lacks closure as a gestalt without those other effects. This entails a double consequence. First, since we expect a *telos*, we lean forward in time and anticipatorily scan the imminent temporal horizon in 'search' of the prospecting threat. Second, since this delayed outcome is expected to be either shocking or horrific the experience of time in-between becomes more accentuated; the duration of time is both *protracted* and perceived as *denser* than average scenes. The experience becomes literally in-*tense*. Think of a clock on a desk. We experience its ticking very differently if we expect the tick-tock to continue monotonously for hours or if we know that a shrill, biting alarm will start anytime soon. In the latter case, we will not only await the outcome and therefore look ahead to it, but also experience a certain tension. Similarly, it makes a difference if a scene plays out rather uneventfully or if we know that it leads up to a potentially biting shock or overwhelming form of horror. In the chapters on direct horror and shock I have briefly hinted at the respective subjective temporalities. It is now—in connection with more extended dread scenes—that I want to take up the question of inner duration more thoroughly.

A number of concepts have been introduced over the years in order to distinguish various kinds of time at the movies. Laura Mulvey, for instance, knows three forms of "cinematic time": first, the "past of registration" to which the medium of film is able to refer qua its indexicality; second, the "fictional time of the story"; and, third, the present, or remembered, time of viewing.[77] In his discussion of time in Hollywood cinema, on the other hand, Richard Maltby distinguishes between *film* time and *movie* time.[78] The former describes the amount of time a movie requires of its audience. It is determined by the length of the film as well as the projection speed and can be objectively measured with a stopwatch. Hence the film time of Martin Scorsese's *Cape Fear* would be 128 minutes. Movie time, on the other hand, refers to the time represented within the narrative (and is therefore equivalent with Mulvey's "fictional time"). It involves flashbacks and flashforwards, ellipses, parallel narratives and slow-motion sequences. Hence the movie time of *The Silence of the Lambs* would comprise several years: from the flashbacks of Clarice Starling's childhood to her present investigation of the Buffalo Bill case. Within movie time one can further distinguish between duration of the *story* and duration of the *plot*. Story duration includes the entire time span of the narrative, including events referred to along the way or inferred by the viewer. Plot duration refers only to those events actually presented on the screen. Both plot duration and story duration can be deduced from the narrative. However, as helpful as these distinctions may be, none of these *objective* categories reveals anything about the viewer's *subjective* temporal experience.

In the majority of cases we are not conscious of the passage of time in everyday life. Subjective inner duration seems roughly in synchronicity with the objective time of the clock.[79] Occasionally, however, we become aware of time as a gestalt. In everyday life our experience of time often changes as we step from one realm of social reality to another, depending on the interplay of subjectivity and objectivity, of self and situation.[80] This is true for the movie theater as well: our temporal experience shifts when a terror scene follows an erotic scene or when a moment of shock bursts into a run-of-the-mill dialogue passage. Hence time experience stands out either when there is a marked *difference* to the preceding scene or when the temporal aspect of the scene *itself* is so striking that it moves from the background towards the center of our field of consciousness. It is therefore necessary to introduce a third temporal category: *experienced* time. Experienced time cannot be measured nor can it be inferred from something objective like story or plot. As a subjective category, it can only be described in relation to other categories. This largely neglected aspect of movie-going is central to the pleasure of frightening films.

Following Husserl's groundbreaking essay on internal time-consciousness, phenomenology has developed a nuanced description of how we experience time.[81] As often, phenomenology implies a critique of the objectifying models of the natural sciences, which argue on an abstract level remote from subjective experience. In this case phenomenology asserts that our experience of time does not correspond to the mathematical model of separate points on an axis of time. We do not experience a succession of isolated 'nows,' of momentary presences, of distinct experiential flashes. If we did, there would be no sense of duration and continuity, but only a staccato-like jumping from one experience to the next. In reality, the experience of time is not characterized by gaps but by varying forms of *continuous flow*, of *permanent goings-on*, no matter how strenuous our everyday life, how jagged the day-in, day-out. The various moments are always connected, even if some moments are more accentuated, more *out*-standing, experienced as thicker than others.

Perceptions, emotions and other varieties of consciousness are all experienced as spread out in time. Thus an event always comes into presence from the imminent future and then trails off into the close past. Three technical terms help to distinguish the different phases of internal time-consciousness: now-consciousness, retention and protention. According to Husserl's account, the 'now' of now-consciousness has a double temporal fringe. On the one hand, *retention* (the 'past-of-the-present-moment') points to what has passed: it retains the primal impression just elapsed. To be conscious of the present's occurrence is to be conscious of the "comet tail" that trails behind it, as Husserl famously put it.[82] On the other hand, *protention* (the 'future-of-the-present-moment') implies what is about to come: it provides the anticipatory horizon of ongoing, present experience.[83] Protention is not identical with projection just as retention does not imply clear-cut memory. Both are much more elementary and make more complex projections and memories possible. "What distinguishes retention from recollection, and protention from 'secondary expectation,' is not the length of their term but their functioning as horizons for ongoing, present experience," Dave Carr notes.[84] Depending on the situation, the immediate past and future acquire varying degrees of prominence.

This is very much true for our experience of films as well. Every filmic narrative (just as every scene *within* a narrative) has a distinct direction: it moves *forward*. Like a sentence or a melody, a narrative cannot be reversed but presses ahead continuously. Even movies like *Memento* (2000) or *Irréversible* (2002)—that seemingly inverse the direction of the narrative, but in fact merely change the order of the narrative's *content*—function accordingly. While this is generally true, we experience some filmic modes as more heavily inclined toward the future than those more deeply embedded in the present. Our attitudes can vary from a neutral act of awaiting the termination of the scene to lively anticipation. The crucial factor is the weight given to the outcome, or rather the intensity of the viewer's interest concerning the things to follow. Broadly speaking, Hollywood movies are films of action: they contain goal-driven heroes who necessarily prefigure the possible results of their actions. Art cinema, on the other hand, often features reflexive, psychologically ambivalent or even confused characters rooted more strongly in the present since the outcome of their actions is not crucial. The preference of different character types has consequences for the film's forward flow: the reflexive hero who often lacks precise desires and goals entails a looser linkage of events and therefore a more drifting quality of the narrative, whereas the active Hollywood hero has a clear objective and hence implies a tight causal chain leading towards an outcome. Broadly speaking, we can distinguish between a cinema of record, observation, delay and digression and a cinema of linear cause-and-effect action, between a cinema of the time-image and a cinema of the movement-image (in Deleuze's terms).

But even within Hollywood cinema the differences can be considerable, varying between genres, narratives and scenes *within* a narrative. Scenes of dread heavily lean towards the protentional side of our temporal experience. The reason can be found in its aforementioned teleological character. While generally the future is open and at least partially indeterminate, the *degrees* of openness and indeterminacy diverge. In our most *habituated* experiences the openness of the immediate future is rather limited, whereas in the midst of the most *novel* experiences the protentional future is comparatively open. Scenes of dread fall somewhere in between: on the one hand, the protentional future is open (we watch a new film after all); by way of the shocking or horrific telos it is simultaneously determined. Since the outcome will most definitely cut sharply into the continuous flow of our time experience—thus rupturing the comfortable being-in-the-world—we are wary of what is impending. Moreover, we cannot do anything against this narrative determinacy but fearfully anticipate the end by scanning the immediate temporal horizon.

To repeat, scanning the protentional horizon does not imply a full-fledged projection in which we imagine ourselves in a different situation. Calling to mind a future event and anticipating the immediate future as the horizon of the present are clearly not the same.[85] Protention functions as a future *horizon* for an ongoing *present* experience. A full-blown *future* projection, on the other hand, implies a displacement of the self: it is an active, presentive and anticipatory form of imagination and thus a different state of consciousness. In contrast to projection, we do not 'call to mind' a vivid presentation of the future with an image on our 'mental screen' and a sound in our 'mind's ear' when immersed in a scene of terror.[86] There is no anticipating *visualization* of the monster jumping from behind the corner and no *audializing* in advance of the knife entering the victim's body. We are too deeply lost in the film experience to actively untangle ourselves and form a visual and aural presentation of what might occur.

Nor does this protentional anticipation imply that we *project* a state of affairs in which we experience *how* it is to feel in a certain manner. Instead, we protentionally *anticipate* an upcoming lived-body experience. Such intuitive anticipations of sensuous effects are familiar from everyday life. Sitting in the waiting room of my dentist, I am afraid because I anxiously anticipate a great displeasure, but I do not visualize and audialize the doctor working with the drill in my mouth nor do I actively imagine-how the drilling will feel. Or, when I go running, I apprehend the strenuousness of the fast interval that I am about to start, but I do not visualize myself running faster. In both cases I fear—but I do not *pre*-live, as it were— a lived-body experience. Again, this underscores that in scenes of dread we not only fear for someone else, but always also fear for ourselves: we *apprehend* the unknown but potentially overwhelming impact of shock or horror (even if we are simultaneously *drawn to* it).

But the time experience of dread scenes is not only characterized by a strong inclination towards the protentional side. Dread scenes are also a perfect example of how film can manipulate absolute, objective time—or, rather, how it can lay bare the fundamental shortcomings of this concept. Few other aesthetic strategies can make duration so prevalent, thus separating subjective from objective time. Obviously, we do not consciously *reflect* on the characteristics of this time experience while immersed in the filmic world. But compared to the habitual flow of everyday life, time in dread scenes assumes a less peripheral position in our field of consciousness. Hence the pre-reflectively experienced aspects are available for phenomenological description after the fact: in comparison to the distinct, pointed and bound time gestalt of shock, with its marked beginnings and endings, the now of dread scenes unfolds more gradually. Unlike the shock that bursts and even explodes into consciousness, time in dread swells up and distends. And while the brevity of shock insists on the present now, the extended duration of dread leans towards the future. But shock and dread have something in common as well: in both cases time is experienced as protracted and dense.

Let us look at protraction first. Generally, there are three forms of time experience. First, compressed time: inner duration is *shorter* than objective time. Second, synchronicity: experienced time and clock time are roughly *equivalent*. Third, protracted time: inner duration is *longer* than objective time. This is easily understood if we think about entertaining movies that seem to be over much quicker than apparently endless, tedious films of equal length. However, pleasurable moments need not fly by but can be protracted as well. Dread scenes are a case in point. Michael Flaherty lists five sequential factors that produce the experience of protracted time.[87] First, a context that is characterized by circumstances departing fairly severely from the habitual flow of life: in dread it is our expectation of a shocking or horrifying outcome—in other words, a moment of danger. Second, there is an increased emotional concern for understanding the problematic nature of the situation and therefore a state of arousal which stretches experienced time: in dread this is manifest in our future-directed fear. Third, a heightened cognitive involvement with self and situation: glued to the screen we are highly concentrated on what is to come. We might hope for an instant positive resolution of the scene; or we may wish that the ending is stalled, since we expect it to be negative. In any case, the suspended end of the scene—whether positive or negative—achieves a considerable weight. As a consequence, we scan the temporal horizon in order to anticipate the danger of shock and horror. Due to this increased emotional and cognitive attention—point four—the stimulus complexity is raised. This, in turn, leads to the fifth point: the increased stimulus complexity of the situation creates a supercharged experience which is much denser than most other moments. Harking back to the end of *The Silence of the Lambs*: from the moment Clarice opens the cellar door, to the moment she shoots the serial killer, *film* time and *movie* time are identical. But which fully engrossed viewer would have thought that this sequence is—objectively—only six minutes long? Especially if you compare the scene to a funny dialogue passage in a Screwball comedy like *His Girl Friday* (1940) or *Bringing Up Baby* (1938), where time seems to fly by.

Flaherty's concept of protracted time needs elaboration, however. Since he lumps together eventful situations and uneventful moments like boredom, the distinction between *dense* (or *tight*) and *empty* (or *slack*) versions of protracted time is lost. While in dread—a clear-cut example of *dense* protracted time experience—we are highly attentive with a thoroughly narrowed focus, in boredom we concentrate on nothing specific; the field of consciousness remains without stable center. In boredom we experience time as empty precisely because there is no fearful anticipation of the things to come, no dense and tense lived-body experience, no heightened cognitive involvement. Boredom means monotony. Dread, on the other hand, is characterized by a gradual densification of time. The closer we approach the anticipated goal, the denser the time experience becomes. Think of the diegetic doors or closets mentioned previously: they intensify the scene because we reach the goal, expecting the killer behind the door or the monster in the closet. As W.H. Rockett points out, showing a door creates its own teleology, or rather enforces the scene's overall teleological character: "doors are meant to be opened, else they would be walls."[88] If these doors or closets turn out to be fake threats, the dense inner-time experience slackens immediately.

THE LIVED-BODY EXPERIENCE: FEELINGS OF CONSTRICTION AND IMMOBILITY

Apart from the protracted and dense time experience, scenes of dread also involve the viewer's lived body on a more specific level. Throughout this chapter I have alluded to constriction: atmospheric elements like setting, daytime, season and weather evoke it just as much as tightly framed camerawork or somatic empathy with frightened characters. But, again, lived-body constriction is not identical with dread. Setting, daytime, season and weather are not *eliciting* fear, but its concomitant lived-body experience of constriction *supports* the constrictive tendency of fear. In the chapter on direct horror I have expounded Hermann Schmitz' concept of fear as being an experience of *tension*, a feeling in which the constrictive tendency dominates the struggle with its expansive counterpart. Schmitz' German expression *Spannung* underlines the usefulness of this concept even more clearly than the English word 'tension': the German adjective *spannend* is exclusively reserved for films that are frightening or suspenseful.

However, in contrast to the dense, pointed fear of horror and the rupturing, piercing shock, the experience of dread is more extended. This might be a reason why critics and aestheticians often prefer dread to other aesthetic strategies discussed here: its extended, anticipatory character and its gradual coming-into-being grant the viewer a certain freedom to act, while the in-your-faceness of horror and shock is bound to an aesthetics of overwhelming. Moreover, intense moments of shock or somatic empathy are characterized by a strong constrictive attention-shift towards the body. During an experience of dread, on the other hand, I usually do not enter reflective consciousness. Even if I am deeply affected, I am first and foremost immersed in the filmic world. However, this is not to say that overwhelming dread cannot force its way into focal awareness. Two thirds into my first viewing of *The Silence of the Lambs*, a friend and I—both 16 years of age at the time—simultaneously turned our heads and looked at each other. After exchanging frightened glances, we shortly discussed the possibility of leaving the theater: we couldn't bear the terrifying intensity of the movie anymore. Even though we considered ourselves tough teenage boys, we had to admit that this film, so heavily based on dread, was overwhelmingly scary. Annette Hill notes that during scenes of dread frightened spectators use some of the exact same protective measures mentioned in terms of horror: "participants recall placing their hands over their eyes, turning away from the screen, and gripping their companion's arm . . . ."[89] But even if the fearful experience of dread does not enter reflective consciousness, it can be described after the fact. Much of what I have said about the *horrifying* experience of fear is valid for dread as well. This is particularly true for the constrictive element. Hence I will not reiterate Schmitz' argument at this point, but rather I will show how the constrictive experience can be traced otherwise.

First, in line with my argument about the revealing power of ordinary language containing corporeally-rooted expressions that are not mere metaphors but nutshell-phenomenologies, we might have a look at the way we describe frightening films. Our vocabulary for the cinematic experience of fear is dominated by expressions indicating constriction, immobility and imprisonment. We are 'seized' and 'captured' by the film. The movie comes across as 'gripping' or 'enthralling.' We are 'bound' or 'riveted' to our seats. The film is 'spell-*binding*' or 'trans-*fixing*' me. There is no dearth of examples from popular film criticism. Hal Hinson notes about Scorsese's *Cape Fear*: "It's a brutal, demonic film with a grip like a vise; it grabs you early, its fingers around your throat, and never lets go."[90] And Pauline Kael describes the way Brian De Palma plays with the viewer in *Dressed to Kill*: "He pulls you in and draws the wires taut or relaxes them; he practically controls your breathing."[91]

Second, this constrictive, immobilizing tendency can also be judged from postures and largely non-existent body movements. During scenes of dread we do not sit relaxed, but follow the in-*tense* movie motionless and in tension: we are paralyzed by fear. It feels as if we are pushed deep down into the cushions. Our hands grab the armrest. Others have their white-knuckled fists clenched. Some people bite their nails. Other viewers sit—their legs clutched—in a defensive, embryonic position. Again others grind their teeth. Scary scenes might even be literally 'breathtaking.' And we are speechless.

Third, it is not unusual that an implicit wish for an *expansive* change arises during the scene. The longer, the more intense, the more constrictive the scene, the stronger grows our desire for the opposite—an experience free of constriction and isolation. We yearn for the end of darkness and a place full of light. We long for an open vision that replaces the limited sight with panorama and long shots rather than close-ups as our preferred vistas. We no longer want the narrative to take place in a dark cellar or a dense forest but in the wide open countryside. We wish for the end of the character's isolation and his or her reintegration in a setting full of people. And: we hope that the brooding music or the leaden silence will come to an end, replaced by lively music or an encouraging soundtrack with chirping birds and laughing children.

But even if we do not have these implicit wishes *during* the constrictive scene, the dialogic relation between lived-body constriction and expansion becomes evident *afterwards*. This is my fourth point. We feel that constriction lessens and makes way for expansion when the scene is over. Suddenly the body posture is less tense. We might even change our seating position, something we did not dare during the constrictive and immobilizing sequence. It is not for no reason that we talk about *relief* once the scene is over and the weight of the terrifying experience is, as it were, lifted from our shoulders. Heaving the proverbial deep *sigh of relief* is a way to expand outwardly by exhaling. Freeing our lungs we 'let go' or 'let off steam'— oxygen withheld during the dread scene that had 'taken our breath away.' This is particularly salient if the endangered character in the previous scene has had a hard time breathing him- or herself, because he or she was overly frightened and immersed in water. As we have seen, the spasmodic in- and exhaling or breath-holding not only *indicates* the constriction of the character but via somatic empathy *affects* the viewer. Sometimes the viewer's relieved breathing-out even takes the form of laughter. Subsequently we take a deep breath that fills our lungs again. Hence the screenwriter Kevin Williamson notes that when the first intense sequence in *Scream* is over and another frightening sequence starts to follow: the spectators "have just caught their breath—and now here we go again." [92] Just like the experience of inner time, the lived-body experience of a frightening film changes from situation to situation, constantly moving in and out: relief follows constriction, tightening replaces expansion.

In my critique of catharsis I have mentioned that the viewer enjoys *both* lived-body metamorphoses: the movement into and out of constriction, out of expansion and back into it. The strong form of constriction felt in an extended dread scene in a dark, labyrinth-like cellar is countered by a deeply felt form of expansion if the situation is over and the protagonist escapes into the bright daylight of a summer morning. Quite the opposite happens when the shock intensification strategy that I have called 'disrupted relief' catches the viewer by surprise: the pleasurably felt expansion is countered by the shock's radical constriction. Again, this pleasurable in-and-out and up-and-down is the reason why the rollercoaster metaphor sounds so convincing when it comes to somatic types of film. Not surprisingly, these phenomenological metamorphoses take place most easily if my lived body is flexible and elastic rather than tight and rigid. Coming home from soccer training or running exercises, my body feeling tense and exhausted, I am often insensitive to the emotional and affective temptations of the movies.

THE SOCIAL EXPERIENCE: A COLLECTIVITY OF FEELING OVERCOMING ISOLATION

Another aspect of fear is the experience of personal isolation. This element was touched upon briefly when I mentioned that the movie *supports* fear by evoking an atmosphere of isolation. The film uses appropriate stylistic means and creates corresponding atmospheres, for instance by tightly framing an isolated character with whom we empathize and who is lost in a dark, cut-off, labyrinth-like place far away from help, confronted by a dangerous monster.

I presume that the experience of isolation in fear needs more elaboration than the readily accessible lived-body constriction. Since it is the cornerstone on which—at least part of—my argument about the pleasurable collectivity of scary movies is built, I will start with an explanation of what I mean by 'experience of isolation in fear.' Most emotional experiences put us in a specific relation to our social environment; they imply that we cannot be indifferent to others but demand responsiveness. Take joy: experiencing a truly joyful moment opens us to the world. We lose our inhibitions and fear of contact. We want to communicate our joyfulness. We feel an urge to embrace the world. When we are sad, on the other hand, we often withdraw. We rest in bed and stare at the wall or pull the blankets over our head. These 'opening' and 'withdrawing' tendencies are mirrored in our reactions to joyful and sad films. After a feel-good comedy we leave the theater in a chattering mood of hilarity, while a deeply felt melodrama tends to individualize us and constrict us in our own (pleasurable) sadness.[93] Another emotion with a particular forceful social aspect is shame. In shame one feels singled out, cut off from but also exposed in front of a—real or imagined—group. As a result, the individual tries to escape the piercing gaze of others by attempting to vanish or to gain renewed access to the group. Think of the wish to be 'swallowed up by the earth' or the subservient expression of giggling that tries to cover up the scream of shock mentioned in Chapter 5.

Similarly, fear is an emotion that carries a sense of personal phenomenological detachment, of feeling separated, of isolation from the world.[94] What Elaine Scarry notes about pain is apposite in case of fear as well: it brings about a split between one's sense of one's own reality and the reality of other persons.[95] Fear throws me radically back upon myself. The emotion centripetally constricts my lived body. I want to escape *Away!* from constriction—but cannot. As a consequence, I feel enclosed and separated. In fear the taken-for-granted being-with-others in which we feel at home literally becomes what the English translators of Freud have dubbed 'uncanny': *un-heim*-lich. A moment of transformation occurs, in which our social environment changes from a familiar home into a place in which we feel *un-home*-ly. Unlike shame, this separation does not imply a feeling of hostility from others, however. Instead, fear seems to spin an isolating cocoon around me. In shame, the others are opponents whose opposition we try to overcome by disappearing from their gaze or by begging for re-entrance into their world through gestures of humility. In fear, the others have simply gone or seem to be far away. As a consequence, fear is dominated by a longing for a return of the group or, conversely, a wish for our save re-integration. Fighting fear not only implies a tendency to flee (Schmitz's *Away!* urge), but to flee into the arms of someone else coming to rescue us from isolation.

The fact that we generally take for granted the familiarity of home in our—real or imagined—social environment can be judged by experiences in which this background phenomenon has disappeared. Children beg their parents to leave the door ajar when they have to go to bed so light can enter as a sign of mom and dad's presence. Waking up from a nightmare, they overcome the isolating experience of fear by crawling into their parents' bed. The psychologist C. W. Valentine once admitted that he feels a tinge of fear walking through lonely woods at night. His fear vanishes, however, when he carries one of his children.[96] Of course, the child cannot mean protection in a *physical* but very much in a *phenomenological* sense. It provides the comforting feeling of companionship that alleviates the isolation of fear. Obviously, the film experience knows its own examples of fearful isolation. In her review of *The Blair Witch Project* Mary Elizabeth Williams gives us a consumer-friendly advice: "It is, quite simply, a movie you have to see, and preferably with a friend. Because this is a film you're going to need to talk about when it's over, and afterward you definitely won't want to walk home alone."[97] This was exactly what I thought when I watched a horror film in a multiplex theater in downtown Los Angeles late at night. Surprisingly, I was the only one present. Under these circumstances even an otherwise stupid film like *White Noise* (2005) became truly frightening. I constantly had to turn around and check if someone else—friend or foe— was lurking behind me. Desperately looking for the reassuring presence of my co-viewers, I missed what is habitually taken for granted. Sitting in a movie theater alone is a highly unusual case, however. More often, the isolating experience of fear occurs in private surroundings, as this viewer comment underscores: "When I'm watching a film in my own home [. . .] it doesn't feel very safe. If I'm the only one there I can't watch certain films because I will become too frightened to carry on watching."[98] Don't we all know instances when we have watched a genuinely scary film alone and felt a strong wish for someone else to be present? When we had to call a friend just to hear his or her soothing voice?

It is here that the social experience of the movie theater becomes salient. Precisely because we feel phenomenologically isolated in fear, we look for personal contact or intersubjective reassurance to re-gain a state of psychological belongingness. In contrast to the solitary viewing position at home, in the movie theater the social element is always already given (not counting obscure multiplexes in downtown LA). During scenes of dread we do not turn into what David Riesman famously called a 'lonely crowd,' because the redemptive experience of the group is always near: we can overcome personal isolation by relating to others. These moments of sociality are rewarding, because we experience them not only as reassuring but also as pleasurably collective. To be sure, feelings of collectivity occur in other genres as well. The comedy with its collective laughter is the most noticeable case in point. What makes thrillers and horror films unique, is their peculiar *dialectic* of fearful isolation and relief through feelings of belongingness. The viewer can vacillate between both poles, with fear stimulating the yearning for the group. Call it the cinema of fear's complementary effect: just as red and green are brightest when put together side by side, positive feelings of collectivity can stand out particularly against the backdrop of fearful isolation.

Each viewer has a personal tipping point beyond which he or she feels unable to bear the fearful experience. When we feel too threatened by what we expect and hence the isolation of fear becomes unpleasant, we deliberately withdraw from the immersion to emerge in the cinematic here. However, rather than merely pulling out of an *unpleasant* individualized immersion into an *aversive* individualized state of extrication, we may more productively slip into a pleasurable *collective* experience. Thus dread becomes the basis of a *co-existentialist* rather than an *integrationist* account. Fear is no longer enjoyed in and of itself but serves as a negative means to a positive end.

How does the viewer counter the unpleasantness of fearful detachment? For one, the viewer may establish *direct* contact. Searching for glimpses of other frightened spectators and engaging in fleeting acts of gazing reassurance is one possibility; talking to one's neighbor about the frightening situation one is caught in can be another. Harking back to the terrifying experience of my first viewing of *The Silence of the Lambs*: when discussing the possibility of leaving the theater, my friend and I admitted to ourselves that we felt the same. This helped. We both stayed and enjoyed the rest of the film. Another way of creating closeness is reaching out for someone else. Catching hold of a hand or leaning against the shoulder of a partner are visible signs of mutual incorporation: by literally escaping into the hands or the embrace of another with which I momentarily 'fuse,' we create a quasi-double-body that is less isolated and hence less prone to fear. What is more, the personal touch reduces lived-body constriction and immobility: the viewer is flooded by an expansive feeling of belongingness and the movement temporarily ruptures rigid immobility. Expanding into the social realm the frightened viewer gets away from him- or herself—and thus soothes the *Away!* tendency: "A person who clings to someone else fearfully tries to relieve his or her own self by transferring it to the other self [. . .]. A person who fuses with someone else gets away from him- or herself," Hermann Schmitz notes.[99] Generations of men have tried to profit from this urge towards personal contact: it was—and still is—one of the peculiar male adolescent strategies of dating to take a girl to a horror movie, so she would come closer little by little during a scary scene. This is why critic Marc Savlov can call the film *Deep Blue Sea* "a terrific first-dater": it guarantees that your companion will be "grappling with the armrests and suddenly, perilously [be] perched atop your lap."[100] Among psychologists this phenomenon is called the "bonding effect of anxiety."[101]

The importance of small subgroups established via direct visual, aural or haptic contact cannot be overestimated. However, I prefer to take a closer look at those more comprehensive and complex audience groups that derive from emotional intersubjectivity. It is therefore necessary to give a short introduction into the field of emotional interrelatedness. How do we grasp the emotions of other viewers apart from direct contact? How do we gain knowledge that we *share* an emotional state? And how are we *influenced* by others emotionally? Following Max Scheler I want to distinguish three major forms of social emotionality at the movies: emotional contagion, fellow-feelings and feelings-in-common.[102]

In comparison to the potentially contagious emotional expressions of hilarity with its conspicuous three-dimensional displays (loud laughter, knee-clapping, stomping feet and back-and-forth movements of the body), scenes of dread differ markedly. While fear certainly 'communicates' powerfully to ourselves, it does not 'speak' in a clear and straightforward 'voice' to our cinematic environment. This is especially true for the surroundings of the multiplex theater where the enhanced hiding effect strongly hampers the communicativeness of emotions anyway (see Chapter 2). Hence emotional contagion through the fearful experience of other *viewers* seems unlikely. What might be the case in a situation of mass panicking, rarely if ever applies to dread scenes.[103]

The situation is somewhat different in regard to fellow-feelings (*Mitgefühl*), and it changes completely when it comes to feelings-in-common (*Miteinanderfühlen*). Scheler illustrates the difference between these forms of emotional intersubjectivity with a compelling example. A couple stands at the coffin of their beloved child. Both parents feel the 'same' sorrow, the 'same' anguish. It is not that the husband feels sorrow and the wife feels it also. No, they feel together: they share a *feeling-in-common*. Scheler calls this common emotionality an 'immediate community of feeling.'[104] By focusing on the death of their child, they relate to *one* phenomenological fact. Sharing a common emotional field, their emotional distance is reduced. However, they do not *consciously* reflect on the fact that they share these 'same' feelings. Their consciousness is mostly dedicated to sorrow and anguish. In contrast, their friend, who also attends the funeral, does not share this emotional field. He does not relate to the death of the child as much as to the suffering of the parents. Through an act of emotional understanding, he feels *for* them, but cannot really feel *together with* them. An emotional distance separates him from their feelings: instead of feelings-in-common he experiences fellow-feelings. The death of the child (the intentional object of the parents) and the suffering of the couple (the friend's intentional object) are *two* phenomenological facts.

If we apply these concepts to our discussion of dread, where can we pinpoint instances of fellow-feelings, and where would feelings-in-common show up? Picture a situation in which you are watching a boring horror film with your friend. During a dread scene that you couldn't care less about you suddenly realize that your friend fearfully peaks through her fingers and cowers in her seat. In an act of fellow-feeling you feel sorry for her or maybe even envy her strong emotional reaction. Just like the friend attending the funeral you feel *for* rather than *together with* her. Unlike the friend, you are not scared; nor do you devote your attention primarily to the film. What is at stake is more than a cognitive *understanding* of her experience, but it does not imply *sharing* her emotions. You are affected emotionally because you pity or envy her, but a certain phenomenological distance exists due to different intentional objects.

This is not the case in Scheler's 'immediate community of feeling,' where the members of the group have the same intentional object. The cinema is particularly suitable for this kind of group experience precisely because it privileges the sharing of the film as the prime intentional object. In comparison to literature, for instance, the cinematic experience relies predominantly on 'objective' *perception* out-there rather than 'subjective' *imagination* in-here. This is quite different in reading, where we not only remain solitary but also enter our own imaginative worlds—worlds that are hardly ever experienced as *ours* and almost always as *mine*.[105] The 'objective' un-stoppable unfolding of the movie in the theatrical surroundings also distinguishes film-going from the 'subjective' act of reading insofar as the latter can be interrupted at will, resulting in very different reading tempos. Even if a group of people sat in the same room and started reading Stephen King's *Carrie* together, they would hardly be shocked or grossed-out simultaneously. Furthermore, the group experience in the movie theater is facilitated by the fact that *we*, the audience, have all decided to come together and watch exactly *this* film.

To be sure, during moments of feeling-dread-in-common the viewers do not have to share *identical* emotions (Scheler indicates this by putting scare quotes around the word 'same'). Some will find the scene scarier than others. But *identical* emotions are not mandatory; it is enough if the viewers are *similarly* afraid to feel frightened *together*. If fear becomes the prevailing emotion experienced with individual nuances, there is a unity in diversity. While in fellow-feelings a discrepancy between me and you can be felt, the experience of feelings-in-common reduces the phenomenological distance. In dread this comes handy: distance reduction alleviates fearful isolation! Moreover, it certainly makes a difference whether there are three persons feeling in common or three hundred. Just as in Scheler's example it would relieve the common sorrow more effectively if not only the parents would suffer but also the three siblings, in the cinema we experience differently when seated in a crowded auditorium rather than alone at home: a problem shared is a problem halved.

How conscious are we about the sharing of an emotion like dread? Just as the parents at the grave, most of the time the viewers are not consciously relating to their feelings-in-common. It is a taken-for-granted background assumption of our cinematic experience—an assumption that becomes foregrounded in moments of crisis. In my description of the multiplex experience I have pointed out that sharing emotions is precisely what we expect, if only tacitly. If all others are immersed in the filmic world (or at least seem to be, because they behave according to cultural norms), we implicitly assume that they not only see and hear the same, but also think and *feel* alike. This is all the more true for scenes of dread. In the grip of a terrifying scene the audience is enveloped by an atmosphere of attention and captivation. This shared atmosphere is established *ex negativo*: through the absence of movements and sounds. Watching silently and in frightening anticipation the immobile and fearfully constricted viewers do not move in their seats. They do not yawn, laugh derisively or otherwise display their displeasure. They do not talk, look on their watches or show their distraction or even boredom in any other way. The background of pure silence is charged with attention and reverberates from one consciousness to the other.[106] The little that enters our focused field of consciousness underscores a common frightening immersion. Only if someone deliberately steps out of the group by commenting condescendingly on the intense atmosphere the background assumption of collectivity is shattered. But, importantly, the 'immediate community of feeling' is foregrounded also in another moment of crisis: precisely when the viewer is overwhelmed by fear and therefore *actively* intends the collective viewing situation in order to counter isolation. Actively reflecting on the collective experience, the viewer does not just enter into a state of mere individualized avoidance (e.g., looking away), but more productively chooses a state of collective *integration*. The likelihood of this active step increases the more frightening the movie. The vacillating movement between immersion and collectivity becomes more fluid.

The pleasurable collectivity in the shared isolation of dread creates a feeling of belongingness quite different from the forms of collectivity that I have described in the last chapter. Just as the lived body in dread is not as aggressively foregrounded as in shock, the social experience in dread does not enter consciousness as forcefully as in moments of startle. Temporally, spatially and emotionally immersed in the filmic world the viewer directs his or her consciousness predominantly to the *filmic there* and backgrounds the sharing of emotions in the *theatrical here*. In comparison, what I have dubbed the 'collective body' depends on a foregrounding of collectivity through joint, forceful emotional expressions, exemplified first and foremost by simultaneous screaming in shock, moaning in disgust and laughing hilariously. These are the moments when the social group united through feelings-in-common suddenly jumps to a higher level of collectivity. Since the 'collective body' depends on the *active doing* of a substantial part of the audience, however, it is not as easily established as the *ex-negativo*-collectivity of feeling-dread-in-common with its absence of movement and aural expression. Moreover, precisely because dread communicates less obviously, a pleasurable feeling-in-common is not as easily destroyed: while the expressivity of screaming, moaning and laughing can quickly produce a collective body for some, it can just as easily shatter the feelings of belongingness of others. If you find a comedy like *There's Something About Mary* (1998) utterly gross and stupid and someone next to you laughs hysterically, you realize that there are differences in thought and feeling between you and him. And if you remain completely unaffected by the torture scenes in *Hostel* or *Saw*, while the whole audience moans loudly—you sense that in a very specific way you do not belong to this group. In both cases feelings of collectivity evaporate or were not existent in the first place.

The scenes discussed in this chapter were hitherto identified as suspense. Yet, the current concept of suspense is overly broad and hence too fuzzy since it lumps together scenes that can be distinguished productively.[107] Scenes of dread with their formal and experiential characteristics occur sufficiently often to merit a separate name (even if dread still remains part of the larger category of suspense). Introducing the new subcategory of cinematic dread implies sharpening our understanding of the various shades of suspense. This will become even more obvious with the introduction of the second subcategory of suspense discussed in the next chapter: cinematic terror. Chapter 7 will be comparatively short since concepts that had to be defined previously will play a significant role again, e.g., empathy, lived-body constriction or inner-time consciousness.

7 Apprehensive Agitation
A Phenomenology of Cinematic Terror

[T]error is a passion which always produces delight when it does not press too close.

(Edmund Burke)[1]

So when God keeps the future hidden, He is saying that things would be very dull without suspense.

(Alfred Hitchcock)[2]

CINEMATIC TERROR: THE DEFINITION

- Fleeing a fugitive serial killer, a heavily frightened teenage girl runs across a dark, deserted small-town street. She arrives at the house of a befriended family, whose son she baby-sits during this last October night. While the killer closes in, the girl desperately searches her pockets for the keys. Since she cannot find them, she hysterically screams for the boy who sleeps on the second floor. Eventually, the lights go on in the boy's room. He drowsily asks who is out there and then moves on to open the door. While the killer approaches, the girl hammers against the door, constantly peaks over her shoulder to observe the stalker and begs the boy to hurry up. All the while the threatening situation is underscored by an insistent, rhythmical synthesizer sound. Inside the house, the still half-asleep boy slowly approaches the door. When he finally opens it, the girl rushes inside, and locks it immediately.
- Trying to escape a masked murderer who has cornered her in a garage, a young high-school girl remains stuck in the small opening of the garage door reserved for pets. The sadistic killer pushes the opening button of the electric garage door, and the girl gets relentlessly pulled towards the ceiling. Accompanied by a thunderously loud soundtrack with a dense, booming orchestral score, she screams, kicks her legs and frantically tries to remove her body from the fatal trap, all of which is shown through a rapid bombardment of cuts and, at times, extreme camera angles. Not able to move forwards or backwards, the girl gradually approaches her imminent death.

- Evading a horde of aliens a crew of astronauts is forced to dive through the flooded bottom of a spaceship. Struggling its way through the water, the group suddenly becomes aware of two monsters who swiftly gain ground. The comparatively slow and quiet scene all of a sudden increases pace and volume. As a female crew member falls behind and one of the aliens comes closer and closer, the music turns into a wild torrent, the editing into a violent stream. The panicking woman, gripped by mortal fear, tries to escape, swimming for her life—but the murderous alien inexorably closes in.

Taken from the movies *Halloween*, *Scream* and *Alien: Resurrection* these scenes exemplify an aesthetic strategy I call 'cinematic terror,' a frightening subcategory of suspense. In terms of narrative content the paradigm case of terror involves a vulnerable, extremely frightened character escaping from a threatening monster or killer gradually coming closer. Call this the chase-and-escape-scenario. Terror derives from the quick and loud perceptible temporal approach of a horrifying threat. Even if the outcome of the scene is as yet uncertain, a negative ending seems highly probable since the source of the danger draws near perceptibly and is therefore a known quantity to us, the viewers. While in chase-and-escape scenes the character is informed about the advancing threat, this is not always the case—think of an unknowing character rushing toward an abyss. The crucial prerequisite of terror is the fact that *we* know the nature of the threat, since for us it is by definition always perceptibly coming closer—"not yet there, but already present," in the words of Béla Balázs.[3]

As a consequence, the scene frightens us because the approaching threat relentlessly urges us to fear with or for the character *and* to fearfully anticipate a negative ending for ourselves: the confrontation with a scene of horror. In other words, similar to dread, terror is an anticipatory type of cinematic

Figure 7.1 Cinematic terror: *Alien: Resurrection*.

fear in which we both feel *for the endangered character* and fearfully expect a threatening outcome that promises to be horrifying—though not shocking!—to *us*. (The reason why the viewer, unlike in dread, is not afraid of a cinematic shock, will become obvious with further reading). However, since we can follow the temporal approach of the treat and hence are able to extrapolate the moment of collision as well as the kind of horror that might await us at the end of the scene, the horizon of expectations shrinks in comparison to the more open dread scene: the potential confrontation with horror is more determined. In light of Hermann Schmitz' advanced notion of intentionality we might therefore distinguish terror from dread as follows: In dread we fearfully anticipate a strongly expected, but *vaguely to moderately determined* threat to the character (concentration section) as well as our endangerment due to a vaguely to moderately determined confrontation with horror *and* shock (anchoring point). In terror, on the other hand, we fearfully anticipate both a strongly expected and *highly determined* threat to the character (concentration section) and our endangerment due to a highly determined confrontation with horror *only* (anchoring point).

In an essay on Hitchcock's strategies of suspense, Richard Allen distinguishes between a *pure* and an *impure* type: while in the former we are informed about the—most likely negative—outcome, in the latter the narrative is suppressive about what will happen to the character, even if something is fearfully expected.[4] If I remained purely on the level of narrative content, my definitions of terror and dread would overlap with Allen's definitions of pure and impure suspense. However, as previously indicated, fine-grained emotion categories should not be based solely on their intentional objects and appraisals but need to take into account experiential differences as well. Since they are strongly related to the aspect of film form and style, a definition of suspense needs to include formal and stylistic features—features that, in turn, are strongly intertwined with the narrative content. I argue that prototypical terror, as a frightening subcategory of suspense, is characterized by loudness and agitation. But why the frantic camera movement, fast editing, accelerated mise-en-scène and abundance of noise, screams and loud forward-driven music? These characteristics suggest themselves once we consider *frightening* escape scenes, chase scenes, rescue scenes or countdown scenes as the epitome of terror: they are not only scenes of heavy action, but also present scenarios in which time is perpetually running out. Hence acceleration and agitation are a logical consequence. A slow and quiet chase-and-escape scene might evoke all kinds of responses, but it is hard to imagine as being fearful.

Astonishingly, the level of film form and style has hardly played a role in most theories of suspense. This disregard is remarkable insofar as the same propositional content can have entirely opposed effects: a director can use the same narrative for thrilling or comic ends, depending on how he or she presents it. I see at least two reasons why film form and style have been ignored so often. First, theories of suspense often—explicitly or implicitly—tried to encompass *all* narrative media. However, a transmedial perspective ignores the distinct possibilities as well as limits of media (like film and literature) in favor of their commonalities. As a consequence, transmedial theories of suspense choose comprehensiveness over acuity. This is unfortunate. While there might be (rather strong) similarities in terms of narrative content and (rather lose) analogies in terms of aesthetic strategies, the experiential differences between suspense in a Stephen King novel and suspense in a Wes Craven film are considerable. Second, theories of suspense often—explicitly or implicitly—overemphasized the thinking part, thus ignoring the viewer's lived-body and temporal experience. Take Carroll's theory of suspense, the most influential in recent years: "suspense is (1) an emotional concomitant to the narration of a course of events (2) which course of events points to two logically opposed outcomes (3) whose opposition is made salient (to the point of preoccupying the audience's attention) and (4) where one of the alternative outcomes is morally correct but improbable (although live) or at least no more probable than its alternative, while (5) the other outcome is morally incorrect or evil, but probable."[5] Even though he talks about emotion, he is predominantly interested in the viewer's morally-inflected *cognitive* response: weighing between an unlikely-good and a likely-bad outcome. Treating the viewer as hardly more than a computing device asked to process the probability of two outcomes, in his strong reliance on cognition and narration Carroll, just as most other suspense theorists, misses the *formal* as well as *experiential* aspect. While dread and terror often involve similar intentional objects and appraisals, form and experience strongly diverge. In this chapter I will support the argument that in terror three aspects are particularly salient: a narrative, a formal and an experiential level.

Suspenseful scenes occur in many genres: westerns, detective movies, film noirs, adventure films, disaster movies and more. This can be explained by the fact that the larger category of suspense does not necessarily imply fear but can evoke less intense experiences as well. While in frightening types of suspense like terror or dread I am *scared*, in a non-frightening suspense scene I am merely *captivated*—for instance when a group of burglars screws its heist and tries to escape the police in a caper movie or when the crucial game is on the verge of being lost in a sports movie. In accordance with my overarching project of answering the paradox of fear, I will focus my discussion on those suspense moments that are aimed at *scaring* the audience, leaving out suspense as a general form of hope for a good outcome and apprehension of a negative ending. Moreover, according to Carroll suspense encompasses the movie's macro- and the micro-level: a film can generate suspense on the level of the whole narrative as well as on the basis of a particular sequence. Again, this is not how I will conceptualize terror. The following discussion is restricted to a description of the micro-level: I will look at terror only as a *situational* affective event rather than an overarching narrative structure.

THE NARRATIVE ASPECT: PERCEPTIBLE
APPROACH OF A HORRIFYING OUTCOME

On the level of narrative content, the viewer's knowledge of the perceptible temporal approach of a horrifying outcome is the first prerequisite for terror—be it a chasing monster, an abyss the character drives towards, a snaphook on the verge of loosening, or a ticking time bomb about to explode. What makes a terror scene frightening is the degree of *horror* at stake: the more, the scarier. And this is meant in a double sense. The potentiality of horror matters because I fearfully *anticipate* what could follow in the imminent future. As a vulnerable viewer I am threatened by horrifying—though not shocking—sound-supported moving-images. It clearly makes a difference in terms of fright if I expect a time bomb to tear apart the likable hero (resulting in my confrontation with violent horror) or explode somewhere in the desert, unnoticed by anyone (entailing no horror at all).

Yet in many cases of terror the prospect of horror also comes into play because I am horrified by the immoral and cruel intention that I have to observe at this very moment. In fact, horror colors many terror scenes with its dark hue, because I am forced to perceive a monster (or monstrous behavior): the masked killer in *Scream* chasing Sidney (Neve Campbell) through the house with his knife, Michael Myers hunting Laurie (Jamie Lee Curtis) in *Halloween*, the angry monsters closing in on the spaceship crew in the underwater scene from *Alien: Resurrection* . . . In those scenes I am not only frightened because I vividly anticipate the killer slashing an innocent girl in an immoral and brutal act of violence any time *soon*, but also because I am appalled by the immorality and cruelty of the monster's intention and behavior *right now*. Obviously, this only goes for scenes with a human or anthropomorphized opponent. When the threat derives from natural disasters, bad material, the character's own mistakes or pure bad luck, horror does not color the scene.

As a second precondition for terror the outcome must remain *open*—even if the probability of a horrifying end is quite high. If it is unambiguously obvious how the scene ends since no opposing option is left, there will be no terror. Interestingly, uncertainty about the outcome on the *internal* narrative level is sufficient. In other words, the viewer might bring *external* non-narrative knowledge about the ending to the scene and yet experience terror. This is evident in scenarios that are based on well-known historical facts. We experience terror even though we know that the showdowns in *Apollo 13* (1995), which are based on the disastrous space mission of the same name, and *The Day of the Jackal* (1973), which deals with the Petit-Clamart assassination attempt on Charles de Gaulle, end positively.[6] Moreover, it is undoubtedly true that people can experience terror even if they have seen the movie once, twice or three times before and are therefore acquainted with the outcome. Furthermore, familiarity with the workings of a genre does not prevent terror. Even if I am completely sure that the 'final girl' always survives the slasher film, I can be anxiously captivated by a terror scene. *External* knowledge exists as background awareness that usually does not interfere. Its existence in the background of awareness merely implies that we can draw upon it if needed. It lowers the threshold which we are not supposed to cross if the terror scene should work. Hence it can help to prevent terror if we *actively* draw upon it and thus deliberately disentangle ourselves from the state of fearful immersion. Until we have crossed this threshold, however, we are just as much in the grip of terror as if we had no knowledge about the outcome at all. An absence of external knowledge might therefore enhance terror only insofar as we cannot easily cross the threshold in order to reach safe grounds.

Note that the actual outcome is not crucial for terror (just as a dread scene is frightening no matter how it ends). Carroll is right in pointing out that suspense pertains to the moments *leading up* to the outcome but not to the outcome itself.[7] Look at the scenes described at the beginning of the chapter: while example 2 (*Alien: Resurrection*) and 3 (*Scream*) end negatively, in example 1 (*Halloween*) there is no collision between character and approaching threat and hence no horrifying outcome. Still, viewers will experience terror in example 1 as well. What is more, presupposing an information *surplus* on the viewer's part—the hallmark of Hitchcock's suspense definition—is unnecessary.[8] Although the *spectator* needs to know the threat, he or she does not have to know *more* than the characters. This can be gauged from terror scenes with characters informed about the approaching threat—as in most chase-and-escape, rescue and countdown scenes. In fact, we shall see that informed characters enable the viewer to empathize somatically and thus increase the peculiar effect of anxious agitation: The viewer follows threatened characters running away in fear with affective and motor mimicry.

Often the necessary *temporal* approach of the negative outcome can be judged from the diminishing *spatial* distance between the (relatively) 'good' character trying to flee and the (comparatively) 'bad' character or event closing in. As the threat approaches spatially and temporarily, danger and fright grow. Conversely, when the distance increases and the threat diminishes, terror decreases. This is the case first and foremost in *escape* scenes, arguably the most prevalent form of terror in horror movies and thrillers. The movies *Scream* and *Scream 2* contain a number of moments in which the masked killer chases the protagonist Sidney through various houses. She manages to escape his knife only by a hair's breadth, fighting him, shaking him off, kicking his stomach, ducking away, rushing up the staircase, slamming a door into his face, and managing to shut the door right in time . . . The intensity of the scenes partly derives from our growing *anticipation* of the impending moving-images and sounds of an innocent girl being killed in a violent, sadistic way. In escape scenes the escapee and the threat can be conjoined through crosscutting between two settings. Or they might be staged in depth—a particularly potent means of intensification. The camera captures the victim in the foreground and the approaching killer in the background, thus underscoring the ever-more imminent threat—as when

Figure 7.2 Chase-and-escape terror: Leatherface (Gunnar Hansen) and Sally (Marilyn Burns) in *The Texas Chainsaw Massacre*.

Sally (Marilyn Burns) runs away from Leatherface (Gunnar Hansen) at the end of *The Texas Chainsaw Massacre*.

A similar thing can be said about the *hampered-escape scene*, a recurrent version of escape terror. As the threat inexorably approaches, a character tries to flee but cannot: because the protagonist is injured, because she is tied to a railroad track, because the exits are blocked, because the car ignition does not work . . . The frantic character moves nervously, while crosscutting or staging in-depth indicate that the threat approaches quickly. *Countdown* scenes, on the other hand, imply that a single character or a group is running out of time. Here the diminishing temporal distance between the status quo and the approaching horrifying end can be judged from a deadline, a ticking time bomb, or an alarm that might go off any time soon. It also includes scenes that contain ropes and cables about to tear apart or snap-hooks and fixings on the verge of loosening. Terror is carried to an extreme when the horrifying conclusion comes within hair's breadth. Shortly before the film reaches the eventual horrifying point of collision, the distance between 'good' and 'bad' has diminished to a minimum, while the threat—and thus terror—has been maximized. One could call this particularly intense and stressful version the *in-the-nick-of-time scenario*.

THE FORMAL ASPECT: ACCELERATION AND AGITATION

However, the perceptible temporal approach of a highly likely horrifying outcome is merely a necessary not a sufficient condition. Prototypical moments of terror are defined not only by their characteristic narrative development, but also in terms of film form and style: they generally involve an *acceleration* or, more broadly speaking, an *agitation* on various grounds. While this element does not play a role in most suspense theories, it certainly should. In fact, the narrative development and the formal agitation go hand in hand. As we have seen, the narrative always involves some sort of contest about time—a contest that becomes more and more intense the closer the horrifying outcome approaches and the less time remains. This is true not only for escape, chase or rescue scenes, but certainly also in countdown scenarios where the opponent is time itself. Now, in order to underscore the growing intensity of the temporal contest the film needs to foreground the loss of time itself and therefore accelerates and agitates the scene: the less time remains, the more one has to speed up.

The acceleration and agitation of the scene can be achieved through various strategies. Among the most widespread and potent means there is, first of all, the dollying, tracking, craning, panning, tilting, zooming, shaking and under-cranking of the *camera*. The chase-and-escape scenes in *Scream*, for instance, are captured with a highly mobile Steadycam that follows the characters running through the house and up and down the staircases. There is, second, a swift increase of the *editing* pace and thus a rapid decrease of the shot length. In the example from *Scream* mentioned at the beginning of this chapter the cutting rate is extremely accelerated in comparison to previous scenes, with 23 cuts in 22 seconds.

And there is, third, the accelerated *mise-en-scène*. Think of the running, jumping, swimming, wildly gesticulating or otherwise rapidly moving characters, who try to chase, escape, or hide. Consider clouds of steam or smoke, darting flames, muzzle flashes, flying sparks, blinking lights, alarm signals or lightning flashes. They can set the filmic world in motion just as objects thrown or hurled through the air can create rapid movement within the

Figure 7.3 Extreme camera angle: The death of Tatum Riley (Rose McGowan) in *Scream*.

diegesis. Another potent means of accelerating the mise-en-scène are objects put between the rapidly moving camera and the rapidly moving character (or object) to be followed. When the Cary Grant and Audrey Hepburn characters are involved in a chase-and-escape scenario at the end of *Charade* (1963), for instance, there are fences, trees, bushes, railings, the outside wall of a subway train and stone columns that accelerate the scene.

A fourth important factor contributing to the impression of speed and agitation is *sound*—voice, noise and music in particular. We hear the often thunderously loud sound of gunshots, fast running feet, screeching car wheels, doors slammed shut or fearful characters breathing fast. We hear characters frantically crying for help, exchanging rapidly delivered dialogue lines, warning one another or cursing each other. We hear the voice of a board computer informing us about the impending self-destruction of a spaceship or the monster howling while approaching rapidly. And we hear, of course, (loud) music. The importance of musical accompaniment, the score, can be gauged by watching a terror sequence without sound: the degree of immersion is immediately reduced. This is why terror scenes are almost always under-*scored*. Music works so well as a form of attachment glue for a time-focused aesthetic strategy like terror, because it is a particularly time-bound form of art itself. The game of retention and protention is conspicuously at work here (in fact, Husserl used music as the prime example for his phenomenology of inner-time consciousness) and hence can be used to enforce the aspect of forward-leaning temporality in terror. Of course, filmmakers cannot use *any* kind of music. They have to accompany moments of terror with a particularly forceful kind of *forward*-driven music: marches with drums and winds; fast piano or string music; voluminous, dissonant orchestral sound; or insistent, rapidly hammering and fastening electronic beats (that sometimes connote a character's fast heartbeat) . . . Often, the music starts out comparatively slow, then gains pace and accelerates gradually until it eventually turns into a wild storm of rhythm and beat.

THE EXPERIENTIAL ASPECT: ANXIOUS AGITATION AND PROTRACTED TIME

The Viewer's Anxious Agitation

The narrative and formal aspects are linked to the experiential one: the viewer experiences terror in a state of anxious restlessness and agitation. It is precisely this specific and conspicuous lived-body experience that allows us to separate terror and dread. Again, category formation should build on lived experience. The frightened stillness in dread and the restless agitation in terror are sufficiently different to merit two categories. But how does the viewer's agitation come about?

First, all kinds of somatic empathy with the characters come into play and are wildly intermingled. There is *motor* mimicry: the running, jumping, fighting or otherwise frantically moving protagonist behaves very differently from a character in a dread scene. There is *affective* mimicry by way of the fear and even panic he or she expresses via face and voice. And there is *sensation* mimicry: it comes into play through the pain or exhaustion the character experiences or the lack of oxygen we feel in an underwater chase-and-escape scene such as the one from *Alien: Resurrection* described at the beginning. I would assume that this is one of the cases where the hard-science approach to film studies could support my point. The discovery of mirror neurons and the use of PET scans or fMRI images might yield scientific evidence to my phenomenological descriptions.[9]

However, it would be reductive to deduce the viewer's lived-body agitation in terror from character empathy alone. This becomes obvious in suspenseful car chase scenes. Think of the classic scenarios in *Bullitt* (1968), *Duel* (1971) or *Death Proof* (2007). It would be astonishing if the viewer's agitation derived wholly from the few scattered character shots. Even stronger support for this argument derives from scenes in which characters are entirely uninformed about an approaching danger—scenes in which a mountaineer's rope is about to loosen, in which a submarine is about to be hit by an undiscovered torpedo, in which a car is about to lose a wheel. While the characters remain relaxed because of ignorance, the tempo of the film often accelerates considerably. There might be crosscutting between the rope and the character. Or the camera might follow the torpedo rushing through the water, underscored by a thunderous soundtrack. In those scene we cannot empathize with the *character*; instead we empathize with the *film* and its accelerated editing, mise-en-scène, camera movements and music. What I have implicitly presumed in earlier chapters must now be stated more explicitly: the viewer experiences the film as a subject-object (or quasi-subject) of its own. Vivian Sobchack and—more recently—Daniel Frampton have vividly underlined this point.[10]

Sobchack argues that we perceive the film as a dynamic gestalt that is itself invisible but visibly expresses its own perception—the film is a visual subject-object. "The film lives its perception without volition—if within the vision—of the spectator. It visibly acts visually and, therefore, expresses and embodies intentionality in existence and at work in a world," Sobchack notes.[11] Likewise, Frampton asserts that the viewer feels the presence of an organizing and thoughtful agent or intentionality. It is this *filmic intentionality* that we empathize with just as much as we empathize with the characters. We do not merely feel with or for a character, but empathize with the film more generally. Conceiving of the film as a form of intentionality helps to account for and integrate into our experience the various forms of film style. Sobchack maintains that through its intentional perceptive activity and visible behavior the filmic subject-object expresses a specific personal style. Similarly, Frampton observes different types of "cinematic form of behavior"[12] If this is true, it certainly makes a difference if a film develops ('behaves') slowly and without a clearly defined *telos* or moves extremely fast towards a horrifying goal.

Thomas Elsaesser talks about the "energy emanating from the viewing situation" in the cinema: pinned to the seat the viewer cannot choose the motility he or she prefers, but depends on the movie's tempo and rhythm.[13] If terror scenes are by definition scenes of action (even though not every action scene is a terror scene), a strong discrepancy between the viewer's motionless viewing position and his or her experience of filmic movement and acceleration entails. While passively bound to the theater seat, the viewer is simultaneously 'set in motion' by empathically observing the onscreen action. But this discrepancy need not be a problem. Quite the contrary: often it comes as a relief. "Whenever for some reason or other the energy [of the viewing situation is] not managed by a film, or where tension is not 'objectified' in terms of conflict, suspense etc. the audience often produces 'fall-out' reactions, such as restlessness, aggressiveness, (irritation, protective laughter, verbal comment) or a feeling of boredom, claustrophobia," Elsaesser notes.[14]

In dread, the slow movement of the character and the film in general are somewhat congruent with the filmgoer's viewing position—which enhances lived-body constriction precisely because there is no 'inner motion' that compensates for the passivity of the viewing situation. In terror, on the other hand, the viewer 'runs' with the character or the accelerated film. Drawing on his or her embodied memory (or carnal knowledge) of how it feels to escape while bound to Sidney (in *Scream*) or Sally (in *The Texas Chainsaw Massacre*) in empathic motor mimicry, the viewer's body is strongly implicated. However, comparable to those nightmares in which one tries to escape but somehow is not able move on, the threat closes in and one feels not fast enough. Bodily tension accumulates and is released only once the scene is over or the character has managed to escape in the nick of time. Hence dread is defined by an experience of *immobility* and *dead silence*, whereas terror puts the viewer into a state of *acceleration* and *agitation*. While in dread the viewer is pressed *deep down* into and *bound to* her seat, in terror she seems to be sitting *on the edge* of her seat.

But lest we make the mistake of a purely mechanistic stimulus-response argument, let me hasten to add: just because there is a lot of action going on does not explain the peculiar agitated state of terror. If we think of montage sequences, music-clip-like intermezzi or purely spectacular destruction scenes, we have to conclude that not every fast or agitated scene is terrifying. In fact, the bombardment of a strong sound and image input can become tiresome. This is why formal *and* narrative aspects are conjoined in my account. In contrast to montage sequences or music-clip intermezzi, terror scenes are teleologically directed toward their solution: we strongly anticipate a horrifying outcome to the characters and ourselves (and are often horrified by a current act of immoral and cruel intention). The outcome is crucial not simply as a cognitive weighing of good and bad. We anticipatorily fear with or for a character who faces a horrifying end (the concentration section of terror). *And* we anxiously anticipate a strong, potentially overwhelming experience that might happen to ourselves: a moment of cinematic horror (the anchoring point of terror). Likewise, we are agitated not only because of character empathy, but due to empathy with the agitated subject-object of the film as whole.

If we take this argument seriously, there is an important corollary to my description of the agitated viewing experience: it could provide a more fine-grained answer to Carroll's 'paradox of suspense.' Carroll is perplexed by the fact that people can consume the same suspense fiction again and again with no loss of affect. How is recidivism possible, he wonders, if most suspense theories rely on the recipient's uncertainty about the outcome? Unlike Carroll, who takes into account both film *and* literature, I want to restrict my answer to the film experience. Here are three additions to Carroll's purely cognitive answer. First, in a cinematic terror scene the viewer is affected by pre-cognitive somatic empathy no matter if he or she knows the outcome or not: particularly the 'inner motions' of *motor* mimicry (running, jumping, fighting etc.) as well as the direct emotional contagion via facial expression of *affective* mimicry (extreme anticipatory fear) are hardly avoidable. The same goes for my second argument: the general acceleration and agitation of the scene and hence the empathy with the film as a subject-object. It affects the spectator despite prior viewings. My third point pertains to those terror scenes in which we are anxiously appalled by the sheer viciousness of the intention portrayed. The disproportional immorality and disturbing cruelty affects us and is therefore still valid even if we have seen this mean act before. Hence Carroll is right: the spectator who feels suspense on second and third viewing is far from irrational.

Dense and Protracted Time

Back in 1924 film theorist Béla Balázs argued that chase-scene suspense ranges among the most reliable effects of the movies because of its foregrounding of time. In his study *Der sichtbare Mensch*, which contains some of the most valuable early remarks on the phenomenology of time at the movies, he notes: "There is no other art that could represent danger like the movies. In every other representation it is either not yet there or already there. But the fate of the reels, the danger in sight, which is not yet there, but already present, is a special film motive. In chase scenes the movie can divide and stretch the minutes of fear and hope into visible dramatic seconds through its 'soon, soon!' and 'still not yet' and thus show not only the impact of fate but also fate itself in its silent flight through time."[15] No doubt, time is crucial in terror. The visible *temporal* approach of the threat pushes time to the fore precisely because the characters can never have enough of it. As in a sandglass their remaining amount of time is relentlessly decreasing. No matter if they flee from the bloody hands of the serial killer, try to keep the hungry monster at bay or rush towards the rescue of the endangered heroine—the characters are always short of time, losing time, running out of time. In countdown scenes the salience of time is particularly obvious: clocks or time bombs are recurrently on display.

Yet the viewers not only *perceive* the significance that time has for the characters, but also directly *experience* it in their embodied here and now. Obviously, no direct correlation exists. A fictive experimental film *thematizing* time by adding the displays of numerous clocks would not necessarily foreground the lived *experience* of time. However, in terror it is the experience of inner-time that becomes accentuated itself. Since the viewer hopes that the extremely rapidly and perceptibly approaching horrifying outcome might be averted as soon as possible, experienced time is *protracted*: the positive ending never comes fast enough but is always somehow delayed. Hence urgent questions arise: When is the killer finally shaken off? When does the engine start at last? When is the time bomb eventually defused? Again, Balázs is perceptible here. With regard to suspense scenes in Griffith films with a catastrophe approaching fast, Balázs notes that narrative tempo and formal tempo diverge and therefore create a protracted time experience: "The tempo of the plot and the tempo of the images diverge here. *The tempo of the plot seems to stand still* whereas the tempo of the images becomes more and more agitated and hurried. *The images are quicker and shorter, and with this rhythm boost the atmosphere to utmost excitement.* However, the plot does not move forward. This breathless state of the last instant is often extended to a whole act. The axe is already lifted up, the fuse is already burning, but a storm of images still rushes past [. . .]. With the accelerando of the second-long images simultaneously comes a *ritardando of the hours*."[16] Just like dread, then, terror foregrounds inner-time experience. But where do terror and dread differ?

Let us hark back to my example of the clock on the desk whose shrill, biting alarm will go off any time soon. We experience a difference when we don't know the exact alarm time, but know that it will start any second (as, so to speak, in dread) or when we know the time of the alarm and have the dial of the clock approaching the deadline visibly in front of us (as, so to speak, in terror). In both cases we know that something will occur and we therefore anticipate. However, in case of dread the approaching *telos* is invisible and its temporal arrival less determined. And this underdetermination is also true for the threat to both the characters and the viewers. In our fear *for Clarice* we have to take into account Jame Gumb's numerous options—options that could potentially exceed our means of psychic self-protection; in our fear *for ourselves* we have to anticipate horror *and* shock. In terror, on the other hand, the approach of the threat is perceptible and the outcome therefore more determined. In our fear *for Sally* we see that Leatherface approaches with his chainsaw and we can therefore limit the outcome options; in our fear *for ourselves* we do not have to anticipate shock but only horror—and type of horror that is itself more determined, because the horizon of expectations is foreseeable. As a consequence, dread differs from terror in its heightened form of anticipation: since the threatening object is clearly visible in terror, we do not have to scan the filmic world and its temporal horizon as thoroughly as in dread. In dread we focus intensely on a more *open* temporal horizon, whereas in terror we are glued to the *approaching* threat. Plus: there is often a somewhat stronger focus on the now in terror, whereas in dread there is the double *future* potential of horror and shock. While in dread we anxiously ask "*What* is going to happen? And *when* will it take place?" during moments of terror we fearfully exclaim to ourselves "*This* should not happen! Please escape soon!" Nevertheless, in *both* cases we experience time as extremely dense. In terror the narrative also pushes towards a *telos*: the time experience is leaning towards its protentional side (even if we are often simultaneously appalled by the viciousness happening right now). Just as in dread, the fact that the scene progresses unstoppably and irreversibly increases our emotional involvement: we cannot keep the source of threat at bay but visibly and mercilessly approach it. As if sitting in a rollercoaster on the way up, we are 'in the hands' of a machine whose grip we are unable to escape.

We finally have to come back to the question why terror involves the anticipation of horror but not shock. Hitchcock famously distinguished between surprise and suspense. Surprise implies the unanticipated, disruptive outcome of a scene: the sudden explosion of a bomb under the protagonist's table. Suspense, on the other hand, derives from the viewer knowing that something negative will happen: a bomb is planted under the protagonist's table without his knowledge.[17] In Hitchcock's account surprise and suspense are mutually exclusive. This is true—but not the way he thought. Hitchcock argued that the audience cannot be forewarned and surprised by one and the same threat; in other words one cannot anticipatorily fear an outcome and be shocked by the very same ending. For Hitchcock suddenness and unexpectedness are crucial elements of surprise. Since in terror the temporal approach of the threat is perceptible, it cannot suddenly and unexpectedly take us by surprise. However, as I have argued in my discussion of cinematic shock, we can strongly anticipate an outcome—and nevertheless be shocked. For instance, the film might deliberately distract us or the shock may be stronger than expected. Just think of the bomb-under-the-table scenario: Even if a countdown indicated the exact time of the explosion, the detonation might still shock us because of we are momentarily sidetracked or because the impact is stronger than expected (due to sheer loudness or a forceful-object strategy). This is certainly one of the reasons why *dread* scenes work so effectively: Even though we strongly expect a moment of shock, we are still afraid of its affective impact.

Hence shock and terror must be mutually exclusive in a different way. Since prototypical terror scenes are by definition accelerated and agitated, their high speed and sound intensity do not allow for the rupture of a rapid visual change and a stabbing increase of loudness that are essential for cinematic shocks (see Chapter 5). Speaking in gestalt theoretical terms, the discrepancy between the preceding moment of terror and the potential shock is not strong enough so that the latter could stand as a figure on the ground of the former. In contrast to the vulnerable stillness of dread, the agitation of terror makes us invulnerable to shock. Harking back to the example from *Scream* at the beginning of this chapter: the scene does not evoke the kind of anticipatory fear of shock known from dread simply because the rupture could not be effective enough. The scene is so loud and fast-paced that we intuitively feel: the figure of shock cannot stand out from its ground. What we *are* anticipatorily afraid of is the personal horror we would have to endure if the imminent and anticipated violent killing of the high-school girl became true—both in terms of character empathy and our own fear of horrific moving-images and sounds.

TERROR VS. DREAD: SIMILAR BUT UNEQUAL

Since the distinction between terror and dread might belong to the more controversial claims of this study, let me summarize the most important points. In both cases the viewer is curious and fearful about the outcome and therefore anticipatorily directed toward the *telos*. In both cases he or she potentially leans toward the future and scans the immediate temporal horizon. And in both cases the event is known to include a danger not only to the character but also to the viewer—which is the reason why he or she anxiously expects the outcome in the first place. As a result of this emotional involvement, both aesthetic strategies are strongly immersive. Much like dread, terror implicates all forms of immersion: *spatial immersion* since often enough the agitation of the scene derives from an accelerated movement through filmic space; *temporal immersion* since the viewer anticipates the horrifying outcome, while simultaneously hoping for a positive ending; *emotional immersion* since the viewer fearfully follows the action and anticipates the danger that awaits him- or herself at the end of the scene.

What are the main differences between dread and terror? While the paradigm case of terror is the chase-and-escape scenario, alone-in-the-dark scenes best exemplify dread. While in terror I know the nature of the threat due to its perceptible approach, in dread the exact nature of the danger that threatens the characters and me as a viewer is still uncertain. In terror I can approximate the time of horror's arrival, whereas in dread I cannot judge the temporal advent of horror and shock (even if I expect it anytime soon). Terror is hectic, loud and fast, whereas dread is almost unmoving, quiet and slow. While in terror we are afraid of a fairly determined form of horror (but no shock), in dread we fear shock and a rather undetermined form of horror. Moreover, in those cases where a horrifying monster chases the character with an immoral and cruel intention, the viewer's fear is not primarily directed to the future (as in dread), but remains partially rooted in the present: I am not only anticipating in suspense, but I am also observing in a state of horrifying suspense—the cinematic horror that shines through the monster's immoral and cruel intention colors my experience.

The results are different phenomenologies: a character slowly and quietly entering a lonely, dark place clearly yields a different experience than an agitated escape scene crosscutting from a panicking character to a furious monster. Phenomenologically, the former is defined by dead silence in which one could hear a needle drop: we hardly dare to breathe, let alone move in our seats. The latter is experienced as an inner acceleration and agitation that keeps the viewer on the edge of the seat. But if the *phenomenological experience* (as well as the formal and stylistic aspect) is different in both cases, why rely exclusively on the *narrative level* as a basis of category formation?

It has been a crucial if implicit assumption of this study that the aesthetic strategies discussed here—horror, shock, dread and terror—are not mutually exclusive but can be combined and permutated in various ways. This certainly goes for dread and terror as well. Often enough, both aesthetic strategies easily and swiftly succeed each other or even alternate. The alternation enables a quick succession of arousing lived-body metamorphoses that are experienced as pleasurable. What is more, precisely because dread scenes are dominated by stillness and quietude the fastness and agitation of the terror sequence can stand out (or vice versa): dread marks the ground for the figure of terror (or vice versa).

To be sure, the two categories blur at their respective fringes, which implies that we cannot separate them neatly once and for all. This is necessarily so since my discussion of categories relies on the prototype view: instances of a category vary in the degree to which they *share* certain properties, and consequently vary in the degree to which they *represent* the category. Since terror and dread—two types of anticipatory fear at the movies—are related, it is unavoidable that less representative instances shade into each other. Since my distinction between dread and terror depends strongly on narrative *and* formal differences, the categories can overlap once the narrative and formal ingredients are mixed.

Just take the scene from *The Pelican Brief* in which a group of killers chase a young law student (Julia Roberts) and a journalist (Denzel Washington) through a parking garage. The two amiable protagonists manage to escape the line of fire by a hair's breadth and hide quietly and hardly breathing between the rear of a car and a concrete wall. One of the killers slowly, cautiously and very quietly looks for them between the parked vehicles. The smooth camera tracks her slowly. The soundtrack becomes quiet. Only some ambient sounds and the approaching footsteps can be heard. The killer looks around keenly, when she spots the protagonists' reflection in an outside mirror. With her handgun in firing position she gradually comes creeping up, step-by-step, without the protagonists realizing it . . . How do we categorize this scene? On the one hand, the threat visibly approaches, and thus points toward terror. On the other hand, the scene contains an important feature of dread: the stillness of the scene, which enables the expectation of both horror *and* shock. (A moment of shock, indeed, brings the scene to a close when a dog suddenly starts to bark inside one of the cars).

Of course, granting that there are overlaps does *not* imply that the respective prototypes are not quite different. The fact that we cannot separate these categories neatly should not prevent us from categorizing. As mentioned, I consider it useful to find other, more fine-grained categories to describe a wider range of aesthetic strategies and emotions for which we hitherto do not have a name.

The phenomenological investigations have yielded two central pleasures of horrifying, shocking, dreadful and terrifying encounters with movies: a) precious moments of subjective intensity including some remarkable metamorphoses of the lived body and a foregrounding of time and b) valuable moments of collectivity. In the final chapters I will argue that these pleasures are intricately and inseparably interwoven with the current state of advanced modernity. The paradoxical problem why we experience pleasure in the face of fear can be resolved more convincingly if we do not simply claim pleasures *per se* but take into account the socio-cultural questions to which the fearful pleasures respond. Putting the cinema of fear into this larger framework, however, implies a change of perspective: from the *micro*-analytical poetics and phenomenology of threatening aesthetic strategies and their concomitant fearful lived-body, time and collective experiences to a speculative *macro*-analysis of the cinema's place within advanced modernity and its counterbalancing function vis-à-vis the transformations brought about by the processes of civilization and modernization.

Part III

8 Moments of Intensity
Lived-Body Metamorphoses and Experienced Time

If people choose to spend some time with a movie rather than with their lives, it must be because the movie gives them something their lives do not.

(Gerald Mast)[1]

Fulfillment of a human need for enjoyment and, in particular, for enjoyable excitement which balances the even control of feelings in non-leisure life is, I believe, one of the basic functions which human societies have to satisfy.

(Norbert Elias)[2]

INTRODUCTION: COUNTERBALANCING THE CHANGES OF ADVANCED MODERNITY

In his essay, "The Metropolis and Mental Life" (1903), Georg Simmel claims that faced with the unpredictable, rapid, overwhelming effects of the modern city individuals have to find modes of adaptation to maintain their psychic integrity. Against the intensified nervous activity of the city they develop their intellect as a protective organ.[3] In contrast to small-town and rural dwellers, people from the city cannot respond emotionally but have to react with blaséness and reserve. As a consequence, there is a blunting of sensitivity to the differences among things: everything appears in a "homogenous, flat and gray color."[4] Walter Benjamin's critical evaluation of modernity contains a comparable thesis about a lack of experience. In modernity individuals are confronted with constant fragmentary stimulations that he calls "chocks." Whether at the assembly line or on the battlefield, whether in street traffic or in confrontations with urban masses, in modernity the experience of "chock" has become the norm. Against this sensory bombardment the self erects "consciousness" as a constant stimulus protection. This protective shield prevents the integration of stimuli into non-superficial, penetrating *experiences*. Everything remains on the level of *events* instead.[5] The everyday world of modernity is described as a disenchanted realm of mechanistic and habituated actions. Performing routine habits, we dwell in the world mostly instrumentally and goal-oriented and are thus deprived of deep and penetrating experiences possible first and foremost under non-instrumental, non-routinized circumstances. Around the very same time, John Dewey expressed similar thoughts about experience: "Ordinary experience is often infected with apathy, lassitude and stereotype. We get neither the impact of quality through sense nor the meaning of things through thought. The 'world' is too much with us as burden or distraction. We are not sufficiently alive to feel the tang of sense nor yet to be moved by thought. We are oppressed by our surroundings or are callous to them."[6] Because of distraction and dispersion, extraneous interruptions or inner lethargy experiences are either inchoate; or they are dominantly practical and consist of overt doings that might be efficient but are too automatic to become experiences in an emphatic sense.[7]

Read after more than 70 years, these theories of modernity sound surprisingly well and alive. Blunting of sensitivity and reserve (Simmel); stimulus protection and routinization (Benjamin); apathy and automatization (Dewey)—however we describe the reactions to the overwhelming, accelerated effects of advanced modern life, in either case we face an overflow that we have to be aware of and respond to so that we often cannot integrate them and round them out into deep experiences. Even if objectively there is an overabundance of sensory stimulation, subjectively we often feel a lack of stimulation-as-deep-experience. As a consequence, life is frequently considered 'flat' and 'superficial.' In order to have a 'deep,' 'penetrating' experience it needs to be 'en-grossing'—or rather we need to be 'in' it. The 'deeper' the experience, the more appropriate it is to describe ourselves as being 'in' it.[8] We are lost 'in' thought; we are immersed 'in' a game; we are 'in' love—these are experiences with depth and therefore stand out from everyday life.

In order to get from superficial event to penetrating experience, a deep and complete interpenetration of self and the world of objects and events is required.[9] When this interpenetration of self and world is missing, things are *somehow* experienced but not in the way that Dewey vigorously calls "*an* experience": a vital, enduring moment that stands out from what went before and what came after.[10] In Dewey's understanding a true experience needs to be rounded out as a consciously attended, sufficiently complex and integral event without holes and dead centers so that its close is a consummation and not a cessation. He writes: "we have an experience when the material experienced runs its course to fulfillment. Then and then only is it integrated within and demarcated in the general stream of experience from other experiences."[11]

If we add the suggestions of Simmel, Benjamin and Dewey, we have to conclude that an experience is vital only if it is non-automatic and non-routinized; uninterrupted and without dead centers; integrated and rounded out; deep and penetrating. In modern life these precious moments are not easy to grasp. In the following sections I will look at our desire for vital experiences from two angles: *disembodiment* and *acceleration*. Disembodiment and acceleration are two of the prices to be paid for the numerous benefits that come with the processes of civilization and modernization. As a consequence, we have to actively pursue the pleasurable experience of the *lived* body and the deep experience of *time* by other means. I will argue that aesthetic experience—and the fearful cinematic situation of the multiplex more specifically—is one possibility our differentiated societies provide us to gain deep lived-body and time experiences. Encounters with aesthetic objects like frightening movies thus acquire a counterbalancing potential.

A similar thing is true for the transformations of collectivity, which will be at the heart of Chapter 9. Advanced modernity is characterized by a destabilization of institutions that in pre-modern and earlier modern societies helped to bind people together. Today, the social order of the nation state is in decline. The importance of class has long decreased. God and religion lose their binding power over their adherents and become a pastime choice among many. The tight knot of the family is untied. Local milieus are less closely bound. Active participation in community organizations crumbles. The once lifelong social frame of work as a vocation with special skills is on the wane . . . I do not claim that these developments follow a straight, linear trajectory with no pushs and pulls and possibilities for reversal. But I *do* presuppose a certain direction: the process of modernization de-traditionalized and, more positively connoted, individualized western societies. While the modern individual gains enormously in individuality and freedom, he or she has to find new forms of collectivity. Belongingness is also individualized.

Not surprisingly, the swift and ever-changing maelstrom of modernity has swept along numerous metaphors of transformation that oscillate ambivalently between admiration and condemnation, between gratitude and fear. In one of the most famous passages from the *Communist Manifesto*, for instance, Marx and Engels write: "All fixed, fast-frozen relations, with their train of ancient and venerable prejudices and opinions are swept away, all new-formed ones become antiquated before they can ossify. All that is solid melts into air . . ."[12] One consequence of this transformation of traditions is an oft-uttered, oft-described, oft-lamented feeling of disintegration and even loneliness—a feeling which the collective experience of fearful movies can counter with a particular form of post-traditional belongingness.

To be sure, there is a certain limit of how far we can take the counterbalancing effect of the movies. Obviously, the cinematic experience is transitory and fleeting. When the film is over after 120 minutes or so, we are released into our normal everyday lives. On the one hand, this is a blessing, because we *cannot*—and therefore do not *have* to—inhabit the filmic world for good. But there is also a flipside to it. Aesthetic experience, once finished, often leaves a feeling of loss. We look back with nostalgia precisely because the intense pleasures of aesthetic experience evaporate as quickly as the perfume-smell of a stunningly beautiful passerby.

DISEMBODIMENT IN ADVANCED MODERN SOCIETIES

The notion of *dis-embodiment* seems apposite to me. In its reliance on the phenomenological term *embodiment* it describes best what I imply here. It is neither the loss of the body per se nor the decline of sensory stimulation that is at stake, but the waning of deep and comprehensive lived-body experiences (*Leiberfahrungen*). The fact that we are in the midst of an ongoing process of disembodiment—or bodily suppression—has four reasons. First, increasing social interdependence necessitates both conscious and internalized forms of self-control, which result in a *leveling of affectivity*. As a university teacher in a modern urban environment I am much more dependent on others—and therefore have to weigh my reactions to them in a much more nuanced way—than, say, a medieval farmer. Second, due to the differentiation of our complex life-world into isolated spheres the body *comes into play increasingly selective*. In the office I use my eyes, my brain, my hands, whereas in the gym I predominantly work out with my arms and legs. Third, as a consequence of industrialization and technological innovation everyday life is largely sedentary: the body *remains (comparatively) inactive*. On the way to work I sit in my car; in the office I sit behind the computer; at night I sit at the dinner table and in front of the television. Fourth, in everyday life the body is often *functionalized for routine instrumental purposes*. When we take the subway to the office and toil away nine hours behind the desk, the body functions more as an automated means to an end than something to be experienced in its own right. As Gernot Böhme comments laconically: "In our world you cannot afford to be a truly sensual human being—at any rate, this is not recommendable while driving a car."[13] As a consequence, everyday life allows only scattered moments of deeply felt experience, short stints in the realm of the sensual.

Of course, the body is far from absent in today's culture. In its objectified, represented form it is everywhere around us: in the media and in advertising, at the movies and other forms of art, in medical and various academic discourses (from philosophy and cultural studies to neuroscience and gender studies). The celebration of youth, fitness, wellness, health and beauty is indicative for the value of the body as a communicative signifier and symbolic practice. Moreover, numerous institutions and leisure practices exist that grant us an experience of the body: from playing soccer, working-out at the gym or visiting yoga classes to roller-coaster riding, bungee-jumping and free-climbing, from the ecstasy-high at a techno rave or rollerblading through the city to a wellness massage or a three-star seven-course dinner. With some justification one can speak of a "body boom" (Karl-Heinrich Bette) or a "somatic turn" (Richard Shusterman).[14]

How can we reconcile this *simultaneity of body suppression and body boom*? There is a correlation at work: the body boom is nothing else than the flipside of body suppression. What is taken away by the habituated-instrumental, self-controlled, selective and comparatively rare experience of the body in everyday life needs to be added by scattered and temporary body revalorizations. Structural characteristics of modernity like differentiation, rationalization, domestication of nature or industrialization have brought this simultaneity into being—or, more accurately, modernity has *increased* and *accelerated* a tendency that has existed all along. In fact, the process of civilization *always* means suppression of the body. Just think of the (speculative) account Freud develops in *Civilization and its Discontents* (1929): since the human drives cannot be satisfied at will, they must be bridled. In exchange for security and communality, eros has to be held in check by taboos, and aggression needs to be controlled by (internalized) rules and laws.[15] The process of modernization merely adds another turn of the screw and thus necessitates increased counterstrategies of body revalorization. These counterstrategies are, of course, themselves subject to characteristics of modernity like differentiation and rationalization. Since a return to a pre-modern *status ante* is impossible, these strategies of body revalorization are bound to counter in a differentiated and rationalized manner. Hence they never work comprehensively.

Even if my accounts of disembodiment and revalorization of the body imply long-term changes in a specific direction, I do not argue for a straight, linear increase without pushes and pulls. Nor do I claim that both developments run exactly parallel. Both assumptions would be distorting and naïve. What I do claim, is that today we are trapped in the predicament of a simultaneity of the non-simultaneous. From an evolutionary perspective advanced modern societies and the body of modern man are in disharmony because bodily evolution could not keep pace with the speed of change. This discrepancy results in diseases of civilization and feelings of lack.

This is not to say that one should endorse an essentialist, monolithic body ontology. No doubt, we need to contextualize the body historically and culturally. But while we readily admit that the body is *co*-constructed according to *different* historical and cultural discourses and practices of race, class, gender, ethnicity, age etc., there is always a slight danger of overlooking our *common* embodiment. The body subsists through cultural and historical influence—even while it is always already intertwined with it. Carol Bigwood coins the fitting oxymoron of the body as an "indeterminate constancy": "we exist simultaneously in cultural and natural ways that are inextricably tangled. We are always already situated in an intersubjective (and thereby already cultural), spatiotemporal, fleshy (and thereby already natural) world before we creatively adopt a personal position in it."[16] If this is the case, we have to deal with the fact that there are limits to the 'plasticity' of the body. Man is a highly malleable and variable being, but one can only go so far before the body reclaims its rights. Writes Richard Shusterman: "Evolutionary adaptation alone will be far too slow to keep pace with our environment's heightened rate of rapid change. [. . .] the rapid changes of advanced technological society have created a crisis for our bodies, which demands an increased level of somatic attention."[17]

Hence we feel forced to counter the lack of deep and comprehensive lived-body experiences by revalorizing the body in various ways.

Roots of Disembodiment: The Civilizing Process and Modernization

A certain abstraction, control and distancing of the body is *always* part of an individual's development. The body is never naturally given. It cannot be experienced in a pre-cultural fullness and entirety. Such an essentialist understanding of the body cannot even be thought. In order to develop a stable identity the individual has to manage, repress and distance itself from the discontinuous and threatening aspects of the body: blood, urine, feces, pus, sweat, body odor etc. Developing a discrete, differentiated corporeality not only requires an initial separation from the mother's womb, but an ability to decide which parts and products of one's body are dirty and socially unacceptable. In other words, the individual's enculturation entails the control, repression or hiding of certain aspects of the body. But while this might be an aspect of the human condition *in general*, there is always a strong influence of the specific *cultural* context on one's attitude towards the body. Hence Norbert Elias writes: "The learning of self-control [. . .] is a human universal, a common condition of humanity. [. . .] What can change, and what in fact have changed during the long development of humanity, are social standards of self-control and the manner in which they are made to activate and to pattern an individual's natural potential for delaying, suppressing, transforming, in short, for controlling in various ways elementary drives and other spontaneous feeling impulses."[18] The historical processes of civilization and modernization have pushed the degree of disembodiment to a degree that demands increasing care for the body.

As Elias demonstrates, the marginalization and strong control of the body is a necessary, unavoidable, unplanned and in its specific manifestations often coincidental by-product of what he calls "the civilizing process."[19] It implies that human behavior has to change towards disembodiment once a society becomes increasingly complex. The growing socio-economic differentiation necessitates a higher level of social interdependence. Once individual members depend more strongly on each other and once their actions have to be coordinated more minutely, they need to modulate and regulate their behavior so that it becomes more calculable and stable and less spontaneous and affective. *Conscious* self-restraint as well as internalized, *quasi-automatic* self-control work hand in hand to keep the emotions in check and help to defer the gratifications of our drives and wishes. Consequently, in complex societies there is only a comparatively limited scope for the experience of strong feelings.[20] Conditions of high excitement—strong antipathies, hot anger or wild hatred just as much as unconditional devotion or unrestrained hilarity—are disqualified as strange or even abnormal. As a result, individuals in complex societies have a different amount and quality of emotional experiences—and hence of the lived body—than their counterparts in less civilized societies.

This is also the case due to a straightforwardly positive development, namely the relief of crises and threat situations still encountered in rural, less industrialized societies. Seriously critical situations that generate a tendency to act in a highly excited manner have strongly decreased: famines, floods, epidemics, violence by socially superior persons or by strangers have been brought under stricter control than ever before. The economic fluctuations and crises of today's affluent societies are less liable to elicit strong, spontaneous excitement. Fluctuations of this type are more impersonal; the sorrows and the joys connected with them are in a different key. Hence uncontrolled and uncontrollable outbreaks of strong communal excitement have become less frequent. In both cases—regulated behavior and relief of external causes—there is a similar effect: the emotional amplitude decreases; the affective ups and downs are less extreme; the transitions from one emotion to the next slow down. The lived body and its emotional metamorphoses are not experienced as deeply and radically anymore.

However, disembodiment derives not only from the *leveled affectivity* characteristic of the civilizing process, but also from the increasingly *selective* and *inactive use* of the body due to such developments as differentiation, industrialization and technological innovation commonly associated with modernization. One only has to think of two institutions characteristic of complex societies in order to illustrate how differentiation affects the body: money and law. By way of the introduction of money as an impartial, indirect means for the exchange of goods the individual and its body necessarily recede into the background: the expressive, verbal faculties of bartering, necessary in a society based on direct exchange, are no longer in place. The active, bodily performance of the bargaining consumer becomes replaced by passive inspecting and buying. And when law and order become monopolized in the political hands of the territorial state, the strong connection between bodily and social power is untied. Since bodily violence is sanctioned *and* professed by the state, random acts of cruelty by the 'fittest' are held in check. Today, no matter if physically strong or weak, individuals have equal rights in court. As a result, in a highly differentiated modern society the body is functionally relevant only in very selective aspects.[21] Capitalism asks for the consuming body, sports for the muscular body, science for the embodied mind etc.

Industrialization and technological innovation imply massive benefits and gains, but they are also further driving forces behind the backgrounding of the body. A plethora of material practices in our life-world supports this claim. Factories, machines and robots have largely replaced the human hand and thus loosened the strong tie between labor and the body. Hard labor made way for white-collar office work at the computer. At work and beyond, technologies of rapid communication allow us to transcend the limits once imposed by the body, cutting the link between participation and presence: telephone, radio, television and internet enable active involvement in events thousands of kilometers away even if we have moved corporeally only from bedroom to living room. Writing an email does not only imply that I can remain seated in front of the computer in order to contact someone else, but also that I can refrain from using voice, facial expressions and gestures. Or think of current forms of transportation. Distances are not laboriously crossed by foot, on horse or via stagecoach but in comfortable, highly accelerated machines that easily fuse with our bodies. In fact, one of the goals of traveling today is to efface the body as thoroughly as possible: the seated, immovable passenger is passively transported like a package and thus does not register the sensual quality of movement.[22] Today we do not move about on our own but we are mostly moved by machines. Conversely, what we would normally have to approach spatially comes to us directly: the home delivery of books, DVDs, pizzas or groceries is a case in point. These random examples illustrate that our technological culture is largely a sedentary one that gives insufficient due to a body otherwise experienced more often and comprehensively.

This backgrounding of our lived bodies is evident also in a very different arena: in intellectual discourses and their Cartesian dream of getting rid of the stubborn flesh and freeing (transcendental) consciousness from its captivation in corporeal prison. The long and powerful intellectual legacy of Cartesianism with its strong anti-somatic undertones runs parallel to and is interlinked with the processes of civilization and modernization. Propagating and perpetuating the highly selective and rationalized use of the body, we can find it in various discourses. I pick out three examples. First, the recent end-of-the-millennium techno-hype discourse: in the accounts of Jean Baudrillard, Hans Moravec or Marvin Minsky the body was decontextualized from its life-world, reduced to a text or digital sign in cyberspace or conceived of as a post-human techno body. The fantasies of disembodiment were particularly aggressive in futuristic dreams of the coming cyberspace: a virtual realm that would allow us to leave our obsolete bodies behind. Technology supposedly enables us to exist as pure consciousness, thus overcoming the complexity, the dirt, the transience, the material demands and limitations of the flesh.

A second contemporary version of the dream of Cartesianism are the strong naturalist positions within philosophy of mind, such as "reductionism" or "eliminative materialism." While reductionists claim that intentionality and subjective experiences can be reduced to purely physico-chemical terms, eliminative materialists hold that intentionality is an outmoded myth altogether and notions such as belief, desire, fear or joy will soon be antiquated and can therefore be eliminated.[23] Neuroscientific research will eventually show that there is no physical correlate to such "qualia" as love or pain and hence these subjective experiences cannot be real. At the other end of the philosophical spectrum, poststructuralism ironically (and maybe unwittingly) advocates disembodiment as well. This is my third example. By emphasizing that the body is largely a product of conventional cultural forms of practice and discourse, poststructuralism likewise tends to negate the lived body as incarnated being-in-the-world.[24] Yet the body is neither pure physical materiality nor the mere product of cultural practices and discourses; it is neither untouched nature prior to culture nor a pure cultural construct beyond nature. Edward Casey argues: "Only if the body were obdurate matter on the one hand or an epiphenomenon of spirit on the other, could we usefully apply the designations 'nature' or 'culture' to it in some exclusive way. But body is not such matter and no such epiphany of spirit. It has its own unique realm or type of being, one that lends itself to both natural and cultural modulations."[25] Technophiles, radical materialists and poststructuralists tend to treat the body as mere object. The subjectively lived body is ignored for the sake of the argument. But the body cannot be reduced to just another thing in the world—even if we sometimes treat it as such.

Reactions to Disembodiment: The Rise of Modern Hedonism

However, we have to be careful not to fall into the trap of an overly narrow and pessimistic cultural critique. Avoiding a history of decline is advisable not only because the processes of civilization and modernization have brought enormous benefits, but also because we would overlook the diversity of simultaneous counter-movements against disembodiment. Three of the most celebrated cultural theorists are indicative here—albeit *ex negativo*. In the work of Weber, Adorno and Foucault a critique of modernity is wedded to the idea of rationalization and instrumental reason as the historical forces behind the yoking of the human body. The vital dimension and the freedom of the body are suppressed by bureaucratic plans and organized codes of behavior (Weber), violently pressed into habitual schemata and thus disciplined (Foucault) or psychologically deformed by the manipulations of quasi-totalitarian mass media (Adorno).[26] While these accounts of the rationalized, disciplined and manipulated body are valuable as hyperbolizing and admonishing social critiques, they rely on a quasi-behaviorist understanding of the body. The human body comes across as passive, palpable material but never experiences let alone opposes its own rationalization, disciplining and manipulation.[27] The body is an object, but not subjectively lived. The individual is passive and docile, but does not actively counter bodily denigration. In terms of the body, the works of Weber, Adorno and Foucault come across as one-sided histories of decline, since they refrain from taking into account the rich empirical evidence of simultaneous bodily empowerment and institutions that provide counterbalancing lived-body experiences.

In the following I will briefly jump back in time and focus on an exemplary historical moment—the late 18th and early 19th century—in order to *illustrate* how the process of disembodiment described by Weber, Adorno and Foucault provokes various movements of body revalorization. When modernity and the industrial revolution got fully underway, the processes of change were accompanied by a number of counteracting developments that did not take place coincidentally but have to be understood as complements of what had broken away.[28] At the exact same time when according to Weber, Adorno and Foucault asceticism and the disciplinary suppression of the body prevailed, ideas, discourses and practices sprang to life or gained in significance that held the value of emotions, the sensual and the body in high esteem.[29] Thus the 'return of the body' is not an exclusively contemporary development. The paradoxical *simultaneity* of suppression and revalorization of the body can be charted through diverse stages of modernity. They go hand in hand.

What follows is a very rough sketch of how modern hedonism sprang to life when a new Romantic ethic developed into a dynamic counter-current to the ascetic, rationalized strand within modernity.[30] In late 18th and early 19th century a sentimental Pietistic undercurrent within Protestantism established a social ethic that stood in opposition to the one described by Weber and which involved fundamental changes in beliefs, values and attitudes.[31] Against the rigorist doctrines of Calvin an alternative grew which valued *high affectivity*.[32] A hedonistic, consumption-oriented Romantic ethic thus began to balance the ascetic, production-oriented Protestant ethic. The birth of modern hedonism implied a strong revaluation of emotions and the body with a strong acceptance of Romantic love. As the very opposite of instrumental reason, Romantic love cherishes emotionality pure and simple. And it brought about a "leisure revolution" that included theater-going, horse-racing, dancing and the development of the modern form of sports.[33] Even more interesting for my account: the hunger for strong sensations via fiction grew. People began to read books that relied on such 'negative' emotions as sorrow and pity, fear and disgust.

The most popular genres in this regard were, of course, the sentimental novel and the gothic novel. The official function of the former—epitomized by Laurence Sterne's *Sentimental Journey* (1768) and, in the U.S., Susanna Rowson's *Charlotte Temple* (1791)—was to evoke moral emotions. However, the didactic aims were often not more than a thin veneer behind which the sentimental novel tried to hide its serialized succession of intense emotional pleasures.[34] Around the same time, a second type of literature became hugely popular: the gothic novel, a precursor of today's horror movies. The gothic novel is exemplified by Horace Walpole's *The Castle of Otranto* (1764), Ann Radcliffe's *The Mysteries of Udolpho* (1794), and, in the U.S., Charles Brockden Brown's *Wieland* (1798). Substituting dread and a frightening flirtation with death for the sentimental novel's love and titillation of sex, the advent of the gothic novel brought a considerable change in emotional climate. Fred Botting explains: "Through its presentations of supernatural, sensational and terrifying incidents, imagined or not, Gothic produced emotional effects on its readers rather than developing a rational or properly cultivated response. Exciting rather than informing, it chilled their blood, delighted their superstitious fancies and fed uncultivated appetites for marvelous and strange events."[35] Frightening fictions with an entertainment function did not exist at all times. To be sure, fear played an important role in religious and literary writing. Greek mythology and the Bible come to mind. So do Dante's *Inferno*, Milton's *Paradise Lost* or Shakespeare's *Macbeth*. Monsters can be found in *Beowulf*, the legend of St. George and Siegfried's adventures. But fictions that treat frightening and shocking subject matter do not necessarily result in fear and shock. Nor did fear play the same quantitative role in earlier fiction. Plus, fear often served a moral purpose but was rarely used for pleasurable ends. The first type of literature geared to the pleasure of fear was precisely the English gothic novel.[36]

Why did it come into being at this time and at this place? With the gothic novel a shift occurred from the social utility of earlier didactic forms of literature to the more 'gratuitous' indulgences in fantasies of fear. This emphasis on emotion and the body has to be seen *also* as part of the new hedonistic ethic and a response to the disembodiment brought about by the kind of modernization described by Weber, Adorno and Foucault. Taking into consideration the composition of the gothic novel's readership explains why it originated and flourished precisely in the country where modernity was most advanced. In Great Britain the genre found adherents especially among women confined to their homes and thus susceptible to a comparatively disembodied life of "rest and inaction" (Edmund Burke).[37] But gothic novels were also popular among men who needed relief from the monotony at work in the urban metropolises. In 1800 the poet William Wordsworth has already pointed out this nexus when he wrote about urban men and how "the uniformity of their occupations produces a craving for extraordinary incident."[38] In both cases we are dealing with groups of individuals whose life-style was part of the growing lack of genuine lived-body experiences within modernity.

However, answering the disembodied monotony of everyday life with reading might not seem such a good idea if one takes into account the less-than-active body of the reader. In fact, around 1800 a change of mentality transformed the habits of reading towards even more inactive forms. While in earlier times it was not uncommon to stand or even walk, at the end of the 18th and the beginning of the 19th century the act of reading became more and more sedentary: the reader sits at a table, assimilates the chair to his or her body and remains immobile.[39] What is more, since the sedentary form of reading with the person sitting upright at the desk was strongly associated with work, readers even started to prefer lying in bed or spread out on a *chaise longue* while reading for leisure. Yet to claim that the body does not come into play in reading is a valid argument only if one ignores the *aisthetic* aspect of aesthetic experience. While a one-sided perspective would stress the disciplined body, we should not overlook what is gained through immobilization: only if the reader wholly devotes his or her attention to the aesthetic object can he or she fully experience the *emotional* aesthetic effects predominant in the sentimental or the gothic novel. Given that a mobile reading body would partially undermine the book's emotional effect, certain reading experiences *presuppose* an immobilized position. The recipient *immobilizes* his or her body in order to *excite* the body. In this respect reading emotional fiction foreshadows a contemporary form of countering disembodiment: the experience of frightening movies.

Against Disembodiment: Lived-Body Metamorphoses and Scary Movies

The sentimental and the gothic novel are two examples for the historical development that Winfried Fluck sees at work in American culture as a whole: a tendency towards ever more direct, bodily forms of aesthetic experience.[40] The increasingly emotional-somatic character and the growing popularity of contemporary frightening movies can serve as another illustration. After having pictured in very broad brushstrokes the rise of modern hedonism in general and the arrival of the gothic novel more specifically, I finally want to return to the cinema of fear's lived-body metamorphoses as a contemporary example of countering the disembodiment of our life-world.

In the face of a threatening movie routine perception and response are out of order, and a transformation from non-emotional life to highly emotional experiences takes place. We feel the field of consciousness reorganized and flexibly shifting emphasis; our bodily experience instantly becomes more complex; a gradual, sometimes abrupt sensual metamorphosis takes place. Suddenly, the hitherto occluded, absent body comes to the fore and tacit corporeal dimensions are brought into awareness. Obviously not even the most radical of all aesthetic experiences will be able to draw attention *exclusively* to the body. If this were the case, our viewing would be suspended and the cinematic surroundings would drop from awareness. But in order to have a strong corporeal experience the lived body need not be the sole object of attention. In some moments the body might *dominate* the center of our field of consciousness, even if it is not the only focus— consider scenes of shock or somatic empathy. In these instances the body becomes strongly foregrounded and claims focal awareness, while the film as intentional object loses its center-stage position and is pushed somewhat to the periphery. But even in moments of deep immersion in which my attention is almost fully captivated by the movie, I often have a strong bodily experience. In order to enjoy a heightened state of bodily stimulation I do not need to be focally aware of it. When I play soccer or go to the gym, I am not necessarily consciously reflecting on the pleasure of my body. In fact, as Don Ihde notes, our greatest feelings of aliveness come from experiences of being *lost* in a (bodily) activity.[41] While we are wholly involved in the movie, we are unable or unwilling to make the emotional experience an object of conscious reflection. However, some experiences are so dense that even their peripheral aspects can be recuperated after the fact.

The emotional experiences of frightening movies change from situation to situation, involving a nuanced spectrum of the lived body. I will shortly reiterate three aspects focused upon throughout this study: constriction, kinaesthesia and depth. First, during a horrifying or terrifying scene the threatening film appears (overly) close phenomenologically: the viewer experiences the fear vis-à-vis the importunate, threatening object's proximity as a *constriction* of the lived body. However, fear is also characterized by an expansive, if hampered *Away!*-tendency: an ultimately futile impulse to escape the lived body's constriction. We desperately want to jump out of our skin, as it were, by expanding *Away!* somewhere, but cannot flee constriction. As a consequence, there is a pulsating *tension*, between dominant constriction and attempted expansion. This shifting between constriction and expansion is particularly dense and compressed in shock. Since its initial radical constriction would be an unbearable state, however, it is immediately followed by expansion. This rapid back-and forth movement between opposed somatic poles can be experienced as pleasurable. To repeat, the viewer feels and enjoys *both* lived-body metamorphoses: the movement into and out of constriction, out of expansion and back into it.

Second, terror and dread imply specific kinds of *kinaesthesia*. The viewer experiences terror in a state of anxious restlessness and agitation. While passively bound to the theater seat, the viewer is simultaneously 'set in motion' by empathically observing the onscreen action. Dread, on the other hand, is defined by frightened stillness: one could hear a needle drop, we hardly dare to breathe, let alone move in our seats. Hence terror puts the viewer into a state of *acceleration* and *agitation*, whereas dread is defined by an experience of *immobility* and *dead silence*.

Third, there are considerable differences in *depth*. Not all emotions are on one level; some emotions affect us deeply, while others remain superficial. Sue L. Cataldi notes "that our deeper emotions are determined on the basis of increased proximity to the 'self'; and that the deepest emotions permeate or overwhelm the self and are experienced by the whole of our being."[42] Some emotional lived-body experiences at the movies seem to be a fully integrated, close part of the self. Strong versions of fear such as horror and dread are cases in point; they imply a *wholesale* emotional captivation. Other lived-body experiences come across as a more *localized*, loosely attached, somewhat distanced part of the self. Among more distanced parts one can further distinguish between various *regions* of the body brought into play. For instance, the body *surface* may be thematized: the film makes our skin crawl, hair stands up or we have goose pimples. Or we might also experience *gut* reactions. The visceral response of nausea caused by cinematic disgust is focused around the stomach and/or the gorge. Painful somatic empathy often affects distinct local regions of the body and therefore touches us merely partially. The differences in depth are mirrored in their psychological longevity. While disgust and painful somatic empathy tend to disappear quickly, horror or dread can stay with us and even haunt our dreams and daydreams. Cataldi writes: "Our deepest emotional experiences [...] are usually accompanied by realizations that we are perceiving the world or ourselves in a new or different 'light.' Any emotional experience about which it seems appropriate to say that the emotional experiencer is 'not [entirely] the same [person]' afterward is a deep emotional experience."[43] To be sure, emotional depth has nothing to do with intensity. Flat feelings and emotions like somatic empathy or disgust can 'hit' us pathically with great force and therefore be experienced as overwhelmingly intense, but they are not as deep and long-lasting as cinematic dread or horror.

In sum, cinematic fear is a volitionally pursued, pleasurable foregrounding of the body. This foregrounding is pleasurable because, in the relatively safe environment of the movie theater, it enables a strong *involvement of the self*. Fearful emotions are more than something lived through and thus more than simply happening *to* me. Instead they often imply an experiencing *of* the self. Against the backdrop of a culture of disembodiment, the cinema of fear awakens our slumbering bodies by literally *moving* them into an awareness of aliveness.

Potential Objections

Despite his overly intellectualist solution to the "paradox of horror," Noël Carroll admits that the invigorating effect can supply *part* of the reason why horror stories appeal. However, as an overarching explanation he rejects it as too broad and unspecific. In his opinion, the hypothesis cannot account for our attraction to horror, because it simultaneously explains the appeal of adventure stories and melodramas.[44] But this conclusion is too hasty, since it relies on an overly monolithic understanding of the body. In fact, one can even go further and put the cinema of fear into a much larger framework that includes activities very different from the movies: the framework of entertainment and leisure more generally. Exciting leisure activities bear a potential for aesthetic experience just as literature, painting or the movies do. As (neo-)pragmatist philosophers like John Dewey and Richard Shusterman have underscored, there is a continuity between real life and art and it would be reductive to limit aesthetic experience to the fine arts.[45] From this perspective, frightening movies function within a large array of stimulating opportunities offered in highly differentiated societies—from ego-shooter games to rock climbing, from techno raves to the religious awe of the church, from reading a sentimental novel to bungee-jumping. "The great variety of leisure activities [...] which complex societies have to offer allows individuals a wide choice. They can adopt one or another in accordance with their temperament, their bodily build, their libidinal, affective or emotional needs," Norbert Elias claims.[46]

The birth of the cinema is tied to those dispositives of the 19th and 20th century devoted to perceptual and bodily stimulation—particularly the amusement parks with attractions like the roller coaster and the Ferris wheel, the tunnel of horror and the merry-go-round. This is not to say that all experiences are one and the same. Considering the cinema a leisure institution within the complex, differentiated culture of advanced modernity does not imply that we should overlook what is *specific* about the cinema. Since the pleasurable experience of fear in the (multiplex) cinema is by definition *not* identical with those other entertainment venues, it must be distinguishable and thus stand out in comparison. What Carroll overlooks is the fact that horror films, adventure stories and melodramas (not to speak of soccer games, techno raves or wellness massages) cater to very *different* aspects of the body. Since the use of the body in modern societies is highly selective, different social circumstances bring into play very specific corporeal aspects. Take comedic laughter and melodramatic crying: while the former involves animal functions (with the *muscular* system in particular), the latter implies vegetative functions (with the *secretory* system in specific).[47] Far from making the explanation less specific, comparing frightening movies to other entertainment and leisure experiences helps to identify their *particular* bodily appeal.

There is an enormous richness and finesse of pleasurable lived-body experiences—not only within the field of leisure in general but within filmic genres in specific—which we can and should explore simply in order to realize and understand the many facets of our selves. It seems undeniable to me that horror films and melodramas, romantic comedies and porn movies, thrillers and slapstick films stimulate our bodies in very peculiar ways. The explosive laughter of a Jim Carrey comedy constrasts with the deeply-felt emotionality of *Titanic* (1997) or the shocks of *Scream*. What my phenomenological section underscored was precisely the fact that even if the overall appeal of frightening movies is an emotional-somatic experience, we can still make clear distinctions between those experiences. Just like advanced modernity as a whole the Hollywood cinema is highly differentiated, appealing to diverse audiences with very different emotional-somatic expectations and needs.

At the same time we must not overestimate their potential. The cinema is able to stir emotions powerfully just as it is able to raise powerful emotions. But it can only plough so many fields of our vast emotional landscape. While admiration, joy, pity, sadness, fear and anger are an essential part of the movies, the convincing evocation of true love is up for debate. Even bodily reactions like laughter or crying are brought into play only in certain facets of their repertoire: for instance, in the cinema we do not cry angrily but sadly. Moreover, the cinema stimulates us bodily predominantly via emotions like fear and sensations such as somatic empathy, but it does not enable, for instance, the experience of deep muscular exhaustion. As a consequence, movies respond to disembodiment specifically and selectively rather than comprehensively. This is necessarily so and not an exclusive feature of the cinema: the selective use of the body in highly differentiated societies makes it impossible for one institution or system to counter the denigration of the body single-handedly.[48] It would be a crass overstatement to ascribe a *comprehensive* counterbalancing potential to the movies. In reality, the cinema is only one option among many that brings the body back into play—first and foremost via the specific lived-body experience of emotions—and will therefore always be used in combination with other counterbalancing leisure activities. As Hans Ulrich Gumbrecht notes: "it makes sense to hope that aesthetic experience may give us back at least a feeling of our being-in-the-world [. . .]. But we should immediately add that this feeling, at least in our culture, will never have the status of a permanent conquest. Therefore, it may be more adequate to formulate, conversely, that aesthetic experience can prevent us from completely losing a feeling or a remembrance of the physical dimension in our lives."[49]

Some readers might object to my thesis from a different angle. They could argue that awareness of the body in and of itself is not a sufficient explanation for elucidating the pleasure of frightening films: individuals do not consider every kind of bodily stimulation pleasurable. In fact, some somatic experiences are not enjoyable at all. This is fair enough. But even if horror films make some people sick and others experience thrillers as emotional torture, this does not pose a problem for my argument. As we have seen in the introduction, I assume an active decision-making process that enables the viewer to decide in advance what he or she regards as a pleasurable experience of the body. Just as some people prefer free rock-climbing to hiking in the mountains, choose S/M over 'regular' sex and have a preference for watching wrestling over dressage, so do movie audiences know what they like and what they can't bear.

THE ACCELERATION OF ADVANCED MODERN LIFE

In his groundbreaking study *Beschleunigung* Hartmut Rosa underscores how our experience of time has changed historically. In contrast to earlier periods, modernity—and *a fortiori* advanced modernity—has gradually *accelerated* our being-in-time. In fact, Rosa argues that acceleration is *the* irreducible hallmark of modernity. While sociological classics like Weber, Simmel, Durkheim and Marx have respectively stressed rationalization, individualization, differentiation and domestication of nature (the development of instrumental reason), Rosa describes the process of modernization first and foremost as the steadily increasing acceleration of technological innovation, social change and speed of life.[50]

Technological innovation has accelerated transportation, communication and production: the introduction of the steam engine and the conveyor belt into the factory hall; the construction of the railway network;

the mass spreading of cars, trams, busses and airplanes; the invention of telegraph, telephone, fax and the internet; the development of modern mass media like radio, cinema and television.[51] *The acceleration of social change* results in a radical shrinking of the duration and stability of the present in various social realms: from politics to economics, from the sciences to art, from occupational relations to moral orientations. Our preferences for job, political party, sexual partner or local organization are speeded up just as much as the development of new styles in art or fashion and the change of work and family structures. This transformative social unrest grants plausibility to the metaphors of vaporizing, dissolving, melting and liquefying that have been brought into play by theorists of modernity like Marx, Engels, Berman and Bauman.[52] *The increasing speed of life* becomes manifest in such cultural practices as fast food, speed dating, power napping or multitasking. I will come back to this third characteristic of accelerated advanced modernity and the cinema's specific pleasure vis-à-vis the increasing speed of life. Before, I will look at why the cinema is a pleasure-yielding modern institution also in terms of accelerated technological innovation and social change.

Squeezing In Some Pleasure: The Cinema as Instant Gratification

Rosa claims that in the face of contingency, instability and constant technological and social change, long-term orientations and goals are replaced by attempts to keep the pace and not miss the connection. As a consequence, the pursuit of activities considered valuable loses ground; there is no time left for the 'actually' important things.[53] It seems natural and reasonable to sequence activities and occupations according to their importance and value: the most important thing first, then something less important and so on. However, in functionally differentiated societies with strong interdependencies and long interaction chains this principle of order is more and more replaced by external deadlines. Rosa concludes: "The power of the deadline determines the succession of activities and necessitates that under the condition of short time ressources goals without deadlines gradually disappear from view. They are smothered, as it were, with the burden of 'things-to-do-first' and leave the faint feeling that one doesn't accomplish anything."[54]

How do frightening movies come into play here? More than many other leisure activities the almost constantly available two-hour experience of the cinema fits nicely into the small remaining fragments of unoccupied time. Moreover, the cinema allows bridging breaks easily because it does not demand a high amount of concentration and energy. Third, the experience promises a positive 'input-output relation': little preparation, small time investment and low energy level yield a comparatively strong and pleasurable experience—an experience that involves the very body that modernity denigrates.[55] Hence in an accelerated culture with high rates of instability and change *instant* trumps *deferred* gratification. Long-term experiences that demand high investment of time and concentration are replaced by short-term experiences even though the former are often considered—and *experienced* as—more valuable and satisfying. This is the case because instant gratifications seem to guarantee a greater return of benefit over cost for the individual viewer. The quick 'instant emotions' at the movies—with the 'cheap trick' of shock as their epitome—and the flexible 'instant collectivity'—with the collective body united in screams of shock as paradigmatic—are precisely instant gratifications.

Intense Time Experiences: Scary Movies as Heterochrony

The cinema of fear also promises to fill the empty time-slots with particularly intense and pleasurable time-bound experiences. Michel Foucault has called the cinema a heterotopia: a *counter-site* that is simultaneously a "mythic and real contestation of the space in which we live."[56] But it also provides us with a kind of *counter-time*. As Foucault writes: "Heterotopias are most often linked to slices in time—which is to say that they open onto what might be termed, for the sake of symmetry, heterochronies. The heterotopia begins to function at full capacity when men arrive at a sort of absolute break with their traditional time."[57] Foucault's last sentence must be understood ambiguously: the cinema allows us to push our daily time constraints to the background *and* makes possible experiences of time hardly available outside the cinema. From its inception the cinema has been described as the medium that qua indexicality could record, seize and represent time. But the *experience* of the cinema's "break with traditional time" has rarely been described in detail.

In fact, what we have noticed in terms of discourses of the body is also true for time: most discussions radically objectify it, leaving the subjective experience almost wholly aside. A good example is Mary Ann Doane's otherwise highly perceptive book on cinematic time. She denies that the classical cinema can be considered a heterochrony and even goes so far as to talk about the "timeless space of the theater."[58] The discussion of the protentional aspect and temporal density of dread and terror scenes has underscored that Hollywood cinema is far from timeless, but enables a *different* experience of time—a Foucauldian *hetero*-chrony. As another example of objectified time one could think of Laura Mulvey's definition of spectacle. She describes it as a-temporal, associated with stasis and the antilinear.[59] As the description of the cinematic shock—a spectacle *par excellence*—has clearly shown: Mulvey might be right if we consider objectified narrative time; but the subjective time experience is far from a-temporal. Quite the opposite: in its extremely pointed density time becomes highly palpable.

It is this aspect that makes the cinema of fear so pleasurable in the face of the accelerated speed of life in advanced modernity—Rosa's third characteristic to which I will return now. The accelerated speed of life is a reaction to a paradoxical shortage of time resources. Even though technological innovations grant us more time, we have less time for each act and event than before. This development is *subjectively* experienced as time pressure, stress and the feeling that we 'have no time.'[60] What are the reasons? Time pressure and the feeling of being rushed derive from both the *fear of missing out* on valuable opportunities and the *obligation to adapt* to technological and social changes (which are themselves accelerated, as we have seen). As a consequence, we react by increasing and compressing the act and event episodes per time unit: we accelerate life because we want to *and* we have to. On the one hand, we *want* to experience as many *events* as possible. The cultural driving force behind our tendency to increase the event rate is the idea that a fulfilled life, with all the world options enjoyed to the full, is 'disenchanted' modernity's secularized equivalent to the religious promise of eternal life.[61] This is the reason why we astonishingly often talk about obligations and musts when it comes to leisure activities: I need to go to the gym; I have to see this new show on TV etc. On the other hand, we also *have* to squeeze in as many acts as possible: the rapidly changing life-world forces us to move constantly in order to remain in place.[62] Rosa coins the apposite metaphor *standing on slipping*—not slippery!—*slopes*.

The resulting increase and compression of act and event episodes, however, leads to a fragmentation of time. The intervals become smaller and smaller. We cannot devote thorough-enough attention to each sequence so it can be experienced as a rounded-out whole. We jump from one occupation to the next and rarely have the opportunity to run its course to fulfillment. "No one experience has a chance to complete itself because something else is entered upon so speedily. What is called experience becomes so dispersed and miscellaneous as hardly to deserve the name," John Dewey noted some 70 years ago about the "hurried and impatient environment in which we live."[63] Time is, so to speak, cut into pieces: by our constant availability and the possibility of a plethora of interruptions, by the de-institutionalization of practices and by the surplus of potentially interesting information and commodities that we try to squeeze in so not to miss out. As a result, the fractured moments gain increasingly less weight in terms of deep experience (or *an* experience, as Dewey would say). Precisely because we do not have deep, rounded out, non-automatic and vital experiences the world comes across as superficial, fleeting and increasingly fast.

But if we '*have* no time,' there is also no chance to 'grasp' it. I argue that we pre-reflectively seek out the pleasurable palpable time experience of scary movies precisely because it gives time temporarily back in our hands, as it were. This becomes particularly obvious when we look at the two extremes of time experience: cinematic shock and dread. In the first case the pointed *now* of the *present moment* bursts forth, while in the second case the dense *duration* of time leading up to an *anticipated moment* becomes palpable. Somewhere along this continuum—between the now and the soon-to-come, the present and the approaching *telos*—we can also locate the temporal experience of horror (close to shock) and terror (close to dread). The five types of fear briefly crystallize the fluid, fugitive time of what Zygmunt Bauman calls 'liquid modernity'. It becomes graspable before it is once again torn away by the stream of time.

John Dewey notes, "Continued acceleration is breathless and prevents parts from gaining distinction."[64] In my phenomenologies of shock, horror, terror and dread I showed how time can stand out as a gestalt. Interestingly, in frightening movies time becomes palpable—and thus counters the fragmentation of time experience in accelerated advanced modernity—by both decelerated *and* accelerated forms of time experience: the *stillness of dread* and the *agitation of terror* (which relies precisely on an increasing lack of time). Hence we do not necessarily crave for a decelerated experience of time, but first of all for an *intensive* experience of time *per se*.

Paradoxically, in order to arrive at these treasured subjective experiences, we have to surrender to the objective, depersonalized time of the movies in a double sense. First, we have to follow the exact public timetable of the theater. Here the cinema functions like so many other institutions of advanced modernity that rationalize, externalize, depersonalize time and force us to adapt to its objective schedule: work, school, public offices, busses, trains . . . Furthermore, we give in to the unstoppable and irreversible flow of the movie. We can read as fast or slow as we want or move from painting to painting according to our own will. In the movie theater we are roobed of this freedom.[65] However, handing myself over to the irreversible progression of the mechanical movie has an advantage other forms of art do not possess to the same degree: we are relieved of the burden and responsibility to choose. We are not forced to act instrumentally and goal-oriented. Instead we can dwell in the non-instrumental, non-routinized condition that Benjamin considers a prerequisite for deep experiences. What is more, the unstoppable and irreversible film offers *pre-focussed* aesthetic effects that stand out as integral gestalts and hence promise the kind of rounded-out experience that Dewey favors. We actively give ourselves over to the freedom of passively experiencing time itself. Even if time experience is highly dependent on a rationalized timetable, an inexorable apparatus and a pre-focussed work of art—and is hence determined *externally*—it is still very much experienced internally as *my* very own palpable time.

9 Moments of Collectivity
The Cinema of Fear and Feelings of Belongingness

> *Films like* [I Know What You Did Last Summer] *need audience participation. It's pointless watching it on video or DVD. You have to experience it in the cinema. You feed off everyone else's tension.*
>
> (Jim Gillespie)[1]

> *I wouldn't have wanted to see* Psycho *[for the] first time alone in a theater (and I sometimes feel a slight queasiness if I'm by myself late at night somewhere watching a horror film on TV). But that's what a theatrical experience is about: sharing this terror, feeling the safety of others around you, being able to laugh and talk together about how frightened you were as you leave.*
>
> (Pauline Kael)[2]

CHANGES OF COMMUNITY: INDIVIDUALIZATION AND NEW COLLECTIVITIES

The last section has dealt with the social and cultural framework connected to our pleasurable *lived-body* and *time* experiences. This chapter is devoted to the larger implications of the *collective* experience at the multiplex. The collective experience of frightening movies is a possible answer to an urgent question raised by the rapid transformations of advanced modernity: How can we create bonds and soothe our desire for belongingness in the face of an ever-more individualized, pluralized and de-traditionalized life-world? While in pre-modern societies people were born into classes and religions, tightly-knit families and local communities, the binding (if often suffocating) powers of these institutions have strongly decreased. Social contacts, ties and networks are not a given anymore.[3] Since the growing pluralization and individualization of post-traditional societies prevents a re-integration into the stable communities of old, people often feel disintegrated, think of themselves as isolated, deem to live in solitude—and therefore have to become active and seek out new forms of collectivity.[4]

The dissolution of traditional types of group formation and the rapidly changing forms of community might be illustrated by a quick glance at today's families. Family life is subject to an accelerated change of private partners resulting in a replacement of life-long monogamy by serial monogamy; the coming of the patch-work family with its changing constellations of mothers, fathers, in-laws, step-brothers and sisters; and the hiatus between the generations who live in isolated subcultures, using different technologies, consuming different media or buying in different stores.[5] Or consider the loss of collective time rhythms. Deregulation and de-institutionalization have led to a growing flexibility and a-synchronicity in terms of work-time and leisure, necessitating the active coordination and synchronization of collective action to a hitherto unknown degree.[6]

In his compelling description of the modern condition, Zygmunt Bauman underscores the dilemma of modern man caught between striving for individuality and freedom *and* longing for community and its warm and comforting safety.[7] For Bauman the process of individualization in modernity was a trade-off: security was exchanged for freedom.[8] Freed but insecure the individual started missing something—community. What followed was a dilemma: "Missing community means missing security; gaining community, if it happens, would soon mean missing freedom. Security and freedom are two equally precious and coveted values which could be better or worse balanced, but hardly ever fully reconciled and without friction."[9] Community, to be sure, is an elusive concept. The endless dream of the perfect community is never fulfilled and always frustrated. Yet still: we keep on dreaming. It is Bauman's profound conviction that "[f]reedom and communality may clash and conflict, but a compound lacking one or the other won't make for a satisfactory life."[10] Hence the contemporary form of individualization has ramifications for the communal side. The result is a new fragility of human bonds. What was once a matter of lifetime commitment—workplace, marriage, religion, home—is nowadays swept away by the floods and torrents of 'liquid modernity.' Individualization creates a need to counterbalance the longing for community and security.

Again, we should avoid an overly pessimistic rhetoric of decline. Just as it remains one-sided to claim a history of *bodily suppression* without taking into account the various institutions that provide counterbalancing lived-body experiences, it would be misleading to talk exclusively about *social disintegration*. A negative teleology is inappropriate for two reasons. First, it would be blind to the enormous possibilities and liberties the process of individualization has enabled. The decline of community values, the loss of tradition and the waning of older forms of sociability have also freed the individual from rigid, hierarchical and constricting patterns of community, a fact that Bauman is not oblivious to.[11] And, equally important, there is a simultaneous countercurrent that accompanies the inexorable march of individualization and its negative concomitants of disintegration and isolation and which works at establishing post-traditional collectivities and communities that are *appropriate to* and *in tune with* an individualized society.[12] Individualization does not mean complete disintegration, but changing forms of community. The freedom that comes with individualization entails that we constantly have to choose and decide. What was once largely regulated has become an obligation of the individual. Freed from former constrictions and released into a world of (comparatively strong) autonomy, people are to a much greater extent thrown upon themselves and responsible for their own lives. This also goes for one's interpersonal relations. Where once predefined and tight social bonds existed, the individual now has to be active, inventive and resourceful in weaving his or her own social web of belongingness.[13] What is there to be done?

Turning back the clock is impossible. Contemporary answers such as American communitarianism appear to be nostalgic, self-contradictory attempts not in tune with individualized modernity.[14] Since the radical changes of interpersonal relations (due to such developments as urbanization, mobilization, globalization, secularization and, more generally, individualization) have made it more difficult to build lasting bonds, one practical and practicable answer to our search for belongingness is given by fluctuating associations, temporary milieus and short-term collectivities. These groups leave enough space to individuality, the right to self-assertion and the wish to lead a life of one's own. Short-term collectivities seem to be the lowest common denominator. They offer a relief from loneliness, but do not take into custody our individuality. They allow for feelings of collectivity, while at the same time asking for minimal obligations. As Bauman informs us, the creation and dismantling of these short-term communities must be determined by the choices made by those who compose them: "In no case should the allegiance, once declared, become irrevocable: the bond made by choices should not inconvenience, let alone preclude, further and different choices."[15] Since short-term communities rest on *individual* choice, they transform the concept of 'community' from a sought-after, but also feared adversary of individual freedom of choice into a reconfirmation of individual autonomy. For Bauman communities in advanced modernity come in various colors and sizes, but if located on the Weberian axis that stretches from 'light cloak' to 'iron cage', they are all remarkably close to the first pole.[16]

Short-term collectivities are often built around a spectacle in whose cloakroom the 'light cloak' is safely stored for a short period of time. Bauman therefore dubs the group of spectators a 'cloakroom community': "Cloakroom communities need a spectacle which appeals to similar interests dormant in otherwise disparate individuals and so bring them all together for a stretch of time when other interests—those which divide them instead of uniting—are temporarily laid aside, put on a slow burner or silenced altogether."[17] The occasion of the spectacle (or maybe less polemically: the event) makes the highly individualized participants look more uniform than usual for a reasonably short period of time. It may not come as a surprise that I believe the cinema in general and the cinema of fear in specific enable such a "cloakroom community." Of course, the cinema should not be seen as a privileged way of arousing feelings of collectivity. Soccer games and pop concerts, techno raves and carnivals, beer festivals and theater performances work in similar (albeit not identical) ways. Nor do I claim that the cinema is necessarily more effective. It remains one option among many, with particular characteristics and facets to be summarized below. Since my point is to explain why fearful cinematic encounters can be pleasurable, I cannot sidestep the pivotal role of its specific collective experience.

CINEMA AND COLLECTIVITY: GENRE BUFFS, FANS, DISCURSIVE 'COMMUNITIES'

I am certainly not the first who stresses the cinema's potential for group formation and the establishment of various forms of 'community.'[18] In recent years important empirical studies have dealt with the nexus between cinema-going and collectivity. Researchers like Henry Jenkins, Annette Kuhn, Rick Altman or Bruce Austin have researched different forms of interpersonal relations based on fandom, film connoisseurship or genre attachment. Their studies are important, because they highlight functions of the cinema reaching beyond the tight boundaries of aesthetic experience proper to which I have restricted my attention. As a consequence, the 'communities' these authors describe are ultimately different from the kind of collectivity I have in mind. This is not to say that they exclude each other. They might, in fact, overlap or even have a reinforcing effect. However, three crucial discrepancies exist.

I begin with Rick Altman's thesis about like-minded *genre buffs* forming an imagined, "constellated community." Altman maintains that watching a genre film requires the acceptance of certain genre *premises* and the expectance of certain genre *pleasures*. Common acceptance and expectance lead to identification with those who have 'signed the generic contract' as well. Altman calls these imagined groups of genre aficionados "constellated communities." Comparable to a group of stars their members cohere only through repeated acts of imagination. "By taking a particular type of film-viewing pleasure I imagine myself as connected to those who take a similar type of pleasure in similar circumstances," he notes.[19] Genres invite this kind of connection by employing certain strategies. Take the inclusion of ironic references to the genre. The *X Files* (1998) movie, for instance, contains a scene in which somebody urinates on an old *Independence Day* (1996) poster—thus reciprocating a joke about the 'X-files' television series in *Independence Day*.[20] And in *Armageddon* (1998) we see a dog sink its teeth into a small, plastic Godzilla—thus attacking the merchandising product of the same-named 1998 summer blockbuster rival. A certain degree of pop culture literacy and what might be called 'genre buffism' is necessary to understand these in-jokes and intertextual references; grasping allusions helps to increase the feeling of having earned a membership to the club. This club might exist literally, but more often than not it remains imagined, gathering in spatial separation (as the metaphor of the 'constellated stars' indicates). How genre connoisseurs construct themselves as a "constellated community" can best be followed on websites dedicated to particular genres. These 'communities' exist in imagined cyberspaces, but not in cinematic places proper. They are not tied to a common experience, but as 'imagined communities' include solitary viewings.

In contrast, Henry Jenkins and Annette Kuhn describe *fandom* as something more than an 'imagined community.'[21] Both envisage fandom as a way of constituting alternative 'communities' that are often face-to-face. Through talk with fellow fans, membership in fan clubs, attendance at conventions, exchange of letters etc. the devotion to a star or a series brings fans into contact with other, like-minded people in their countries and even around the world. In this respect, Jenkins' detailed description of fan-music making ('filking') is exemplary. Fans regularly gather at conventions in order to sing self-made songs dealing with TV series, films like *Star Trek* (1982), *Star Wars* (1977) or *Indiana Jones and the Last Crusade* (1989) and fan culture itself. During these filking events fans *actively* participate in performing and singing together as a group, thus resolving the differences separating them and providing a common basis for interaction. Often humor—another means for creating bonds—plays an important role; as do filk songs that distinguish fans from normal consumers. These are not communities in any strong sense but come close to what Robert Bellah et al. call "lifestyle enclaves": they bring together those who share similar tastes and lifestyles; the participants are not interdependent and do not act politically; and they are segmental insofar as they involve only the private life of the individual (i.e. his or her leisure and consumption segment). As Bellah et al. write: "We might consider the lifestyle enclave an appropriate form of collective support in an otherwise radically individualizing society."[22] Just as in Altman's case, the 'communal' fandom activities described by Jenkins and Kuhn do not take place *inside* the cinema, even if the films constitute the fundament on which fans build their 'communities.' They are the means to an end.

This is also true for a third example of movie collectivity: the *discursive 'community'* formed in the wake of special events like blockbusters, unexpected successes or filmic scandals. Widespread media exposure via commercials, ads, or special reports can build a diffuse social pressure to watch the film, thus turning the movie into a must that must not be missed. Giving in to social pressure rewards the viewer with a feeling of belonging to those in the know as well as a certain discourse-ability, as Bruce Austin argues.[23] The significance of the first weekend for a film's box-office performance certainly owes much to the wish to become part of the discursive 'community.' You do not want to be left out when others discuss the phenomenal scare tactics of *The Blair Witch Project* or the moral question posed by *Indecent Proposal* (1993) in the school yard or an internet chat-room.

The various 'communities' described by Altman, Jenkins, Kuhn and Austin have one thing in common: they are established outside the cinema.

They take place at fan conventions, in the minds of genre buffs, in internet chat-rooms or around coffee-machines in the office. The literature on fandom focuses almost exclusively on ethnographies of fan activities *before* or *after* the cinematic experience. What they do not take into account is the actual experience of group formation happening *inside* the cinema *during* the act of experiencing aesthetically. Here I would locate my *first* point of departure.

The *second* discrepancy relates to the question of *identity* and *value*. Fans devote time and money to construct a 'community' that consists of individuals sharing a taste for stars, films or genres. In other words, they share a common cultural identity that coheres around a minimum of common values or, at least, a common taste. These values or tastes can have a subversive political tinge. Horror fan subculture, for instance, derives a sense of imagined subcultural homogeneity through opposing censorship and searching for 'banned' or 'uncut' material.[24] The glue for this 'community' also stems from acts of distinction. The in-group is drawn closer together by distancing itself symbolically from those who do not belong to the club. There is an inside (the fans) and an outside (the others), a 'we' and a 'they.'[25] This is not the case in collectivities based on collective cinematic emotions.

The third discrepancy has to do with the degree of *participatory activity*. Practices like 'filking,' editing fanzines or becoming the member of a genre fan club need to be distinguished from the mostly passive attitude in aesthetic experience. When it comes to what Scheler calls the 'immediate community of feelings' established during a terrifying film there is little active participation involved. The group experience is readily available through the individuals' bodies and their emotional reactions. The viewers' activity remains restricted to their decision to *attend* the film, to *behave* according to the cultural norms of the theater and to *re-act* appropriately in certain moments (for instance, by laughing or screaming together).

UNITED WE STAND IN FEAR: COLLECTIVITY AT THE MULTIPLEX

The pleasurable collectivity at the multiplex is popular because it does not oppose but remains in tune with the high degree of individualization characteristic of advanced modern societies. The cinema of fear enables a collectivity that does not demand too much in terms of shared values, commitment and time investment; that has minimal claims to the individual's freedom; that represents a somewhat adequate balance between individuality and collectivity. As my phenomenological description has revealed, one of the most salient features of scary movies at the multiplex is an aesthetic experience of individualized immersion. The pleasure of fearful individualized immersion implies an experience not only of something that happens *to* the self but more emphatically an experience *of* the self; pleasure always means that *I* am affected.[26] But in the movie theater the I is always pleasurably affected with *others*. It is my lived body that is affected, but I know—or at least *believe* that I know—that others are affected equally. The encounter is merely "almost" private. The cinematic experience always involves a grain of the social. During specific pleasurable moments, it is much more than this.

In frightening movies the collective aspect comes into play predominantly on three levels: as essential but tacit background; as actively intended group of feelings-in-common; and as the heightened form of group feeling that I call collective body. The three levels open up a spectrum that reaches from being attached as a group of physically close viewers to the intersubjective intimacy of phenomenologically close spectators, from simply not being alone to an emphatic feeling of belongingness.

Since no one is forced to attend a multiplex screening, these easily-established short-term collectivities exist only if a sufficient number of individuals participate. In times of ever-more perfect home viewing conditions, actively opting for the collective viewing situation inside the theater (rather than watching a video tape or a DVD) should not be underestimated. In the theater we deliberately take the active attention of aesthetic attitude and surrender to the bodily and temporal dictates of the cinematic situation in order to arrive at a public experience that we share as a *physically close group*. The cinematic situation coordinates and synchronizes otherwise highly individualized agendas and thus gathers a variety of people around a common activity: the largely passive consumption of the movie. This collectivity is unified through the perception of the aesthetic object and only occasionally directs attention towards itself. There is little social interaction, but apart from the physical closeness we also take for granted a heightened state of *intersubjective objectivity*: due to the strong *hiding effect* of the multiplex in combination with the immersive quality of fearful moments like dread or terror we tacitly presuppose that the other viewers not only see and hear but also think and feel alike. It is *my* self that becomes the point of origin for my understanding of the group: it simply cannot be that the others do not think and feel like I do. Unless we are proven otherwise by viewers who make their non-conformity explicit, we can indulge in our highly individual thoughts and feelings *and* assume a collectivity according to our own likeness. This pleasurably flatters what Bellah et al. call our "narcissism of similarity."[27]

These feelings-in-common largely form a tacit background, but under certain circumstances I focus more actively on the group experience. The feelings-in-common become more centrally aware. As we have seen in the chapter on dread, fear is an emotion that carries a sense of personal detachment. When we feel too threatened by the film and hence the isolation of fear becomes overwhelming—in other words, when pleasure turns into a negative experience—we can deliberately withdraw from immersion and let ourselves fall into the safety net of the group. Precisely because we feel psychologically isolated in fear, we look for intersubjective reassurance or even personal contact to re-gain a state of belongingness. These moments of sociality are rewarding, because we experience them not only as reassuring but also as pleasurably collective. By actively focusing on the fact that our co-viewers are also quietly following the film, we might be rewarded with the reassuring impression that they are similarly afraid. But the viewer may also establish *direct* visual, aural or haptic contact: searching for glimpses of other frightened viewers; talking to one's neighbor; pressing the hand or leaning against the shoulder of one's partner.

As these examples make clear, the cinematic collectivity can also involve some form of common activity. The third version of fearful pleasurable collectivity is connected precisely to the *active* doing of the collective scream—an activity that is more encompassing than the small subgroups established via direct contact. This corporeal reaction is not a simple reflex answering a moment of frightening shock, but a conventionalized and thus legitimate *common* response (rare are those who scream alone at home). Screaming implies both actively reaching out to others and being passively reached by them. By screaming we cry out loud that we have a similar fearful experience. The taken-for-granted background suddenly comes to the fore: we become aware that others are present and feel the same. Again, this can be reassuring; the isolation of fear vanishes. Moreover, when the shocking scene is particularly intense (and thus encourages a *uniform reaction*) and the screaming crowd is sufficiently big and densely seated (and thus enforces a *fusion* of the individual viewers' reactions), collective screaming is not just reassuring but leads to the pleasurable experience of a collective body, i.e. the spontaneous formation of a comprehensive quasi-*Leib*.

Significantly, these various forms of collectivity are united through the body. In the rough, swift-changing climate of advanced modernity, the stable commonality of our bodies is positively conservative. While everything around is continuously involved in change, the body's 'indeterminate constancy' is "the last shelter and sanctuary of continuity and duration," as Bauman puts it.[28] Via intense emotions and somatic responses like screaming the body becomes the most easily accessible instrument for creating a bond between the heterogeneous visitors of the movie theater. Since our bodily reactions are both *strongly felt* and experienced as *inevitable*, they are able to foster an intersubjective understanding of affective equality. Hence strong forms of fear like horror, shock, dread and terror level social, economic, ethnic, gender, age and religious differences. If everybody is horrified or shocked, it is not social distinction that counts but social connection. This is presumably the reason why Hitchcock after the enormous success of *Psycho* felt so "tremendously satis[fied] . . . to be able to use the cinematic art to achieve something of a mass emotion."[29]

PLEASURABLE VACILLATIONS: BETWEEN INDIVIDUALITY AND COLLECTIVITY

The cinema as a whole has to be located somewhere on a continuum between the extreme individuality and solitude of reading and the strong collectivity and conformity of mass sports events. When we read, there is no actual collectivity involved. We enter into a private dialogue with the text.[30] On the other end of the continuum, we have mass sports events like basketball or soccer games. During such events we leave parts of our individuality behind and take over the identity of the group we identify with. When we support a team—say the UCLA Bruins in college basketball—we scream and shout the letters "U-C-L-A!" not a-synchronically but at the same time, thus indicating that we leave behind what distinguishes us from the rest and are willing to merge into a larger whole. The synchronicity of screams creates a powerful collectivity of which we are an integral part. Obviously, we are part of this specific group only because we have chosen it as an expression of our *individual* identity. Nevertheless, we temporarily give up an individualized stance *during* the collective experience.

The pleasure of fear derives from the fact that it offers a bit of both: a strong individualized immersion *and* a collective experience, with both elements dialogically intertwined. In scary movies the viewers sometimes vacillate fluidly between two extremes: they can almost reach the individuality of reading (during states of deep immersion) but also come close to the collectivity of mass sports events (during instances of intense collective screaming). To be sure, the collectivity stays mostly in the background as a necessary fundament. But throughout the film this background becomes foregrounded and is perceived more centrally. What is more, if we are part of an audience that agrees to play by the (display) rules—viewers who do not stress social distinction by standing out from the group as individuals—the collective aspect comes to the fore precisely when it does *not* conflict with our wish for individualized immersion but is, in fact, longed for and needed. These are the moments when we seek the presence of others; when we need the confirmation that we are not alone; moments of loneliness due to fear. During these moments the unique pleasure of cinematic fear derives from the graceful back-and-forth movement of a pendulum swinging between two positive ends: from the pleasure of a powerful lived-body and time experience in individualized immersion to enjoyable feelings of belongingness in our collective cinematic experience.

This specific multiplex collectivity is formed on the site that many critics accuse of being overly individualized, anonymous and sterile.[31] According to these commentators, the multiplex is a place that supports and even accelerates the loss of community. However, the quality of the multiplex comes from its ability to let us eat our cake and have it. Ed Tan may be right when he asserts, "the sense that one is part of a community of likeminded individuals can probably be more easily acquired by seeking the company of family and friends or joining in the social life offered by clubs, societies, and cafés."[32] What the cinema of fear at the multiplex can offer, however, is the simultaneity of both: individuality *and* collectivity. During the two hours or so in the multiplex we can predominantly indulge in our individual experience that involves keeping social distance to others while *at the same time* entertain the comforting idea that we are part of a larger whole—a collectivity that for the most part even appears to us as sculpted in the likeness of our own experience. As such, the multiplex can be seen as a symptomatic place. It is the institutionalized expression of an attempt to reconcile a dilemma that determines modern societies as a whole: the conflicting wish for individuality *and* community.

To be sure, cinematic collectivity is comparatively flat, fleeting and anonymous. If the aesthetic object vanishes or attention is dispersed otherwise, the instability of the group and the precariousness of its cohesion become blatantly obvious. After the movie we avoid each other and go home separately, even though we might have enjoyed a pleasurable experience of collectivity a minute before. Obviously, these weak bonds do not mobilize solidarity, result in reciprocity or create strong in-group loyalty. And they do not pacify the considerable worries about political fragmentation, the loss of shared values and goals, the waning of public engagement, the vanishing of a stable public sphere, the fear of rampant narcissism, me-first individualism and the instrumental use of others.[33] Without question, the short-term collectivity offered by the multiplex is very different from the communitarian vision of a good society with shared values, mutual trust and solidarity.

Yet admitting the limits of cinematic collectivity and refraining from hyperbolizing the curative power of aesthetic experience should not obscure the fact that the cinema *does* function as a temporary alleviation for many viewers. In fact, the experience of frightening movies at the multiplex enables a form of group experience with many advantages. First, apart from the compliance with the cultural norms of the theater, there are little common values that have to be established or fought over—it remains a mere collectivity of feelings. Second, the cinematic collectivity does not demand long-term commitments, mutual obligations and cooperation and thus does not impose restrictions on one's individual way of life. As a result, there is no danger of authoritarianism and the pressure to conform, characteristics of many emphatic forms of community. Third, thanks to the existing institution of the cinema the group is established as easily as it is dispersed afterwards. It does not demand a common history with specific memories and a strong incentive to build this collectivity; nor does it require any efforts to secure its future existence. We can easily dip in and get out without much ado. Fourth, unlike many long-term communities (but also in contrast to fan groups and genre buffs) the short-term cohesion of the cinematic audience does not depend on othering. No actual outsider, enemy or scapegoat is needed. Togetherness derives from common fear of the movie. Since there are in principle no barriers, fearful collectivities are inclusive rather than exclusive: they do not rely on out-group antagonism.[34] Small wonder that this particular form of collective experience—despite strong competitors from other media—is still cherished in individualized advanced modern societies like ours.

10 The End

THE MISSING

"This is beginning," Detective Somerset alias Morgan Freeman declares in *Seven* at the start of a long and painful investigation. At the very end, I have to admit that this book is in many ways only a beginning. A number of aspects have necessarily not found their way into the preceding pages. My suggestion to expand the research scope of film phenomenology into the directions of emotions, film form and style as well as reception surroundings leaves many aspects untouched—even when it comes to the cinema of fear. One could easily round out my study by drawing a comparison to the experience of watching scary movies in the private sphere of the home: alone, in a dark living-room, on a computer screen, at night. Furthermore, there are more types of fear to be discussed—types like the uncanny or even the sublime, which are more difficult to delineate. The abstractions that I had to make in my typology of the five types of fear, moreover, entailed the neglect of *unique-individual* solutions in favor of *recurrent-typical* strategies. Hence I have not talked about particular styles of auteurs. And with the possible exception of *Henry—Portrait of a Serial Killer*, I have not taken into account arthouse or even experimental approaches to frightening the audience—think of David Lynch, Abel Ferrara, Michael Almereyda or, from a non-American perspective, Lars von Trier, Park Chan-Wook and Takashi Miike.

In addition, a number of questions related to the experience of sound, music and particularly color had to remain open. Last, since this study was not primarily intended as an investigation into genres but sought to answer the aesthetic paradox of pleasurable *fear*, it had to ignore other emotional or somatic pleasures often gained from horror movies and thrillers. In order to be truthful to the genres that figured so prominently in the preceding pages one would have to take into account *disgust* and—particularly in regard to the horror film—*laughter* and *erotic titillation*.

One of my underlying arguments was that horror films and thrillers watched inside the multiplex often entail deep immersive experiences. However, when we looked at the five types of fear, we saw that considerable

Figure 10.1 Arthouse horror: Henry (Michael Rooker) in *Henry—Portrait of a Serial Killer*.

differences existed in terms of their immersive potential. Following from this, it might be worthwhile to think more thoroughly about how frightening films form a continuum, ranging from strongly immersive to particularly extricating movies. On the one end of the spectrum one would have to locate movies that rely heavily on dread, terror and suggested horror and do completely without shocks and overwhelming direct horror—films like the original version of *The Haunting* (1963), *The Blair Witch Project* and *The Silence of the Lambs*. At the opposite end we would find films that are heavy on the shock and direct horror side—slasher movies like *Scream* or *The Evil Dead* which repeatedly jolt the viewer out of the filmic world and draw him or her back into theatrical space. The latter are more interactive and hence more consciously collective insofar as they *perceptibly* foreground the shared reactions. This is even more obvious once we do not focus on fear alone but take into account audience responses to disgusting and funny moments. Witty, allusive movies like *Scream 2*, horror comedies like *An American Werewolf in London* (1987) or trashy, gross-out splatter-films like *The Evil Dead 2* come to mind. William Paul observes, correctly I think, that these movies "work best within the context of a crowded theater—because their aesthetic *is* rousing rabble."[1]

WHY CINEMATIC FEAR IN A CULTURE OF FEAR?

"Why do so many fearful Americans enjoy movies that scare them at the exact historical moment when they have more than enough of it in everyday life?", I asked at the very beginning. It is now time to come back to this question. Americans can enjoy the kinds of fear discussed in this study in the face of real-life fears sociologists and historians like Barry Glassner and Peter Stearns talk about simply because the two types of fear easily co-exist. Fear is not a monolithic block. As Oswald Hanfling has pointed out: "Such words as 'fear' cover a wide range of situations, and the feelings cannot be described as 'the same' or 'similar' without the reference to their circumstances. [. . .] what if one were asked whether, say, fear of being chased by a bull is similar to fear of taking an exam or of being betrayed in love? The experience of fear is multifarious . . ."[2] In what way is the fear of climate change, road rage or terrorist attacks different from direct or suggested horror, shock, dread or terror?

First of all, they entail different temporal and lived-body experiences. As argued in Chapter 9, due to the developments of civilization *imminent* fears are largely exterminated. Today most of our fears are directed towards the future. Philip Fisher elaborates: "Only a civilization that has partly tamed or thinned out the traditional objects of fear—constant war, predatory animals, the variations of nature—can then, as a result, begin to expose itself to a long-term future as part of its daily imagination. [. . .] As a society that has successfully conquered or reduced imminent fear, we live more and more in an extended future."[3] In comparison to cinematic fear the kinds of fear that Fisher, Glassner and Stearns talk about are less imminent; they are less transformative; they are less dense in terms of their temporal experience; and they are less concrete as a gestalt. In fact, they are less embodied. Instead, we experience them as comparatively vague, future-oriented and cognitive.

Second, and more importantly, there are differences in terms of pleasure. Emotions are almost always *double-faced*. However, in the literature on emotions the flipside of the coin is often overlooked. This is certainly true for fear, which is rarely described other than negatively. As this study has shown, under certain circumstances fear can have a positive, pleasurable side. Now, if this is the case, the paradox of fear must evaporate. Pleasurable fear—Angst-Lust—does exist: In its *cinematic* variant fear can enable precious moments of lived-body and temporal intensity just as it may allow for valuable instances of collectivity and belongingness. Precisely because negative, long-term, real-life fear and positive, imminent, cinematic fear are hardly on the same level, there is no need to draw a tight connection between them: the latter does not control, master or cathartically purge the former. Hence cinematic fear does not help us to face up to the angst of contemporary life. Instead, it is more plausible to look at how the experience of scary movies counterbalances the transformations brought about by the processes of civilization and modernization.

This counterbalancing function also offers an explanation for the demise of certain genres: they were not capable of offering specific gratifications sought by the audience. The renewal of a genre depends on its variability and openness towards the integration of new contents, stylistic as well as aesthetic devices that strive to grant certain pleasures. Since the adaptability of genres is not unlimited, the gratification of specific wishes, desires and needs cannot be guaranteed by every genre alike. Hence some genres fall from grace, while others rise. This argument further explains the enormous popularity of frightening movies at this particular stage of advanced modernity.

LEGITIMATE PLEASURES? THE CINEMA OF FEAR'S PLACE IN MODERNITY

While the pleasures of fear as such should not be overly controversial, some commentators might question the social *value* of these types of lived-body, time and collective experience. We should not forget that, as a quintessential institution of modernity, the cinema cannot inhabit a place 'beyond' but is right at the center of the problem. My argument that the cinema of fear counterbalances negative transformations of modernity might therefore raise objections among pessimistic cultural critics. Are frightening films a double-edged sword not only in terms of their (sometimes questionable) forms of representation and their (unproved but possibly negative) media-effects but also in terms of the pleasures they entail? I don't think so.

We may start with the question of technology. In the midst of a high-tech world of computers, cyberspace, biotechnology and high-speed trains the cinema as a modern institution *par excellence* certainly does not remain unaffected. I have highlighted some technological changes in terms of exhibition. On the level of production, one only has to consider digital cameras, digital sound and digital special-effects. Today the cinema employs more high technology than ever before. Hence the cultural critic might point out that the cinema furthers the imbalance in our culture's overvaluation of technology and devaluation of bodily being. But isn't this an overly one-side perspective on technology? It is precisely the cinema's advanced technology that affords us some of our most affective and sought-after lived-body experiences—experiences that counterbalance the disembodying tendencies of other technological innovations.

Next we might have a look at the question of time. When we watch a frightening film on a Saturday evening, we surely have to submit to the external time dictates of the movie theater and the internal time regulation of the projected film, whose rationalization, efficiency, regimentation, irreversibility und fragmentation might be considered an expression of the problematic time experience of modernity more generally.[4] On the other hand, this surrendering yields a strong reward: the cinema of fear's palpability of time counters precisely modernity's loss of time experiences in an ever more accelerated world.

Or take the problem of social disintegration. The cultural critic might claim that the cinema propels disintegration because it soothes us and hence prevents more committed, long-lasting, 'real' communities. But doesn't the cinema at the same time respond positively to the fluctuation of social contacts by, first of all, uniting scattered individuals at a public venue? And doesn't the cinema's anonymous instant collectivity of feelings, moreover, create a post-traditional form of belongingness that is much more adequate to and in tune with individualized advanced modernity than the cultural critic's communitarian dream?

Last, consider the problem of disembodiment. It is true that the cinema asks for a docile, disciplined body. If the viewer did not sit still and follow the movie quietly, there would be no aesthetic attitude appropriate to frightening strategies like dread or suggested horror. Then again, the viewer's body can become the site of the specific frightening experience elaborated on throughout this study only because it is disciplined. While the viewer is disembodied in one sense, he or she simultaneously experiences a strong revalorization of the body in another sense.

Hence I consider it a wise move to discard the cultural critic's pessimistic and hasty claim that frightening movies *exacerbate* matters. Instead I want to underscore, once again, the cinema of fear's *alleviating* function vis-à-vis the powerful and persistent transformations of advanced modernity. It was a central goal of this book to complement the numerous denouncements and disparagements by providing a strong argument for the counterbalancing effect of scary movies. The oft-derided and condemned but hugely popular cinema of fear surely yields beneficial pleasures.

Notes

NOTES TO THE INTRODUCTION

1. Edmund Burke. 1958. *A Philosophical Enquiry into the Origin of Our Ideas of the Sublime and the Beautiful*. London: Routledge. p. 44.
2. Quoted from Stanley Wiater. 1992. *Dark Visions. Conversations with the Masters of the Horror Film*. New York: Avon Books. p. 11.
3. Quoted from Sidney Gottlieb (ed.). 1995. *Hitchcock on Hitchcock. Selected Writings and Interviews*. Berkeley: University of California Press. p. 116/117.
4. St. Augustine. 1838. *The Confessions of St. Augustine*. Oxford: Rivington. p. 29/30.
5. Immanuel Kant. 2001. *Critique of the Power of Judgment*. Cambridge: Cambridge University Press.
6. David Hume. 1965. "Of Tragedy." In *Of the Standard of Taste. And Other Essays*, 29–37. Indianapolis: Bobbs-Merrill. Friedrich Schiller. 2003. "On the Reason Why We Take Pleasure in Tragic Subjects." In *Friedrich Schiller. Poet of Freedom*, Vol. 4, 267–283. Washington, DC: Schiller Institute.
7. Joseph Addison. 1712. "Why Terrour and Grief are Pleasing to the Mind when Excited by Descriptions." In *The Spectator*. No. 418, June 30, [no page number]. John Aikin and Anna Laetitia Aikin. 1792. "On the Pleasure Derived From Objects of Terror." In *Miscellaneous Pieces in Prose*. London: Johnson. 117–138. See also the extended bibliography in Carsten Zelle. 1990. "Über den Grund des Vergnügens an schrecklichen Gegenständen im achtzehnten Jahrhundert." In *Schönheit und Schrecken. Entsetzen, Gewalt und Tod in alten und neuen Medien*, eds. Peter Gendolla and Carsten Zelle, 55–91. Heidelberg: Winter.
8. Carsten Zelle. 1987. *Angenehmes Grauen. Literaturhistorische Beiträge zur Ästhetik des Schrecklichen im achtzehnten Jahrhundert*. Hamburg: Meiner.
9. Noël Carroll. 1990. *The Philosophy of Horror, or Paradoxes of the Heart*. New York: Routledge. p. 10. See also Andrew Tudor. 1997. "Why Horror? The Peculiar Pleasures of a Popular Genre." In *Cultural Studies*. Vol. 11, No. 3, 443–463 and Michael Levine. 2004. "A Fun Night Out. Horror and Other Pleasures of the Cinema." In *Horror Film and Psychoanalysis. Freud's Worst Nightmare*, ed. Steven Jay Schneider, 35–54. Cambridge: Cambridge University Press.
10. See, for instance, Barry Glassner. 1999. *The Culture of Fear. Why Americans Are Afraid of the Wrong Things*. New York: Basic. David L. Altheide. 2002. *Creating Fear. News and the Construction of Crisis*. New York: Aldine. The culture-of-fear thesis in Moore's documentary is largely based on Glassner's book.

11. Peter N. Stearns. 2006. *American Fear. The Causes and Consequences of High Anxiety*. New York: Routledge. p. 202.
12. Politicians try to gain votes and create new laws. Television stations and newspapers aim to expand their audience and readership. Advocacy groups attempt to win support for their cause. Advertisers and companies want to sell more products.
13. Glassner, p. xxviii.
14. Stearns, p. 154/155.
15. Matt Hills. 2005. *The Pleasures of Horror*. London: Continuum. p. 5.
16. Carl Plantinga. 2009. *Moving Viewers. American Film and the Spectator's Experience*. Berkeley: University of California Press. p. 39.
17. Pierre Bourdieu. 1987. *Distinction. A Social Critique of the Judgment of Taste*. Cambridge: Harvard University Press.
18. Hills, p. 94.
19. Hills, p. 74.
20. The idea of aesthetic experience as self-expansion and imaginary role-play is presented in various articles by Winfried Fluck. See 2005. "California Blue. Americanization as Self-Americanization." In *Americanization and Anti-Americanism. The German Encounter with American Culture after 1945*, ed. Alexander Stephan, 221–237. New York: Berghahn.
21. Daniel Shaw. 2001. "Power, Horror and Ambivalence." In *Film and Philosophy*. Horror Special Edition. 1–12.
22. This therapeutic understanding, reintroduced by Jacob Bernays in the mid-19th century, stresses the medical sense of the metaphor. Jacob Bernays. 1857. *Grundzüge der verlorenen Abhandlung des Aristoteles über Wirkung der Tragödie*. Breslau: Trewenát.
23. Aristotle. 1997. *Poetics*. London: Penguin. p. 10 (emphasis added).
24. "The suspense thriller is a genre which uses thrills—which are [. . .] a vicarious psychological experience which provides the spectator with a particular kind of catharsis," Charles Derry asserts, but never explains what he means precisely. Charles Derry. 1988. *The Suspense Thriller. Films in the Shadow of Alfred Hitchcock*. Jefferson: McFarland. p. 19.
25. To be sure, there is one area in which the concept of catharsis has been used more sophisticatedly: the debate about media effects. A prominent strain of the discussion revolves around aggression as a response to screen violence and the possible purging of it. However, in my search for the aesthetic pleasures of fear the catharsis of aggression through the vicarious experience of violence seems not an appropriate candidate, since in its exclusive concern with *aggression* it cannot account for the paradox of *fear*.
26. Norbert Elias. 1994. *The Civilizing Process. Sociogenetic and Psychogenetic Investigations*. Malden: Blackwell. p. 170.
27. Thomas Scheff. 1979. *Catharsis in Healing, Ritual, and Drama*. Berkeley: University of California Press. p. 51.
28. See the entries on the 'pleasure principle (p. 322–325),' the 'Nirvana principle' and the 'principle of constance' in J. Laplanche and J.-B. Pontalis. 1988. *The Language of Psycho-Analysis*. London: Karnac.
29. Ernest Schachtel. 1984. *Metamorphosis. On the Development of Affect, Perception, Attention, and Memory*. New York: Da Capo. p. 9.
30. See Pinedo, Isabel Cristina. 2004. "Postmodern Elements of the Contemporary Horror Film." In *The Horror Film*, ed. Stephen Prince, 85–117. New Brunswick: Rutgers University Press. p. 29.
31. See Norbert Elias and Eric Dunning. 1986. *Quest for Excitement. Sport and Leisure in the Civilizing Process*. Oxford: Basil Blackwell. p. 63/64.

32. Elias/Dunning, p. 82.
33. Friedrich Nietzsche. 1968. *The Will to Power*. New York: Vintage. p. 452.
34. Ed S. Tan. 1996. *Emotion and the Structure of Narrative Film. Film as Emotion Machine*. Mahwah: Lawrence Erlbaum Associates. Torben Grodal. 1997. *Moving Pictures. A New Theory of Film Genres, Feelings, and Cognition*. Oxford: Clarendon. Noël Carroll. 1998. *A Philosophy of Mass Art*. Oxford: Clarendon. Greg M. Smith. 2003. *Film Structure and the Emotion System*. Cambridge: Cambridge University Press. Murray Smith. 1995. *Engaging Characters. Fiction, Emotion, and the Cinema*. Oxford: Clarendon Press.
35. Noël Carroll. 1999a. "Film, Emotion, and Genre". In *Passionate Views. Film, Cognition and Emotion*, ed. Carl Plantinga and Greg M. Smith, 21–47. Baltimore: Johns Hopkins University Press. p. 29.
36. Carroll (1999a), p. 25.
37. Steven Shaviro. *The Cinematic Body*. 1993. Minneapolis: University of Minnesota Press. Barbara M. Kennedy. 2000. *Deleuze and Cinema. The Aesthetics of Sensation*. Edinburgh: Edinburgh University Press. Anna Powell. 2005. *Deleuze and Horror Film*. Edinburgh: Edinburgh University Press.
38. Kennedy, in fact, considers her form of aesthetics "an empiricism." Kennedy, p. 31.
39. Here is Barbara Kennedy on *William Shakespeare's Romeo and Juliet* (1996): "The languorous liquidity and fluidity of the colors and tones lend a sensuality to the mood and feel of the sequence. [. . .] Colors—greens, turquoises, blues, opals, lavenders—are painted across a canvas which fades and wipes into a liquidity of sensuality and sensation." Kennedy, p. 175.
40. Kennedy, p. 112 and 31.
41. Hills, p. 24.
42. Powell, p. 201.
43. Powell, p. 8 and 3.
44. Herbert Spiegelberg. 1982. *The Phenomenological Movement. A Historical Introduction*. The Hague: Martinus Nijhoff. p. 680.
45. Vivian Sobchack. 1992. *The Address of the Eye. A Phenomenology of Film Experience*. Princeton: Princeton University Press. Vivian Sobchack. 2004. *Carnal Thoughts. Embodiment and Moving Image Culture*. Berkeley: University of California Press. For further investigations into film and phenomenology see Allan Casebier. 1991. *Film and Phenomenology. Toward a Realist Theory of Cinematic Representation*. Cambridge: Cambridge University Press. Laura U. Marks. 2000. *The Skin of the Film. Intercultural Cinema, Embodiment, and the Senses*. Durham: Duke University Press. Jennifer M. Barker. 2009. *The Tactile Eye. Touch and the Cinematic Experience*. Berkeley: University of California Press.
46. Sobchack (2004), p. 56/57.
47. Hans Ulrich Gumbrecht. 2004. *Production of Presence. What Meaning Cannot Convey*. Stanford: Stanford University Press. p. 109.
48. Richard Shusterman. 2000b. *Pragmatist Aesthetics. Living Beauty, Rethinking Art*. Lanham: Rowman and Littlefield. p. 268.
49. Motion Picture Association of America: *Entertainment Industry Market Statistics 2007*. p. 24.
50. Motion Picture Association: *Motion Picture Statistics*. p. 10. Motion Picture Association: *2006 US Theatrical Market Statistics*. p. 6.
51. Quoted from Robert Blanchet. 2003. *Blockbuster. Ästhetik, Ökonomie und Geschichte des postklassischen Hollywoodkinos*. Marburg: Schüren. p. 225/226 (emphasis added).
52. Motion Picture Association: *2006 US Theatrical Market Statistics*. p. 18.

53. See Paul Griffith. 2004. "Is Emotion a Natural Kind?" In *Thinking About Feeling. Contemporary Philosophers on Emotions*, ed. Robert C. Solomon, 233–249. New York: Oxford University Press. See also the detailed discussion in Jesse Prinz. 2004. *Gut Reactions. A Perceptual Theory of Emotions*. Oxford: Oxford University Press.
54. For the experience of *disgust*, which also dominates many horror films and thrillers but is not connected to the paradox of fear, see Julian Hanich. 2009. "(Dis-)Liking Disgust: The Revulsion Experience at the Movies." In *New Review of Film and Television Studies*. Vol. 7, No. 3, 293–309.
55. Hermann Schmitz. 1969. *Der Gefühlsraum*. Bonn: Bouvier. p. 306–320.
56. Prinz, p. 75.
57. See the discussion of LeDoux in Jon Elster. 1999. *Strong Feelings. Emotion, Addiction, and Human Behavior*. Cambridge: MIT Press. p. 31–35.
58. Carl Plantinga and Greg M. Smith (ed.). 1999. *Passionate Views. Film, Cognition and Emotion*. Baltimore: Johns Hopkins University Press. p. 6.
59. Jean-Paul Sartre writes: "We have to speak of a world of emotions as one speaks of a world of dreams or of worlds of madness." Jean-Paul Sartre. 2002. *Sketch for a Theory of the Emotions*. London: Routledge. p. 54.
60. In a number of articles neuroscientist James A. Coan has provided experimental evidence for the relieving quality of social proximity and physical contact with others in the face of threat. See James A. Coan. 2008. "Toward a Neuroscience of Attachment." In *Handbook of Attachment*. Vol. 2, ed. Jude Cassidy and Phillip R. Shaver, 241–265.
61. See John Dewey's characterization of experience: "Experience is a matter of interaction of organism with its environment [. . .] The self acts as well as undergoes, and its undergoings are not impressions stamped upon an inert wax but depend upon the way the organism reacts and responds." John Dewey. 1980. *Art as Experience*. New York: Perigee. p. 246.
62. See Sue L. Cataldi. 1993. *Emotion, Depth, and Flesh. A Study of Sensitive Space*. Albany: State University of New York Press. p. 43.
63. See, for instance, the definition of Robert Bellah et. al.: "a *community* is a group of people who are socially interdependent, who participate together in discussion and decision making, and who share certain *practices* [. . .] that both define the community and are nurtured by it. Such a community is not quickly formed. It almost always has a history and so also is a community of memory, defined in part by its past and its memory of its past." Robert Bellah, Richard Madsen, William M. Sullivan, Ann Swidler and Stven M. Tipton. 1985. *Habits of the Heart. Individualism and Commitment in American Life*. New York: Harper and Row. p. 333 (emphasis in the original).
64. Various names have been coined for the contemporary stage of Western societies: from 'post-modernity' to 'late modernity,' from 'second modernity' to 'liquid modernity'. In their opposition to 'classic,' 'high,' 'first,' or 'solid' modernity all concepts carry slightly (or not so slightly) different meanings. In order to indicate a certain distance from these highly charged concepts I prefer the more neutral expression 'advanced modernity.'
65. Charles Taylor. *The Malaises of Modernity*. Reprinted as Charles Taylor. 1992. *The Ethics of Authenticity*. Cambridge: Harvard University Press.
66. Daniel Patrick Moynihan. 1996. "Defining Deviancy Down." In *The Essential Neo-Conservative Reader*, ed. Mark Gerson, 356–371. Reading: Addison-Wesley.
67. Hills, p. 205.
68. See, for instance, Yvonne Leffler. 2000. *Horror as Pleasure. The Aesthetics of Horror Fiction*. Stockholm: Almqvist & Wiksell. One important

exception is the detailed literature on suspense, listed at the end of my chapter on dread.
69. George Lakoff and Mark Johnson. 1999. *Philosophy in the Flesh. The Embodied Mind and Its Challenge to Western Thought.* New York: Basic Books. p. 19 (emphasis in the original).
70. As Daniel Frampton notes: "a filmgoer may be unable to describe a feeling after seeing something and [will therefore] have to drag their friends to see what they mean." Daniel Frampton. 2006. *Filmosophy.* London: Wallflower. p. 194.
71. Note that my suggestions concern only the most common aesthetic strategies of not more than two genres.
72. Maltby, p. 1.
73. Carroll (1999a), p. 34.
74. Steve Neale. 1990. "Questions of Genre". In *Screen.* Vol. 31, No. 1, 45–66. p. 65.
75. Jörg Schweinitz. 1994. "'Genre' und lebendiges Genrebewusstsein. Geschichte eines Begriffs und Probleme seiner Konzeptualisierung in der Filmwissenschaft." In *Montage/AV.* Vol. 3, No. 2, 99–118. p. 113.
76. This can be judged from the heated controversy that followed the publication of Noël Carroll's *The Philosophy of Horror.* This seminal book has not only caused numerous reactions when it came out, but is still able to spark protest—as we shall see in my own discussion in Chapter 1.
77. Schweinitz, p. 109 (my translation).
78. David Bordwell. 1989. *Making Meaning. Inference and Rhetoric in the Interpretation of Cinema.* Cambridge: Harvard University Press. p. 147.
79. See Rick Altman. 1999. *Film/Genre.* London: Bfi.
80. Steve Neale has shown how the meaning of the term *melodrama* had changed over time. Analyzing the use of the word in the American trade press, Neale argues that in the 1930s and 1940s melodrama almost implied the opposite of its common-sense meaning today: from an action-oriented to a sentimental genre. Steve Neale. 1993. "Melo Talk: On the Meaning and Use of the Term 'Melodrama' in the American Trade Press." In: *Velvet Light Trap.* No. 32, 66–89.
81. See Edward E. Smith and Douglas Medin. 1981. *Categories and Concepts.* Cambridge: Harvard University Press. David Bordwell argues: "The processes by which people construct a fuzzy category [like genre] do not define it but rather provide a loose set of more or less central, more or less strongly linked expectations—default hierarchies—that are taken to hold good unless contradicted by other information." Bordwell (1989), p. 148.
82. Neale (1990), p. 66.
83. Ernest Klein. 1966. *A Comprehensive Etymological Dictionary of the English Language.* Amsterdam: Elsevier. p. 744.
84. Klein, p. 1611.
85. Martin Rubin. 1999. *Thrillers.* Cambridge: Cambridge University Press. p. 8.
86. Rubin, p. 264.
87. Michael Sragow. 1992. "The Current Cinema: Tricks" In *The New Yorker.* August 24. p. 77. Barry Keith Grant. 1998. "Rich and Strange: The Yuppie Horror Film." In *Contemporary Hollywood Cinema,* ed. Steve Neale and Murray Smith, 280–293. London: Routledge.
88. Richard Dyer. 1997. "Kill and Kill Again." In *Sight and Sound.* Vol. 7, No. 9, 14–17. p. 14.
89. Neale (1990), p. 55.
90. A similar argument can be found in David Bordwell. 2006. *The Way Hollywood Tells It. Story and Style in Modern Movies.* Berkeley: University of California Press. p. 51–58.

91. Carol J. Clover. 1992. *Men, Women, and Chainsaws. Gender in the Modern Horror Film*. Princeton: Princeton University Press. As *Variety* noted in October 2006: "Studio execs have noticed for the past few years [. . .] that females under 25 made up a large chunk of B.O. bucks. Exit polls show that slightly more women than men saw 'Grudge 2' over its opening weekend. [. . .] But even as a string of gorier, harder-edged slasher pics—including the 'Saw' franchise—have entered the market, they are pulling in women." Ian Mohr: "Girls' Fright Out. Horror Pics Bank on New Femme Fanbase." In: *Variety*. October 22, 2006. www.variety.com/indexasp?layout=print_story&articleid=VR1117952345&categoryid=1019.
92. Apart from the studies footnoted above, there are, for instance, Peter Hutchings. 2004. *The Horror Film*. London: Longman. Steffen Hantke (ed.). 2004. *Horror Film. Creating and Marketing Fear*. Jackson: University Press of Mississippi. Kevin Heffernan. 2004. *Ghouls, Gimmicks, and Gold. Horror Films and the American Movie Business 1953–1968*. Durham: Duke University Press. Joseph Maddrey. 2004. *Nightmares in Red, White and Blue. The Evolution of the American Horror Movie*. Jefferson: McFarland. Rick Worland. 2007. *The Horror Film. An Introduction*. Malden: Blackwell.
93. Despite its wide application as a communicative generic concept in both everyday speech and the media, academics have devoted less critical scrutiny to the thriller than to many other genres. Comparable to the melodrama, the thriller defies generic descriptions in terms of iconography, content and narrative perspective. Given that emotions were neglected in film studies for the longest time, one of the reasons for this lack of critical attention might be the fact that the thriller is a genre whose prime feature is precisely the evocation of a strong emotional experience. For literature on the thriller, see Rubin and Derry.
94. Gerhard Schulze. 2005. *Die Erlebnisgesellschaft. Kultursoziologie der Gegenwart*. Frankfurt/Main: Campus. p. 40–42.
95. Tan, p. 10 (emphasis in the original).
96. Tan, p. 16.

NOTES TO CHAPTER 1

1. Maurice Merleau-Ponty. 2002. *The Phenomenology of Perception*. London: Routledge. p. xxiv.
2. Simon Glendinning. 2007. *In the Name of Phenomenology*. New York: Routledge. p. 29.
3. Maurice Roche. 1973. *Phenomenology, Language and the Social Sciences*. London: Routledge. p. 13.
4. Don Ihde. 1977. *Experimental Phenomenology. An Introduction*. New York: Putnam. p. 73.
5. Ihde, p. 47/48.
6. Francisco J. Varela and Jonathan Shear. 1999. "First-Person Methodologies: What, Why, How?" In *Journal of Consciousness Studies*. Vol. 6, No. 2–3, 1999, 1–14. p. 3.
7. Bruce Mangan. 1999. "The Fringe: A Case Study in Explanatory Phenomenology." In *Journal of Consciousness Studies*. Vol. 6, No. 2–3, 249–252. p. 250.
8. This exclusion of competing experiences is also called 'restriction of consciousness' (*Enge des Bewusstseins*). Bernhard Waldenfels. 2004. *Phänomenologie der Aufmerksamkeit*. Frankfurt/Main: Suhrkamp. p. 103.
9. Sobchack (2004), p. 5.

10. Schmitz (1969), p. 149.
11. Pierre Vermersch. 1999. "Introspection as Practice." In *Journal of Consciousness Studies*. Vol. 6, No. 2–3, 17–42. p. 19.
12. Varela/Shear, p. 14.
13. Sobchack (2004), p. 5. The quote comes from Paul Ricoeur. 1977. *The Rule of Metaphor. Multi-Disciplinary Studies of the Creations of Meaning in Language*. Toronto: University of Toronto Press.
14. www.rollingstone.com/reviews/movie/5948711/review/5948712/seven [last accessed: 23 July 2009].
15. www.washingtonpost.com/wp-srv/style/longterm/movies/videos/singlewhitefemalerhinson_a0a79d.htm [last accessed: 23 July 2009].
16. rogerebert.suntimes.com/apps/pbcs.dll/article?AID=/19990701/REVIEWS/907010301/1023 [last accessed: 23 July 2009].
17. George Lakoff and Mark Johnson. 1980. *Metaphors We Live By*. Chicago: University of Chicago Press. p. 19.
18. Lakoff/Johnson (1980), p. 15. Interestingly, the authors also point out the literal debasement of *emotions* in ordinary language, exemplified by the 'rational is up; emotion is down' concept.
19. Jack Katz. 1999. *How Emotions Work*. Chicago: University of Chicago Press. p. 11.
20. Glendinning, p. 227/228.
21. Sobchack (2004), p. 5.
22. Herbert Spiegelberg. 1975. "How Subjective is Phenomenology?" In *Doing Phenomenology. Essays on and in Phenomenology*, 72–79. The Hague: Martinus Nijhoff. p. 78.
23. See Janet Staiger. 1992. *Interpreting Films. Studies in the Historical Reception of American Cinema*. Princeton: Princeton University Press. Melvyn Stokes and Richard Maltby (ed.). 2000. *Identifying Hollywood's Audiences*. London: Bfi.
24. Stephen Prince. 2004. "Violence and Psychophysiology in Horror Cinema." In *Horror Film and Psychoanalysis. Freud's Worst Nightmare*, ed. Steven Jay Schneider, 241–256. Cambridge: Cambridge University Press. p. 249.
25. Joseph Levine. 1983. "Materialism and Qualia: The Explanatory Gap." In *Pacific Philosophical Quarterly*. Vol. 64, No. 4, 354–361.
26. Katz, p. 341.
27. In Germany the interest in Schmitz' oeuvre has been growing over the last couple of years. Studies by Hilge Landweer and Gernot Böhme are cases in point. Hilge Landweer. 1999. *Scham und Macht. Phänomenologische Untersuchungen zur Sozialität eines Gefühls*. Tübingen: Mohr Siebeck. Gernot Böhme. 1995. *Atmosphäre. Essays zur neuen Ästhetik*. Frankfurt/Main: Suhrkamp.
28. I will strategically employ Schmitz' perceptive phenomenological *descriptions*. It would lead me astray, however, to introduce his complex *concept* of emotions as atmospheres.
29. Smith/Medin, p. 2.
30. For the difference between aesthetic object and work of art, see Mikel Dufrenne. 1973. *The Phenomenology of Aesthetic Experience*. Evanston: Northwestern University Press. p. 204 and 218.

NOTES TO CHAPTER 2

1. Anne Friedberg. 1993. *Window Shopping. Cinema and the Postmodern*. Berkeley: University of California Press. p. 6.

2. Mark Kermode. 1993. "Terror Terror" [interview with horror director Joe Dante]. In *Sight and Sound*. Vol. 3, No. 6, 7–8.
3. Dufrenne, p. 16.
4. Roman Ingarden. 1973. *The Literary Work of Art*. Evanston: Northwestern University Press. Wolfgang Iser. 1978. *The Act of Reading. A Theory of Aesthetic Response*. London: Routledge.
5. Dufrenne, p. 406.
6. Carroll lists various means how the pre-focussed and selected film can *hold* as well as *guide* the viewer's attention. Noël Carroll. 2003. "Film, Attention, and Communication. A Naturalistic Account." In *Engaging the Moving Image*, 10–58. New Haven: Yale University Press.
7. Linda Singer. 1990. "Eye/Mind/Screen: Toward a Phenomenology of Cinematic Scopophilia." In *Quarterly Review of Film and Video*. Vol. 12, No. 3, 51–67. p. 54.
8. Thomas Elsaesser. 1981. "Narrative Cinema and Audience-Oriented Aesthetics." In *Popular Television and Film*, ed. Tony Bennett, Susan Boyd-Bowman, Colin Mercer and Janet Woollacott, 270–282. London: Bfi. p. 270.
9. Frampton, p. 206.
10. Laura Mulvey. 2006. *Death 24x a Second. Stillness and the Moving Image*. London: Reaktion Books. p. 171.
11. Mulvey (2006), p. 184.
12. In an empirical study Annette Hill found out: "When watching a video in the home environment, participants are aware there is more scope for audience interaction. One participant comments: 'I notice more reactions when I watch videos at home with family or friends. In the cinema there is the big screen and darkness." Annette Hill. 1997. *Shocking Entertainment. Viewer Response to Movie Violence*. Luton: University of Luton Press. p. 28.
13. See Barry Schwartz. 2004. *The Paradox of Choice. Why More is Less*. New York: HarperCollins.
14. Singer, p. 53/54.
15. Obviously, there would be more to say about the multiplex. Since I am interested exclusively in aesthetic experience, I will not elaborate here. A complete account would have to stress the geographical location; the computerized box office; the enormous concession stands; the aspect of plurimediality and intermediality; the association with larger leisure opportunities within or close to shopping malls and restaurants etc. See Charles R. Acland. 2000. "Cinemagoing and the Rise of the Megaplex." In *Television and New Media*. Vol. 1, No. 3, 355–382.
16. Acland writes: "What everyone comes to see [in the megaplex], evidently, is their own film; the quality being offered is the possibility of experiencing, unencumbered by other distractions, one's own event." Acland, p. 371.
17. Following Lakshmi Srinivas' ethnographic study on movie-going habits in India, we sense the specificity of the American way. In contrast to the U.S. "where film-viewing is an atomized and highly disciplined activity" (p. 160), Srinivas argues that in India the *social* experience of movie going is more important than the film itself. People usually go to the movies in large groups. They dress up for these occasions and go to be seen and to see others. There are family members of all ages, including toddlers and grandparents. Often people join a group for an evening at the movies even though they might not be keen on the respective film or have seen it already. And while in the U.S. it is not uncommon to go to the movies alone, in India this is considered an anti-social and unnatural act. Amongst the huge audiences socializing takes place in various ways. People talk to each other. They pass around coffee.

They shout out loud, applaud, and respond to the screen. They hum or sing along with the songs. Some whistle or make vulgar comments. In sum: "Socializing in the theatre with friends and family takes priority over seeing the film," Srinivas argues (p. 164). Lakshmi Srinivas. 2002. "The Active Audience: Spectatorship, Social Relations and the Experience of Cinema in India." In *Media, Culture and Society.* Vol. 24, No. 2, 155–173.
18. Srinivas, p. 171.
19. V.F. Perkins. 1972. *Film as Film. Understanding and Judging Movies.* Harmondsworth: Penguin. p. 134.
20. Douglas Gomery. 1992. *Shared Pleasures. A History of Movie Presentation in the United States.* London: Bfi. p. 76.
21. Gomery, p. 107.
22. Phil Hubbard. 2003. "A Good Night Out? Multiplex Cinemas as Sites of Embodied Leisure." In *Leisure Studies.* Vol. 22, No. 3, 255–272. p. 261.
23. Siegfried Kracauer. 1987. "Cult of Distraction. On Berlin's Picture Palaces." In *New German Critique.* No. 40, 91–96. p. 94.
24. Singer, p. 52/53.
25. Gomery, p. 117/118.
26. See Janet Staiger. 2000. *Perverse Spectators. The Practices of Film Reception.* New York: NYU Press.
27. Gomery, p. 100.
28. Gianluca Sergi. 2003. "Blockbusting Sound. The Case of *The Fugitive.*" In *Movie Blockbusters,* ed. Julian Stringer, 141–152. London: Routledge. p. 152.
29. Barbara Flückiger. 2001. *Sound Design. Die virtuelle Klangwelt des Films.* Marburg: Schüren. See especially p. 237–243.
30. Gomery, p. 100.
31. Gianluca Sergi. 1998. "A Cry in the Dark. The Role of Post-Classical Film Sound." In *Contemporary Hollywood Cinema,* ed. Steve Neale and Murray Smith, 156–165. London: Routledge. p. 161.
32. For useful introductory overviews into the functions of emotions, see: Dacher Keltner and James J. Gross. 1999. "Functional Accounts of Emotions." In *Cognition and Emotion.* Vol. 13, No. 5, 505–521. For the communicativeness of emotions, see Keith Oatley. 1996. "Emotions: Communications to the Self and Others." In *The Emotions. Social, Cultural and Biological Dimensions,* ed. Rom Harré and W. Gerrod Parrot, 312–316. London: Sage.
33. Ursula Hess and Gilles Kirouac. 2000. "Emotion Expression in Groups." In *Handbook of Emotions. Second Edition,* ed. Michael Lewis and Jeanette Haviland-Jones, 368–381. New York: Guildford. p. 374.
34. Katz, p. 152.
35. Perkins, p. 134.
36. Tan, p. 36.
37. Tan, p. 81/82.
38. Lambert Wiesing. 2006. "Von der defekten Illusion zum perfekten Phantom. Über phänomenologische Bildtheorien." In *. . . kraft der Illusion,* ed. Gertrud Koch and Christiane Voss, 89–101. Munich: Fink. p. 93. See also the discussion in Bernhard Waldenfels. 2000. *Das leibliche Selbst. Vorlesungen zur Phänomenologie des Leibes.* Frankfurt/Main: Suhrkamp. p. 48–62.
39. For a distinction between 'illusion' and 'delusion' see John L. Austin. 1962. *Sense and Sensibilia.* Oxford: Clarendon. p. 20–26.
40. Menachem Brinker. 1977. "Aesthetic Illusion." In *The Journal of Aesthetics and Art Criticism.* Vol. 36, No. 2, 191–196. p. 192/193.
41. Wiesing (2006), p. 89.
42. Sobchack (1992), p. 179 (emphases in the original).

43. See Gertrud Koch. 2003. "Filmische Welten. Zur Welthaltigkeit filmischer Projektionen." In *Dimensionen ästhetischer Erfahrung*, ed. Joachim Küpper and Christoph Menke, 162–175. Frankfurt/Main: Suhrkamp.
44. For the differences in active and passive attention between theater and film, see Carroll (2003).
45. See Marie-Laure Ryan. 2001. *Narrative as Virtual Reality. Immersion and Interactivity in Literature and Electronic Media*. Baltimore: The Johns Hopkins University Press. Judith H. Murray. 1997. *Hamlet on the Holodeck. The Future of Narrative in Cyberspace*. New York: Free Press.
46. Ryan, p. 14.
47. Ryan, p. 90.
48. Murray, p. 98/99.
49. Koch, p. 166.
50. Ryan, p. 140.
51. Helmuth Plessner. 1970. *Philosophische Anthropologie*. Frankfurt/Main: Fischer. p. 138.
52. Elsaesser, p. 273.
53. Elsaesser, p. 271 and 272.
54. See Richard Allen. 2001. "Cognitive Film Theory." In *Wittgenstein, Theory and the Arts*, ed. Richard Allen and Malcolm Turvey, 174–209. London: Routledge.
55. Ryan, p. 348.
56. Jon Elster, for instance, writes: "It seems to be a fairly robust fact about the emotions that each of them goes together with one or several spontaneous action tendencies that, if unchecked, will result in action. Jon Elster. 2004. "Emotion and Action." In *Thinking About Feeling. Contemporary Philosophers on Emotions*, ed. Robert C. Solomon, 151–162. Oxford: Oxford University Press. p. 151.
57. Linda Williams. 2002. "Learning to Scream." In *Horror, the Film Reader*, ed. Mark Jancovich, 163–168. London: Routledge. p. 163.
58. I neglect the unlikely possibility of watching the film alone. In years of excessive cinemagoing it happened to me only once. Even in this unusual case other viewers were present through their absence in the atmosphere of an auditorium that was built for them in the first place.
59. Motion Picture Association: *Motion Picture Statistics*. p. 10. Motion Picture Association: *2006 US Theatrical Market Statistics*. p. 6. Admittedly, this rise in numbers of spectators does not take into account the general increase of the U.S. population, which certainly contributes to this growth.
60. Daniel Stern. 2004. *The Present Moment in Psychotherapy and Everyday Life*. New York: Norton. p. 101.
61. Vivian Sobchack. 1999. "Toward a Phenomenology of Nonfictional Film Experience." In *Collecting Visible Evidence*, ed. Jane M. Gaines and Michael Renov, 241–254. Minneapolis: University of Minnesota Press, 1999. See Jean-Paul Meunier. 1969. *Les Structures de l'experience filmique: L'Identification filmique*. Louvain: Librairie Universitaire.
62. Drew Leder. 1990. *The Absent Body*. Chicago: University of Chicago Press.
63. John Searle. 1992. *The Rediscovery of the Mind*. Cambridge: MIT Press. p. 175.
64. Searle, p. 184/185.
65. I am certainly not alone in taking this position. The psychologist Daniel Stern, for instance, notes: "the participation in rituals, artistic performances, spectacles, and communal activities like dancing or singing together can result in a transient (real or imagined) intersubjective contact. All participants assume that others experience what is happening roughly as they do." Stern, p. 109.

66. See Gary Edgerton. 2002. "The Multiplex. The Modern American Motion Picture Theater as Message." In *Exhibition. The Film Reader*, ed. Ina Rae Hark, 155–159. London: Routledge.

NOTES TO CHAPTER 3

1. Siegfried Kracauer. 1997. *Theory of Film. The Redemption of Physical Reality*. Princeton: Princeton University Press. p. 58.
2. Quoted from Wiater, p. 22.
3. Plantinga (2009), p. 106.
4. Stephen Prince. 2000. "Graphic Violence in the Cinema: Origins, Aesthetic Design, and Social Effects." In *Screening Violence*, ed. Stephen Prince, 1–44. London: Athlone. p. 10–19.
5. The example comes from Noël Carroll. 1999b. "Horror and Humor." In *The Journal of Aesthetics and Art Criticism*. Vol. 57, No. 2, 145–160. p. 147.
6. Carroll (1990), p. 24 and 27–35.
7. Prince (2000), p. 18.
8. Carroll (1990), p. 182.
9. Mirjam Schaub. 2005. *Bilder aus dem Off. Zum philosophischen Stand der Kinotheorie*. Weimar: VDG. See particularly p. 48–56.
10. Carroll (1990), p. 243/245. Or take this example from *The Silence of the Lambs*: an autopsy is performed on a corpse found in water. We can study the grossed-out, horrified faces of the attendant characters. We get to hear detailed descriptions of the wounds. We can see the unfocused contours of the victim at the lower edge of the frame. But it takes roughly 80 seconds from the moment the characters first confront the victim until the camera discloses *parts* of the bloated body, and another 100 seconds till the corpse is *fully* revealed.
11. I introduce the new terms *ontological* as well as *phenomenological* distance because the previous use of notions like "aesthetic, "psychic" or "psychological" distance seems too muddled. These expressions were often not clearly set apart and used interchangeably.
12. Stanley Cavell. 1979. *The World Viewed. Reflections on the Ontology of Film*. Enlarged Edition. Cambridge: Harvard University Press. p. 24. It is precisely this ontological boundary that films like Woody Allen's *The Purple Rose of Cairo* (1985) and *Last Action Hero* (1993) with Arnold Schwarzenegger explored.
13. Burke, p. 40; Kant, p. 144; Jean-Jacques Rousseau. 2000. *Confessions*. Oxford: Oxford University Press. p. 168.
14. Béla Balázs. 2001. *Der sichtbare Mensch oder die Kultur des Films*. Frankfurt/Main: Suhrkamp. p. 82. Kracauer, p. 58.
15. Tan, p. 77.
16. Mulvey (2006), p. 171. Cavell, p. 40.
17. See the discussion of Renoir in Sobchack (2004), p. 268–275.
18. In his book *Offensive Films* Mikal Brottman introduces a category called *cinéma vomitif* that includes films like *Blood Feast* (1963), *The Texas Chainsaw Massacre* or *Death Scenes* (1989). These movies aim at the arousal of "strong sensations in the lower body—nausea, repulsion, weakness, faintness, and loosening of bowel or bladder control—normally by way of graphic scenes featuring the by-products of bodily detritus: vomit, excrement, viscera, brain tissue and so on." Mikal Brottman. 1997. *Offensive Films. Toward an Anthropology of* Cinéma Vomitif. Westport: Greenwood. p. 11.
19. W. J. T. Mitchell. 2005. *What Do Pictures Want? The Lives and Loves of Images*. Chicago: The University of Chicago Press. p. 8 and 32/33.

268 Notes

20. Erwin Straus. 1930. "Die Formen des Räumlichen." In *Der Nervenarzt*. Vol. 3, No. 11, 633–656. p. 641.
21. Erwin Straus. 1956. *Vom Sinn der Sinne. Ein Beitrag zur Grundlegung der Psychologie*. Second Edition. Berlin: Springer, 1956. p. 393 (my translation). Similar to Erwin Straus, Laura Marks underscores that instances of visuality mark a continuum between the distant and the embodied, the optical and the haptic. Marks, p. 132.
22. Straus (1930), p. 640. In German the expression 'ins Auge stechen' exists: something is so striking that it stabs the eye.
23. Charles Baudelaire. 1974. *Selected Poems of Charles Baudelaire*. New York: Grove Press.
24. Cataldi, p. 139.
25. David Freedberg. 1989. *The Power of Images. Studies in the History of Response*. Chicago: University of Chicago Press. p. xxii and 1.
26. Freedberg, p. 438.
27. Freedberg, p. 438.
28. Wiesing (2006), p. 89–101.
29. Moritz Geiger. 1928. *Zugänge zur Ästhetik*. Leipzig: Der Neue Geist. p. 140.
30. Wiesing (2006), p. 98.
31. Lambert Wiesing. 2005. *Artifizielle Präsenz. Studien zur Philosophie des Bildes*. Frankfurt/Main: Suhrkamp. p. 36.
32. Mitchell, p. 11, 10, 55, 93 and 7.
33. Mitchell, p. 8.
34. Wiesing (2006), p. 100.
35. Straus (1930), p. 642.
36. Straus (1930), p. 645.
37. Oswald Hanfling. 1996. "Fact, Fiction and Feeling." In *British Journal of Aesthetics*. Vol. 36, No. 4, 356–366. Malcolm Turvey. 2006. "Imagination, Simulation, and Fiction." In *Film Studies*. Vol. 8, 116–125. p. 125.
38. Needless to say, not everybody everywhere at every time responds identically. Freedberg, p. 445. W.J.T. Mitchell argues in a similar direction when he notes the universal tendency to ascribe a magical, life-like quality to images: "the phenomenon of the living image or animated icon is an anthropological universal, a feature of the fundamental ontology of images as such." Mitchell, p. 11.
39. Clover, p. 168.
40. Susan Sontag. 1977. *On Photography*. New York: Farrar, Straus and Giroux. p. 168/169 (emphasis added).
41. Sontag, p. 169.
42. Incidentally, this points to another discrepancy between the cinema and home-viewing: the social pressure of the movie theater keeps audiences much longer in their seats, whereas home-viewers can turn off their video recorders or DVD players quite easily. Hill, p. 61. As a consequence, some viewers choose specific films to be watched at home, because there is more opportunity for permanent avoidance. Hill, p. 65.
43. Aurel Kolnai. 2004. *On Disgust*. Chicago: Open Court, 2004. p. 97 (emphasis added).
44. Hill, p. 47 (emphasis added).
45. See Jean-Paul Sartre. 2004. *The Imaginary. A Phenomenological Psychology of the Imagination*. London: Routledge.
46. Brinker, p. 195.
47. Pauline Kael. 1994. *For Keeps*. New York: Dutton. p. 783.
48. Quoted from Hill, p. 70.

49. See Alex Neill. 1996. "Empathy and (Film) Fiction." In *Post-Theory. Reconstructing Film Studies*, ed. David Bordwell and Noël Carroll, 175–194. Madison: The University of Wisconsin Press.
50. For a psychoanalytic account of *Angst-Lust*, see Michael Balint. 1959. *Thrills and Regressions*. New York: International Universities Press.
51. Moritz Geiger. 1913. "Beiträge zur Phänomenologie des ästhetischen Genusses." In *Jahrbuch für Philosophie und phänomenologische Forschung*. Vol. 1, No. 2, 567–684. Halle/Saale: Niemeyer. p. 625 (my translation).
52. Kolnai, p. 38 (emphasis added).
53. See Schmitz (1969).
54. Max Pagès. 1974. *Das affektive Leben der Gruppen. Eine Theorie der menschlichen Beziehung*. Stuttgart: Klett. p. 172.
55. Hermann Schmitz. 1965. *Der Leib*. Bonn: Bouvier.
56. Vivian Sobchack. 2006. "Peek-a-Boo! Thoughts on Seeing (Most of) *The Descent* and *Isolation*." In *Film Comment*, 38–41. p. 41.
57. See Murray Smith, p. 98–102. Christine Noll Brinckmann. 1999. "Somatische Empathie bei Hitchcock: Eine Skizze." In *Der Körper im Bild: Schauspielen, Darstellen, Erscheinen*, ed. Heinz-B. Heller, Karl Prümm and Birgit Peulings, 111–120. Marburg: Schüren. I introduce the term 'sensation mimicry,' because the expressions *motor* and *affective* mimicry do not capture all of the empathizing experiences described later.
58. Sobchack (2004), p. 76/77 (emphasis added).
59. This is confirmed by empirical audience research. Hill, p. 36.
60. Sobchack (2004), p. 76.
61. Mary Ann Doane. 2003. "The Close-Up. Scale and Detail in the Cinema." In *Differences. A Journal of Feminist Cultural Studies*. Vol. 14, No. 3, 89–111. p. 109.

NOTES TO CHAPTER 4

1. Quoted from Wiater, p. 79.
2. Gotthold Ephraim Lessing. 1984. *Laocoon. An Essay on the Limits of Painting and Poetry*. Baltimore: The Johns Hopkins University Press. p. 19.
3. Only at the end of the scene does suggested horror make way for direct horror, when an openly disgusting and brutal shot is briefly shown.
4. Schaub, p. 55.
5. Marshall McLuhan. 1964. *Understanding Media. The Extensions of Man*. Routledge: London. p. 22/23.
6. To be sure, arguing that imagining and perceiving are two distinct accesses to the world does not imply that they are mutually exclusive and cannot occur simultaneously. It is true that we cannot perceive and imagine the *same* thing in the *same* respect. But when it comes to *different* things—the dominant case in the film experience—we face no problem.
7. Let me make one remark in defense of the much-maligned direct horror, though. There is a great amount of artistry involved in creating a convincing monster or a realistic bodily mutilation, and many people lament the distancing, de-immersive effect of unrealistic monsters, the visibility of fake blood or the conspicuousness of computer-generated imagery (CGI).
8. Edward S. Casey. 1976. *Imagining. A Phenomenological Study*. Bloomington: Indiana University Press. p. 141 (original emphasis).
9. Casey (1976), p. 107.
10. Casey (1976), p. 91.
11. Casey (1976), p. 92.

12. Sartre (2004), p. 15 (emphasis added).
13. At times, we have a more active control over the imagined content and seem to be more consciously contributing to it. A movie like Ingmar Bergman's *Saraband* (2003) is dominated by close-ups of people looking backward in time, recounting events from their past. Relying mostly on verbal descriptions, the film does not guide imagination as straightforwardly as the examples cited before. There is, then, a wide continuum of filmic imaginations ranging from comparatively self-controlled and voluntary (albeit guided) to involuntary and uncontrollable forms such as many cases of suggested horror.
14. Dennis Giles. 1984. "Conditions of Pleasure in Horror Cinema." In *Planks of Reason. Essays on the Horror Film*, ed. Barry Keith Grant, 38–52. Metuchen: Scarecrow. p. 41.
15. Giles, p. 40.
16. Robert Sokolowski. 2000. *Introduction to Phenomenology*. Cambridge: Cambridge University Press. p. 70.
17. Giles, p. 48.
18. Merleau-Ponty, p. 472.
19. Casey (1976), p. 26.
20. Quoted from Perkins, p. 141 (emphasis in the original).
21. See Manfred Pfister. 1993. *The Theory and Analysis of Drama*. Cambridge: Cambridge University Press. p. 204–208.
22. Sobchack (1992), p. 292 (emphasis added).
23. "To be in musical space means more than mere existence at a particular place, and therefore has nothing to do with one's physical location," Thomas Clifton reminds us. Thomas Clifton. 1983. *Music as Heard. A Study in Applied Phenomenology*. New Haven: Yale University Press. p. 141.
24. Roman Polanski. 1984. *Roman Polanski. Autobiographie*. Bern: Scherz. p. 231.
25. Hill, p. 97.
26. Quoted from Hill, p. 98.

NOTES TO CHAPTER 5

1. On the audio commentary of the *Lord of Illusions* DVD.
2. Quoted from Richard Dyer. 1999. *Seven*. London: Bfi. p. 23.
3. For an account that considers 'startle' closely related to fear, see Jenefer Robinson. 1995. "Startle". In *The Journal of Philosophy*. Vol. XCII, No. 2, 53–74.
4. Robinson, p. 72.
5. David Denby. 1999. "The Spook Doctor. A Horror Film Exorcised of Cheap Thrills." In *The New Yorker*. August 23 and 30, 201.
6. On the audio commentary of the *Hellraiser* DVD.
7. Quoted from Robert Baird. 2000. "The Startle Effect. Implications for Spectator Cognition and Media Theory." In *Film Quarterly*. Vol. 53, No. 3, 12–24. p. 23.
8. Baird, p. 23.
9. Baird, p. 22.
10. David Scott Diffrient. 2004. "A Film Is Being Beaten. Notes on the Shock Cut and the Material Violence of Horror." In *Horror Film. Creating and Marketing Fear*, ed. Steffen Hantke, 52–81. Jackson: University Press of Mississippi.
11. Baird, p. 13.
12. Baird, p. 15.

13. At various points in his essay Baird talks about "brief" shock cuts. This expression is a logical misnomer, since *cuts* cannot be brief—only *shots* can. In the following I will use the expression 'shock cuts' for the actual transition from one shot to the next, while I will introduce the notion of 'shock shot' for the brief intervals that Baird has in mind.
14. Baird, p. 16.
15. My distinction of screen space and offscreen space is based on Noël Burch. 1981. "*Nana*, or the Two Kinds of Space." In *Theory of Film Practice*, 17–31. Princeton: Princeton University Press.
16. Burch, p 18.
17. See David Bordwell. 1997. *On the History of Film Style*. Cambridge: Harvard University Press.
18. On the audio commentary of the *Evil Dead* DVD.
19. Michel Chion. 1994. *Audio-Vision. Sound on Screen*. New York: Columbia University Press. p. 132.
20. This example, by the way, is also a perfect specimen of those scenes that producer Val Lewton once termed "busses": scenes in which something as trivial and benign as a bus bursts into the frame and causes a jolt. Diffrient argues that the term was introduced with the Lewton-produced Jacques Torneur film *Cat People* (1942). Diffrient, p. 62.
21. Chion, p. 10/11.
22. Dewey, p. 237 (emphasis in the original).
23. Hans Jonas. 2001. *The Phenomenon of Life. Toward a Philosophical Biology*. Evanston: Northwestern University Press. p. 149.
24. Jonas, p. 139.
25. Spiegelberg (1982), p. 683.
26. Spiegelberg (1982), p. 687.
27. Spiegelberg (1982), p. 687.
28. See Sobchack (2004), p. 286–318.
29. Sobchack (2004), p. 314.
30. Chion, p. 155.
31. Chion, p. 155.
32. Chion, p. 58.
33. Chion, p. 84/85 (emphasis added).
34. Schmitz (1965), p. 174/175.
35. Thomas Morsch. 2007. "Verkörperte Wahrnehmung. Körperliche Erfahrung als ästhetische Erfahrung im Kino." Dissertation. Freie Universität Berlin. p. 276.
36. Baird, p. 13 and 23.
37. Hermann Schmitz. 1966. *Der Leib im Spiegel der Kunst*. Bonn: Bouvier. p. 24.
38. Hermann Schmitz. 1995. "Gefühle in philosophischer (neuphänomenologischer) Sicht." In *Die Wiederentdeckung des Gefühls. Emotionen in der Psychotherapie und menschlichen Entwicklung*, ed. Hilarion Petzold, 47–81. Paderborn: Jungfermann. p. 53.
39. Baird, p. 22.
40. Baird, p. 22/23.
41. Plessner, p. 76.
42. For the concept of body foreground and background, see Leder and Katz.
43. Quoted from Laurent Bouzereau: "Ultraviolent Movies." www.fridaythe13thfilms.com/disc/essays/ultraviolent.html [last accessed: 23 July 2009].
44. Stern, p. 128.
45. Erving Goffman. 1963. *Behavior in Public Places. Notes on the Social Organization of Gatherings*. New York: Free Press. p. 14.

46. Stern, p. 111.
47. Katz, 319/320.
48. Pinedo (2004), p. 109.
49. Hermann Schmitz. 1990. *Der unerschöpfliche Gegenstand. Grundzüge der Philosophie*. Bonn: Bouvier. p. 137–140 and 151–153.
50. Scheler classifies what I call the 'collective body' and what Schmitz terms 'solidarian incorporation' among his larger category of 'emotional identification' (*Einsfühlung*). Max Scheler. 1954. *The Nature of Sympathy*. New Haven: Yale University Press. p. 36.
51. Goffman, p. 214.

NOTES TO CHAPTER 6

1. Burke, p. 58/59.
2. Quoted from Wiater, p. 87.
3. My definition of cinematic dread differs from what some scholars call "art-dread." See Carroll (1990); Cynthia Freeland. 2004. "Horror and Art-Dread." In *The Horror Film*, ed. Stephen Prince, 189–205. New Brunswick: Rutgers University Press.
4. My distinction between dread and horror resembles the one Aurel Kolnai makes between *timor* and *pavor*. On the one hand there is fear as a worrying "about an unwelcome event or as a presumption of danger;" on the other hand there is fear "in the face of something." In the first case, the *anticipation of a danger* causes fear. In the second case, the *danger itself* is the reason for fear. Kolnai, p. 36.
5. Will H. Rockett. 1982. "The Door Ajar. Structure and Convention in Horror Films that Would Terrify." In *Journal of Popular Film and Television*. Vol. 10, No. 3, 130–136. p. 131.
6. Schmitz (1969), p. 316/317.
7. Plantinga (2009), p. 73.
8. As an example for the latter approach read Alex Neill's discussion of a scene in Robert Wise's *The Haunting* (1963). Neill, p. 180.
9. Dyer (1999), p. 65.
10. Deborah Knight and George McKnight. 1999. "Suspense and Its Master." In *Hitchcock: Centenary Essays*, ed. Richard Allen and Sam Ishii Gonzalés, 107–121. London: Bfi. p. 108.
11. Richard Allen. 2003. "Hitchcock and Narrative Suspense." In *Camera Obscura/Camera Lucida*, ed. Richard Allen and Malcolm Turvey, 164–182. Amsterdam: Amsterdam University Press. p. 163.
12. Hans J. Wulff. 1996. "Suspense and the Influence of Cataphora on Viewers' Expectations." In *Suspense. Conceptualizations, Theoretical Analyses, and Empirical Explanations*, ed. Hans J. Wulff, Peter Vorderer and Mike Friedrichsen, 1–17. Mahwah: Lawrence Erlbaum Associates. p. 7.
13. Leffler, p. 190.
14. Wulff, p. 6.
15. David Bordwell. 1985. *Narration in the Fiction Film*. Madison: The University of Wisconsin Press. p. 11 and 12.
16. Richard Maltby. 2003. *Hollywood Cinema*. Second Edition. Malden: Blackwell. p. 312.
17. Maltby, p. 354.
18. Mary Ann Doane. 2002. *The Emergence of Cinematic Time. Modernity, Contingency, the Archive*. Cambridge: Harvard University Press. p. 195.

19. David Bordwell, Kristin Thompson and Janet Staiger. 1985. *The Classical Hollywood Cinema. Film Style and Mode of Production to 1960.* London: Routledge. p. 54.
20. J.P. Telotte. 1982. "Through a Pumpkin's Eye: The Reflexive Nature of Horror." In *Film/Literature Quarterly.* Vol. 10, No. 3, 139–149. p. 143.
21. Bordwell (1985), p. 163.
22. Giles, p. 42.
23. Giles, p. 44.
24. See Edward Branigan. 1984. *Point of View in the Cinema. A Theory of Narration and Subjectivity in Classical Film.* Berlin: Mouton. p. 103–109.
25. Maltby, p. 435.
26. This is does not go for every kind of offscreen sound. For instance, we do not look for the source of ambient sounds. Michel Chion therefore distinguishes between *active* and *passive* offscreen sound. Chion, p. 85.
27. Chion, p. 69.
28. Chion, p. 133.
29. Yvonne Tasker. 2002. *The Silence of the Lambs.* London: Bfi, 2002. p. 64.
30. Maltby, p. 429–431.
31. Quoted from Maltby, p. 429.
32. Bordwell/Thompson/Staiger, p. 19–21.
33. Bordwell (1985), p. 20.
34. Maltby, p. 468/469.
35. Jeffrey Sconce. 1993. "Spectacles of Death: Identification, Reflexivity, and Contemporary Horror." In *Film Theory Goes to the Movies,* ed. Jim Collins, Hilary Radner and Ava Preacher Collins, 103–119. New York: Routledge. p. 113.
36. Bordwell (1985), p. 37.
37. Bordwell (1985), p. 39.
38. K.J. Donnelly. 2005. *The Spectre of Sound. Music in Film and Television.* London: Bfi. p. 88.
39. Donnelly, p. 105.
40. Donnelly, p. 95.
41. Quoted from Wiater, p. 127.
42. The German philosopher Gernot Böhme was foremost in reintroducing the concept to aesthetic debates. Gernot Böhme. 1998. *Anmutungen. Über das Atmosphärische.* Ostfilden: Edition Tertium. Böhme's ideas are heavily influenced by Hermann Schmitz, whose phenomenological lived-body philosophy also plays an important role in my account.
43. The idea that atmospheres (or what he calls "moods") facilitate emotions is also held by Greg M. Smith, one of the few film studies scholars who have dealt with atmospheres, albeit from a cognitive perspective. Greg M. Smith, p. 42.
44. Peter Weir's extraordinary Australian film *Picnic at Hanging Rock* (1975) comes to mind as a rare exception.
45. Gaston Bachelard. 1970. *The Poetics of Space.* Boston: Beacon. p. 47.
46. Bachelard, p. 199 (translation slightly modified).
47. On the DVD audio commentary of the movie *Seven.*
48. Clover, p. 31.
49. Clover, p. 31.
50. In the Production Notes on the *Haunting* DVD.
51. Bachelard, p. 18.
52. Bachelard, p. 20.
53. Apart from creating an atmosphere the descent often has a semantic meaning, turning it into an "expressive space" that connotes the way to hell or into the unconscious. On "expressive space" see Maltby, p. 314.

54. Giles, p. 43.
55. On the bonus track of the *Dark Water* DVD, chapter "The Sounds of Terror."
56. On the audio commentary of the *Blair Witch Project* DVD.
57. Connelly, p. 90 and 91.
58. Bachelard, p. 186 (emphasis in the original).
59. Bachelard, p. 185 (emphasis added).
60. On the audio commentary of the *Blair Witch Project* DVD.
61. Bachelard calls the forest "shattered, closed, serried." Bachelard, p. 186.
62. *Film* time is the amount of time a movie requires of its audience, whereas *movie* time refers to the time represented within the narrative (see also further reading in this chapter). Maltby, p. 419/420.
63. Böhme (1998) p. 31 and 39.
64. Quoted from Jens Soentgen. 1998. *Die verdeckte Wirklichkeit. Einführung in die Neue Phänomenologie von Hermann Schmitz*. Bonn: Bouvier. p. 67 (my translation).
65. See Noël Carroll. 1996. "The Paradox of Suspense." In *Suspense. Conceptualizations, Theoretical Analyses, and Emperical Explorations*, ed. Peter Vorderer, Hans J. Wulff and Mike Friedrichsen, 71–92. Mahwah: Lawrence Erlbaum Associates.
66. Carl Plantinga. 1999. "The Scene of Empathy and the Human Face." In *Passionate Views. Film, Cognition and Emotion*, ed. Carl Plantinga and Greg M. Smith, 239–255. Baltimore: Johns Hopkins University Press.
67. Murray Smith, p. 98.
68. Murray Smith, p. 99.
69. Murray Smith, p. 92.
70. Plantinga (1999), p. 243/244.
71. Murray Smith, p. 82.
72. Murray Smith, p. 188.
73. In her particular case, our extra-filmic knowledge might come into play as well: Jodie Foster's film biography brings to mind other victim roles, for instance the child-like prostitute she played in *Taxi Driver* (1976) and her impersonation of a rape victim in *The Accused*.
74. Robin Wood. 2002. *Hitchcock's Films Revisited*. New York: Columbia University Press. p. 146.
75. Rockett (1982), p. 132. Consider also the quotes from Burke and Gordon early on in this chapter.
76. Will H. Rockett. 1988. *Devouring Whirlwind. Terror and Transcendence in the Cinema of Cruelty*. New York: Greenwood. p. 50.
77. Mulvey (2006), p. 191.
78. Maltby, p. 419/420.
79. Michael G. Flaherty. 1999. *A Watched Pot. How We Experience Time*. New York: New York University Press. p. 18.
80. Flaherty, p. 4/5.
81. See Edmund Husserl. 2008. *On the Phenomenology of the Consciousness of Internal Time (1893–1917)*. New York: Springer.
82. See David Carr. 1986. *Time, Narrative, and History*. Bloomington: Indiana University Press. p. 21.
83. The expressions 'past-of-the-present-moment' and 'future-of-the-present-moment' come from Stern, p. 27.
84. Carr, p. 24 (emphasis in the original).
85. Carr, p. 22.
86. This distinguishes dread from suggested horror in which we often *imagine* a clearly discernible, textually dense, straightforward presentation of a violent or monstrous scene.

87. Flaherty, p. 91–97.
88. Rockett (1982), p. 131.
89. Hill, p. 34.
90. www.washingtonpost.com/wp-srv/style/longterm/movies/videos/capefear-rhinson_a0a719.htm [last accessed: 23 July 2009].
91. Kael, p. 830.
92. On the audio commentary of the *Scream* DVD (Dimension Collector's Series).
93. See Julian Hanich. 2008. "A Weep in the Dark. Tears and the Cinematic Experience." In *Passionate Politics. The Cultural Work of American Melodrama*, ed. Ilka Saal and Ralph Poole, 27–45. Newcastle: Cambridge Scholars Publishing, 2008.
94. The aspect of personal isolation is part of many phenomenological, psychological or psychoanalytic accounts of fear. Phenomenologist Hermann Schmitz notes that fear pushes you into the forsakenness of individual isolation ("Verlassenheit, Verlorenheit"). Hermann Schmitz. 1964. *Die Gegenwart*. Bonn: Bouvier. p. 208. Psychosociologist Max Pagès argues that fear is "an experience of isolation and loneliness." Pagès, p. 170 (my translation).
95. Leder, p. 74.
96. C. W. Valentine. 1991. "The Innate Bases of Fear." In *The Journal of Genetic Psychology*. Vol. 152, No. 4, 501–527. p. 508.
97. www.salon.com/ent/movies/review/1999/07/13/blair/index.html?CP=SAL&DN=110 [last accessed: 23 July 2009].
98. Quoted from Hill, p. 63.
99. Schmitz (1964), p. 182/183.
100. www.austinchronicle.com/gyrobase/Calendar/Film?Film=oid%3A139794 [last accessed: 23 July 2009].
101. There might be an evolutionary explanation to the conjunction between fear and affection: it could have evolved to help our ancestors join forces in dangerous situations, when there was safety in numbers. Dylan Evans. 2003. *Emotion. A Very Short Introduction*. Oxford: Oxford University Press. p. 85. The classic psychological experiment can be found in: Donald G. Dutton and Arthur P. Aron. 1974. "Some Evidence for Heightened Sexual Attraction Under Conditions of High Anxiety." In *Journal of Personality and Social Psychology*. Vol. 30, No. 4, 510–517.
102. See Scheler.
103. Obviously, we *can* be (and often *are*) infected by the silent, attentive *atmosphere* during a dread scene—but this does not go for the fearful aesthetic *emotion* of dread.
104. Scheler, p. 12.
105. Hence we can at best experience an *imagined* community.
106. Dufrenne, p. 49/50.
107. For literature on suspense, see for instance Carroll (1990) and (1996); Derry; Leffler; Gottlieb; Rubin; Knight/McKnight; Allen (2003); François Truffaut. 1985. *Hitchcock*. Revised Edition. New York: Simon and Schuster.

NOTES TO CHAPTER 7

1. Burke, p. 46.
2. Quoted from Gottlieb, p. 140.
3. Balázs, p. 81 (my translation). My definition of terror differs from other scattered usages in film studies, for instance in Rockett (1982 and 1987) and Isabel Cristina Pinedo. 1997. *Recreational Terror. Women and the Pleasures of*

Horror Film Viewing. Albany: State University of New York Press. It vaguely resembles what 19th-century Gothic novelist Ann Radcliffe noted about terror: it arouses the soul and the higher faculties to a state of attention, expectation and curiosity. Ann Radcliffe. 1826. "On the Supernatural in Poetry." In *The New Monthly Magazine and Literary Journal*, 145–152. p. 149.
4. Allen (2003), p. 169–176.
5. Carroll (1996), p. 78.
6. Rubin, p. 32.
7. Carroll (1996), p. 74.
8. Truffaut, p. 73.
9. For the large amount of literature on mirror neurons see for instance: Vittorio Gallese. 2000. "The Inner Sense of Action: Agency and Motor Representation." In *Journal of Consciousness Studies*. Vol. 7, No. 10, 23–40.
10. See Chapters 3 ("Film's Body") and 5 ("Filmind") in Sobchack (1992) and Frampton respectively.
11. Sobchack (1992), p. 167.
12. Frampton, p. 96.
13. Elsaesser (1981), p. 271 and 272.
14. Elsaesser (1981), p. 273. I have already quoted parts of this passage in the multiplex chapter.
15. Balázs, p. 81 (my translation).
16. Balázs, p. 91 (my emphases and my translation). See also his remarks on the phenomenology of time at the movies on p. 86.
17. Truffaut, p. 73.

NOTES TO CHAPTER 8

1. Gerald Mast. 1983. *Film/Cinema/Movie. A Theory of Experience*. Chicago: University of Chicago Press. p. 24.
2. Elias/Dunning, p. 60.
3. Georg Simmel. 2002. "The Metropolis and Mental Life." In *The Blackwell City Reader*, ed. Gary Bridge and Sophie Watson, 11–19. Malden: Blackwell. p. 12.
4. Simmel, p. 14.
5. Benjamin's loss-of-experiences thesis is present in his famous essay on "The Work of Art in the Age of Mechanical Reproduction" from 1935/36 (In Clive Cazeaux. 2002. *The Continental Aesthetics Reader*. London: Routledge. p. 322–343), but it got fully worked out only in the 1940 article "On Some Motifs in Baudelaire" (In Walter Benjamin. 1988. *Illuminations*. New York: Schocken. p. 155–200).
6. Dewey, p. 260.
7. Dewey, p. 35 and 38.
8. Cataldi, p. 2 and 122.
9. Dewey, p. 19.
10. Dewey, p. 36.
11. Dewey, p. 35.
12. Karl Marx and Friedrich Engels. 1967. *The Communist Manifesto*. London: Penguin. p. 223.
13. Böhme (1995), p. 17 (my translation).
14. Karl-Heinrich Bette. 1998. *Körperspuren. Zur Semantik und Paradoxie moderner Körperlichkeit*. Berlin: de Gruyter. p. 1. Richard Shusterman: 2000a. *Performing Live. Aesthetic Alternatives for the Ends of Art*. Ithaca: Cornell University Press. p. 154.

15. Sigmund Freud. 1961. *Civilization and its Discontents*. New York: Norton.
16. Carol Bigwood. 1998. "Renaturalizing the Body (with the Help of Merleau-Ponty). In *Body and Flesh. A Philosophical Reader*, ed. Donn Welton, 99–114. Malden: Blackwell. p. 109.
17. Shusterman (2000a), p. 164.
18. Elias/Dunning, p. 45.
19. See Elias.
20. To be sure, since the 1960s the suppression of emotions and affects—particularly in terms of sexuality—has decreased in Western societies and has made way for what Cas Wouters calls "informalization." However, Wouters' argument does not contradict Elias' thesis of the civilizing process but rather extends it. Times of informalization still have a high demand for individual regulation of drives and emotions since former norms and rules of conduct have disappeared and now need to be negotiated anew. What has changed is the *mechanism* of self-regulation: what was once internalized has to follow *rational* conduct and goal-oriented motivations. See Cas Wouters. 1979. "Informalisierung und der Prozess der Zivilisation." In *Materialien zu Norbert Elias' Zivilisationstheorie*, ed. Peter Gleichmann, Johan Goudsblom and Hermann Korte, 279–298. Frankfurt/Main: Suhrkamp.
21. Bette, p. 19/20.
22. See Hartmut Rosa. 2005. *Beschleunigung. Die Veränderung der Zeitstrukturen in der Moderne*. Frankfurt/Main: Suhrkamp. p. 438.
23. David R. Cerbone. 2006. *Understanding Phenomenology*. Stocksfield: Acumen. p. 172.
24. Bigwood, p. 102.
25. Edward S. Casey. 1998. "The Ghost of Embodiment. On Bodily Habitudes and Schemata." In *Body and Flesh. A Philosophical Reader*, ed. Donn Welton, 207–225. Malden: Blackwell. p. 209.
26. For a critique of Adorno and Foucault, see Axel Honneth. 1999. "Foucault und Adorno. Zwei Formen einer Kritik der Moderne." In *Die zerrissene Welt des Sozialen. Sozialphilosophische Aufsätze*, 73–92. Frankfurt/Main: Suhrkamp. For a critique of Weber, see Bryan S. Turner. 1984. *The Body and Society. Explorations in Social Theory*. Oxford: Basil Blackwell. p. 163/164.
27. Honneth (1999), p. 87.
28. I will not discuss the vexing question when *exactly* the civilizing process and the process of modernization got underway. Since I am interested in the directionality of these processes and the changes they brought about, I allow myself to leave the problem of origins aside. It is important for my argument, however, to note that the end of the 18th and the beginning of the 19th century implied a considerable, effective push—even if these developments were doubtlessly set into motion earlier. For the problem of dating the start of modernity, see Stephen Toulmin. 1990. *Cosmopolis. The Hidden Agenda of Modernity*. New York: Free Press. p. 3–13.
29. However, it would be a crass simplification to assume a monocausal connection that regards these developments as an *exclusive* reaction to disembodiment. Hence Bette warns that we also have take into account, among other developments, the altered time and social structures of modernity—aspects that will occupy us later. Bette, p. 17.
30. See Axel Honneth. 1995. *Desintegration. Brüchstücke einer soziologischen Zeitdiagnose*. Frankfurt/Main: Fischer. p. 39–47.
31. Colin Campbell. 1987. *The Romantic Ethic and the Spirit of Modern Consumerism*. Oxford: Basil Blackwell.
32. Honneth (1995), p. 46.
33. Elias/Dunning, p. 19–62.

34. Ann Jessie Van Sant. 1993. *Eighteenth-Century Sensibility and the Novel. The Senses in Social Context.* Cambridge: Cambridge University Press. p. 117/118.
35. Fred Botting. 1996. *Gothic.* London: Routledge. p. 4.
36. This argument is put forward in Werner Wolf. 1995. "Angst und Schrecken als Attraktion. Zu einer gender-orientierten Funktionsgeschichte des englischen Schauerromans im 18. und frühen 19. Jahrhundert." In *Zeitschrift für Anglistik und Amerikanistik.* Vol. XLIII, No. 1, 37–59. Richard Alewyn. 1974. "Die Lust an der Angst." In *Probleme und Gestalten. Essays,* 307–330. Frankfurt/Main: Insel. Carroll (1990).
37. Wolf, p. 41. David H. Richter thinks that women were especially sensitive to this mode of aesthetic experience because "increased leisure time without opportunity for useful work might conduce toward ennui, lassitude, and desires for escape." David H. Richter. 1996. *The Progress of Romance. Literary Historiography and the Gothic Novel.* Columbus: Ohio State University Press. p. 123.
38. Quoted from Wolf, p. 42.
39. Erich Schön. 1987. *Der Verlust der Sinnlichkeit oder Die Verwandlungen des Lesers. Mentalitätswandel um 1800.* Stuttgart: Klett-Cotta. p. 63–97.
40. Fluck, p. 118.
41. Ihde, 44/45.
42. Cataldi, p. 173.
43. Cataldi, p. 151.
44. Carroll (1990), p. 167.
45. See Richard Shusterman. 1997. "The End of Aesthetic Experience." In *The Journal of Aesthetics and Art Criticism.* Vol. 55, No. 1, 29–41.
46. Elias/Dunning, p. 44. The opportunities are in fact so varied and differentiated that one philosopher—Shusterman—has suggested a whole discipline to study them. He calls it *somaesthetics*: "Somaestethics is devoted to the critical, ameliorative study of one's experience and use of one's body as a locus of sensory-aesthetic appreciation (*aesthesis*) and creative self-fashioning." Shusterman (2000a), p. 138.
47. Plessner, p. 127.
48. Bette, p. 49.
49. Gumbrecht, p. 116.
50. Rosa, p 114/115 and 124–138
51. Rosa, p. 79.
52. Marshall Berman. 1988. *All That Is Solid Melts Into Air. The Experience of Modernity.* New York: Penguin. Zygmunt Bauman 2000. *Liquid Modernity.* Cambridge: Polity.
53. Rosa, p. 221.
54. Rosa, p. 221/222 (my translation).
55. Rosa, p. 224/225.
56. Michel Foucault. 1986. "Of Other Spaces." In *Diacritics.* Vol. 16, No. 1, 22–27. p. 24.
57. Foucault, p. 26.
58. Doane (2002), p. 139.
59. Laura Mulvey. 1986. "Visual Pleasure and Narrative Cinema." In *Narrative, Apparatus, Ideology,* ed. Philip Rosen, 198–209. New York: Columbia University Press.
60. Rosa, p. 214.
61. Rosa, p. 279–294.
62. Rosa, 199/200.
63. Dewey, p. 45.

64. Dewey, p. 36.
65. Doane (2002), p. 108.

NOTES TO CHAPTER 9

1. Ironically, director Jim Gillespie formulates this argument on the *I Know What You Did Last Summer* DVD—precisely the medium that undermines the very collective experience he talks about.
2. Kael, p. 783.
3. Ulrich Beck and Elisabeth Beck-Gernsheim. 2002. "Institutionalized Individualism." In *Individualization. Institutionalized Individualism and its Social and Political Consequences*, xx–xxv. London: Sage. p. xxii.
4. See Robert Bellah et al. and Amitai Etzioni (ed.). 1998. *The Essential Communitarian Reader*. Lanham: Rowman and Littlefield.
5. See Rosa, p. 181 and 186–189.
6. Rosa, p. 197 (see also p. 205).
7. Individuality/freedom and community/security are the two poles in the "dyad of *sine qua non* human values." Bauman (2000). 170.
8. Zygmunt Bauman. 2001. *Community. Seeking Safety in an Insecure World.* Cambridge: Polity. p. 22. For a comparable view on modernity see Berman.
9. Bauman (2001), p. 4/5.
10. Bauman (2001), p. 60.
11. Axel Honneth recommends an analytical distinction between three dimensions of individualization: 1) *differentiation* (*Ausdifferenzierung*) refers to the growing differentiation of ways of life due to the institutionalized expansion of individual choices: more economic freedom, more alternatives of action on the level of institutions; liberation from social norms and codes of behavior etc. 2.) *isolation* (*Vereinzelung*) involves the destruction of intersubjective experiences of community relations and the growing isolation of the individual due to a loss of social contacts 3) *autonomization* (*Autonomisierung*) implies all the processes that enable individuals to respond in a reflexive, self-confident manner to alternatives of action. Honneth (1995), p. 25.
12. See Honneth (1995), p. 27.
13. Beck/Beck-Gernsheim, p. 4.
14. Bauman (2000), p. 169/170.
15. Bauman (2001), p. 65. See particularly Chapter 5: "Two Sources of Communalism." p. 58–73.
16. Bauman (2000), p. 169.
17. Bauman (2000), p. 200.
18. I put inverted commas around the word 'community', since I do not consider these various forms of cinematic collectivity a community in any strong sense (see the introduction).
19. Altman, p. 162.
20. Stephen Keane. 2001. *Disaster Movies. The Cinema of Catastrophe.* London: Wallflower. p. 100.
21. Henry Jenkins. 1992. *Textual Poachers. Television Fans and Participatory Culture.* New York: Routledge. p. 250–267. Annette Kuhn. 1999. "'That Day *Did* Last Me All My Life': Cinema Memory and Enduring Fandom". In *Identifying Hollywood's Audiences. Cultural Identity and the Movies*, ed. Melvyn Stokes and Richard Maltby, 135–146. London: Bfi.
22. Bellah et al., p. 73.
23. Bruce A. Austin. 1989. *Immediate Seating. A Look at Movie Audiences.* Belmont: Wadsworth. p. 156/157.

24. Hills, p. 105.
25. Jenkins, p. 273.
26. Geiger (1913), p. 613.
27. Bellah et al., p. 72.
28. Bauman (2000), p. 183.
29. Truffaut, p. 282.
30. Reading can, of course, become the fundament for an 'imagined community.' See Dufrenne, p. 64.
31. See, for instance, the article by Hubbard.
32. Tan, p. 31.
33. See the discussion of these issues in Taylor.
34. This is, of course, not to say that scary movies on the *representational* level do not rely on othering. What I am talking about is the *actual* cinematic audience.

NOTES TO CHAPTER 10

1. William Paul. 1994. *Laughing Screaming. Modern Hollywood Horror and Comedy*. New York: Columbia University Press. p. 21.
2. Hanfling, p. 359.
3. Philip Fisher. 1998. "The Aesthetics of Fear." In *Raritan*. Vol. 18, No. 1, 40–72. p. 46.
4. See Doane (2002), p. 162.

Bibliography

Acland, Charles R. 2000. "Cinemagoing and the Rise of the Megaplex." In *Television and New Media*. Vol. 1, No. 3, 355–382.
Addison, Joseph. 1712. "Why Terrour and Grief are Pleasing to the Mind when Excited by Descriptions." In *The Spectator*. No. 418, June 30, [no page number].
Aikin, John and Anna Laetitia Aikin. 1792. "On the Pleasure Derived From Objects of Terror." In *Miscellaneous Pieces in Prose*, 117–138. London: Johnson.
Alewyn, Richard. 1974. "Die Lust an der Angst." In *Probleme und Gestalten. Essays*, 307–330. Frankfurt/Main: Insel.
Allen, Richard. 2001. "Cognitive Film Theory." In *Wittgenstein, Theory and the Arts*, ed. Richard Allen and Malcolm Turvey, 174–209. London: Routledge.
Allen, Richard. 2003. "Hitchcock and Narrative Suspense." In *Camera Obscura/Camera Lucida*, ed. Richard Allen and Malcolm Turvey, 164–182. Amsterdam: Amsterdam University Press.
Altheide, David L. 2002. *Creating Fear. News and the Construction of Crisis*. New York: Aldine.
Altman, Rick. 1999. *Film/Genre*. London: Bfi.
Aristotle. 1997. *Poetics*. London: Penguin.
Austin, Bruce A. 1989. *Immediate Seating. A Look at Movie Audiences*. Belmont: Wadsworth.
Austin, John L. 1962. *Sense and Sensibilia*. Oxford: Clarendon.
Bachelard, Gaston. 1970. *The Poetics of Space*. Boston: Beacon.
Baird, Robert. 2000. "The Startle Effect. Implications for Spectator Cognition and Media Theory." In *Film Quarterly*. Vol. 53, No. 3, 12–24.
Balázs, Béla. 2001. *Der sichtbare Mensch oder die Kultur des Films*. Frankfurt/Main: Suhrkamp.
Balint, Michael. 1959. *Thrills and Regressions*. New York: International Universities Press.
Barker, Jennifer M. 2009. *The Tactile Eye. Touch and the Cinematic Experience*. Berkeley: University of California Press.
Baudelaire, Charles. 1974. *Selected Poems of Charles Baudelaire*. New York: Grove Press.
Bauman, Zygmunt. 2001. *Community. Seeking Safety in an Insecure World*. Cambridge: Polity.
Bauman, Zygmunt. 2000. *Liquid Modernity*. Cambridge: Polity.
Beck, Ulrich and Elisabeth Beck-Gernsheim. 2002. "Institutionalized Individualism. " In *Individualization. Institutionalized Individualism and its Social and Political Consequences*, xx–xxv. London: Sage.
Bellah, Robert, Richard Madsen, William M. Sullivan, Ann Swidler and Stven M. Tipton. 1985. *Habits of the Heart. Individualism and Commitment in American Life*. New York: Harper and Row.

Benjamin, Walter. 1988. "On Some Motifs in Baudelaire." In: *Illuminations*, 155–200. New York: Schocken.
Benjamin, Walter. 2000. "The Work of Art in the Age of Mechanical Reproduction." In *The Continental Aesthetics Reader*, ed. Clive Cazeaux, 322–343. London: Routledge.
Berman, Marshall. 1988. *All That Is Solid Melts into Air. The Experience of Modernity*. New York: Penguin.
Bernays, Jacob. 1857. *Grundzüge der verlorenen Abhandlung des Aristoteles über Wirkung der Tragödie*. Breslau: Trewenát.
Bette, Karl-Heinrich. 1998. *Körperspuren. Zur Semantik und Paradoxie moderner Körperlichkeit*. Berlin: de Gruyter.
Bigwood, Carol. 1998. "Renaturalizing the Body (with the Help of Merleau-Ponty). In *Body and Flesh. A Philosophical Reader*, ed. Donn Welton, 99–114. Malden: Blackwell.
Blanchet, Robert. 2003. *Blockbuster. Ästhetik, Ökonomie und Geschichte des postklassischen Hollywoodkinos*. Marburg: Schüren.
Böhme, Gernot. 1998. *Anmutungen. Über das Atmosphärische*. Ostfilden: Edition Tertium.
Böhme, Gernot. 1995. *Atmosphäre. Essays zur neuen Ästhetik*. Frankfurt/Main: Suhrkamp.
Bordwell, David. 1989. *Making Meaning. Inference and Rhetoric in the Interpretation of Cinema*. Cambridge: Harvard University Press.
Bordwell, David. 1985. *Narration in the Fiction Film*. Madison: The University of Wisconsin Press.
Bordwell, David. 1997. *On the History of Film Style*. Cambridge: Harvard University Press.
Bordwell, David and Noël Carroll (ed.). 1996. *Post-Theory: Reconstructing Film Studies*. Madison: University of Wisconsin Press.
Bordwell, David; Kristin Thompson and Janet Staiger. 1985. *The Classical Hollywood Cinema. Film Style and Mode of Production to 1960*. London: Routledge, 1985.
Bordwell, David. 2006. *The Way Hollywood Tells It. Story and Style in Modern Movies*. Berkeley: University of California Press.
Bourdieu, Pierre. 1987. *Distinction. A Social Critique of the Judgment of Taste*. Cambridge: Harvard University Press.
Bouzereau, Laurent: "Ultraviolent Movies." www.fridaythe13thfilms.com/disc/essays/ultraviolent.html.
Botting, Fred. 1996. *Gothic*. London: Routledge.
Branigan, Edward. 1984. *Point of View in the Cinema. A Theory of Narration and Subjectivity in Classical Film*. Berlin: Mouton.
Brinckmann, Christine Noll. 1999. "Somatische Empathie bei Hitchcock: Eine Skizze." In *Der Körper im Bild: Schauspielen, Darstellen, Erscheinen*, ed. Heinz-B. Heller, Karl Prümm and Birgit Peulings, 111–120. Marburg: Schüren.
Brinker, Menachem. 1977. "Aesthetic Illusion." In *The Journal of Aesthetics and Art Criticism*. Vol. 36, No. 2, 191–196.
Brottman, Mikal. 1997. *Offensive Films. Toward an Anthropology of* Cinéma Vomitif. Westport: Greenwood.
Burch, Noël. 1981. "*Nana*, or the Two Kinds of Space." In: *Theory of Film Practice*, 17–31. Princeton: Princeton University Press. .
Burke, Edmund. 1958. *A Philosophical Enquiry into the Origin of our Ideas of the Sublime and the Beautiful*. London: Routledge.
Campbell, Colin. 1987. *The Romantic Ethic and the Spirit of Modern Consumerism*. Oxford: Basil Blackwell.

Carr, David. 1986. *Time, Narrative, and History*. Bloomington: Indiana University Press.
Carroll, Noël. 1998. *A Philosophy of Mass Art*. Oxford: Clarendon Press.
Carroll, Noël. 2003. "Film, Attention, and Communication. A Naturalistic Account." In *Engaging the Moving Image*, 10–58. New Haven: Yale University Press.
Carroll, Noël. 1999a. "Film, Emotion, and Genre". In *Passionate Views. Film, Cognition and Emotion*, ed. Carl Plantinga and Greg M. Smith, 21–47. Baltimore: Johns Hopkins University Press.
Carroll, Noël. 1999b. "Horror and Humor." In *The Journal of Aesthetics and Art Criticism*. Vol. 57, No. 2, 145–160.
Carroll, Noël. 1996. "The Paradox of Suspense." In *Suspense. Conceptualizations, Theoretical Analyses, and Emperical Explorations*, ed. Peter Vorderer, Hans J. Wulff and Mike Friedrichsen, 71–92. Mahwah: Lawrence Erlbaum Associates.
Carroll, Noël. 1990. *The Philosophy of Horror, or Paradoxes of the Heart*. New York: Routledge.
Casebier, Allan. 1991. *Film and Phenomenology. Toward a Realist Theory of Cinematic Representation*. Cambridge: Cambridge University Press.
Casey, Edward S. 1976. *Imagining. A Phenomenological Study*. Bloomington: Indiana University Press.
Casey, Edward S. 1998. "The Ghost of Embodiment. On Bodily Habitudes and Schemata." In *Body and Flesh. A Philosophical Reader*, ed. Donn Welton, 207–225. Malden: Blackwell.
Cataldi, Sue L. 1993. *Emotion, Depth, and Flesh. A Study of Sensitive Space*. Albany: State University of New York Press.
Cavell, Stanley. 1979. *The World Viewed. Reflections on the Ontology of Film*. Enlarged Edition. Cambridge: Harvard University Press.
Cerbone, David R. 2006. *Understanding Phenomenology*. Stocksfield: Acumen.
Chion, Michel. 1994. *Audio-Vision. Sound on Screen*. New York: Columbia University Press.
Clifton, Thomas. 1983. *Music as Heard. A Study in Applied Phenomenology*. New Haven: Yale University Press.
Clover, Carol J. 1992. *Men, Women, and Chainsaws. Gender in the Modern Horror Film*. Princeton: Princeton University Press.
Coan, James A. 2008. "Toward a Neuroscience of Attachment." In *Handbook of Attachment*. Vol. 2, ed. Jude Cassidy and Phillip R. Shaver, 241–265.
Denby, David. 1999. "The Spook Doctor. A Horror Film Exorcised of Cheap Thrills." In *The New Yorker*. August 23 and 30, 201.
Derry, Charles. 1988. *The Suspense Thriller. Films in the Shadow of Alfred Hitchcock*. Jefferson: McFarland.
Dewey, John. 1980. *Art as Experience*. New York: Perigee.
Diffrient, David Scott. 2004. "A Film Is Being Beaten. Notes on the Shock Cut and the Material Violence of Horror." In *Horror Film. Creating and Marketing Fear*, ed. Steffen Hantke, 52–81. Jackson: University Press of Mississippi.
Doane, Mary Ann. 2003. "The Close-Up. Scale and Detail in the Cinema." In *Differences. A Journal of Feminist Cultural Studies*. Vol. 14, No. 3, 89–111.
Doane, Mary Ann. 2002. *The Emergence of Cinematic Time. Modernity, Contingency, the Archive*. Cambridge: Harvard University Press.
Donnelly, K. J. 2005. *The Spectre of Sound. Music in Film and Television*. London: Bfi.
Dufrenne, Mikel. 1973. *The Phenomenology of Aesthetic Experience*. Evanston: Northwestern University Press.

Dutton, Donald and Arthur P. Aron. 1974. "Some Evidence for Heightened Sexual Attraction Under Conditions of High Anxiety." In *Journal of Personality and Social Psychology*. Vol. 30, No. 4, 510–517.
Dyer, Richard. 1997. "Kill and Kill Again." In *Sight and Sound*. Vol. 7, No. 9, 14–17.
Dyer, Richard. 1999. *Seven*. London: Bfi.
Ebert, Roger: "The Haunting." rogerebert.suntimes.com/apps/pbcs.dll/article?AID=/19990701/REVIEWS/907010301/1023.
Edgerton, Gary. 2002. "The Multiplex. The Modern American Motion Picture Theater as Message." In *Exhibition. The Film Reader*, ed. Ina Rae Hark, 155–159. London: Routledge.
Elias, Norbert. 1994. *The Civilizing Process. Sociogenetic and Psychogenetic Investigations*. Malden: Blackwell.
Elias, Norbert and Eric Dunning. 1986. *Quest for Excitement. Sport and Leisure in the Civilizing Process*: Oxford: Basil Blackwell.
Elsaesser, Thomas. 1981. "Narrative Cinema and Audience-Oriented Aesthetics." In *Popular Television and Film*, ed. Tony Bennett, Susan Boyd-Bowman, Colin Mercer and Janet Woollacott, 270–282. London: Bfi.
Elster, Jon. 2004. "Emotion and Action." In *Thinking About Feeling. Contemporary Philosophers on Emotions*, ed. Robert C. Solomon, 151–162. Oxford: Oxford University Press.
Elster, Jon. 1999. *Strong Feelings. Emotion, Addiction, and Human Behavior*. Cambridge: MIT Press.
Etzioni, Amitai (ed.). 1998. *The Essential Communitarian Reader*. Lanham: Rowman and Littlefield.
Evans, Dylan. 2003. *Emotion. A Very Short Introduction*. Oxford: Oxford University Press.
Fisher, Philip. 1998. "The Aesthetics of Fear." In *Raritan*. Vol. 18, No. 1, 40–72.
Flaherty, Michael G. 1999. *A Watched Pot. How We Experience Time*. New York: New York University Press.
Fluck, Winfried. 2005. "California Blue. Americanization as Self-Americanization." In *Americanization and Anti-Americanism. The German Encounter with American Culture after 1945*, ed. Alexander Stephan, 221–237. New York: Berghahn.
Flückiger, Barbara. 2001. *Sound Design. Die virtuelle Klangwelt des Films*. Marburg: Schüren.
Foucault, Michel. 1986. "Of Other Spaces." In *Diacritics*. Vol. 16, No. 1, 2227.
Frampton, Daniel. 2006. *Filmosophy*. London: Wallflower.
Freedberg, David. 1989. *The Power of Images. Studies in the History of Response*. Chicago: University of Chicago Press.
Freeland, Cynthia. 2004. "Horror and Art-Dread." In *The Horror Film*, ed. Stephen Prince, 189–205. New Brunswick: Rutgers University Press.
Freud, Sigmund. 1961. *Civilization and Its Discontents*. New York: Norton.
Friedberg, Anne. 1993. *Window Shopping. Cinema and the Postmodern*. Berkeley: University of California Press.
Gallese, Vittorio. 2000. "The Inner Sense of Action: Agency and Motor Representation." In: *Journal of Consciousness Studies*. Vol. 7, No. 10, 23–40.
Geiger, Moritz. 1913. "Beiträge zur Phänomenologie des ästhetischen Genusses." In *Jahrbuch für Philosophie und phänomenologische Forschung*. Vol. 1, No. 2, 567–684. Halle/Saale: Niemeyer.
Geiger, Moritz. 1928. *Zugänge zur Ästhetik*. Leipzig: Der Neue Geist.
Giles, Dennis. 1984. "Conditions of Pleasure in Horror Cinema." In *Planks of Reason. Essays on the Horror Film*, ed. Barry Keith Grant, 38–52. Metuchen: Scarecrow.

Glassner, Barry. 1999. *The Culture of Fear. Why Americans Are Afraid of the Wrong Things*. New York: Basic.
Glendinning, Simon. 2007. *In the Name of Phenomenology*. New York: Routledge.
Goffman, Erving. 1963. *Behavior in Public Places. Notes on the Social Organization of Gatherings*. New York: Free Press.
Gomery, Douglas. 1992. *Shared Pleasures. A History of Movie Presentation in the United States*. London: Bfi.
Gottlieb, Sidney (ed.). 1995. *Hitchcock on Hitchcock. Selected Writings and Interviews*. Berkeley: University of California Press.
Grant, Barry Keith. 1998. "Rich and Strange. The Yuppie Horror Film." In *Contemporary Hollywood Cinema*, ed. Steve Neale and Murray Smith, 280–293. London: Routledge.
Paul Griffith. 2004. "Is Emotion a Natural Kind?" In *Thinking About Feeling. Contemporary Philosophers on Emotions*, ed. Robert C. Solomon, 233–249. New York: Oxford University Press.
Grodal, Torben. 1997. *Moving Pictures. A New Theory of Film Genres, Feelings, and Cognition*. Oxford: Clarendon.
Gumbrecht, Hans Ulrich. 2004. *Production of Presence. What Meaning Cannot Convey*. Stanford: Stanford University Press.
Hanfling, Oswald. 1996. "Fact, Fiction and Feeling." In *British Journal of Aesthetics*. Vol. 36, No. 4, 356–366.
Hanich, Julian. 2008. "A Weep in the Dark. Tears and the Cinematic Experience." In *Passionate Politics. The Cultural Work of American Melodrama*, ed. Ilka Saal and Ralph Poole, 27–45. Newcastle: Cambridge Scholars Publishing.
Hanich, Julian. 2009. "(Dis-)Liking Disgust: The Revulsion Experience at the Movies." In: *New Review of Film and Television Studies*. Vol. 7, No. 3, 293–309.
Hantke, Steffen (ed.). 2004. *Horror Film. Creating and Marketing Fear*. Jackson: University Press of Mississippi.
Heffernan, Kevin. 2004. *Ghouls, Gimmicks, and Gold. Horror Films and the American Movie Business 1953–1968*. Durham: Duke University Press.
Hess, Ursula and Gilles Kirouac. 2000. "Emotion Expression in Groups." In *Handbook of Emotions. Second Edition*, ed. Michael Lewis and Jeanette Haviland-Jones, 368–381. New York: Guilford.
Hill, Annette. 1997. *Shocking Entertainment. Viewer Response to Movie Violence*. Luton: University of Luton Press.
Hills, Matt. 2005. *The Pleasures of Horror*. London: Continuum.
Hinson, Hal: "Cape Fear." In: *Washington Post*. www.washingtonpost.com/wp-srv/style/longterm/movies/videos/capefearrhinson_a0a719.htm.
Hinson, Hal: "Single White Female." In: *Washington Post*. www.washingtonpost.com/wp-srv/style/longterm/movies/videos/singlewhitefemalerhinson_a0a79d.htm.
Honneth, Axel. 1995. *Desintegration. Brüchstücke einer soziologischen Zeitdiagnose*. Frankfurt/Main: Fischer.
Honneth Axel. 1999. "Foucault und Adorno. Zwei Formen einer Kritik der Moderne." In *Die zerrissene Welt des Sozialen. Sozialphilosophische Aufsätze*, 73–92. Frankfurt/Main: Suhrkamp.
Hubbard, Phil. 2003. "A Good Night Out? Multiplex Cinemas as Sites of Embodied Leisure." In *Leisure Studies*. Vol. 22, No. 3, 255–272.
Hume, David. 1965. "Of Tragedy." In *Of the Standard of Taste. And Other Essays*, 29–37. Indianapolis: Bobbs-Merrill.
Husserl, Edmund. 2008. *On the Phenomenology of the Consciousness of Internal Time (1893–1917)*. New York: Springer.

Hutchings, Peter. 2004. *The Horror Film*. London: Longman.
Ihde, Don. 1977. *Experimental Phenomenology. An Introduction*. New York: Putnam.
Ingarden, Roman. 1973. *The Literary Work of Art*. Evanston: Northwestern University Press.
Iser, Wolfgang. 1978. *The Act of Reading. A Theory of Aesthetic Response*. London: Routledge.
Jenkins, Henry. 1992. *Textual Poachers. Television Fans and Participatory Culture*. New York: Routledge.
Jonas, Hans. 2001. *The Phenomenon of Life. Toward a Philosophical Biology*. Evanston: Northwestern University Press.
Kael, Pauline. 1994. *For Keeps*. New York: Dutton.
Kant, Immanuel. 2001. *Critique of the Power of Judgment*. Cambridge: Cambridge University Press.
Katz, Jack. 1999. *How Emotions Work*. Chicago: University of Chicago Press.
Keane, Stephen. 2001. *Disaster Movies. The Cinema of Catastrophe*. London: Wallflower.
Keltner, Dacher and James J. Gross. 1999. "Functional Accounts of Emotions." In *Cognition and Emotion*. Vol. 13, No. 5, 505–521.
Kennedy, Barbara M. 2000. *Deleuze and Cinema. The Aesthetics of Sensation*. Edinburgh: Edinburgh University Press.
Kermode, Mark. 1993. "Terror Terror." In *Sight and Sound*. Vol. 3, No. 6, 7–8.
Klein, Ernest. 1966. *A Comprehensive Etymological Dictionary of the English Language*. Amsterdam: Elsevier.
Knight, Deborah and George McKnight. 1999. "Suspense and Its Master." In *Hitchcock: Centenary Essays*, ed. Richard Allen and Sam Ishii Gonzalés, 107–121. London: Bfi.
Koch, Gertrud. 2003. "Filmische Welten. Zur Welthaltigkeit filmischer Projektionen." In *Dimensionen ästhetischer Erfahrung*, ed. Joachim Küpper and Christoph Menke, 162–175. Frankfurt/Main: Suhrkamp.
Kolnai, Aurel. 2004. *On Disgust*. Chicago: Open Court.
Kracauer, Siegfried. 1987. "Cult of Distraction. On Berlin's Picture Palaces." In *New German Critique*. No. 40, 91–96.
Kracauer, Siegfried. 1997. *Theory of Film. The Redemption of Physical Reality*. Princeton: Princeton University Press.
Kuhn, Annette. 1999. "'That Day *Did* Last Me All My Life': Cinema Memory and Enduring Fandom". In *Identifying Hollywood's Audiences. Cultural Identity and the Movies*, ed. Melvyn Stokes and Richard Maltby, 135–146. London: Bfi.
Lakoff, George and Mark Johnson. 1980. *Metaphors We Live By*. Chicago: University of Chicago Press.
Lakoff, George and Mark Johnson. 1999. *Philosophy in the Flesh. The Embodied Mind and Its Challenge to Western Thought*. New York: Basic Books.
Landweer, Hilge. 1999. *Scham und Macht. Phänomenologische Untersuchungen zur Sozialität eines Gefühls*. Tübingen: Mohr Siebeck.
Laplanche, J. and J.-B. Pontalis. 1988. *The Language of Psycho-Analysis*. London: Karnac.
Leder, Drew. 1990. *The Absent Body*. Chicago: University of Chicago Press.
Leffler, Yvonne. 2000. *Horror as Pleasure. The Aesthetics of Horror Fiction*. Stockholm: Almqvist & Wiksell.
Lessing, Gotthold Ephraim. 1984. *Laocoon. An Essay on the Limits of Painting and Poetry*. Baltimore: The Johns Hopkins University Press.
Levine, Joseph. 1983. "Materialism and Qualia: The Explanatory Gap," In *Pacific Philosophical Quarterly*. Vol. 64, No. 4, 354–361.

Levine, Michael. 2004. "A Fun Night Out. Horror and Other Pleasures of the Cinema." In *Horror Film and Psychoanalysis. Freud's Worst Nightmare*, ed. Steven Jay Schneider, 35–54. Cambridge: Cambridge University Press.
Maddrey, Joseph. 2004. *Nightmares in Red, White and Blue. The Evolution of the American Horror Movie*. Jefferson: McFarland.
Maltby, Richard. 2003. *Hollywood Cinema*. Second Edition. Malden: Blackwell.
Mangan, Bruce. 1999. "The Fringe: A Case Study in Explanatory Phenomenology." In *Journal of Consciousness Studies*. Vol. 6, No. 2–3, 249–252.
Marks, Laura U. 2000. *The Skin of the Film. Intercultural Cinema, Embodiment, and the Senses*. Durham: Duke University Press.
Marx, Karl and Friedrich Engels. 1967. *The Communist Manifesto*. London: Penguin.
Mast, Gerald. 1983. *Film/Cinema/Movie. A Theory of Experience*. Chicago: University of Chicago Press.
McLuhan, Marshall. 1964. *Understanding Media. The Extensions of Man*. Routledge: London.
Merleau-Ponty, Maurice. 2002. *The Phenomenology of Perception*. London: Routledge.
Meunier, Jean-Paul. 1969. *Les Structures de l'experience filmique: L'Identification filmique*. Louvain: Librairie Universitaire.
Mitchell, W. J. T. 2005. *What Do Pictures Want? The Lives and Loves of Images*. Chicago: The University of Chicago Press.
Mohr, Ian: "Girls' Fright Out. Horror Pics Bank on New Femme Fanbase." In: *Variety*. October 22, 2006. www.variety.com/indexasp?layout=print_story&articleid=VR1117952345&categoryid=1019.
Morsch, Thomas. 2007. "Verkörperte Wahrnehmung. Körperliche Erfahrung als ästhetische Erfahrung im Kino." Dissertation. Freie Universität Berlin.
Motion Picture Association of America: *Entertainment Industry Market Statistics 2007.*
Motion Picture Association: *2006 US Theatrical Market Statistics.*
Moynihan, Daniel Patrick. 1996. "Defining Deviancy Down." In *The Essential Neo-Conservative Reader*, ed. Mark Gerson, 356–371. Reading: Addison-Wesley.
Mulvey, Laura. 2006. *Death 24x a Second. Stillness and the Moving Image*. London: Reaktion Books.
Mulvey, Laura. 1986. "Visual Pleasure and Narrative Cinema." In *Narrative, Apparatus, Ideology*, ed. Philip Rosen, 198–209. New York: Columbia University Press.
Murray, Judith H. 1997. *Hamlet on the Holodeck. The Future of Narrative in Cyberspace*. New York: Free Press.
Neale, Steve. 1993. "Melo Talk: On the Meaning and Use of the Term 'Melodrama' in The American Trade Press." In *Velvet Light Trap*. No. 32, 66–89.
Neale, Steve. 1990. "Questions of Genre". In *Screen*. Vol. 31, No. 1, 45–66.
Neill, Alex. 1996. "Empathy and (Film) Fiction." In *Post-Theory. Reconstructing Film Studies*, ed. David Bordwell and Noël Carroll, 175–194. Madison: The University of Wisconsin Press. .
Nietzsche, Friedrich. 1968. *The Will to Power*. New York: Vintage.
Oatley, Keith. 1996. "Emotions: Communications to the Self and Others." In *The Emotions. Social, Cultural and Biological Dimensions*, ed. Rom Harré and W. Gerrod Parrot, 312–316. London: Sage.
Pagès, Max. 1974. *Das affektive Leben der Gruppen. Eine Theorie der menschlichen Beziehung*. Stuttgart: Klett.
Paul, William. 1994. *Laughing Screaming. Modern Hollywood Horror and Comedy*. New York: Columbia University Press.

Perkins, V.F. 1972. *Film as Film. Understanding and Judging Movies*. Harmondsworth: Penguin.
Pfister, Manfred. 1993. *The Theory and Analysis of Drama*. Cambridge: Cambridge University Press.
Pinedo, Isabel Cristina. 2004. "Postmodern Elements of the Contemporary Horror Film." In *The Horror Film*, ed. Stephen Prince, 85–117. New Brunswick: Rutgers University Press.
Pinedo, Isabel Cristina. 1997. *Recreational Terror. Women and the Pleasures of Horror Film Viewing*. Albany: State University of New York Press.
Plantinga, Carl. 2009. *Moving Viewers. American Film and the Spectator's Experience*. Berkeley: University of California Press.
Plantinga, Carl and Greg M. Smith (ed.). 1999. *Passionate Views. Film, Cognition and Emotion*. Baltimore: Johns Hopkins University Press.
Plantinga, Carl. 1999. "The Scene of Empathy and the Human Face." In *Passionate Views. Film, Cognition and Emotion*, ed. Carl Plantinga and Greg M. Smith, 239–255. Baltimore: Johns Hopkins University Press.
Plessner, Helmuth. 1970. *Philosophische Anthropologie*. Frankfurt/Main: Fischer.
Polanski, Roman. 1984. *Roman Polanski. Autobiographie*. Bern: Scherz.
Powell, Anna. 2005. *Deleuze and Horror Film*. Edinburgh: Edinburgh University Press.
Prince, Stephen. 2000. "Graphic Violence in the Cinema: Origins, Aesthetic Design, and Social Effects." In *Screening Violence*, ed. Stephen Prince, 1–44. London: Athlone.
Prince, Stephen. 2004. "Violence and Psychophysiology in Horror Cinema." In *Horror Film and Psychoanalysis. Freud's Worst Nightmare*, ed. Steven Jay Schneider, 241–256. Cambridge: Cambridge University Press.
Prinz, Jesse. 2004. *Gut Reactions. A Perceptual Theory of Emotions*. Oxford: Oxford University Press.
Radcliffe, Ann. 1826. "On the Supernatural in Poetry." In *The New Monthly Magazine and Literary Journal*, 145–152.
Richter, David H. 1996. *The Progress of Romance. Literary Historiography and the Gothic Novel*. Columbus: Ohio State University Press.
Ricoeur, Paul. 1977. *The Rule of Metaphor. Multi-Disciplinary Studies of the Creations of Meaning in Language*. Toronto: University of Toronto Press.
Robinson, Jenefer. 1995. "Startle". In *The Journal of Philosophy*. Vol. XCII, No. 2, 53–74.
Roche, Maurice. 1973. *Phenomenology, Language and the Social Sciences*. London: Routledge.
Rockett, Will H. 1988. *Devouring Whirlwind. Terror and Transcendence in the Cinema of Cruelty*. New York: Greenwood.
Rockett, Will H. 1982. "The Door Ajar. Structure and Convention in Horror Films that Would Terrify." In *Journal of Popular Film and Television*. Vol. 10, No. 3, 130–136.
Rosa, Hartmut. 2005. *Beschleunigung. Die Veränderung der Zeitstrukturen in der Moderne*. Frankfurt/Main: Suhrkamp.
Rousseau, Jean-Jacques. 2000. *Confessions*. Oxford: Oxford University Press.
Rubin, Martin. 1999. *Thrillers*. Cambridge: Cambridge University Press.
Ryan, Marie-Laure. 2001. *Narrative as Virtual Reality. Immersion and Interactivity in Literature and Electronic Media*. Baltimore: The Johns Hopkins University Press.
Sartre, Jean-Paul. 2002. *Sketch for a Theory of the Emotions*. London: Routledge.
Sartre, Jean-Paul. 2004. *The Imaginary. A Phenomenological Psychology of the Imagination*. London: Routledge.

Savlov, Marc: "Deep Blue Sea." In: *Austin Chronicle.* www.austinchronicle.com/gyrobase/Calendar/Film?Film=oid%3A139794.
Schachtel, Ernest. 1984. *Metamorphosis. On the Development of Affect, Perception, Attention, and Memory.* New York: Da Capo.
Schaub, Mirjam. 2005. *Bilder aus dem Off. Zum philosophischen Stand der Kinotheorie.* Weimar: VDG.
Scheff, Thomas. 1979. *Catharsis in Healing, Ritual, and Drama.* Berkeley: University of California Press.
Scheler, Max. 1954. *The Nature of Sympathy.* New Haven: Yale University Press.
Schiller, Friedrich. 2003. "On the Reason Why We Take Pleasure in Tragic Subjects." In *Friedrich Schiller. Poet of Freedom,* Vol. 4., 267–283. Washington, DC: Schiller Institute.
Schmitz, Hermann. 1969. *Der Gefühlsraum.* Bonn: Bouvier.
Schmitz, Hermann. 1965. *Der Leib.* Bonn: Bouvier.
Schmitz, Hermann. 1966. *Der Leib im Spiegel der Kunst.* Bonn: Bouvier.
Schmitz, Hermann. 1990. *Der unerschöpfliche Gegenstand. Grundzüge der Philosophie.* Bonn: Bouvier.
Schmitz, Hermann. 1964. *Die Gegenwart.* Bonn: Bouvier.
Schmitz, Hermann. 1995. "Gefühle in philosophischer (neuphänomenologischer) Sicht." In *Die Wiederentdeckung des Gefühls. Emotionen in der Psychotherapie und menschlichen Entwicklung,* ed. Hilarion Petzold, 47–81. Paderborn: Jungfermann.
Schön, Erich. 1987. *Der Verlust der Sinnlichkeit oder Die Verwandlungen des Lesers. Mentalitätswandel um 1800.* Stuttgart: Klett-Cotta.
Schulze, Gerhard. 2005. *Die Erlebnisgesellschaft. Kultursoziologie der Gegenwart.* Frankfurt/Main: Campus.
Schwartz, Barry. 2004. *The Paradox of Choice. Why More is Less.* New York: HarperCollins.
Schweinitz, Jörg. 1994. "'Genre' und lebendiges Genrebewusstsein. Geschichte eines Begriffs und Probleme seiner Konzeptualisierung in der Filmwissenschaft." In *Montage/AV.* Vol. 3, No. 2, 99–118.
Sconce, Jeffrey. 1993. "Spectacles of Death: Identification, Reflexivity, and Contemporary Horror." In *Film Theory Goes to the Movies,* ed. Jim Collins, Hilary Radner and Ava Preacher Collins, 103–119. New York: Routledge.
Searle, John. 1992. *The Rediscovery of the Mind.* Cambridge: MIT Press.
Sergi, Gianluca. 1998. "A Cry in the Dark. The Role of Post-Classical Film Sound." In *Contemporary Hollywood Cinema,* ed. Steve Neale and Murray Smith, 156–165. London: Routledge.
Sergi, Gianluca. 2003. "Blockbusting Sound. The Case of *The Fugitive.*" In *Movie Blockbusters,* ed. Julian Stringer, 141–152. London: Routledge.
Shaviro, Steven. 1993. *The Cinematic Body.* Minneapolis: University of Minnesota Press.
Shaw, Daniel. 2001. "Power, Horror and Ambivalence." In *Film and Philosophy,* Horror Special Edition, 1–12.
Shusterman, Richard. 2000a. *Performing Live. Aesthetic Alternatives for the Ends of Art.* Ithaca: Cornell University Press.
Shusterman, Richard. 2000b. *Pragmatist Aesthetics. Living Beauty, Rethinking Art.* Lanham: Rowman and Littlefield.
Shusterman, Richard. 1997. "The End of Aesthetic Experience." In *The Journal of Aesthetics and Art Criticism.* Vol. 55, No. 1, 29–41.
Simmel, Georg. 2002. "The Metropolis and Mental Life." In *The Blackwell City Reader,* ed. Gary Bridge and Sophie Watson, 11–19. Malden: Blackwell.
Singer, Linda. 1990. "Eye/Mind/Screen: Toward a Phenomenology of Cinematic Scopophilia." In *Quarterly Review of Film and Video.* Vol. 12, No. 3, 51–67.

Smith, Edward E. and Douglas Medin. 1981. *Categories and Concepts*. Cambridge: Harvard University Press.
Smith, Greg M. 2003. *Film Structure and the Emotion System*. Cambridge: Cambridge University Press.
Smith, Murray. 1995. *Engaging Characters. Fiction, Emotion, and the Cinema*. Oxford: Clarendon Press.
Sobchack, Vivian. 2004. *Carnal Thoughts. Embodiment and Moving Image Culture*. Berkeley: University of California Press.
Sobchack, Vivian. 2006. "Peek-a-Boo! Thoughts on Seeing (Most of) *The Descent* and *Isolation*." In *Film Comment*, July/August 38–41.
Sobchack, Vivian. 1992. *The Address of the Eye. A Phenomenology of Film Experience*. Princeton: Princeton University Press.
Sobchack, Vivian. 1999. "Toward a Phenomenology of Nonfictional Film Experience." In *Collecting Visible Evidence*, ed. Jane M. Gaines and Michael Renov, 241–254. Minneapolis: University of Minnesota Press.
Soentgen, Jens. 1998. *Die verdeckte Wirklichkeit. Einführung in die Neue Phänomenologie von Hermann Schmitz*. Bonn: Bouvier.
Sokolowski, Robert. 2000. *Introduction to Phenomenology*. Cambridge: Cambridge University Press.
Sontag, Sontag. 1977. *On Photography*. New York: Farrar, Straus and Giroux.
Spiegelberg, Herbert. 1975. "How Subjective is Phenomenology?" In *Doing Phenomenology. Essays on and in Phenomenology*, 72–79. The Hague: Martinus Nijhoff.
Spiegelberg, Herbert. 1982. *The Phenomenological Movement. A Historical Introduction*. The Hague: Martinus Nijhoff.
Sragow, Michael. 1992. "The Current Cinema: Tricks" In *The New Yorker*. August 24.
Srinivas, Lakshmi. 2002. "The Active Audience: Spectatorship, Social Relations and the Experience of Cinema in India." In *Media, Culture and Society*. Vol. 24, No. 2, 155–173.
Staiger, Janet. 1992. *Interpreting Films. Studies in the Historical Reception of American Cinema*. Princeton: Princeton University Press.
Staiger, Janet. 2000. *Perverse Spectators. The Practices of Film Reception*. New York: NYU Press.
St. Augustine. 1838. *The Confessions of St. Augustine*. Oxford: Rivington.
Stearns, Peter N. 2006. *American Fear. The Causes and Consequences of High Anxiety*. New York: Routledge.
Stern, Daniel. 2004. *The Present Moment in Psychotherapy and Everyday Life*. New York: Norton.
Stokes, Melvyn and Richard Maltby (ed.). 1999. *Identifying Hollywood's Audiences. Cultural Identity and the Movies*. London: Bfi.
Straus, Erwin. 1930. "Die Formen des Räumlichen." In *Der Nervenarzt*. Vol. 3, No. 11, 633–656.
Straus, Erwin. 1956. *Vom Sinn der Sinne. Ein Beitrag zur Grundlegung der Psychologie*. Second Edition. Berlin: Springer.
Tan, Ed S. 1996. *Emotion and the Structure of Narrative Film. Film as Emotion Machine*. Mahwah: Lawrence Erlbaum Associates.
Tasker, Yvonne. 2002. *The Silence of the Lambs*. London: Bfi.
Taylor, Charles. 1992. *The Ethics of Authenticity*. Cambridge: Harvard University Press.
Telotte, J.P. 1982. "Through a Pumpkin's Eye: The Reflexive Nature of Horror." In: *Film/Literature Quarterly*. Vol. 10, No. 3, 139–149.
Toulmin, Stephen. 1990. *Cosmopolis. The Hidden Agenda of Modernity*. New York: Free Press.

Travers, Peter: "Seven." In: *Rolling Stone.* www.rollingstone.com/reviews/movie/5948711/review/5948712/seven.
Truffaut, François. 1985. *Hitchcock.* Revised Edition. New York: Simon and Schuster.
Tudor, Andrew. 1997. "Why Horror? The Peculiar Pleasures of a Popular Genre." In *Cultural Studies.* Vol. 11, No. 3. 443–463.
Turner, Bryan S. 1984. *The Body and Society. Explorations in Social Theory.* Oxford: Basil Blackwell.
Turvey, Malcolm. 2006. "Imagination, Simulation, and Fiction." In *Film Studies.* Vol. 8, 116–125.
Valentine, C. W. 1991. "The Innate Bases of Fear." In: *The Journal of Genetic Psychology.* Vol. 152, No. 4, 501–527.
Van Sant, Ann Jessie. 1993. *Eighteenth-Century Sensibility and the Novel. The Senses in Social Context.* Cambridge: Cambridge University Press.
Varela, Francisco J. and Jonathan Shear. 1999. "First-Person Methodologies: What, Why, How?" In *Journal of Consciousness Studies.* Vol. 6, No. 2–3, 1–14.
Vermersch, Pierre. 1999. "Introspection as Practice." In *Journal of Consciousness Studies.* Vol. 6, No.2–3, 17–42.
Waldenfels, Bernhard. 2000. *Das leibliche Selbst. Vorlesungen zur Phänomenologie des Leibes.* Frankfurt/Main: Suhrkamp.
Waldenfels, Bernhard. 2004. *Phänomenologie der Aufmerksamkeit.* Frankfurt/Main: Suhrkamp.
Wiater, Stanley. 1992. *Dark Visions. Conversations with the Masters of the Horror Film.* New York: Avon Books.
Wiesing, Lambert. 2005. *Artifizielle Präsenz. Studien zur Philosophie des Bildes.* Frankfurt/Main: Suhrkamp.
Wiesing, Lambert. 2006. "Von der defekten Illusion zum perfekten Phantom. Über phänomenologische Bildtheorien." In . . . *kraft der Illusion*, ed. Gertrud Koch and Christiane Voss, 89–101. Munich: Fink.
Williams, Linda. 2002. "Learning to Scream." In *Horror, the Film Reader*, ed. Mark Jancovich, 163–168. London: Routledge.
Williams, Mary Elizabeth: "The Blair Witch Project." In: *Salon.com.* www.salon.com/ent/movies/review/1999/07/13/blair/index.html?CP=SAL&DN=110.
Wolf, Werner. 1995. "Angst und Schrecken als Attraktion. Zu einer gender-orientierten Funktionsgeschichte des englischen Schauerromans im 18. und frühen 19. Jahrhundert." In *Zeitschrift für Anglistik und Amerikanistik.* Vol. XLIII, No. 1, 37–59.
Wood, Robin. 2002. *Hitchcock's Films Revisited.* New York: Columbia University Press.
Worland, Rick. 2007. *The Horror Film. An Introduction.* Malden: Blackwell.
Wouters, Cas. 1979. "Informalisierung und der Prozess der Zivilisation." In *Materialien zu Norbert Elias' Zivilisationstheorie*, ed. Peter Gleichmann, Johan Goudsblom and Hermann Korte, 279–298. Frankfurt/Main: Suhrkamp.
Wulff, Hans J. 1996. "Suspense and the Influence of Cataphora on Viewers' Expectations." In *Suspense. Conceptualizations, Theoretical Analyses, and Empirical Explanations*, ed. Hans J. Wulff, Peter Vorderer and Mike Friedrichsen, 1–17. Mahwah: Lawrence Erlbaum Associates.
Zelle, Carsten. 1987. *Angenehmes Grauen. Literarhistorische Beiträge zur Ästhetik des Schrecklichen im achtzehnten Jahrhundert.* Hamburg: Meiner.
Zelle, Carsten. 1990. "Über den Grund des Vergnügens an schrecklichen Gegenständen im achtzehnten Jahrhundert." In *Schönheit und Schrecken. Entsetzen, Gewalt und Tod in alten und neuen Medien*, ed. Peter Gendolla and Carsten Zelle, 55–91. Heidelberg: Winter.

Index

A

Abbott & Costello Meet Frankenstein 85
absorption. *See also* appreciation; enthrallment; immersion; involvement 52, 54–55, 57–58, 64, 65, 73
Accused, The 185, 274n73
action movie 10, 30, 31, 34, 144
action tendency 19, 20, 23, 71, 266n56
Addiction, The 35
Addison, Joseph 4
admiration 13, 65, 235
Adorno, Theodor W. 9, 229–231
advanced modernity. *See* modernity
aesthetic attitude 52–54, 70, 247, 256
aesthetic experience 7, 8, 11, 14, 16, 25, 28, 52–53, 67, 88, 147, 223, 231, 232, 234, 236, 244, 250, 258n20, 278n37
Aikin, John and Laetitia 4
Alien 127, 130, 162
Alien 3 7, 109, 110, 162
Alien: Resurrection 28, 35, 173, 177–178, 185, 203, 206, 207, 211
Alighieri, Dante 231
Allen, Richard 160–161, 204
Almereyda, Michael 252
Alone in the Dark 178
Altman, Rick 244, 245
À ma soeur 129
Amenábar, Alejandro 35
American Werewolf in London, An 253
Amityville Horror, The 30
Anaconda 30, 84
anchoring point 157–159, 204, 213
Andrej Rubljov 89
Angel Heart 108, 109, 117
anger/rage 11, 64, 65, 75, 128, 226, 235

Antonioni, Michelangelo 94
Apollo 13 206
appreciation. *See also* enthrallment 64–65, 96, 137
Aristotle 8, 9, 10
Armageddon 244
Army of Darkness 8
art-horror 5, 85
Astronaut's Wife, The 167
atmosphere
  in the film 37, 43, 47, 48, 162, 170–179, 207, 273n58
  in the movie theater 50, 54, 56, 60, 200, 266n58
Augustine, St. 4, 9
audience response
  closing one's eyes 62, 71, 95, 115, 146
  covering one's ears 20, 23, 62, 71, 95, 96, 97, 101, 103, 115, 137, 146
  covering one's eyes 95, 96, 101, 114, 146, 193,
  crying and weeping 64, 114, 235, 150
  laughing 8, 39, 50, 69, 73, 75, 76, 77, 85, 149–153, 194, 195, 197, 198, 200, 201, 212, 235, 241, 246, 252
  leaving the theater 88, 89, 93, 95
  looking away 20, 23, 55, 71, 95, 96, 97, 98, 101, 103, 105, 114, 193, 200
  moaning 73, 76, 77, 201
  screaming 23, 57, 71, 73, 76, 77, 127, 149–153, 195, 201, 238, 246, 248, 249
  touching someone 22, 71, 76, 193, 198, 248

Austin, Bruce A. 244, 245

B
Bachelard, Gaston 172, 173–174, 175–176, 274n61
Bad Influence 33
Baird, Robert 130, 131, 133, 147, 149, 271n13
Balázs, Béla 88, 203, 213, 214
Barker, Clive 3, 127, 129, 130, 153
Barrymore, Drew 185
Basic Instinct 6, 33, 34, 35, 167, 168, 169
Baudelaire, Charles 90
Baudrillard, Jean 228
Bauman, Zygmunt 37, 237, 240, 242–243, 248, 279n7
Beck, Ulrich 37
Bellah, Robert 37, 245, 247, 260n63
belongingness. *See* collectivity
Benjamin, Walter 143, 221–222, 240, 276n5
Berman, Marshall 237
Bette, Karl Heinrich 37, 224, 277n29
Bigwood, Carol 225
Birds, The 40, 84
Blair Witch Project, The 11, 12, 30, 35, 93, 119, 129, 175–177, 196, 245, 253
Blink 185
Body
    bodily tension 10–12, 103, 140, 148, 188, 192, 193, 212, 233, 241
    and disembodiment 12, 25, 37, 222–223, 225–234, 235–236, 255–256, 277n29
    lived-body (*Leib*) 9, 15, 22, 24, 25, 27, 38–39, 40–41, 43, 47, 49, 63, 67, 101–106, 140, 147–150, 169–170, 172, 178, 182–183, 192–195, 196, 201, 211–212, 217, 223, 226–229, 232–233, 235, 236, 254–255
    physiological body (*Körper*) 14, 15, 20–21, 22, 46–47, 49, 102, 147–148, 149
    transformation/metamorphosis of the 8–10, 22, 24, 28, 32, 40, 47, 49, 71, 147, 150, 194–195, 217–218, 227, 232, 233, 254
    bodily constriction 22, 24, 102–103, 140, 148–149, 170, 171, 172, 174, 177, 183, 192–195, 196, 198, 201, 212, 233

bodily expansion 22, 24, 103, 140, 148–149, 194–195, 233
Böhme, Gernot 224, 263n27, 273n42
Bone Collector, The 33, 178
Bordwell, David 53, 136, 168, 261n81
Botting, Fred 230–231
Bourdieu, Pierre 6
Bourne Identity, The 34
Bowling for Columbine 5
Boyle, Danny 35
Braindead 85
Brakhage, Stan 65, 68
Bram Stoker's Dracula 6
Branagh, Kenneth 6
Branigan, Edward 165
Breillat, Catherine 129
Bresson, Robert 89, 93
Bringing Up Baby 192
Brinker, Menachem 66
Brood, The 116
Brown, Charles Brockden 230
Bullitt 211
bungee jumping 10, 97, 224, 234
Burch, Noël 135
Burke, Edmund 3, 4, 88, 155, 159, 186, 202, 231

C
Cabin Fever 175
Candyman 6, 42
Cape Fear 33, 35, 85, 132, 178, 188, 193
Carpenter, John 81, 129, 130, 153
Carr, Dave 189
Carroll, Noël 4 5, 12, 13, 85, 86, 100, 180, 205, 207, 213, 234 235, 261n76, 264n6, 266n44, 267n5
Casey, Edward 112, 113, 229
Casino 31
Cataldi, Sue L. 233
catharsis 8–12, 194, 254, 258n24, 258n25
Cavell, Stanley 87, 88
Cell, The 34
Chan-Wook, Park 252
Charade 210
Chion, Michel 136, 144–145, 166, 273n26
Chung Kuo 94
civilizing process, the 10, 12, 25, 218, 223, 225, 226–229, 254, 277n20, 277n28
Clover, Carol 35, 94
cognitive pleasure 5, 7, 29, 46, 48, 100

cognitive film theory 12–13, 14, 19, 21
Coleridge, Samuel 98
collective body 78, 150, 151, 152, 153, 201, 238, 247, 248, 272n50
collectivity, feeling of 22, 24–25, 39–40, 50, 72–77, 150–154, 195, 197–201, 223, 238, 241–251, 253–256, 272n50
concentration section 157–159, 204, 213
contagion, emotional 183, 198, 213
Coppola, Francis Ford 6
Copycat 34, 162, 185
Craven, Wes 28, 205
Cronenberg, David 116, 144
Cunningham, Sean S. 150
cultural capital 6
culture of fear 5, 254

D
Dante, Joe 52
Dark Half, The 135, 174
Dark Water 30, 174, 175
Da Vinci Code, The 35
Dawn of the Dead (1978) 30
Dawn of the Dead (2004) 4
Day After Tomorrow, The 31
Day of the Jackal 206
Death Proof 211
De Bont, Jan 173
Deep Blue Sea 30, 134, 185, 198
Deep Rising 30, 131–132, 135
Deleuze, Gilles 12, 13–15, 190
Deleuzian film theory 12, 13–15
Denby, David 129
Denis, Claire 35
de Palma, Brian 35, 193
Descent, The 83
Dewey, John 137, 227, 234, 239–240, 260n61
Die Hard 144
Diffrient, David Scott 130, 271n20
direct horror (as type of fear) 19, 27, 81–103, 109, 110–111, 112, 113, 114, 115, 116, 136, 137, 138, 253, 269n7
disgust 5, 8, 13, 18, 19, 33, 48, 55–56, 76, 83, 85, 90, 99, 100, 102, 104, 112, 153, 201, 230, 233–234, 252, 253, 267n10
displeasure 36, 71, 82, 100, 101, 186, 187, 190, 200
disrupted relief 138, 139–141, 145, 148, 195

distance
  ontological 87–89, 93, 94, 95, 97, 104, 126, 131, 147, 267n11
  phenomenological 69, 93–95, 97, 98, 100, 101, 106, 126, 146, 147, 149, 153, 160, 187, 199, 200, 267n11
Doane, Mary Ann 164, 238
documentary consciousness 92–93
documentary film 6, 29, 74
Donnelly, K.J. 175
Don't Look Now 24
Dracula 129
dread (as type of fear) 10, 19, 20, 21, 22, 23, 25, 27, 28, 33, 34, 37, 40, 48, 49, 50, 68, 69, 70, 71, 74, 78, 83, 100, 105, 109, 115, 124, 126, 128, 131, 134, 136, 138, 139, 140, 141, 145, 146, 148, 150, 154, 155–201, 203, 204, 205, 207, 210, 211, 212, 214, 215, 216, 217, 218, 233, 234, 238, 239, 240, 247, 248, 253, 256, 272n3, 272n4, 274n86, 275n103
Dressed to Kill 155, 156, 185, 193
Duel 211
Dufrenne, Mikel 53
Dumont, Bruno 129
Durkheim, Émile 236
DVD 17, 54, 56, 228, 241, 247, 268n42, 279n1
Dyer, Richard 34, 160

E
Ebert, Roger 43
Elias, Norbert 10, 12, 37, 221, 226, 234, 277n20
Elsaesser, Thomas 55, 69–70, 212
emotions
  communicativeness of 63, 64, 152, 198, 201, 246, 248
  difficulty of defining 18–19, 21, 128
  experience of 11, 13, 19, 21–23, 28, 33, 41, 44, 49, 64, 69, 76, 102, 104, 232–234, 260n59, 262n93
  film studies and 12–16, 26, 45, 48–50, 252
  intentionality of 19–20, 21, 74, 82–82, 128, 157–158, 204, 228
  negative view of 5, 8–10, 26, 254, 263n18
  repression/control of 9–12, 63, 226/227, 277n20

empathy. *See also* somatic empathy; sympathy 37, 99, 134, 143, 144, 158, 180–183, 201, 211, 213, 216
End of Days, The 88
Engels, Friedrich 223, 237
enthrallment. *See also* appreciation 64–66
erotic excitement 11, 32, 105, 252
Evil Dead, The 4, 8, 11, 30, 40, 84, 130–131, 135, 175, 253
Evil Dead II, The 84–85, 253
Exorcist, The 35, 53, 89
extrication 24, 49, 69, 71, 82, 101, 126, 154, 197, 253

F

fans 6, 168, 244–246, 250
Fatal Attraction 33, 185
fear. *See also* direct horror; dread; shock; suggested horror; terror.
 bodily experience of 8, 10–12, 13, 16, 19–24, 31–32, 39–40, 47, 101–103, 104, 105, 192–195, 198, 200, 210–213, 223, 232–234, 235–236, 254, 256
 categorizing types of 18–19, 21, 27–28, 37, 85, 97, 107, 128, 160, 201, 203, 204, 205, 210, 217–218
 collective experience of 22, 24, 40, 76–77, 139, 150–153, 172, 195–201, 223, 246–248, 249–251, 253
 definition of (cinematic) 18–24
 pleasure of 3–5, 8, 10, 12, 13, 14, 15, 17, 24–26, 31, 40, 82, 88, 99–101, 103, 130, 186, 188, 218, 231, 236, 246–247, 248, 255–256, 275n101
 temporal experience of 19, 22, 103, 104, 147–148, 156–157, 160, 161, 186–192, 205, 213–215, 238–240, 254
feelings-in-common 76, 198–199, 200, 201, 247
fellow-feelings 198–200
Ferrara, Abel 35, 252
film studies 12, 16, 26, 29, 36, 45, 46, 47, 48, 211, 262n93
Final Analysis 33, 178
Fincher, David 6, 35, 86
Fisher, Philip 254
Flaherty, Michael 191–192

Fog, The 142
Foster, Jodie 181, 185, 274n73
Foucault, Michel 229–230, 231, 238
Frampton, Daniel 211, 261n70
Freedberg, David 91
Freud, Sigmund 11, 196, 225
Friday the 13th 129, 139, 150, 162
Friedberg, Anne 52
function of frightening films, 4, 5–8, 9, 12, 16, 221
 counterbalancing 12, 24–25, 221–223, 229, 235–236, 243, 250, 254, 255, 256
Fright Night 178
Fugitive, The 31

G

Geiger, Moritz 100
genre, importance of 5–6, 8, 28–36, 90, 145, 156, 161–162, 244–245, 246, 255, 261n81
Giles, Dennis 114, 115, 125, 165, 174
Gillespie, Jim 241, 279n1
Glendinning, Simon 38, 44
Godard, Jean-Luc 16
Goethe, Johann Wolfgang von 7
Goffman, Erving 150, 152
Gomery, Douglas 60, 61
Gordon, Stuart 108, 155, 186
Grodal, Torben 12
Grudge, The 30
Grudge 2, The 30, 262n91
Gumbrecht, Hans Ulrich 16, 236

H

Halloween 11, 117–118, 120, 129, 161, 165, 169, 202, 203, 206, 207
Hand that Rocks the Cradle, The 33
Hanfling, Oswald 254
Hannibal 35, 84
Haunting, The (1963) 253
Haunting, The (1999) 30, 43, 173, 185
Hell Night 178
Hellraiser 7, 129
Henry—Portrait of a Serial Killer 6, 11, 81, 82, 84, 87, 89, 119, 121, 123, 252
hiding effect 63, 73, 198, 247
High Noon 31
Hill, Annette 96, 98, 125, 193, 264n12
Hills, Matt 5–6, 8
Hills Have Eyes, The (1977) 175
Hills Have Eyes, The (2006) 30, 104, 175

Hills Have Eyes II, The (2007) 88
Hinson, Hal 43, 193
His Girl Friday 192
Hitchcock, Alfred 3, 4, 40, 71, 105, 167, 182, 202, 204, 207, 215, 248
home/non-theatrical viewing 17, 54, 56, 228, 241, 242, 247, 264n12, 268n42, 279n1
horror film 5, 6, 13, 30–32, 33, 34, 35, 39, 54, 69, 70, 76, 84, 86, 87, 89, 94. 104, 126, 127, 129, 130, 144, 145, 150, 161, 166, 168, 172, 173, 175, 178, 197, 207, 230, 235, 236, 241, 252, 253, 260n54
   slasher film 7, 30, 34, 35, 161, 162, 187, 206, 253, 262n91
   splatter film 8, 84, 85, 160, 253
Hostel 30, 35, 110, 201
House of Frankenstein 85
House of 1000 Corpses 12, 81, 82, 88
Hubbard, Phil 59
Hume, David 4
Husserl, Edmund 38, 40, 188–189, 210

I

Ihde, Don 39, 232
I Know What You Did Last Summer 7, 141, 142, 154, 173, 185, 241
illusion, critique of film as 14, 66–67, 91–92, 93, 98, 126
immersion 24, 49, 64–71, 75, 76, 77, 82, 89, 91, 96, 99, 100–101, 115, 126, 137, 146, 147, 149, 153, 153, 160, 197, 200, 207, 210, 216, 232, 246, 248, 249, 252, 253
Indecent Proposal 245
Independence Day 244
Indiana Jones and the Last Crusade 245
Ingarden, Roman 53, 111, 114, 123
Innocent Blood 129, 135
Inside Man 34
interest, cognitive 4, 18, 86, 87, 99–100, 169, 180, 182, 186, 189
interpretation 7, 16
Interpreter, The 35
interobjectivity 143–144
intertextuality 6, 7, 244
Interview with the Vampire 35
Invasion of the Body Snatchers, The 28

involvement. *See also* immersion 64–65, 67, 70
Irréversible 189
Iser, Wolfgang 53, 111, 114

J

Jackson, Samuel L. 185
Jacob's Ladder 33, 127, 136
Jaws 35, 84, 105, 170, 175, 177, 185
Jenkins, Henry 244, 245
Jennifer Eight 34, 165, 178, 185
Jeunet, Jean-Pierre 35
Johnson, Mark 27, 43, 263n18
Jonas, Hans 137–138
Jordan, Neil 35

K

Kael, Pauline 98, 193, 241
Kant, Immanuel 4, 88
Katz, Jack 44
Kauffman, Philip 144
Kennedy, Barbara M. 13, 14, 15, 259n38, 259n39
kinaesthesia 14, 233
King, Stephen 55, 199, 205
Kiss the Girls 34, 175
Klute 129
Knight, Deborah 160
Kolnai, Aurel 95, 102, 272n4
Kracauer, Siegfried 60, 81, 88
Kubrick, Stanley 95
Kuhn, Annette 244, 245

L

Lakoff, George 27, 43, 263n18
Lang, Fritz 116
Last Broadcast, The 175, 176
Leder, Drew 74
LeDoux, Joseph 20
Leigh, Janet 185
Lessing, Gotthold Ephraim 108
Levine, Joseph 47
Lost Highway 11, 35
Lost World: Jurassic Park 2, The 7, 30, 35, 88
Lynch, David 35, 252

M

Malice 33, 140, 167
Maltby, Richard 164, 165, 168, 187–188
Marathon Man 104, 106, 179
Marx, Karl 223, 236, 237
Mary Shelley's Frankenstein 6

Index

Mast, Gerald 221
Max, Arthur 172
McKnight, George 160
McLuhan, Marshall 70, 111, 112
M – Eine Stadt sucht einen Mörder 116
melodrama 11, 13, 76, 77, 102, 150, 195, 234, 235, 261n80, 262n93
Memento 189
Merleau-Ponty, Maurice 38, 40, 115–116
Meunier, Jean-Pierre 74
Miike, Takashi 252
Millan, Scott 175
Milton, John 231
Mimic 131, 142, 167, 173
mimicry, affective 103, 104, 182, 183, 207, 211, 213, 269n57
  motor 103, 104, 182, 183, 207, 211, 212, 213, 269n57
  sensation 103, 104, 182, 183, 211, 269n57
Minsky, Marvin 228
Misery 104
Mitchell, W.J.T. 92, 268n38
modernization 12, 25, 218, 223, 226–229, 231, 236, 254, 277n28
modernity 12, 25, 37, 218, 221–226, 229, 230, 231, 235–243, 248, 255–256, 260n64, 277n29
monster 4, 5, 7, 11, 82–87, 93, 97, 98, 99, 109, 110, 118, 124, 131, 134, 142, 153, 162, 165, 195, 203, 206, 210, 216–217, 231, 269n7
Moore, Michael 5, 257n10
Moravec, Hans 228
Motion Picture Association 18, 90
Mouchette 89
Moynihan, Daniel Patrick 26
multiplex cinema 16–18, 35, 36, 52, 56–64, 66, 69, 71, 72–73, 75, 77, 94, 100, 138, 144–145, 171, 177, 196, 198, 200, 223, 235, 241, 246, 247, 249, 250, 252, 264n15
Mulvey, Laura 55, 88, 187–188, 238
Musil, Robert 178

N

narrative closure 11, 12, 68
Neale, Steve 29, 34, 251n80
Neco z Alenky 31
Nietzsche, Friedrich 7, 12
Nightbreed 81, 82, 83
Night of the Living Dead 178
Nightwatch 34, 178
Nightmare on Elm Street, A 173, 174
Nine ½ Weeks 168
Ninth Gate, The 35
Nolan, William F. 170
No Way Out 173

O

Omen, The 7
Open Water 175, 177, 185
Others, The 35

P

Pacific Heights 33
Pakula, Alan J. 35
paradox of fear 3–5, 6, 8, 16, 25, 70, 77, 205, 218, 252, 254, 258n25, 260n54
paradox of horror 4, 234
paradox of suspense 180, 213
Peckinpah, Sam 84
Pelican Brief, The 35, 217
Penn, Arthur 84
Perkins, V.F. 58, 63
phenomenology
  characteristics of 13, 15, 16, 38–48, 53, 57, 66, 69, 170, 171, 188
  critique and limits of 14, 41, 42, 43, 45
  film and 15, 36, 40, 48–51, 67, 69, 70, 252
phenomenological description 13, 14, 15, 17, 23, 25, 38, 40, 42, 43, 44–46, 48–49, 51, 112, 171, 188, 191, 246
Pinedo, Isabel Cristina 151
Pitt, Brad 6
pity 9, 13, 99, 199, 230, 235
Plantinga, Carl 12, 13, 158, 183
Plato 9
Platoon 31
pleasure 3, 4, 5, 6, 8, 9, 10, 11, 12, 13, 14, 17, 24, 25, 26, 27, 29, 32, 34, 40, 51, 65, 67, 68, 70, 88, 97, 99, 100, 101, 103, 114, 117, 125, 130, 139, 152, 164, 185, 186, 188, 218, 218, 223, 230, 231, 232, 236, 237, 244, 246, 247, 248, 249, 252, 254, 255, 256
Plessner, Helmuth 149
Polanski, Roman 35, 125
Pollack, Sidney 35

Poltergeist 140
pornography 11, 16, 26, 32, 76, 153, 235
Powell, Anna 14, 15
Prince, Stephen 46, 84, 86
process of civilization. *See* civilizing process
Psycho (1960) 35, 71, 84, 98, 105, 133, 155, 156, 158, 159, 170, 185, 241, 248
Psycho (1998) 35
Pulp Fiction 85

R
Radcliffe, Ann 230, 276n3
Raimi, Sam 8, 136, 144
Raising Cain 35, 131
reading 16, 55–56, 70, 72, 199, 231–232, 234, 249, 280n30
règle du jeu, La 89
Relic, The 173
relief, feeling of 9, 10, 30, 32, 100, 164, 183, 194, 197, 212
Renoir, Jean 89, 93
Reservoir Dogs 84, 125
Reynolds, Scott 127
Ricoeur, Paul 43
Riesman, David 197
Riget/The Kingdom 35
Ring, The 30, 35
Ring 2, The 30
Rockett, Will H. 186, 187, 192, 275n3
role-play, imaginary 7, 8, 258n20
rollercoaster 3, 10, 224, 235
Ronin 31
Rosa, Hartmut 37, 236–239
Rosemary's Baby 11–12, 124–125
Roth, Eli 175
Rousseau, Jean-Jacques 9, 88
Rowson, Susanna 230
Rubin, Martin 32
Ryan, Marie-Laure 67–68, 70

S
sadness 12, 43, 44, 75, 195, 235
Sartre, Jean-Paul 114, 260n59
Savini, Tom 97
Savlov, Marc 198
Saw 30, 35, 201, 262n91
Saw II 104, 262n91
Scary Movie 129
Schaub, Mirjam 86, 110
Scheff, Thomas 10
Schiller, Friedrich 4

Scheler, Max 198–200, 246, 272n50
Schmitz, Hermann 19, 42, 49, 102–103, 147–148, 151–152, 157–158, 192–193, 196, 198, 204, 263n27, 263n28, 272n50, 273n42, 275n94
Schoeffter, Conrad 18
Schroeder, Barbet 43
Schulze, Gerhard 35
Schütz, Alfred 38
Schweinitz, Jörg 29
Sconce, Jeffrey 168
scopophilia 6, 164
Scorsese, Martin 35, 188, 193
Scott, Ridley 35
Scream 7, 28, 30, 35, 120, 123, 161, 166, 185, 194, 202, 203, 206, 207, 209, 212, 216, 235, 253
Scream 2 6, 30, 207, 253
Searle, John 74
self-expansion 7, 258n20
self-reflexivity 7, 95
setting, 33, 167, 170–178, 192, 194
 the forest as 119, 175–178, 194, 274n61
 the labyrinth as 33, 48, 155, 167, 173, 174, 176, 181, 194, 195
Seven 6, 33, 34, 35, 43, 86–87, 104, 118–119, 123, 127, 160, 163, 172, 175, 178, 252
Shakespeare, William 231
shame 18, 56, 63–64, 148, 151, 152, 195, 196
Shaviro, Steven 13, 15, 16
Shaw, Daniel 8
Shining, The 95, 98, 173
shock (as type of fear) 8, 9, 19, 20, 22, 23, 27, 28, 31, 32, 33, 34, 37, 39, 40, 48, 49, 50, 56, 69, 71, 76, 89, 98, 100, 104, 105, 109, 127–154, 156, 158, 159, 160, 161, 162, 166, 168, 169, 175, 179, 180, 185, 186, 187, 188, 190, 191, 193, 195, 201, 204, 214, 215, 216, 217, 218, 232, 233, 235, 238, 239, 240, 248, 253, 271n13
Shusterman, Richard 16, 224, 225, 234, 278n46
Shyamalan, M. Knight 176
Signs 6, 35
Silence of the Lambs, The 7, 11, 24, 34, 35, 40, 84, 99, 121, 122, 129, 154, 155, 156, 158, 159, 164,

174, 178, 180, 181, 183, 184, 185, 186, 188, 192, 193, 197, 214, 253, 267n10
Simmel, Georg 221, 222, 236
Sin City 31
Single White Female 33, 43
Singer, Linda 55
Sixth Sense, The 30, 35
Sleeping with the Enemy 35, 131, 165, 168
Sliver 33, 168
Smith, Greg M. 12, 273n43
Smith, Murray 12, 181, 183, 184
Sobchack, Vivian 15, 16, 41, 43, 45, 67, 74, 103, 105, 106, 115, 119, 143–144, 211
soccer 10, 113, 152, 172, 195, 224, 232, 235, 243, 249
social distinction 6, 75, 246, 248, 249
Sokolowski, Robert 115
somatic empathy 83, 103–106, 112, 126, 138, 177, 180, 182, 192, 193, 194, 211, 213, 232, 233–234, 235
Sontag, Susan 94–95
special effects 6, 7, 18, 65, 84, 86, 96, 97, 255
spectacle 4, 133, 168–169, 185, 238, 243
Spiegelberg, Herbert 15, 45–46, 143
Spielberg, Steven 35, 105, 170
stars (in frightening films) 6, 84, 185–186, 245
startle effect. *See also* cinematic shock 18, 20, 33, 127–130, 133, 135, 139, 140, 141, 145–149, 152, 153, 201, 270n3
Staiger, Janet 46
Star Trek 245
Star Wars 245
Stearns, Peter N. 5, 254
Stern, Daniel 150, 151, 266n65
Sterne, Laurence 230
Stir of Echoes 30
Strangers on a Train 182
Straus, Erwin 90, 268n21
sublime, the 4, 88, 252
suggested horror (as type of fear) 19, 27, 30, 49, 56, 68, 70, 82, 108–126, 160, 252, 253, 256, 269n3, 270n13, 274n86
Svankmajer, Jan 31
sympathy 37, 99, 143, 144, 158, 159, 180, 183–186

synaesthesia 14, 108, 119

T

Tales of Terror 162
Tan, Ed 12, 36, 64–65, 88, 249–250
Tarkovsky, Andrej 89, 93
Taylor, Charles 25
Terminator 2: Judgment Day 31, 42
terror (as type of fear) 4, 8, 19, 20, 21, 22, 23, 24, 27, 28, 33, 34, 37, 48, 49, 50, 68, 69, 71, 78, 83, 99, 100, 109, 115, 128, 138, 139, 145, 148, 158, 159, 161, 179, 183, 188, 190, 202–218, 233, 238, 240, 247, 248, 253, 254, 275n3
Texas Chainsaw Massacre, The (1974) 4, 11, 185, 208, 212, 214, 267n18
Texas Chainsaw Massacre, The (2003) 30
Third Man, The 173
thriller 6, 31–36, 54, 70, 76, 77, 86, 89, 94, 101, 104, 117, 130, 145, 168, 172, 173, 178, 197, 207, 235, 236, 252, 258n24, 262n93
There's Something About Mary 201
Titanic 235
Totally Fucked Up 31
tragedy 4, 8–9, 44, 77
Travers, Peter 43
Trouble Every Day 35
28 Days Later 35
Twentynine Palms 129

U

Unbreakable 108, 109, 117
Unforgiven 31
Unlawful Entry 33
Urban Legend 30, 178
Usual Suspects, The 34

V

Valentine, C.W. 196
Vanishing, The 33, 175
Van Sant, Gus 35
Vermersch, Pierre 42
Vertigo 185
videoplayer/VHS 17, 56, 241, 242, 264n12, 268n42
viewer
    imagination of the 11, 56, 70, 104, 108–125, 157–160, 176,

181–183, 186, 190, 199, 269n6, 270n13, 274n86
immobility of the 70, 94, 193–194, 198, 200, 212, 232, 233
(relative) safety of the 87–89, 93–95, 101, 197, 207, 234, 241, 248
Village, The 176
violence 7, 19, 26, 30, 31, 32, 33–34, 35, 82–87, 89 , 91, 93, 96, 97–99, 102 , 103–106, 109, 111, 114, 115, 120, 121, 131, 137, 146, 157, 158, 206, 207, 227
Virus 7, 173
Von Trier, Lars 35, 252

W

Wait Until Dark 178
Walpole, Horace 230
Weber, Max 229–230, 231, 236, 243
Weir, Peter 6, 273n44
Wes Craven's New Nightmare 7, 30, 127
What Lies Beneath 30, 35, 174
Whispers in the Dark 33
White Noise 196
Wild Orchid 168
Williams, Linda 71
Williams, Mary Elizabeth 196
Williamson, Kevin 194
Witness 6
Woo, John 84
Wood, Robin 185

X

X Files, The 244

Z

Zelle, Carsten 4, 257n7

Printed in Great Britain
by Amazon